Readings in Urban Economics and Spatial Patterns

Edited by Michael R. Greenberg

CENTER FOR URBAN POLICY RESEARCH
Rutgers University—The State University of New Jersey
New Brunswick, New Jersey

THE CUPR SURVEY SERIES

Series Editors George Sternlieb and Virginia Paulus

LAND USE CONTROLS: PRESENT PROBLEMS AND FUTURE
REFORM
Edited by David Listokin
MUNICIPAL NEEDS, SERVICES AND FINANCING: READINGS ON
MUNICIPAL EXPENDITURES
Edited by W. Patrick Beaton
MODELS OF EMPLOYMENT AND RESIDENCE LOCATION
Edited by Franklin J. James
SUBURBANIZATION DYNAMICS AND THE FUTURE OF
THE CITY
Edited by James W. Hughes
READINGS IN URBAN ECONOMICS AND SPATIAL PATTERNS
Edited by Michael R. Greenberg

CONTENTS

I

Introduction

INTRODUCTION

This anthology is intended for persons interested in urban planning, urban studies, community development, urban economics and urban geography. The readings pivot around four fundamental questions:

(1) How is urban land divided among alternative uses?
(2) How do industries choose a location?
(3) Why do some communities sustain economic development, while others decline?
(4) How are the externalities of urban-industrial growth distributed within urban regions?

The nineteen selections provide either concise statements of basic theory, or introductory methodological and systems approaches to one of the four fundamental questions. The first nine selections focus on the problems of intraurban land use and the siting of industries in metropolitan regions. The articles by Hoover and Alonso review classical bid-rent theory. The selections by Hughes, Van Til, and Simmons deal with social area analysis and intraurban population migration. The Applebaum and Berry readings focus upon the location of retail activities and the Economic Development Administration and Christian selections upon industrial location.

Six selections are devoted to metropolitan economic development. Hansen's article overviews growth center theory while Ullman's considers the export and local market bases of the central city. Next, Morrill presents a concise statement challenging conventional wisdom about threshold sizes for developing growth centers. The selections by the Bureau of Labor Statistics, James and Hughes, and the Economic Development Administration present approaches for tracing the multiplier effect in economic development.

The final four readings concentrate on environmental externalities. The Council on Environmental Quality identifies areas of critical environmental impact. Slavin outlines approaches for shifting the focus of land use decision-making. Carey and associates present a water quality monitoring system for an urban region. Greenberg and Hordon review the complexities of environmental impact analysis.

In addition to the nineteen selections, a supplementary bibliography is included with the references divided in approximately equal numbers among the four questions posed, and further subdivided according to degree of difficulty. Each reference is classified as introductory, intermediate, or advanced.

A SUGGESTED STUDY SEQUENCE

The following study sequence presupposes no previous training in economics, geography, or urban planning. It is designed to accommodate the needs of several types of readers. These would include the student who wishes a single, and broad exposure to the subjects treated; the more advanced student who wishes to concentrate on one or more of the questions around which the readings pivot; and the nonstudent who wishes an orderly introduction to the field.

I have found it useful to begin with the subject that the reader is likely to find most familiar from everyday experience—basic intraurban land use. Economic and sociological reasons for the spatial distribution of land use will help to put the mass of buildings, parks, highways, ethnic and class enclaves and sprawling suburbs into conceptually simple perspective (Readings 1-5). Once the basic theories of land use are understood, factors associated with the siting of industry and retailing activities in central cities and suburbs can be examined (6-9). Next, balanced and unbalanced economic growth theories can be used to help explain the economic development of metropolitan regions (10-12). Then, methods used to simulate alternative development patterns can provide an insight into the complexities of planning regional economic development (13-15).

Finally, some of the environmental consequences of an urban-industrial society may be explored (16-19). The reader should seek to understand environmental standards and their scientific bases, environmental data, simple simulation approaches, alternative proposed solutions to environmental degradation—such as land use control and regionalization of treatment facilities—and the estimated costs and benefits of a cleaner environment.

FIELD WORK

One cannot become a doctor solely by attending lectures and reading texts and journal articles. Time must be devoted to experimentation in the laboratory and the hospital. Similarly, one cannot adequately grasp the theories of urban social science without dealing with real world information. The retention of the basic theories and methods tends to increase by several magnitudes if each of the four focal questions is built around a field problem.

The reader can collect, map, and perform simple statistical correlations on socioeconomic data and try both to validate and to supplement the results with field observations. Similarly, central place theory may be examined in the field by classifying clusters of stores in the central place hierarchy or by interviewing shoppers to test range-of-good theories. An alternative to devising field problems is to use an existing document, such as a master plan, which would be reviewed critically, with an eye to identifying important deficiencies and suggesting alternative plans.

ADVANCED STUDY

Too frequently students graduate, find employment, and run up against a problem—a lack of technical preparation. Enthusiasm is useful, but it is not a substitute for familiarity with the tools used to construct and to evaluate a master plan, an economic development plan or an environmental impact statement. I am well aware of the fact that methods are a stumbling block for many students, and I have tried to take this into account in choosing the readings in this volume. Nevertheless, the reader should not assume that skills are easily learned on the job or that methodological sections of reports may be skimmed.

Accordingly, I urge all readers of this book who wish to pursue an interest in the four pivotal questions to seek courses which stress methods used in economic and environmental studies. A partial list of important techniques include interindustry analysis, econometrics, economic base analysis, linear programming, factor analysis, demographic projections, environmental simulation models, and cost-benefit and cost-effectiveness analyses. In short, there is no substitute for the professional skills and maturity required to ask intelligent questions about the choice of assumptions and the selection and testing of models.

ACKNOWLEDGMENTS

Acknowledgment is made to the authors and publishers below who have granted permission to reprint material and who reserve all rights in the articles appearing in this anthology.

Applebaum, William, "Chapter Seven," in *Shopping Center Strategy.* New York: International Council of Shopping Centers, 1970, pp. 165-191. This work was completed as part of the author's research activities at Harvard University.

Alonso, William, "A Theory of the Urban Land Market," *Papers and Proceedings of the Regional Science Association,* Vol. 6, 1960, pp. 149-157.

*Berry, Brian J.L., *Commercial Structure and Commercial Blight* (excerpts). Chicago, Illinois: Dept. of Geography, 1963, pp. 179-203 (Research Paper No. 85).

*Carey, George, Leonard Zobler, Michael R. Greenberg and Robert Hordon. *Urbanization, Water Pollution, and Public Policy* (excerpts). New Brunswick, N.J.: Center for Urban Policy Research, Rutgers University, 1972.

Christian, Charles M. and Sari J. Bennett, "Industrial Relocations from the Black Community of Chicago," *Growth and Change,* April 1973, pp. 14-20.

Greenberg, Michael and Robert Hordon, "Environmental Impact Statements: Some Annoying Questions." Reprinted by permission of the *Journal of the American Institute of Planners,* Vol. 40, No. 3, May 1974.

Hansen, Niles M., "Development Pole Theory in a Regional Context," *KYKLOS,* Vol. 20, 1967, pp. 709-725.

Hoover, Edgar, "Land Use Competition" (excerpts), from *The Location of Economic Activity.* Copyright © 1948 McGraw-Hill Book Company. Used by permission of McGraw-Hill Book Company.

*Hughes, James, *Urban Indicators, Metropolitan Evolution and Public Policy* (excerpts). New Brunswick, N.J.: Center for Urban Policy Research, Rutgers University, 1972.

*James, Franklin and James W. Hughes, *Economic Growth and Residential Patterns* (excerpts). New Brunswick, N.J.: copyright © Center for Urban Policy Research, Rutgers University, 1972, pp. 15-29.

Management and Economics Research, Inc., "Economic and Fiscal Impacts of a New Autonomous Enterprise in an Area." In *Industrial Location as a Factor in Regional Economic Development.* Washington, D.C.: Government Printing Office, 1967.

Management and Economics Research, Inc., "Plant Location Decision-

Making," in *Industrial Location as a Factor in Regional Economic Development*. Washington, D.C.: Government Printing Office, 1967, pp. 11-30.

Morrill, Richard L., "On the Size and Spacing of Growth Centers," *Growth and Change*, April 1973, pp. 21-24.

Simmons, James, "Changing Residence in the City," Reprinted by permission from the *Geographical Review*, Vol. 58, 1968, copyrighted by the American Geographical Society of New York.

Slavin, Richard, "Toward a State Land Use Policy: Harmonizing Development and Conservation," *State Government*, Winter 1971, pp. 2-11.

Ullman, Edward L. "The Nature of Cities Reconsidered," *Papers and Proceedings of the Regional Science Association*, Vol. 9, 1962, pp. 7-23.

*U.S. Bureau of Labor Statistics, *Patterns of U.S. Economic Growth* (excerpts). Washington, D.C.: Government Printing Office, 1970, pp. 1-10.

*U.S. Council on Environmental Quality, *Fourth Annual Report of the Council on Environmental Quality* (excerpts). Washington, D.C.: Government Printing Office, 1973.

Van Til, Sally Bould and Jon Van Til, "The Lower Class and the Future of Inequality," *Growth and Change*, January 1973, pp. 10-16.

*The editor has given his own title to the excerpts chosen from this work.

II

Intra-Urban Land Use

1

Edgar M. Hoover

LAND USE COMPETITION

6·1 *Processing Advantages and Transfer Advantages of Sites*

A producer requires a site on which to operate and can afford to pay different rents for different sites, depending on their advantages for his business. These advantages are of two sorts.

In some uses the value of a site depends primarily on the access the site affords to other parties with whom the occupant may want to trade. A good site in this sense is one entailing low *transfer costs*. For downtown urban land uses in general, transfer costs are the important locational factor, and land is rented, bought, and sold on the basis of its positional advantages alone.

At the other extreme are types of land use for which transfer costs are unimportant compared with differences in *processing costs* at good and bad sites. The more valuable the product in relation to its distribution costs per mile the greater is the significance of resource quality as against access to markets. Metal ore mining is an example—the chemical and physical make-up of the site rather than its location is the main basis of value. Other factors of intrinsic quality are the availability of water on the site in adequate amount and quality, the suitability of the soil and climate for agriculture, the natural flora and fauna (for trapping, fishing, hunting, forestry, or grazing), the amenities of the site (climate, view, and terrain), and finally those features of the site which determine construction and maintenance costs (primarily terrain, soil structure, and climate). All these aspects of intrinsic quality join with the advantages of position, in different combinations for different industries, to determine the economic attractiveness of the site.

11

This distinction between processing and transfer advantages of sites is worth emphasizing. Even if all land were of uniform quality, patterns of differential advantage and preferred land use would still arise on the basis of relative position alone. This is the case first analyzed theoretically more than a century ago by von Thünen [2] and exemplified most nearly in plains regions where the pattern of occupance is based almost entirely on transfer relations.

For the purposes of the present analysis it is appropriate to devote attention mainly to position. On the basis of its transfer advantages, a site can attract a wide variety of bidders. It is this competition of alternative uses which sets the over-all pattern of rents and land utilization. Specific quality advantages of a site, on the other hand, are often relevant only to one industry and rarely to more than a few.

6·2   Rents as the Outcome of Competitive Bidding for the Use of Sites

In so far as there really is competition and an active and informed pursuit of maximum individual advantage (which is by no means always the case), better sites will be bid up in rent and purchase price. Complete competitive equilibrium, in fact, would imply that rents on better sites were just enough higher to offset the advantages of those sites to the highest bidder, so that no producer would have any further incentive to move. The existing pattern, of course, never attains this state of equilibrium.

The landowner in general will attempt to exact the maximum rent any user will pay for the site; or if he uses it himself, he will choose a form of use that yields as great a return on the land as possible. Thus the outcome of competition for the limited and immobile supply of land tends to allocate each site to the user and type of use capable of paying the *highest rent per acre*.

Note should be made of the distinction between this principle and the one regulating the policies of the individual land user, which is the maximization of the rate of net return on his total

[2] "Der isolierte Staat in Beziehung auf Landwirthschaft und Nationalökonomie," 3 vols., Hamburg and Rostock, 1826–1863. For a more recent and accessible exposition, see R. T. Ely and G. S. Wehrwein, "Land Economics," The Macmillan Company, New York, 1940.

outlay inclusive of rent.[3] The reason for this difference is that for the individual the total resources at his command are fixed but the supply of land may be just as elastic as the supply of any other factor, whereas for the whole economy of an area, the supply of land is fixed.

6·3 Rent Gradients for Specific Types of Land Use

To understand how the process of competitive allocation of sites leads to systematic patterns of land use we must inquire what determines the maximum, or ceiling, rents that particular types of use will pay for different sites. We are interested here not in the location of individual producers but in the location pattern of an industry or type of land use, such as wheat growing or hardware selling. Within any such relatively homogeneous group of producers, the factors of locational preference are similar despite the latitude afforded by the possibility of varying the intensity of land use according to rent charged.

Figure 5·3 showed that with increasing distance from a market there is a rather consistent decline of the ceiling rents payable by any one type of land use. Since increased distribution costs reduce the net receipts of the producer, such producers can afford less rent if they are farther from the market and finally none at all at a point beyond which it would no longer pay to use the land for that purpose even if rent free.

There is such a "rent gradient," or progression of ceiling rents, for each kind of use, and no two such gradients are identical. What determines their shape?

The level of transfer costs naturally influences the slope of rent gradients. When transfer is costly, the ceiling rent for any given kind of use drops off rapidly with increasing distance; but along a route of cheap transfer, the corresponding rent gradient is relatively flat.

The structure of transfer costs influences the shape of rent gradients. It has already been noted that the characteristic long-haul economy of transfer is reflected in an accentuated concavity of the gradients; [4] i.e., ceiling rents fall off rapidly with distance

[3] Cf. Section 5·3.

[4] Cf. Fig. 5·3 and the accompanying discussion.

from market as long as the distance is short but less and less rapidly as longer hauls are involved. Over any stretch of distance for which the rate is uniform, the gradient will be horizontal, except as influenced by considerations other than freight cost. Thus the steplike characteristic of transport-rate progressions may be reflected by steps in the gradient of land use return as well.

As between different products, the slope of the gradient will differ according to the *amount and transferability of the product produced per unit of land*. This is not at all the same thing as the intensity. Intensity of use is measured by the input of capital and labor per unit of land; what is in question here is the cost of delivering the products of a unit of land. Some very intensive uses, like diamond mines, yield compact and easily transferable products; some uses of low intensity, like city parking lots, are forced by transfer considerations to be very close to their markets. Within any single kind of use, however, larger output per unit of land (of a given intrinsic quality) is directly dependent on increased intensity.

Regardless of relative intensity of land use, processes that yield a large volume of output per unit of land, particularly if the product is expensive to distribute, have relatively steep rent gradients. This is because each addition to distance adds a relatively large amount to the expense of distributing the products of an acre and thus makes a relatively large reduction in the rent earnable on an acre.

The ultimate extreme in this direction is the production of direct personal services, such as shoe shining. Where the potential customers pass, *i.e.,* on main shopping streets, the use of space for a shoe-shining establishment may justify paying a high rent; a short distance away on a side street it may be impossible to earn enough to pay any rent at all. In other words, the rent gradient in this kind of use is so steep as to be almost vertical. It is limited by the extent to which the customers themselves are willing to detour in order to get the service, and in the case of small-scale "convenience" transactions this is a very short distance indeed. At the other extreme are land uses producing small amounts of easily transferable products per unit of land. Sheep grazing, for example, is profitably practiced thousands of miles from the markets for wool and mutton.

Evidently the gradients and patterns of ceiling rents will show different characteristic forms for different land uses even in the absence of any intrinsic-quality differentiation in the land itself. Some kinds of use can afford to pay more than others for the occupance of sites convenient to markets.

The same can be said with reference to the effect of procurement costs on the location of different industries around material-supply points. That case, however, is far less significant. It is rare for a number of industries, requiring considerable space, to be competing for sites as close as possible to a single materials source. On the other hand, nearly all types of industry find a *market* in towns and cities, and for many of them the ease of access to that market is the dominant locational factor.

6·4 *Characteristic Patterns of Land Uses around Markets*

The way in which the different slopes of rent gradients around a market produce an orderly sequence of land uses is illustrated schematically in Fig. 6·1. Four representative types of use are included, with the rent gradient for each rising to a peak in the market city, since that would be the optimum location for each use from the standpoint of distribution costs alone. The rent gradients fall at different rates, so that each use in turn appears as the highest bidder.[5] The resulting idealized pattern of land uses—a series of four concentric zones—is indicated mapwise in the lower part of the figure.

In the actual world it is rare to find so neat a pattern. One reason for this is the irregularity with which transfer costs correspond to distance. Another reason is that each product or kind of land use has its own geographic pattern of supply areas and market centers.

In Fig. 6·1 the influence of only a single market center is shown. But some products (such as fluid milk) have a primarily local sale, whereas others (such as wheat) are produced largely for national or even world markets, and their whole geographic price structures are based on the prices quoted at a few major market

[5] The composite gradient of actual rents, as determined by the sequence of "highest bidder" uses, must be even more concave than the gradients for individual uses. Figure 6·1 adequately demonstrates this.

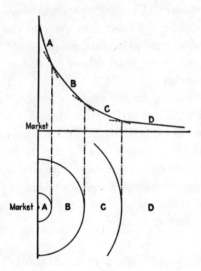

Fig. 6·1 Rent gradients and zones of land use tributary to a single market center. The upper part of the diagram shows the relation between distance from a market and rent in four different types of land use *A, B, C,* and *D.* Each of the four rent gradients is drawn as a solid line over the interval in which the corresponding land use is the highest rent use. The lower part of the diagram is a map of the resulting pattern of land-use zones.

centers. A more complete picture, which takes account of this diversity of patterns, is shown in Fig. 6·2. The flatter rent gradients of the more easily transferable products are intermittently penetrated by the more closely spaced peaks of the steeper local gradients.

The over-all pattern of land uses shows broad regions of supply for the most easily transferable products, interrupted occasionally by smaller enclosed supply areas for less easily transferable products, which are, in turn, interrupted frequently by the very small enclosed supply areas of the least transferable products. The rather complex pattern of land-use areas derived in Fig. 6·2 for only three products under high simplified assumptions should make it clear why in the much more complicated actual world, with many rival products and sets of markets, we see a patchwork that sometimes appears utterly unsystematic.

6·5 *Influence of Differences in Land Quality on Rent Gradients and Land Use*

Little attention has been given thus far to differences in the intrinsic quality of the land, which affect ceiling rents by determining processing costs in specific uses. Areas of especially low processing cost could be shown as humps on the rent gradients; areas of especially high cost (such as swamps, mountains, sterile soil, etc.), by depressions or gaps in the gradients.

The circumstances that make for low processing costs in one type of land use may be less advantageous or even a handicap for another type of use. On industrial sites, for example, soil fertility is irrelevant. Again, most good vineyard land is poor onion land and vice versa. The gradients for different uses have quite different configurations, though all share the tendency to rise with nearness to market centers.

Rent gradients for the production of valuable materials—or more generally, for activities restricted to a few scarce and highly specialized sites—consist only of short segments or isolated stalagmites. In such cases, the presence and the richness of the specific resource in question is a much more important factor than access of market.

6·6   Impediments to Optimum Utilization of Land

The foregoing simplified exposition of the principles of land-use competition ignores practical problems of great importance. Every change in production techniques, markets, transportation rates, etc., alters the conditions of profitable land use and raises, lowers, or reshapes the various gradients. The adjustments consequent to these changes often take a long time and create maladjustments of the locational pattern, which will be given some attention in a later chapter.

It must also be recognized that the land use adopted by the user is not always the best one, despite competitive pressures and incentives. The user may cling to an inferior use because he knows no other; he may be indifferent to the prospect of greater returns; rent charges may fail to be readjusted in response to potential returns; or the user may decide on a use that is most profitable for him in the immediate future but not so good from a long-run standpoint or from a broader social point of view. He may abuse and even destroy the land resources through ignorance or through unwillingness or inability to take a long-range view. He may use his land in such a way as to handicap others,

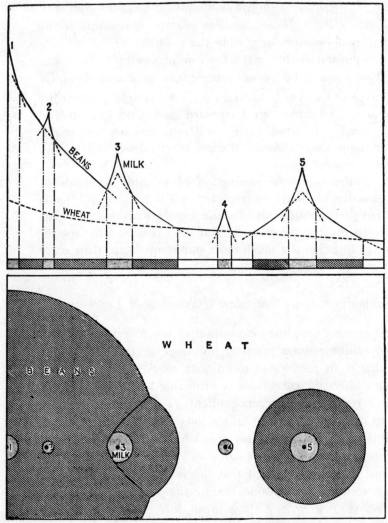

Fig. 6·2 Rent gradients and zones of land use tributary to five market centers, 1, 2, 3, 4, and 5. Three types of land use are involved: milk, beans, and wheat production. It is assumed that a market for milk exists at each of the five market centers, that markets for beans exist at market centers 1, 3, and 5 only, and that a market for wheat exists only at market center 1.

The upper part of the diagram shows the rent gradients for the three types of use, each rent gradient being drawn as a solid line over the interval in which the corresponding land use is the highest rent use.

The resulting progression of land uses along the route running through the five market centers is shown by the shadings on the strip near the middle

e.g., by stream pollution or by cropping practices that lead to erosion and floods, silting of reservoirs, etc. All these problems of locational dynamics and possible conflicts of private with public interest lie, however, beyond the scope of the present chapter.

---

of the figure: Stippled stretches of territory are devoted to milk production; shaded stretches to bean production; and white stretches to wheat production.

The lower part of the diagram is a map of the resulting pattern of land use zones. Dots represent the five market centers. Stippled areas are devoted to milk production; shaded areas to bean production; and white areas to wheat production. The bean-supply areas of market centers 1 and 3 meet along the boundary that curves around market center 3.

2

William Alonso

A THEORY OF THE URBAN LAND MARKET

THE EARLY THEORY of rent and location concerned itself primarily with agricultural land. This was quite natural, for Ricardo and Malthus lived in an agricultural society. The foundations of the formal spatial analysis of agricultural rent and location are found in the work of J. von Thunen, who said, without going into detail, that the urban land market operated under the same principles.[1] As cities grew in importance, relatively little attention was paid to the theory of urban rents. Even the great Marshall provided interesting but only random insights, and no explicit theory of the urban land market and urban locations was developed.

Since the beginning of the twentieth century there has been considerable interest in the urban land market in America. R.M. Hurd[2] in 1903 and R. Haig[3] in the twenties tried to create a theory of urban land by following von Thunen. However, their approach copied the form rather than the logic of agricultural theory, and the resulting theory can be shown to be insufficient on its own premises. In particular, the theory failed to consider residences, which constitute the preponderant land use in urban areas.

Yet there are interesting problems that a theory of urban land must consider. There is, for instance, a paradox in American cities: the poor live near the center, on expensive land, and the rich on the periphery, on cheap land. On the logical side, there are also aspects of great interest, but which increase the difficulty of the analysis. When a purchaser acquires land, he acquires two goods (land and location) in only one transaction, and only one payment is made for the combination. He could buy the same quantity of land at another location, or he could buy more, or less land at the same location. In the

---

[1] *Johan von Thunen*, DER ISOLIERTE STAAT IN BEZIEHUNG AUF LANDWIRTSCHAFT UND NATIONALEKONOMIE, *1st. vol., 1826, 3d. vol. and new edition, 1863.*

[2] *Richard M. Hurd*, PRINCIPLES OF CITY LAND VALUES, *N.Y.: The Record and Guide, 1903.*

[3] *Robert M. Haig. "Toward an Understanding of the Metropolis",* QUARTERLY JOURNAL OF ECONOMICS, *XL: 3, May 1926; and* REGIONAL SURVEY OF NEW YORK AND ITS ENVIRONS, *N.Y.: New York City Plan Commission, 1927.*

analysis, one encounters, as well, a negative good (distance) with positive costs (commuting costs); or, conversely, a positive good (accessibility) with negative costs (savings in commuting). In comparison with agriculture, the urban case presents another difficulty. In agriculture, the location is extensive: many square miles may be devoted to one crop. In the urban case the site tends to be much smaller, and the location may be regarded as a dimensionless point rather than an area. Yet the thousands or millions of dimensionless points which constitute the city, when taken together, cover extensive areas. How can these dimensionless points be aggregated into two-dimensional space?

Here I will present a non-mathematical over-view, without trying to give it full precision, of the long and rather complex mathematical analysis which constitures a formal theory of the urban land market.[4] It is a static model in which change is introduced by comparative statics. And it is an economic model: it speaks of economic men, and it goes without saying that real men and social groups have needs, emotions, and desires which are not considered here. This analysis uses concepts which fit with agricultural rent theory in such a way that urban and rural land uses may be considered at the same time, in terms of a single theory. Therefore, we must examine first a very simplified model of the agricultural land market.

AGRICULTURAL MODEL

In this model, the farmers are grouped around a single market, where they sell their products. If the product is wheat, and the produce of one acre of wheat sells for $100 at the market while the costs of production are $50 per acre, a farmer growing wheat at the market would make a profit of $50 per acre. But if he is producing at some distance-say, 5 miles - and it costs him $5 per mile to ship an acre's product, his transport costs will be $25 per acre. His profits will be equal to value minus production costs minus shipping charges: 100-50-25 = $25. This relation may be shown diagrammatically (see Figure 1). At the market, the farmer's profits are $50, and 5 miles out, $25; at intermediate distance, he will receive intermediate profits. Finally, at a distance of 10 miles from the market, his production costs plus shipping charges will just equal the value of his produce at the market. At distances greater than 10 miles, the farmer would operate at a loss.

In this model, the profits derived by the farmers are tied directly to their location. If the functions of farmer and landowner are viewed as separate, farmers will bid rents for land according to the profitability of the location The profits of the farmer will therefore be shared with the landowner through rent payments. As farmers bid against each other for the more profitable locations, until farmers' profits are

[4]A full development of the theory is presented in my doctoral dissertation, A MODEL OF THE URBAN LAND MARKET: LOCATIONS AND DENSITIES OF DWELLINGS AND BUSINESSES, University of Pennsylvania, 1960.

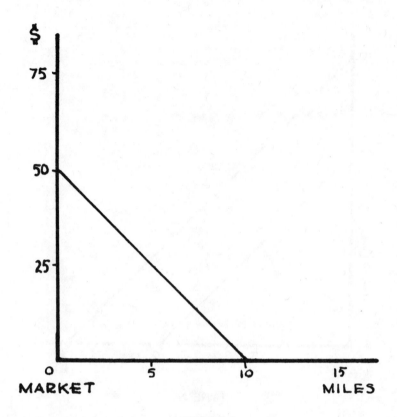

FIGURE I

everywhere the same ("normal" profits), what we have called profits becomes rent. Thus, the curve in Figure 1, which we derived as a farmers'
profit curve, once we distinguish between the roles of the farmer and
the landowner, becomes a bid rent function, representing the price or
rent per acre that farmers will be willing to pay for land at the different locations.

We have shown that the slope of the rent curve will be fixed by the
transport costs on the produce. The level of the curve will be set by
the price of the produce at the market. Examine Figure 2. The lower
curve is that of Figure 1, where the price of wheat is $100 at the mar-
ket, and production costs are $50. If demand increases, and the price
of wheat at the market rises to $125 (while production and transport
costs remain constant), profits or bid rent at the market will be $75;
at 5 miles, $50; $25 at 10 miles, and zero at 15 miles. Thus, each bid
rent curve is a function of rent vs. distance, but there is a family of
such curves, the level of any one determined by the price of the produce at the market, higher prices setting higher curves.

Consider now the production of peas. Assume that the price at the market of one acre's production of peas is $150, the costs of production

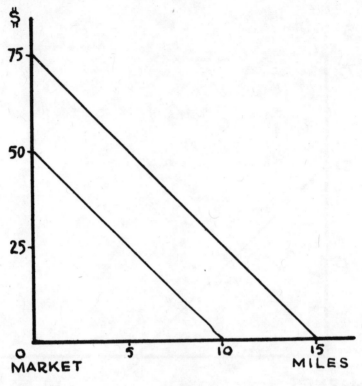

FIGURE 2

are $75, and the transport costs per mile are $10. These conditions will yield curve MN in Figure 3, where bid rent by pea farmers at the market is $75 per acre, 5 miles from the market $25, and zero at 7.5 miles. Curve RS represents bid rents by wheat farmers, at a price of $100 for wheat. If will be seen that pea farmers can bid higher rents in the range of 0 to 5 miles from the market; farther out, wheat farmers can bid higher rents. Therefore, pea farming will take place in the ring from 0 to 5 miles from the market, and wheat farming in the ring from 5 to 10 miles. Segments MT of the bid rent curve of pea farming and TS of wheat farming will be the effective rents, while segments RT and TN represent unsuccessful bids.

The price of the product is determined by the supply-demand relations at the market. If the region between zero and 5 miles produces too many peas, the price of the product will drop, and a lower bid rent curve for pea farming will come into effect, so that pea farming will be practiced to some distance less than 5 miles.

Abstracting this view of the agricultural land market, we have that:

(1) land uses determine land values, through competitive bidding among farmers;

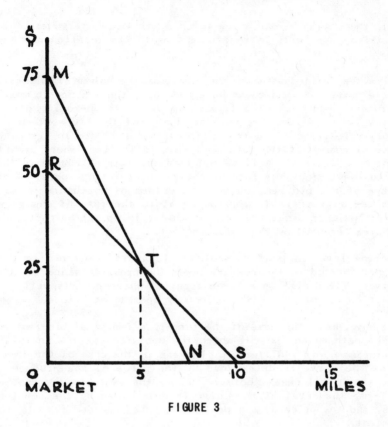

FIGURE 3

(2) land values distribute land uses, according to their ability to pay;
(3) the steeper curves capture the central locations. (This point is a simplified one for simple, well-behaved curves.

Abstracting the process now *from* agriculture, we have:

(1) for each user of land (e.g., wheat farmer) a family of bid rent functions is derived, such that the user is indifferent as to his location along any *one* of these functions (because the farmer, who is the decision-maker in this case, finds that profits are everywhere the same, i.e., normal, as long as he remains on one curve);
(2) the equilibrium rent at any location is found by comparing the bids of the various potential users and choosing the highest;
(3) equilibrium quantities of land are found by selecting the proper bid rent curve for each user (in the agricultural case, the curve which equates supply and demand for the produce).

BUSINESS

We shall now consider the urban businessman, who, we shall assume, makes his decisions so as to maximize profits. A bid rent curve for the businessman, then, will be one along which profits are everywhere the same: the decision-maker will be indifferent as to his location along such a curve.

Profit may be defined as the remainder from the volume of business after operating costs and land costs have been deducted. Since in most cases the volume of business of a firm as well as its operating costs will vary with its location, the rate of change of the bid rent curve will bear no simple relation to transport costs (as it did in agriculture). The rate of change of the total bid rent for a firm, where profits are constant by definition, will be equal to the rate of change in the volume of business minus the rate of change in operating costs. Therefore the slope of the bid rent curve, the values of which are in terms of dollars per unit of land, will be equal to the rate of change in the volume of business minus the rate of change in operating costs, divided by the area occupied by the establishment.

A different level of profits would yield a different bid rent curve. The higher the bid rent curve, the lower the profits, since land is more expensive. There will be a highest curve, where profits will be zero. At higher land rents the firm could only operate at a loss.

Thus we have, as in the case of the farmer, a family of bid rent curves, along the path of any one of which the decision-maker - in this case, the businessman - is indifferent. Whereas in the case of the farmer the level of the curve is determined by the price of the produce, while profits are in all cases "normal", i.e., the same, in the case of the urban firm, the level of the curve is determined by the level of the profits, and the price of its products may be regarded for our purposes as constant.

RESIDENTIAL

The household differs from the farmer and the urban firm in that satisfaction rather than profits is the relevant criterion of optional location. A consumer, given his income and his pattern of tastes, will seek to balance the costs and bother of commuting against the advantages of cheaper land with increasing distance from the center of the city and the satisfaction of more space for living. When the individual consumer faces a given pattern of land costs, his equilibrium location and the size of his site will be in terms of the marginal changes of these variables.

The bid rent curves of the individual will be such that, for any given curve, the individual will be equally satisfied at every location at the price set by the curve. Along any bid rent curve, the price the individual will bid for land will decrease with distance from the center at a rate just sufficient to produce an income effect which will balance to his satisfaction the increased costs of commuting and the bother of a long trip. This slope may be expressed quite precisely in mathematical terms, but it is a complex expression, the exact interpretation of which is beyond the scope of this paper.

Just as different prices of the produce set different levels for the bid rent curves of the farmer, and different levels of profit for the urban firm, different levels of satisfaction correspond to the various levels of the family of bid rent curves of the individual household. The higher curves obviously yield less satisfaction because a higher price is implied, so that, at any given location, the individual will be able to afford less land and other goods.

INDIVIDUAL EQUILIBRIUM

It is obvious that families of bid rent curves are in many respects similar to indifference curve mappings. However, they differ in some important ways. Indifference curves map a path of indifference (equal satisfaction) between combinations of quantities of two goods. Bid rent functions map an indifference path between the price of one good (land) and quantities of another and strange type of good, distance from the center of the city. Whereas indifference curves refer only to tastes and not to budget, in the case of households, bid rent functions are derived both from budget and taste considerations. In the case of the urban firm, they might be termed isoprofit curves. A more superficial difference is that, whereas the higher indifference curves are the preferred ones, it is the lower bid rent curves that yield greater profits or satisfaction. However, bid rent curves may be used in a manner analogous to that of indifference curves to find the equilibrium location and land price for the resident or the urban firm.

Assume you have been given a bid rent mapping of a land use, whether business or residential (curves $brc_{1,2,3}$, etc., in Figure 4). Superimpose on the same diagram the actual structure of land prices in the city (curve SS). The decision-maker will wish to reach the lowest possible bid rent curve. Therefore, he will choose that point at which the curve of actual prices (SS) will be tangent to the lowest of the bid rent curves with which it comes in contact (brc_2). At this point will be the equilibrium location (L) and the equilibrium land rent (R) for this user of land. If he is a businessman, he will have maximized profits; if he is a resident, he will have maximized satisfaction.

Note that to the left of this point of equilibrium (toward the center of the city) the curve of actual prices is steeper than the bid rent curve; to the right of this point (away from the center) it is less steep. This is another aspect of the rule we noted in the agricultural model: the land uses with steeper bid rent curves capture the central locations.

MARKET EQUILIBRIUM

We now have, conceptually, families of bid rent curves for all three types of land uses. We also know that the steeper curves will occupy the more central locations. Therefore, if the curves of the various users are ranked by steepness, they will also be ranked in terms of their accessibility from the center of the city in the final solution.

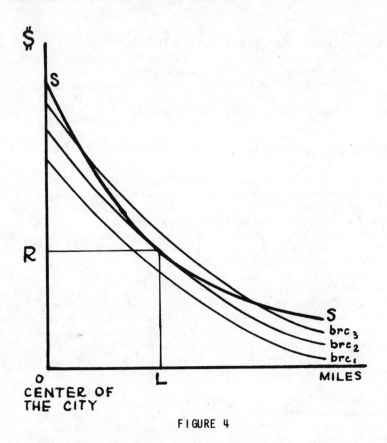

FIGURE 4

Thus, if the curves of the business firm are steeper than those of residences, and the residential curves steeper than the agricultural, there will be business at the center of the city, surrounded by residences, and these will be surrounded by agriculture.

This reasoning applies as well within land use groupings. For instance, it can be shown that, given two individuals of similar tastes, both of whom prefer living at low densities, if their incomes differ, the bid rent curves of the wealthier will be flatter than those of the man of lower income. Therefore, the poor will tend to central locations on expensive land and the rich to cheaper land on the periphery. The reason for this is not that the poor have greater purchasing power, but rather that they have steeper bid rent curves. This stems from the fact that, at any given location, the poor can buy less land than the rich, and since only a small quantity of land is involved, changes in its price are not as important for the poor as the costs and inconvenience of commuting. The rich, on the other hand, buy greater quantities of land, and are consequently affected by changes in its price to a greater degree. In other words, because of variations in density among different levels of income, accessibility behaves as an inferior good.

Thus far, through ranking the bid rent curves by steepness, we have found the relative rankings of prices and locations, but not the actual prices, locations, or densities. It will be remembered that in the agricultural case equilibrium levels were brought about by changes in the price of the products, until the amount of land devoted to each crop was in agreement with the demand for that crop.

For urban land this process is more complex. The determination of densities (or their inverse, lot size) and locations must be found simultaneously with the resulting price structure. Very briefly, the method consists of assuming a price of land at the center of the city, and determining the prices at all other locations by the competitive bidding of the potential users of land in relation to this price. The highest bid captures each location, and each bid is related to a most preferred alternative through the use of bid rent curves. This most preferred alternative is the marginal combination of price and location for that particular land use. The quantities of land occupied by the land users are determined by these prices. The locations are determined by assigning to each successive user of land the location available nearest the center of the city after the assignment of land quantities to the higher and more central bidders.

Since initially the price at the center of the city was assumed, the resulting set of prices, locations, and densities may be in error. A series of iterations will yield the correct solution. In some cases, the solution may be found by a set of simultaneous equations rather than by the chain of steps which has just been outlined.

The model presented in this paper corresponds to the simplest case: a single-center city, on a featureless plain, with transportation in all directions. However, the reasoning can be extended to cities with several centers (shopping, office, manufacturing, etc.), with structured road patterns, and other realistic complications. The theory can also be made to shed light on the effects of economic development, changes in income structure, zoning regulations, taxation policies, and other. At this stage, the model is purely theoretical; however, it is hoped that it may provide a logical structure for econometric models which may be useful for prediction.

3

James Hughes

SOCIAL AREA ANALYSIS

The present state of urban ecological inquiry is the cumulative
result of research efforts carried out during the past 50 years in
a number of subfields in the social sciences. The early traditions
of urban ecology--a discipline which applied certain principles and
processes of biological ecology to the urban milieu--have converged
with the more recent trends in social area analysis in a context of
advancing computer technology and multivariate statistical techniques.
The result has been the emergence of a new approach to the study of
urban spatial structure. This approach, known as factorial ecology,
is a direct outgrowth of an earlier technique--social area analysis--
which we shall now examine.

SOCIAL AREA ANALYSIS

"Social area analysis is one approach to the classic problem of
urban ecology, the succinct description of the location of residential
areas by types within cities in terms meaningful to persons interested
in social differentiation and stratification."[1] Although the technique as it was originally formulated "disclaimed interest in traditional ecological preoccupations with urban spatial structure,"[2] it helped
revitalize interest in this latter concern.

Viewed in its strict sense, social area analysis refers to the specific technique and theoretical elaboration developed by Eshref
Shevky and his associates in their studies of Los Angeles and San
Francisco commencing in the later 1940s.[3] It seeks to relate the
areal differentiation of American cities to basic societal changes.
Three basic constructs are used in describing complex urban social
structures in an industrial society. These constructs--social rank
(economic status), urbanization (family status), and segregation (ethnic status)--are purported to represent the urban social consequence
of a shift from a rural and/or preindustrial way of life to an advanced industrial society. For each of these constructs, an index
was developed, comprising the census variables of Exhibit 2-1. Tract
populations in urban areas are thus defined by their scores on these
two indices. Tracts having high scores on the social rank index tend
to have residents who are employed in white collar occupations, who
have attained high levels of education, and who live in expensive housing. Conversely, low scoring tracts are characterized by blue collar

31

occupations and low rental and educational levels. The second index,
urbanization, measures the population's stage in life cycle. High
scoring tracts are dominated by families in the child-rearing stage,
consequently having many young children and few women in the labor
force and many single-family dwellings. Low scoring tracts have low
rates of fertility, many working females, and high proportions of
multiple-dwelling units. High scores on the third index, ethnic status

---

EXHIBIT 2-1

SOCIAL AREA INDEXES

Social Rank (Economic Status)	Urbanization (Family Status)	Segregation (Ethnic Status)
Occupation	Fertility	Racial and national groups in relative isolation
Schooling	Women at Work	
Rent	Single Family Dwelling Units	

---

reflect strong concentrations of racial minorities while low scores
define areas dominated by native-born white populations.

Tracts can be grouped into social areas (defined) based upon their
scoring pattern for these three indexes. "Employing the concept of
attribute space, a three dimensional space is constructed with the
indexes of social rank, urbanization, and segregation as the three
axes. Tracts near one another in this social attribute space have
similar patterns of scores on the three indexes and are grouped into
a type."[4] Social area analysis thus isolates and classifies census
tracts into social areas in terms of these three basic indexes, which
are assumed to represent the principal dimensions of urban social
structure.

Theoretical Rationale

The theoretical justification for social area analysis was presented[5]
several years after the basic constructs themselves were introduced.
Fundamental to it is the concept of the city as "a product of the
complex whole of modern society; thus the social forms of urban life
are to be understood within the changing character of the larger
containing society."[6] In other words, the social organization of
urban areas might be reasonably explained in terms of the basic
parameters of the larger containing society.

These parameters are based upon three broad postulates, each of which
reflects the increasing scale[7]--the scope and intensity of social
interaction--of modern industrial society (Exhibit 2-2). From these
postulates (Column 1), the forces and trends underlying modern societal
change can be derived (Column 2). The consequences of these trends
are subsequently translated into changes in the structure of a given

EXHIBIT 2-2

STEPS IN CONSTRUCT FORMATION AND INDEX CONSTRUCTION

Postulates Concerning Industrial Society (Aspects of Increasing Scale) (1)	Statistics of Trends (2)	Changes in the Structure of a Given Social System (3)	Constructs (4)	Sample Statistics (Related to the Constructs) (5)	Derived Measures (From Col. 5) (6)	
Change in the range and intensity of relations	Changing distribution of skills: Lessening importance of manual productive operations - growing importance of clerical, supervisory, management operations	Changes in the arrangement of occupations based on function	Social Rank (economic status)	Years of schooling Employment status Class of worker Major occupation group Value of home Rent by dwelling group Plumbing and repair Persons per room Heating and refrigeration	Occupation Schooling Rent	Index I
Differentiation of function	Changing structure of productive activity: Lessening importance of primary production - growing importance of relations centered in cities - lessening importance of the household as economic unit	Changes in the ways of living - movement of women into urban occupations - spread of alternative family patterns	Urbanization (family status)	Age and sex Owner or tenant House structure Persons in household	Fertility Women at work Single-family dwelling units	Index II
Complexity of organization	Changing composition of population: Increasing movement - alterations in age and sex distribution - increasing diversity	Redistribution in space-changes in the proportion of supporting and dependent population - isolation and segregation of groups	Segregation (ethnic status)	Race and nativity Country of birth Citizenship	Racial and national groups in relative isolation	Index III

social system (Column 3). These changes are then redefined as
structural reflections of change or simply constructs (Column 4),
which serve as the basic dimensions for the study of social differentiation of modern industrial society.

In Postulate 1 the process of increasing scale leads to individual
specialization in production by specific process, rather than by
product that was common in the preindustrial city.[8] The increasing
division of labor[9] is accompanied by increased importance of tertiary
and quarternary economic activities, i.e., service industries; this
in turn results in changes in the arrangement of occupations by function
producing a hierarchical ranking of occupational groups according to
levels of skill, education, income and prestige. This structural
change in the social system is represented by the construct of social
rank.

In Postulate 2, changes in the nature of productive activity--i.e.,
the separation of home and work, both spatially and by the separation
of the family organization from the production organization--result
in changes in lifestyle.[10] Alternative family patterns emerge and
women enter the labor force. This structural change in the social
system is represented by the construct of urbanization.

The third postulate, representing the changing composition of the
population, reflects increased mobility and diversity. These, in
turn, lead to territorial redistribution, the isolation and segregation of subgroups; the resulting construct indexes racial segregation.

Having established these three major areas of social differentiation,
Shevky and Bell view individuals and groups in modern society as
being "significantly differentiated with respect to the long term
trends which have been important in the development of the character
of [that] society".[11]

An operable format is achieved by establishing measures revealing
those aspects of the urban population "which are most clearly indicative of the changing distribution of skills, the changing organization of productive activity (especially the changing structure
of the family), and changing composition of the population".[12] These
measures are the social area indexes--social rank, urbanization and
segregation.

This theoretical elaboration stems directly from the concepts of
urbanism formulated by Louis Wirth. "In his view, urbanism was tied,
at least in the West, to large-scale economic and political units,
to a calculating approach to social relationships, to an elaborate
division of labor which obscured simple class differences, and to
an emphasis on readily visible symbols and mass produced goods and
services."[14]

Wirth based his analysis of urban social organization and attitudes
upon three variables--size, density, and heterogeneity. His underlying
propositions, deriving from a description of the city as a relatively large, dense, and heterogeneous permanent settlement, approximate
the postulates employed by Shevky and Bell. Consequently, their urban
constructs reflect Wirth's observations of the decreasing importance
of both primary contacts and of the family as a societal unit.

Two major differences between their analysis and Wirth's are nevertheless apparent; whereas Wirth views the city as the prime mover,
Shevky and Bell see it rather as a mirror of trends in the larger
carrying society. Wirth's analysis was thus considered incomplete
in its underlying assumption:

> it is not the city which is an underlying prime mover
> in the recent transformation of Western society, but
> the necessity of economic expansion itself. Size,
> density, and heterogeneity, important in describing
> the urban ambit, are not the most significant aspects
> of urbanization - for urbanization is a stage of total
> society, as well as of its cities.[15]

In other words, given the societal differentiation of types,
Shevky and Bell suggest that this differentiation finds urban
territorial expression. And second, while Wirth focused on urbanism
as a way of life, the social area scheme "assumed that there is a
continuum of alternative life styles at the same economic level and
that these are concentrated in different urban sub-areas...In this
view, the Shevky-Bell index of urbanization is a putative means of
identifying such variations in 'ways of life'".[16]

Among the critics of social area analysis were Amos Hawley and Otis
Duncan. They concluded that there are

> serious obscurities and gaps in the theoretical form-
> ulations about 'social area analysis' that must be remedied
> before its more ambitious claims are granted...it seems
> to us evident that 'social area analysis' boasts no
> theory that cogently relates hypotheses about areal struc-
> ture to propositions about social differentiation...efforts
> at construction formation...look suspiciously like an
> ex-post facto rationalization for their choice of indexes.[17]

Further reservations about the logic of the theoretical schema were
expressed by B. T. Robson:

> If each of the three steps is followed, it can read-
> ily be seen that there is no logical procedure where-
> by the selection of the particular indexes can be justi-
> fied. At each of the various stages in the argument
> there would appear to be a variety of possible deriva-
> tions in place of those selected by Shevky. Further-
> more, this scale transition in the argument, from the
> scale of a total society to an intraurban level, would
> not appear to be the most fruitful basis on which to
> provide criteria for the selection of variables which
> are diagnostic in the analysis of urban social struc-
> ture.[18]

Robson's argument is weakened, however, by the fact that although
he suggests the possibility of alternative derivations, he offers
no specific substitutes for those used by Shevky and Bell.

Richard Udry, in addressing himself to the scale question, subjected
the Shevky-Bell model to a temporal test and asked: "...how can
you get from the theory of increasing scale to the axes of differenti-

ation of sub-areas? Deductively, you cannot get there from here".[19]
But deductive process was amply illuminated in Shevky and Bell's
theoretical elaboration.

Shevky and Bell, have not been criticized so much for attributing
urban change to changes in society as a whole. The major target for
their critics has been the ex-post facto nature of their theoretical
deductions.

In responding to Udry's criticism and presumably to that of their
other detractors, Bell and Moskos concede the deficiencies of
the theoretical scheme as originally formulated, concluding that "it
needs elaboration in both detail and scope".[20]

Yet the validity of the basic constructs of the social area scheme
is supported by the empirical findings of planners in residential
areas. Hans Blumenfeld, for example, has observed that urban residential areas "are patterned by two factors: family composition and
income...[but] the pattern of segregation by income class is, in
the United States, overlaid and obscured by race segregation".[21] But
the most convincing justification of the Shevky-Bell constructs emerge
from several rigorous empirical tests within appropriate cultural-
temporal contexts.

Empirical Validity

Wendell Bell, in 1955, undertook empirical research "to test the
extent to which the three dimensions are necessary to account for
social differentiation between urban sub-populations in two metropolitan areas, Los Angeles and San Francisco, and to determine whether
the indexes selected to measure the three dimensions are unidimensional measuring instruments".[22] He hypothesized that economic
status, family status, and ethnic status each represent a discrete
social factor which is necessary to account for the differences in
social characteristics between urban populations. A sub-hypothesis
concerned the component variables for each index as originally conceived for the social-area scheme.

Using factor analysis, Bell compared the normative-theoretical
constructs and the rotated factor matrix computed from the empirical
relations in each of the observed areas. In comparing the predicted
with the observed values in each of the two regions, he found substantial support for the two hypotheses,[23] thereby lending some
credence to the Shevky-Bell formulations.

At about the same time, in San Francisco, Robert Tryon attempted to
derive social dimensions empirically by using cluster analysis on 33
variables measuring population, housing, and employment characteristics. The three most independent clusters derived corresponded
strikingly to the three principal social area dimensions, thereby
providing a degree of empirical verification via an alternative
technique.

A more extensive factor analytic test of the model was reported by
VanArsdol, Camilleri and Schmidt on ten United States cities. They
constructed a limited model of urban society on the basis of the ten
cities combined. Their factor analysis showed "that the Shevky census
tract measures differentiate at least three dimensions in the in-

ternal structure of the combined cities and the dimensions are [24]
related to the census tract measures in the manner specified by Shevky"
However, when analyzed separately, six cities verified the existence
of the hypothesized structure while four did not. In two of the latter--
southern cities--fertility was associated with both economic and family
status, while the other two revealed an association between fertility
and economic status. (This anomaly will be discussed in Chapter 3 and
Appendix H.)

Still another factor analytic study was undertaken in Toledo by Anderson and Bean. They extended the number of variables beyond those included in the indexes.[25] Although their findings confirmed the general structure of the Shevky-Bell dimensions, the urbanization index
separated into what was designated a housing factor and an urbanization
factor. Despite this exception, the authors felt that they had established the factorial existence of the social area dimensions.

The weight of the abovementioned support for the social area dimensions
of differentiation in American cities led to several other areas of
inquiry. One of these concerned the technique's applicability in different socio-cultural contexts.

Cross Cultural-Temporal Analyses

An important test of the Shevky-Bell dimensions outside the North
American setting was made by Dennis McElrath in Rome. He investigated
relationships between the variables measuring social rank and urbanization indexes;[26] data limitations and differences necessitated his
use of several surrogate variables. His finding of a high degree of
intercorrelation among the variables composing the two indexes raised
a question about the independence of the two constructs. Although
McElrath chose to evade this question, Robson, in reexamining the
data, concluded that "the utility of the Shevky technique within the
context of Rome would therefore appear to be thrown in doubt".[27]

In a subsequent study of Accra, Ghana, McElrath introduced the idea
that change in the organization of developing societies is accompanied
by changes in the dimensions of social differentiation.[28] Viewing
urban patterns of differentiation as a consequence of the state of
the total society, he raised the question: "Is increasing differentiation, by an increasing number of dimensions, a necessary consequence
of increasing scale?"[29]

McElrath evolved a theoretical frame of reference that was an adaptation of the original social area analysis formulations. He divided
increase in scale into two essential components--industrialization
and urbanization--which subsequently yield four basic dimensions of
social differentiation.[30] His addition of a fourth construct, migrant
status, to the Shevky scheme, has not as yet been generalized empirically. This additional dimension results from McElrath's view
of the urbanization process as yielding "two analytically distinct
divisions within the urban community,"[31] migrant status and ethnic
heterogeneity.

McElrath later constructed a comparative analysis of Accra; Kingston,
Jamaica; San Francisco, and of the combined data of ten United States
cities.[32] Selecting the samples because of their representation of
four levels of societal scale, he focused on the relations between

EXHIBIT 2-3

FRAME OF REFERENCE FOR ANALYSIS OF SOCIAL DIFFERENTIATION
ACCRA, GHANA

	Distributive Changes		Related Dimensions of Differentiation	
	Changes	Measures	Construction	Subarea Measures
Industrialization	Distribution of Skills	Literacy, Schooling Commerce workers Nonmanual workers	Social Rank	Occupation Education
Industrialization	Structure of Production	Nonagricultural workers Industrial diversity Wage and salaried workers Tertiary workers	Family Status	Fertility Women in Labor Force
Urbanization	Aggregation of Population	Urban concentration Metropolitan concentration	Migrant Status	Distance: Birthplace Selection: Age-sex structure
Urbanization	Dispersion of Resources	Measure of external dispersion Immigration rates	Ethnic Status	Cultural visibility (Tribal origin) (National origin) Physical visibility

Source: Dennis McElrath, "Societal Scale and Social Differentiation;
Accra, Ghana," The New Urbanization, Scott Greer, et al.
(New York: St. Martin's Press, 1968), p. 35.

social differentiation and increase in scale.[33]

His findings concerning the dimension of social rank may be generalized as follows:

1. Social rank is an independent dimension of social
    differentiation in cities of society with a low
    level of skills distribution. (Accra, Kingston).

2. Social rank becomes increasingly independent of
    family status as the level of skills distribution
    advances (Rome, U.S.).

3. The independence of social rank varies among urban
    areas of the same large-scale society (the ten
    medium-sized cities and the San Francisco Bay Region).

The dimension of family status follows a somewhat different pattern:

1. Family status does not operate as an independent
    dimension in cities of a society which has undergone
    only limited changes of the structure of production
    (Ghana).

2. Family status operates independently of social rank
    in a society with slightly more advanced production
    structure.

3. Family status becomes increasingly independent of
    social rank as societal scale increases; it reaches its
    greatest independence in a society of largest scale
    (United States).

4. Within large-scale societies, the independence of
    family status varies from one urban area to another,
    with greatest independence in larger metropolitan
    areas.

Because McElrath's findings concern ;g the other two dimensions--
migrant status and ethnic status--however, were not as fruitful, they
can be regarded only as suggestions.

Research along these same lines was undertaken in Cairo, Egypt by Janet
Abu-Lughod, who shares McElrath's interest in relating the type and
complexity of intraurban differentiation to the scale of the larger
containing society. She suggested that "the pattern of social (and
physical) differentiation in preindustrial societies (cities) would be
relatively simple and perhaps unidimensional; as the scale of society
increased, there would be increased complexity of differentiation and
a separation of the axes or dimensions of differentiation".[34]

In her principal-axes factor analysis with oblique rotation, the
significant finding was a close association between certain variables
of family status and those of economic status. In a subsequent
attempt to explain this relationship, Abu-Lughod effectively established the conditions for both association and disassociation between
the family and socio-economic variables. Applying these to McElrath's
findings, Abu-Lughod explained that Accra was

> still ecologically structured according to the prein-
> dustrial principle of ethnicity, linked by endogamy to
> extended kinship networks...Family differences are
> still linked to cultural variations between ethnic and
> tribal groups...When these factors are combined with the
> low level of housing type differentiation...the result is
> weak vectors of residential differentiation, as measured
> by the indices that have proven powerful discriminations
> in Western industrial societies.[35]

Abu-Lughod questioned the broad applicability of the deductive dimensions posited by the social area analysts. She concluded that
a theory of comparative urban ecology can be developed by determining
the actual dimensions of urban social structure revealed through
factor analyses of each city. This application of factor analysis to
ecological study is termed "factorial ecology;" its constructs are not
determined a priori, but are an empirical outcome of the analysis.

Both Abu-Lughod and McElrath concluded that the social area dimensions
serve to represent urban differentiation only in societies of the
largest scale. The indexes therefore would have limited utility in
developing societies, where structural differentiation may be unidimen
sional or in some transient state, i.e., in process of change.   Increa
ing complexity of differentiation, represented by an increasing number
and separation of dimensions, is viewed by these authors as an inevit
able consequence of increasing scale.

This notion about scale was first raised by McElrath in seeking to
determine at what point in scale the two forms of differentiation (social rank and urbanization) emerge, he elaborated the following possible situations:[36]

1. Sub-area populations are not differentiated by
    either dimension of the typology. Presumably this
    would occur in societies of minimum scale according
    to the Shevky formulation.

2. Sub-areas are differentiated by only one dimension
    of the typology. Presumably this would occur at some
    point in scale if primacy exists for either dimension.

3. Sub-area populations are differentiated by both di-
    mensions. This would occur in large scale societies
    either (1) subsequent to situation II if primacy
    occurs or (2) at some point in scale following the
    first situation if no primacy occurs.

Working about the same time as McElrath (1962), Scott Greer introduced the same concept. Considering American society at the turn of
the century as an early phase of increase in scale, Greer suggested
three dimensions of differentiation: "occupational background, cultur
background (or ethos), and rural or urban origins,"[37] all highly inter-
correlated, perhaps unidimensional, phenomena. However, integration
and absorption of immigrants and rural persons into the large-scale
networks of organization

    have separated the dimensions of social rank, ethnicity,
    and life style. Their correlation steadily weakens, as
    there is greater variation of social rank and life style
    within each 'ethnic' segment, greater variation in ethnicity
    and life style at each level of social rank, greater variation
    in social rank, and ethnicity within each life style.[38]

Thus, Greer increased the dynamic scope of the traditional Shevky-Bel
formulations, setting the stage for the later empirical research of
McElrath and Abu-Lughod.

This notion of increasing complexity of differentiation within a

societal unit as a consequence of evolutionary change corresponds
closely to the general systems concept. In biological systems, for
example, evolution is the change from a less to a more complex state
of organization, resulting from deviation amplifying (positive) feedback.[39] The organization of biological wholes is established by
differentiation of an original whole which segregates into parts. This
principle of progressive segregation implies a separation into sub-
ordinate partial systems (subsystems) as a concomitant of the system's
increasing complexity. Of the two types of progressive segregation--de-
cay and growth--the latter corresponds to an evolutionary phenomenon
(See pp. 4 to 7). "The system changes in the direction of increasing
division into subsystems and sub-subsystems of functions. This kind
of segregation seems to appear in systems involving some creative
process or in evolutionary and developmental processes."[40] Such macro-
scopic properties of general systems "apply to social structures.
In a primitive community every member can perform almost anything expected in its connection with the whole; in a highly differentiated
community, each member is determined for a certain performance or
complex of performances."[41] Thus, "the growth of a city first increases
the internal structuredness of the city itself."[42] In other words,
"growth in structural size requires modification in some component
structures--and consequently functions. Stated somewhat explicitly,
growth requires some specialization of functions".[43]

According to the hypotheses of Abu-Lughod, Greer and McElrath, the
notion of increasingly complex differentiation resulting from an increasingly complex community organization would appear to be deducible
from a general systems framework. This increasing complexity may reveal itself through a separation of the dimensions of differentiation
in the urban social structure. These patterns of urban differentiation
can be determined through factorial ecology, a technique that provides
empirical connection to the real world.

However, before examing the factor analytic approach, we should review the spatial aspects of social area analysis wherein the territorial
expression of the constructs is used to evaluate hypothesized patterns
of intraurban structure. Our next area of concern, then, is with the
traditional models of intraurban structure.

CLASSICAL SPATIAL MODELS

The Concentric Zone Model

The concentric zone model was the logical spatial expression of "a conception of the city, the community, and the region, not as geographical
phenomenon merely, but as a kind of social organism,"[44] a line of thought
which emerged from the University of Chicago in the early part of the
century.

The well-developed field of plant ecology, with its extensive theoretical
elaborations and empirical research, influenced the University's Robert
Park to formulate a theory of the human community based on a direct
analogy to plant communities.[45] The new field of human ecology
applied the specific principles and processes of biological ecology
to social science inquiry. Such an intellectual approach appears to
foreshadow von Bertalanffy's system formulations which assumed that
certain principles are universally valid for all systems.

The urban ecologists attempted to transcend superficial analogy, however, by establishing a homology, wherein "the efficient factors are different, but the respective laws are formally identical".[47]   Their concern with a conceptual model applicable to diverse phenomena evidenced during a symposium held by the University of Chicago in 1941. Robert Redfield, one of those attending the symposium, concluded that "the organism and the society are not more analogies; they are varieties of something more general"[48]--the very premise underlying a general system theory.

Park recognized that this premise alone was inadequate to establish a culturally relevant theory. He perceived social organization as occupying two levels--the biotic and the cultural--two distinct aspects of human life which were interrelated but analytically separable. The cultural level corresponded to society and was viewed as a super- structure which "imposes itself as an instrument of direction and control upon the biotic substructure".[49] Cultural forces such as moral order and tradition served to distinguish man from other living ele- ments in nature. The biotic level corresponded to the community and was based on the subsocial forces of competition--the basic natural force of plant ecology. Its guiding laws were those of survival. Park's focus on the community or biotic level rather than on the more complex area of society, recalls Wirth's preoccupation with the city or com- munity itself. Both men regarded the structure of the urban milieu as consequence of the community itself.

Human ecology, in contrast to social area analysis, avoided the role of societal forces, concentrating exclusively on the "natural forces" at work in the community. Ignoring inputs from the broader environ- ment, human ecologists attributed all regularities in the use of urban or community space to the mechanism of competition.

"Community, for Park, was a human aggregation living in a fixed, geo- graphical locale and controlled by the subcultural processes"[50]--i.e., those specific natural processes borrowed or translated from plant communities. For example, competition, a fundamental concept of plant ecology, is a process by which each organism struggles for survival against the environment, other species, and even its own kind, due to an overall lack of resources. Park assumed that man's economic compe- tition for limited space and access for his residences and businesses was a direct social counterpart of the plant world's survival struggle. He regarded such competition as contributing to homogeneous land uses and the segregation of subpopulations into distinct areas.

Change in such areas was construed by Park as the result of three inti- mately connected processes: dominance, invasion and succession. In the biological community, the dominant species controls the environment to the extent that it controls the community and subordinates other species. The human counterparts are industry and commerce [CBD]. Dom- inance results when environmental changes create conditions amenable for other species to thrive, invade an area of the environment and finally succeed the original species. Invasions are of two general types: those resulting in a change of land use and those resulting sim- ply in changes of occupant. This dominance, invasion, succession process would translate itself into the human context as follows: the expansion of the CBD into residential areas or the takeover of a spe- cific neighborhood by successive ethnic groups. Another process close- ly related to competition and having similar relevance in terms of social structure is that of adaption. In biological terms, the pressure

EXHIBIT 2-4

CLASSICAL SPATIAL MODELS

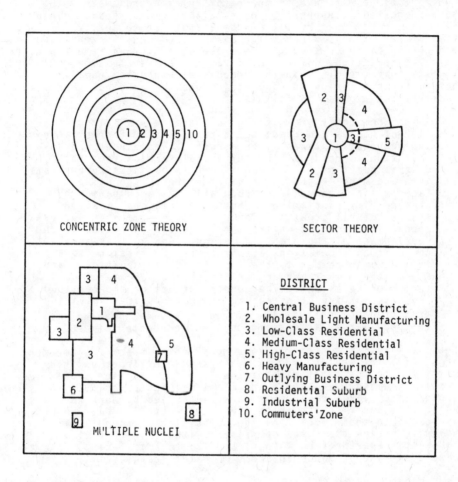

CONCENTRIC ZONE THEORY

SECTOR THEORY

MULTIPLE NUCLEI

DISTRICT

1. Central Business District
2. Wholesale Light Manufacturing
3. Low-Class Residential
4. Medium-Class Residential
5. High-Class Residential
6. Heavy Manufacturing
7. Outlying Business District
8. Residential Suburb
9. Industrial Suburb
10. Commuters' Zone

SOURCE: Chauncy D. Harris and Edward L. Ullman, "The Nature of Cities,"
The Annals, Vol. 242 (November, 1945), p. 13.

of competition forces species to make adaptions to improve their
potential for survival. The human equivalent is the division of labor
which "can be considered as an adaption for survival forced by economic
competition."[5] These, then, are just some of the various processes
of biological ecology which Park applied to the human community. Underlying this view of the community as a mosaic of competing and accom-

modating subgroups regulated only by the market reflected a general
systems orientation. His thinking also reflected the influence of
social Darwinism, a philosophy espoused by Herbert Spencer in the late
nineteenth century. Spencer's doctrine, built upon Darwin's evolutionary tenets, was one of "survival of the fittest" under the indispensabl
conditions of laissez-faire; Park built this point of view into his
ecological model. "Competition, conflict, accomodation and assimilation take place within a framework of rules approximately the same as
those advocated by Herbert Spencer--with room for social evolution,
enterprise, and the survival of those most fit to survive."[53] Going on
step further, Ernest Burgess formulated a concentric zone model of
city growth based on a spatial expression of the abovementioned pro-
cesses--competition, dominance, invasion, and succession. His model
suggests that the city, in the process of expanding radially from its
center, forms a series of concentric zones or annules. McKenzie
describes the process as follows:[54]

> As the community grows there is not merely a multiplica-
> tion of houses and roads but a process of differentiation
> and segregation takes place as well. Residences and in-
> stitutions spread out in centrifugal fashion from the
> central point of the community, while business concentrates
> more and more around the spot of highest land values.
> Each cyclical increase of population is accompanied by
> greater differentiation in both services and location...
> the structural growth of community takes place in succes-
> sional sequence not unlike the successional stages in the
> development of the plant formation...And just as in plant
> communities successions are products of invasion, so also
> in the human community the formations, segregations, and
> associations that appear constitute the outcome of a
> series of invasions...The general effect of the continuous
> processes of invasions and accommodations is to give the
> developed community well-defined areas, each having its
> own peculiar selective and cultural characteristics.

Specifically, the concentric zone model comprises five component
rings: (a) the center or core--the central or inner business
district, (b) the first ring or zone II--a transition area which
is being invaded by business and light manufacturing, (c) the second
ring or zone III--a residential area inhabited by working class
people who have fled the transition area (zone II) but who prefer to
live close to their work, (d) the third ring or zone IV--an
exclusive residential area comprising either single family homes or
high-rental apartment buildings, and (3) the final ring, zone V--the
commuters' zone of suburban areas or satellite cities.[55]

The concentric zone model is essentially a static view at one point
in time of a highly dynamic situation; although the concentric form
remains the basic spatial pattern, its parameters undergo constant
change.

Criticism

The basic critical attack against urban ecology centers on its
distinction between society and community and its analytical focus
on the latter. Although Park contended that society formed a
superstructure lying above the competitive biotic community, he
never clearly established the relationship of societal forces to

community structure. This narrow focus on the city without concern
for its social environment precipitated widespread criticism. For
example, Milla Alihan rejected this dichotomy as unacceptable,
viewing both aspects of urban structure as highly interdependent.[56]

Paradoxically, the subsequent attempt by social area analysts to overcome this objection by linking the areal differentiation of urban
areas (communities) to the basic social trends of industrial society,
itself became an object of criticism.

The most widely known of the many empirical studies that followed
was that of Walter Fiery, who maintained that culture could not be
separated from community.[57] His analysis of Beacon Hill and other
cultural areas in Boston, concluded that sentiment and symbolism
are strong forces which can effectively counteract biotic processes.
Competition in space was simply inadequate to explain complex
cultural phenomena, much less the change in land values resulting
from zoning or political boundaries.

Hoyt's Sector Model

A more important effort, though, in terms of determining a
universal or general urban pattern, was that of Homer Hoyt.[58] A
land economist, Hoyt analyzed the distributions of rent, block by
block, in 142 American cities over time and discovered the following tendencies:[59]

1. The various groups in the social order tend to
    be segregated into rather definite areas accord-
    ing to their income or social positions. While
    there are exceptions to this rule, it appears
    to have fairly general validity.

2. The highest income groups live in the houses
    which command highest prices and rents, while
    the lower-income groups live in houses which are
    offered for the lower prices and rents. Generally
    the low rent areas are located first near the busi-
    ness and industrial center of the city and then
    tend to expand outward on one side or sector of
    the city which is not pre-empted by higher rent
    residential areas or by business and industrial
    districts.

3. The principal growth of American cities has taken
    place by new building at the periphery rather than
    by the rebuilding of older areas. This means
    that some of our cities are beginning to resemble
    a 'hollow shell' with the major demands for land
    uses by-passing many of the 'near-in' areas. In
    other cases these near-in areas become slums with
    little possibility of being rehabilitated through
    ordinary market processes.

Of key significance in Hoyt's scheme is the movement of the high-
rent sector since it tends to pull the growth of the entire city
in the same direction.[60] It moves outward toward other established
areas along major transportation routes, toward open country, and
to high ground. Rent levels within the sector tend to rise toward
the periphery and decline toward the city's center. Moderate-rent

areas occupy a number of sectors and tend to adjoin the high-rent areas, buffering them from the low-rent sectors. Land use patterns, then, tend to be sectoral rather than concentric, as hypothesized by Burgess.

Despite this difference, Robson provides some unique insights into the similarities between the two models.[61]

> The essential difference between his very flexible model and that of Burgess is that Hoyt added a directional component to the evaluation of the spatial patterning of urban residential areas. Nevertheless he still recognized the validity and importance of the centrifugal/ centripetal forces upon which the Burgess model was based... The difference, however, was that Hoyt suggested that ... invasion, therefore the type of social area, differed from sector to sector...While Hoyt's scheme was thus radically different from Burgess in many ways, the dynamic mechanisms which it isolated are perhaps much less different in essence than many commentators have tended to suggest.

In sum, the sector theory maintains that the urban growth process is represented by a distinct axial pattern of sectors; new and future growth occurs at the outer rim of each sector, tending to sustain the sector's present character.

The Multiple Nuclei Model

The multiple nuclei model of Chauncey Harris and Edward Ullman suggests that urban land uses are centered on not one, but a series of nuclei. These nuclei have, in some cities, existed from the very origins of the city while in others, they have resulted from migration and functional specialization. Thus the number of such nuclei is a function both of locational forces and of historical development. Harris and Ullman clarify these factors:

1. Certain activities require special facilities.

2. Certain like activities group together because they profit from cohesion.

3. Certain unlike activities are detrimental to each other.

4. Certain activities are unable to afford the high rents of the most desirable sites.

As a consequence of these factors, the city is seen as comprising multiple nuclei, each containing the following: a) central business district--located at the focus of the intracity transportation facilities, i.e., the most accessible point; b) wholesale and light manufacturing district--near the city's present or former outer edge; c) residential district--some of these are extremely cohesive; most are ethnically and economically segregated; d) minor nuclei--such as outlying business centers and universities; and 3) suburb and satellite--outlying communities characteristic of most American cities.

Its host of possible nuclei distinguishes this model from the concentric and sector models; it suggests that there may be no common
spatial structure among cities. But Harris and Ullman do not reject completely the other models and conclude that most cities "exhibit aspects of the three generalizations of the land use pattern."
Thus at the close of World War II, the suggestion was made that all
three models were applicable--each for different locational dimen-
sions--to describe the internal variation within cities.

SPATIAL ASPECTS OF SOCIAL AREA ANALYSIS

Classical spatial models were fused with social area analysis
techniques by Theodore Anderson and Janice Egeland. They undertook
"a statistical comparison of the concentric zone and sector hypotheses of urban residential structure, where residential structure is measured by the prestige-value (social rank) and the urbanization indices proposed and developed by Shevky and Bell."[62] Four
cities--Akron, Dayton, Indianapolis, and Syracuse--were selected
on the basis of similar population size (200,000-500,000) and geographical configuration (flat and circular, to eliminate topographic
discrepancies.) In each city, a sample of census tracts was drawn
from a predefined grid of sectors and zones. After calculating the
social rank and urbanization indexes for each tract, they performed
an analysis of variance of the two indexes by sectors and zones,
thereby determining the spatial pattern of the social area dimensions. They found that social rank varied principally by sectors
while family status (urbanization) varied primarily in a concentric
fashion. Anderson and Egeland therefore concluded "that Burgess'
concentric zone hypothesis (as modified) is supported with respect
to urbanization but not prestige value, while Hoyt's sector hypothesis is supported with respect to prestige value but not urbanization."[63] However, it must be emphasized that they used the
social area constructs rather than empirically derived factors to
test the spatial pattern.

FACTORIAL ECOLOGY

The use of factor analysis to empirically isolate the dimensions of
urban social structure has been labeled factorial ecology. This
type of analysis, frequently accompanied by an associated mapping
process, emerged directly from social area analysis. Proponents
of the latter technique used factor analysis to validate the normative
constructs. Even the critics of the technique, who felt that the
dimensions should be deduced from each observational area rather than
assumed a priori,[64] drew upon the Shevky-Bell constructs for interpretation of most of the factorial ecologies undertaken during the
1960s. Despite the subsequent displacement of the social area
indexes by a superior methodology,[65] i.e., the factor analytic approach,
the reasoning behind the Shevky-Bell approach has yet to be succeeded.
For example, Berry, in summarizing the results of factor ecological
studies during the past decade, notes that "studies of American
cities have, by and large, succeeded in isolating the three social
area constructs originally proposed by Shevky: social-economic
status, family status, and ethnic status."[66] Each of the constructs
has generally tended to correspond spatially to the classical
models of urban structure in the Anderson and Egeland manner. They
illustrate the territorial distribution of homogeneous subareas of

the community. But these territorial expressions must be viewed in
light of the following statement by Haggett:[67]

> If we ask of a given region whether its settlements
> are arranged in some predictable sequence, or its
> land use zones concentric, or its growth cyclical, then
> the answer largely depends on what we are prepared
> to look for and what to accept as order. Order and
> chaos are not part of nature but part of the human mind.

Recent computer mapping techniques have not lent great supportive
evidence to the Anderson and Egeland patterns.[68]

Cross-National Comparisons

Cross-national comparisons of residential area differentiation in
urban and metropolitan communities were first undertaken by Frank
Sweetser. Utilizing 1960 data, Sweetser employed factor analysis
in his comparative study of Boston and Helsinki.[69] His theoretical
orientation reflects the equifinality concepts previously described:[70]

> It is a sociological commonplace to note that urban-
> industrial societies, regardless of differences in
> antecedent culture or in details of national history,
> tend to develop essentially similar social struc-
> tures, and to undergo change in similar directions as
> a consequence of working out of the same general
> processes in their specific socio-cultural settings.
> At the same time these specific socio-cultural differ-
> ences--along with differences in resources, popu-
> lation, societal scale and the like--produce larger
> or smaller differences in the detailed configuration
> of the basically similar structures in different soci-
> eties or even within the same society from region to
> region, or at different points in time.

His comparison of Helskinki and Boston was but an initial step
toward a more exact formulation of these similarities and differences.

Since it was impossible to replicate any of the Boston variables
directly in the Helsinki data, Sweetser had to use a number of
surrogates. The resulting comparisons of each set of data yielded
similar ecological findings. Three common factors emerged: socio-
economic status, progeniture (familism or stage in life cycle),
and urbanism, with coefficients of congruence between the sets,
respectively, of .744, .792, and .480.[71] The significant loadings
common to both sets are summarized as follows, with loading direction
in parentheses:[72]

Due to the absence of racial variables from the analysis, it was
possible to replicate only two of the Shevky dimensions. Nevertheless, the congruence between the sets of data and between the social
area formulations was so strong that Sweetser concluded:[73]

> Modern factor analysis, using factor structure as a
> model for ecological structure, is the method par

Factor I (socio-economic status)	Factor II (progeniture)	Factor III (urbanism)
(-) low education	(+) fertility	(+) working women
(+) professional managerial occupations	(+) elementary school age population	(-) high school age
(-) blue collar occupations	(-) non-family population	
(+) high school status	(-) retirement age	
(+) college status	(+) new housing	
(-) room crowding		
(-) housing defects		

excellence for comparing cross-nationally (and intra-nationally) the ecological differentiation of residential areas in urban and metropolitan communities.

Applying factor analysis to the samples listed above, Sweetser classified metropolitan ecological factors into either "universal" or "special" factors. Universal factors are assumed to be present in all metropolitan communities of all urban-industrial societies since they derive from the societal and cultural features of these societies. (Sweetser obviously has accepted "the Shevky-Bell argument that there are indeed fundamental dimensions of urban and metropolitan ecological structure arising out of the necessities of societal and cultural change in the process of industrialization-urbanization."[74]) Socio-economic status, familism, and migration status are presented as the universal factors for North American and Scandinavian metropoli.

Special factors derive from the distinctive social structures of individual nations. Sweetser "recognizes that, while universal processes of industrialization-urbanization have their necessities, which produce the universal types of factors, they also allow considerable latitude for distinctive socio-cultural features of national, regional, and local societies to influence ecological dimensions, thus producing special types of ecological factors."[75]

Sweetser raised the important question of metropolitan region delineation, noting that different factor structures emerged when analyses were undertaken for the community as a whole and for distinct sub-areas, as defined by specific zones and sectors. He concluded that specific area delineation gave rise to three modes of ecological differentiation. Of these modes--inner city (urban), urban-suburban (metropolitan), and rural-urban--the first and third represent a distortion from the ideal metropolitan representation. These distortions are an important consideration in this study, since we have chosen operational metropolitan systems as our desired units of analysis.

CURRENT RESEARCH THEMES

The increasing sophistication of available analytical techniques
has raised several important theoretical and empirical questions.
The theoretical concerns focus on explanations of spatial patterns
of human social organization, either through some variant of the
social area analysis technique or a "micromotive" behavioral approach based on the residential location decision.[76]

The latter efforts (Berry and Rees) focus specifically on the behavior of individuals and institutions as a basic process underlying the spatial structuring of a city's population. The residential location decision is viewed as a product of the interaction of
the home demander and the house supplier. The individual choices
of the home buyers and home builders (micro decisionmakers) affect
the ecology of urban areas, generating neighborhoods of homogeneous
residents. As individuals make similar choices with respect to the
market, an orderly social geography results--a geography quite similar to that hypothesized by the social area analysts as resulting
from the broad forces of modern industrial society.

Of the empirical concerns, the most pressing is the delineation
of the observational area--a problem studied by Phillip Rees in
Chicago as well as by Sweetser in Boston.[77] Appendix D presents
an empirical test of the effects of areal delineation and the
possibility of bias through boundary drawing.[78] It is initially
concluded in Appendix D that the SMSA is a valid representation
of a true regional system. This enables us to proceed with our
operational scheme, using the Standard Metropolitan Statistical Area
as our basic observational unit.

Another empirical question centers on the utility of the orthogonal
model. Current research reported by this author in Environment and
Planning substantiates its use at the SMSA scale of analysis.[80]
The basic issue centers on the apriori assumption of independent
dimensions inherent in the orthogonal model. By using alternative
oblique rotations, we can evaluate the validity of such an assumption. Further supportive evidence is included in Chapter 3 of this
study, wherein both orthogonal and oblique solutions have been used
to view the Newark SMSA over time.

SUMMARY

The integration of classical urban ecology, traditional spatial
models of urban structure, and social area analysis has resulted
in an approach to the study of urban spatial structure called
factorial ecology. Although there exists a substantial body of
literature on this subject, and there have been numerous hypotheses
and research areas suggested, few, if any, policy implications have
been proposed. A major objective of this study is to make a
start in bridging the academic-public policy gap.

NOTES

[1] Brian J. L. Berry, "Cities as Systems Within Systems of Cities," in John Friedmann and William Alonso (eds.), Regional Development and Planning (Cambridge, Massachusetts: MIT Press, 1964), pp. 126-127.

[2] Janet Abu-Lughod, "Testing the Theory of Social Area Analysis: The Ecology of Cairo, Egypt," American Sociological Review (April 1969) 198.

[3] Eshref Shevky and Marilyn Williams, The Social Area of Los Angeles (Berkeley and Los Angeles: The University of California Press, 1949); Wendell Bell, "The Social Areas of the San Francisco Region," American Sociological Review, XVIII (February 1953) 29-47; Eshref Shevky and Wendell Bell, Social Area Analysis: Theory, Illustrative Application, and Computational Procedure (Stanford: Stanford University Press, 1955).

[4] Shevky and Bell, op. cit., p. 18.

[5] Ibid.

[6] Ibid., p. 3.

[7] According to Scott Greer, the key meaning of increasing scale is "the organizational transformation of the total society." See Scott Greer, The Emerging City (New York: The Free Press, 1962), p. 67. Increasing scale is defined as the scope and intensity of social relations and is a concept left at the intuitive level.

[8] See Gideon Sjoberg, The Preindustrial City (New York: The Free Press, 1960), especially Chapter VII, "Economic Structure."

[9] For the classic treatment of a direct relationship between the division of labor and urbanization, see Emile Durkheim, The Division of Labor in Society, translated by George Simpson, (Glencoe, Illinois: The Free Press, 1949), especially pp. 256-260.

[10] William Goode suggests "that a crucial linkage between industrialization and the conjugal family is that under industrialization, control over jobs tends to pass from the kin group to non-kin groups. This tends to weaken familial control over behavior and social placement and loosens loyalty at the farther degrees of kinship and affection - the conjugal family." The family loses its specially productive, economic functions, giving rise to variation in family size and subsequently to life style. See William Goode, "World Revolution and Family Patterns," in Silvia Fava, Urbanism in World Perspective (New York: Thomas Y. Crowell, 1968), p. 274 and pp. 281-287.

[11] Shevky and Bell, op. cit., p. 17.

[12] Ibid., p. 5.

[13]Louis Wirth, "Urbanism as a Way of Life," American Journal of Sociology, 44 (1938) 1-24.

[14]Raymond Morris, Urban Sociology (New York: Praeger, 1968), p. 37.

[15]Shevky and Bell, op. cit., p. 8.

[16]Scott Greer, "Urbanism Reconsidered: A Comparative Study of Local Areas in a Metropolis," American Journal of Sociology, 21 (February 1956) 24.

[17]Amos H. Hawley and Otis Dudley Duncan, "Social Area Analysis: A Critical Appraisal," Land Economics 33 (Nov. 1957), 337-340.

[18]B. T. Robson, Urban Analysis: A Study of City Structure (London: Cambridge University Press, 1969), p. 52.

[19]Richard J. Udry, "Increasing Scale and Spatial Differentiation: New Tests of Two Theories from Shevky and Bell," Social Forces, Vol. 42, No. 4, p. 408.

[20]Wendell Bell and Charles C. Moskos Jr., "A Comment on Udry's Increasing Scale and Spatial Differentiation," Social Forces, 42 (May 1964) 416.

[21]Hans Blumenfeld, "The Urban Pattern," The Annals of the American Academy of Political and Social Science, 352 (March 1964) 80.

[22]Wendell Bell, "Economic, Family, and Ethnic Status: An Empirical Test," American Sociological Review, XX (February 1955) 45.

[23]Ibid., p. 51.

[24]Maurice D. VanArsdol, Jr., Santo F. Camilleri, and Calvin F. Schmidt, "An Application of the Shevky Social Area Indexes to a Model of Urban Society," Social Forces, 37 (October 1958) 31. See also: VanArsdol, Camilleri, and Schmidt, "The Generality of Urban Social Area Indexes," American Sociological Review, XXIII (June 1958) 277-284.

[25]Theodore Anderson and Lee L. Bean, "The Shevky-Bell Social Areas: Confirmation of Results and a Reinterpretation," Social Forces, XL (December 1961) 119-124.

[26]Dennis McElrath, "The Social Areas of Rome: Comparative Analysis," American Sociological Review, 27 (June 1962).

[27]Robson, op. cit., p. 56.

[28]Dennis McElrath, "Societal Scale and Social Differentiation: Accra, Ghana," in Scott Greer, Dennis McElrath, David Minar, and Peter Orleans, The New Urbanization (New York: St. Martin's Press, 1968), pp. 33-52.

[29]Ibid., p. 34.

[30]McElrath recognizes the distinction between two concepts of urbanization as emphasized by both John Friedmann and David Popenoe. According to Friedmann, "urbanization refers to processes that: (1) Incorporate a growing proportion of the total population into urban settlement patterns, giving rise to the city as a basic ecological matrix for social life and production and leading to its expansion, multiplication and transformation in space; and (2) Incorporate a growing proportion of the total population into urban social structures and styles of life." John Friedmann, "Two Concepts of Urbanization: A Comment" Urban Affairs Quarterly, I (June 1966) 78. See also: David Popenoe, "On the Meaning of 'Urban' in Urban Studies," Urban Affairs Quarterly, 1 (September 1965) 30.

[31]Dennis McElrath, "Urban Differentiation: Problems and Prospects," Law and Contemporary Problems, 30 (Winter 1965) 104.

[32]VanArdsol, op. cit., p. 34.

[33]McElrath, op. cit., pp. 49-50.

[34]Abu-Lughod, op. cit., p. 199.

[35]Ibid., p. 210.

[36]McElrath, op. cit., p. 386.

[37]Greer, The Emerging City, p. 69.

[38]Ibid., p. 72.

[39]J. W. S. Pringle, "On the Parallel Between Learning and Evolution," in Walter Buckley, Modern Systems Research for the Behavioral Scientist, (Chicago: Aldine, 1968), p. 260.

[40]A. D. Hall and R. E. Fagen, "Definition of System," General Systems, I (1956) 5.

[41]Ludwig von Bertalanffy, General Systems Theory (New York: George Braziller, 1969), p. 70.

[42]Magorah Marayuma, "The Second Cybernetics: Deviation-Amplifying Mutual Causal Processes," in Walter Buckley, Modern Systems Research for the Behavior Scientist, (Chicago: Aldine, 1968), p. 306.

[43]F. Kenneth Berrien, General and Social Systems (New Brunswick, N.J.: Rutgers University Press, 1968), p. 84.

[44]Quoted by Everett C. Hughes in his Preface to Robert E. Park, Human Communities (New York: The Free Press of Glencoe, 1952), p. 5.

[45]R. E. Park, "The City: Suggestions for the Investigation of Human Behavior in the Urban Environment," American Journal of Sociology, XX (1916) 557-612; E. W. Burgess and D. J. Bogue (eds.) Contributions to Urban Sociology (Chicago, 1964), pp. 2-14.

[46]von Bertalanffy, op. cit., p. 84.

[47]Ibid.

[48]Robert Redfield, "Levels of Integration in Biological and Social Systems," in Walter Buckley, Modern Systems Research for the Behavioral Scientist (Chicago: Aldine, 1968), p. 60 (originally published in 1942).

[49]Park, "Human Ecology" in Human Communities, p. 158.

[50]Leonard Reissman, The Urban Process, New York: The Free Press, 1964.

[51]Ibid., p. 100.

[52]For an explanation of the relationship of Social Darwinism to the emerging planning movement, see: Seymour Toll, Zoned American (New York: Grossman, 1969), especially pp. 13-23.

[53]Greer, The Emerging City, p. 8.

[54]R. D. McKenzie, "The Ecological Approach," in Robert E. Park, Ernest W. Burgess, and R. D. McKenzie, The City (Chicago: University of Chicago Press, 1925), pp. 73-77.

[55]Ernest Burgess, "The Growth of a City," in The City, p. 50.

[56]Robson, op. cit., p. 18.

[57]Walter Fiery, "Sentiment and Symbolism as Ecological Variables," American Sociological Review, X (1945) 140-148.

[58]Homer Hoyt, Structure and Growth of Residential Neighborhoods in American Cities (Washington, D.C.: U. S. Government Printing Office, 1939).

[59]Arthur M. Weimer and Homer Hoyt, Principles of Real Estate (New York: The Ronald Press, 1939), pp. 333-334.

[60]Hoyt, op. cit., p. 114.

[61]Robson, op. cit., p. 16.

[62]Theodore R. Anderson and Janice A. Egeland, "Spatial Aspects of Social Area Analysis," American Sociological Review, XXVI (June 1961) 392.

[63]Ibid., p. 398.

[64]Not all studies have sought to test the Shevky-Bell model of urban differentiation. In fact, George Carey, one of the first geographers to apply factor analysis to the investigation of an urban area's ecological structure, used the technique to interpret the distribution of population groups and neighborhoods in the core of New York City--Manhattan. See George W. Carey, "The Regional Interpretation of Manhattan Population and Housing Patterns Through Factor Analysis," Geographical Review (October 1966) 551-569.

[65]Abu-Lughod, op. cit., p. 200.

[66]Brian Berry and Philip Rees, "Factorial Ecology of Calcutta," American Journal of Sociology (March 1969), 459.

[67]Peter Haggett, Locational Analysis in Human Geography, (New York: St. Martin's Press, 1966), p. 3.

[68]See Dieter Gebhard, Factorial Ecology of New York City, Master's Thesis, Rutgers University, 1971.

[69]Frank L. Sweetser, "Factor Structure as Ecological Structure in Helsinki and Boston," Acta Sociologica, VIII (1965) 205.

[70]Ibid., p. 265.

[71]See Harry Harmon, Modern Factor Analysis, (Chicago: University of Chicago Press, 1967), pp. 269-271.

[72]Ibid., p. 219.

[73]Sweetser, op. cit., p. 214.

[74]Frank L. Sweetser, "Ecological Factors in Metropolitan Zones and Sectors," in Mattei Dogan and Stein Rokkan, eds., Quantitative Ecological Analysis in the Social Sciences (Cambridge: MIT Press, 1969), p. 449.

[75]Ibid.

[76]Brian J. L. Berry and Philip Rees, "Factorial Ecology of Calcutta," American Journal of Sociology 75 (March), pp. 445-491.

[77]See Philip Rees, "Concepts of Social Space: Toward an Urban Social Geography," in Brian J. L. Berry and Frank E. Horton, eds., Geographic Perspectives on Urban Systems (Englewood Cliffs, N.J.:   Prentice-Hall, 1970), pp. 306-394; and Frank L. Sweetser, "Ecological Factors in Metropolitan Zones and Sectors," in Mattei Dogan and Stein Rokkan, Quantitative Ecological Analysis in the Social Sciences (Cambridge, Mass.: MIT Press, 1969).

[78]James W. Hughes, "Metropolitan Demarcation: A Case Study of the New York Region," New York Statistician, December, 1972.

[79]K. Haynes, "Spatial Change in Urban Structure: Alternative Approaches to Ecological Dynamics," Economic Geography, 47 (1971), pp. 324-335; A. Hunter, "Factorial Ecology: A Critique and Some Suggestions," Demography 9 (1972), pp. 107-117: R. Johnston, "Some Limitations of Factorial Ecologies and Social Area Analysis," Economic Geography, 47 (1971), pp. 314-323; D. Meyer, "Factor Analysis Versus Correlation Analysis: Are Substantive Interpretations Congruent?" Economic Geography, 47 (1971),pp. 336-343; and P. Rees, "Factorial Ecology: An Extended Definition, Survey and Critique of the Field," Economic Geography, 47 (1971), pp. 220-233.

[80]J. W. Hughes and G. W. Carey, "Factorial Ecologies: Orthogonal and Oblique Solutions--A Case Study of the New York SMSA," Environment and Planning, Vol. IV, No. 2, 1972, pp. 147-162.

4

Sally Bould Van Til and Jon Van Til

THE LOWER CLASS
AND THE FUTURE OF INEQUALITY

IT is a recurrent problem in social science to measure and evaluate the degree to which the poor are different from the rich and to explain why this may be so. Despite Jenny's assertion in *The Threepenny Opera* that "first comes the belly, then come the morals," many social scientists in the 1960s tended to approach the study of the poor with the hypothesis of a *culture of poverty* as the dominant point of reference. In this article,[1] we review this literature and argue that social scientists have sufficiently advanced their research to support two major contentions. These contentions are: (1) that neither of the two most common perspectives adopted regarding the lower class and its culture has proved to be empirically accurate or theoretically useful; and (2) that recent evidence points to a third perspective, *adaptive drift*, as most adequate in dealing with the problem.

Neither of these points is original, but both ought to be stated forcefully, for they reflect genuine advances in social science over the past decade. Despite recent criticism of the appropriateness of social scientists studying the behavior of the poor,[2] the answer does not lie in denying the legitimacy of such research, but rather in coming to grips with the broad social policy implications of the empirical evidence.

Two Common Perspectives

THE two positions most commonly adopted regarding the orientation of the lower class are those of the culture of poverty and the *blocked opportunity* or *situational* hypotheses. A brief identification of each position, as well as substantiation of the contention that

The authors are, respectively, Assistant Professor of Sociology, University of Delaware, and Assistant Professor of Sociology, Swarthmore College.

many social scientists have yet to go beyond these positions, may be provided by quoting from a newly edited textbook put together from the work of about fifty eminent sociologists.

> Although virtually all sociologists agree that the behaviors of different classes have both cultural and situational sources, there is considerable disagreement on the relative importance of the two. Many emphasize the cultural sources and speak of "social class subcultures" or of a "culture of poverty." The latter is believed to be a way of life guided by values transmitted from one generation to another, a collective adaptation of the poor to their adverse conditions.... Other observers believe that the behaviors attributed to the culture of poverty are actually individual responses to the conditions of economic deprivation and social dishonor. According to this point of view, the values of the poor are basically the same as those of higher strata; however, because of situational restrictions, they do not result in the same overt behaviors.[3]

The authors then outline how each perspective interprets lower-class family life, noting the importance of the differences in policy implied by each view.

> If the situational view is correct, once the social environment of the poor is changed, their behavior will quickly come to resemble that of the solid middle classes.... If, however, there is a culture of poverty, many of the poor will not respond readily or at all to increased opportunities and other situational changes. Rather, the values of the poor that are maladaptive in the long run will have to be extinguished, or the society's guardians will have to accept the fact that American middle-class values are perhaps, after all, not the highest point of moral evolution, that other values may be equally suitable to those who hold them.[4]

Our first contention is that the issue, thus framed, presents a false dilemma, for neither of these two commonly held perspectives on the problem is satisfactory.[5] Despite the attractiveness of the culture of poverty hypothesis to some social scientists and the widespread attention it received from its statement by Oscar Lewis, very litte empirical evidence has lent it support. Rejection of the culture of poverty view, however, does not imply acceptance of the situational, blocked opportunity view, which has also proved to be less than adequate.

The Culture of Poverty

The evidence refuting the culture of poverty hypothesis is most clear and comes from careful ethnographic and statistical studies of the behavior and attitudes of the poor. Foremost among the latter is Kriesberg's study of fatherless families among public housing residents, in which he searches exhaustively for cultural differences between his sample of mothers in poverty and a largely near-poor sample of parents in whole families.[6] Neither a homogeneous way of life nor the perpetuation of poverty-specific values is found by Kriesberg. Rather, the poor and the near-poor evince similar high levels of housing aspirations, desire to work, encouragement of achievement and autonomy, and achievement aspiration for their children. The samples differ mainly in the opportunities available to them for jobs, housing, and association with potential neighbors in the various communities in which the projects are located.

Ethnographic studies. Similar conclusions emerge from the major ethnographic studies of black lower-class communities, most notably those of Liebow, Hannerz, and Valentine. Liebow rejects the cultural view in favor of the situational hypothesis.

> We do not have to see the problem in terms of breaking into a puncture proof circle, of trying to change values, of disrupting the lines of communication between parent and child so that parents cannot make children in their own image, thereby transmitting their culture inexorably, ad infinitum.... Of much greater importance for the possibilities of change ... is the fact ... that the son goes out and independently experiences the same failures, in the same areas, and for much the same reasons as his father.[7]

Hannerz expands his analysis beyond the street corner and discovers four major forms of adaptation to ghetto life, among which the "mainstreamers" behave in a fashion which directly refutes almost every contention of the culture of poverty position.[8] Charles A. Valentine, in his ongoing research in Blackston (a large-city neighborhood), reports discovering a greater pattern of institutional participation than the culture of poverty theorist would expect.[9]

Research among Mexican Americans has similarly found the culture of poverty view inadequate. Burma notes that while "present-orientation" is common in this cultural context, it is "closely related to what the parent Anglo culture calls fatalism, the feeling that one's destiny is not in one's own hands."[10] Studies of the Puerto Rican poor in New York also provide little support for a hard culture of poverty hypothesis. Sexton finds the Puerto Rican school child proud of his ethnic heritage and achieving well through the first few years of school.[11] Padilla finds that recent migrants on welfare do not hide that fact, but speak openly of the reasons for dependence on aid.[12] By doing so, they make it clear that they were forced to receive welfare aid, that they had no choice but to take it. And Oscar Lewis, the misreading of whom did much to popularize the concept, noted that "the culture of poverty is both an adaptation and a reaction of the poor to their marginal position in a class-stratified, highly individuated, capitalistic society."[13]

Survey research. Survey research among the poor has also lent little evidence to support the culture of poverty position. With an area probability sample of 1,400 persons, Rokeach and Parker examined differences in the values held by the poor and middle class.[14] Differences in values did exist, but not in areas generally cited as evidence for a self-perpetuating poverty subculture. An exhaustive search of the literature led Rossi and Blum to conclude, similarly, that if one means by the culture of poverty something more than the fact that the poor are different with respect to some behavioral indicators and show higher rates of a wide variety of disabilities, "then the empirical evidence would not support such a view."[15]

Blocked Opportunity

If the culture of poverty hypothesis must be rejected, what of the situational hypothesis? We contend that it too is inadequate, although it is evident that behavior is greatly influenced by what Schorr called the "non-culture of poverty."[16] The extent of existing inequality and the limitations it places upon the poor in achieving the economic security required to support mainstream life-styles are overwhelming. Indeed, pervasive economic insecurity, coupled with severely limited opportunities to achieve economic security, appears to provide sufficient explanation for many of the behavior patterns which have been seen as characteristic of a culture of poverty.[17]

Conceptualized reality. Dissatisfaction with the blocked opportunity model is not due to any question about the reality of such limitations, but rather derives from the failure of the model, as it is often conceptualized, to recognize fully the complex nature of human beings in social life. It is a basic part of the human condition to develop cultural patterns that facilitate adaptation to external situations. Even in one of the most brutal cases of external limitation, the American experience with slavery, cultural forms are now acknowledged to have emerged which provided the basis for interaction. Such patterns have been termed survival techniques, but their essence is neither technical nor rational, but rather affective.[18] The will to survive is not simply an existential decision, but one which rests as well upon the individual's attachment to an ongoing human community, and the basis of that community interaction is cultural. Culture, as Hannerz argues, is itself delimited by environment, an important part of which is social.[19]

Policy implications. On a similar basis we criticize the policy implications of the situational hypothesis. The poor do not live in a cultural vacuum and hence will not react mechanically to new opportunity structures. Past lifeways developed within the stark options of poverty cannot be shed quickly. Early socialization, no matter how limited the environment, is the process of becoming human,[20] and it is not only unrealistic but also arrogant to assume that such socialization is a superficial process which can be swept away by new structural forms.

The poor will alter their behavior when their options increase; the mass media and the public schools provide for their socialization to patterns not found in ghetto streets. But it is doubtful that their past experience will cease to play a role in their behavior. Claude Brown's insight, when he returned to Harlem and became involved in a fracas, is pertinent. "Damn, I thought I had grown out of all that sort of thing. I thought I had grown out of hitting anybody in the street. I thought I had grown out of putting the blame on somebody else. I guess I hadn't."[21] Though evidence is slim in sociological studies, it does point to the persistence of some past behavior patterns among those upwardly mobile from the ranks of the lower class.[22]

Adaptive Drift

THAT the poor, living in poverty, do not respond mechanically to opportunity, as Liebow suggested, is the basic revision of the blocked opportunity model suggested by Hannerz at the end of his ghetto study. The argument was first persuasively stated in Rodman's seminal essay on "The Lower-Class Value Stretch." There Rodman noted that "the lower-class person, without abandoning the general values of the society, develops an alternative set of values. . . . The resultant is a stretched value system with a low degree of commitment to all the values within the range, including the dominant, middle-class values."[23]

The Heterogeneous Poor

Rodman's perspective was substantiated by his own empirical work and by that of S. M. Miller, Frank Riessman, Martin Rein, Pamela Roby, and their associates. Working in Trinidad, Rodman concluded that the lower-class family seeks solutions to its problems by both value-stretching and pragmatic responses. Lower-class individuals are seen as "circumstance-oriented," though their values are "not altogether determined by the circumstances of lower-class life."[24] Miller, Riessman, and Seagull reviewed this literature and found little evidence to support the hypothesized inability of the poor to defer gratification;[25] Miller and Rein summarized their findings as follows.

(1) Great variation occurs among the poor.
(2) There are important differences from many middle-class patterns. . . .
(3) Although many of these patterns and orientations are carried from generation to generation,

contemporary influences are important in maintaining them.
(4) Some positive elements of strength, of coping, exist as well as negative ones that make it difficult to handle life.
(5) Many of the poor are open to change, to taking advantage of new possibilities. But in offering new possibilities, their experiences and orientations must be considered.[26]

Hannerz' work documents how, in the lower-class milieu, basic modes of behavior and outlook develop and become shared. They are learned from experience and maintained both by experience and by interaction. These modes of behavior vary from individual to individual, mixing mainstream and ghetto-specific adaptations. The model is probabilistic, not rigidly deterministic.

> Exposure thus gives practically every ghetto dweller opportunities to familiarize himself with a range of modes of behavior and combinations of modes of behavior, from mainstream-oriented to ghetto-specific ways. It is obvious, however, that man is not a mindless cultural automaton. . . . [A cultural] repertoire to some measure constitutes adaptive potential. . . . As far as the individual's evaluation of a mode of behavior is concerned, it is likely that the more often it occurs in his milieu, the greater will be his readiness to find it not only convenient but also morally appropriate.[27]

Current research by Charles Valentine appears to be confirming much of Hannerz' research, as well as Valentine's earlier contention that neither the cultural nor the situational view was adequate and that a third model involving a "heterogeneous subsociety with variable, adaptive subcultures" was required.[28] Valentine's field research in Blackston has led to the preliminary finding that "the most significant cultural similarities and differences of Blackston are associated with ethnic identity or racial status and not with class lines that would indicate a 'culture of poverty.' "[29]

Biculturalism

Elsewhere, Valentine has argued that a bicultural model is more applicable to the study of Afro-American behavior than either deficit or difference models. He notes that many black Americans "are simultaneously enculturated and socialized in two different ways of life," learning and practicing "both mainstream cultures and ethnic cultures at the same time."[30] This biculturalism has also been noted by Burma in his study of Mexican Americans,[31] as well as Padilla and Lewis in their research on Puerto Ricans in New York.[32] Those studied demonstrated a mixing of traits common to the Spanish-speaking subculture and the subculture of poverty. Much of the overall adaptation, Burma further notes, falls in "areas of indifference to or mesh[es] well with the middle-class Anglo culture and hence [is] subject to no normative stress."[33] Thus, the biculturalism of the black and Mexican American poor appears to be demonstrated along both class and ethnic lines, mixing on the one hand middle-class with lower-class behavior, and on the other ethnic and core cultural adaptations. Separating the class and ethnic factors will require a series of studies in varying lower-class milieux, especially among the infrequently studied native white poor.

Adaptive drift, however, differs from biculturalism in a manner similar to Weber's distinction between caste and ethnic segregation: "ethnic coexistences . . . allow each ethnic community to consider its own honor as the highest one."[34] A bicultural individual obtains in his ethnic identity a sense of dignity and legitimacy which is independent of the mainstream system of stratification. For the poor, however, "the belief in their own specific 'honor' " becomes problematic precisely because of their position at the bottom of the system of stratification.[35] Their ambiguous culture represents an attempt to sustain some aspect of self-respect and legitimacy in spite of their position at the tail end of an unequal distribution of class, status, and power. Poverty-specific patterns, distinct from ethnic or racial differences, arise as a result of this situation. As Lewis has indicated, such conditions are especially favorable in industrialized and industrializing countries with predominantly capitalistic economic systems.[36]

The unequal distribution of rewards is legitimized in capitalistic systems by the achievement ethic which implies that one gets what one deserves. Even without full equality of opportunity, however, this ethic is used to justify the present treatment of the poor as marginal misfits. It is the ideology of the *open class* system which on the one hand provides for the socialization of the poor into mainstream culture, while being used on the other hand to justify their unequal treatment by mainstream institutions. These are the conditions which promote behavior patterns described in our concept of adaptive drift. Unless they see themselves as upwardly mobile, the poor cannot risk total commitment to a system of values which defines them as deserving of less than their fellow human beings. There must be an alternative design for living which provides a safety valve for their feelings of self-worth and self-respect, one which they can drift into and out of as circumstances shift.

The Adaptive Drift Model

We suggest that the phrase *adaptive drift* catches the flavor of this lower-class style. The concept of adaptive drift combines the notions of biculturalism,[37] openness,[38] and adaptation to social-environmental circumstances.[39] By "drift," David Matza referred to the ability of the delinquent to move from the criminal to the conventional milieu, physically, socially, and morally, with a minimum of personal disorganization.[40] The process of drift is not a mechanistic or calculated response. Furthermore, it is one which is circumscribed by the larger social environment. The lower-class drifter is not fully bicultural because he cannot risk commitment to either mode—not to the mainstream one because he is not likely to be accepted as a full participant, and not to the poverty one because it lacks much of the reward provided by the larger system. Thus, the lower-class person remains open.

Lower-class values. Adaptive drift encompasses Rodman's view that lower-class individuals have a wider range of values than middle-class individuals but also possess a lower degree of commitment to any of those values.[41] "As a consequence, they are more open to the possibility of acts that are defined as delinquent by the official representatives of society."[42] Rainwater, similarly, sees a distinctive pattern of lower-class behavior, both existential and evaluative.

> Lower class subculture, then, can be regarded as the historical creation of persons who are disinherited by their society, persons who have adapted to the twin realities of disinheritance and limited functional autonomy for their group by developing existential perspectives on social reality (including the norms and practices of the larger society) that allow them to stay alive and not lose their minds, that allow them some modicum of hope about a reasonably gratifying life, and that preserve for many the slim hope that somehow they may be able to find admittance for themselves and their children to the larger society.[43]

Like Hannerz, Rainwater does not want wholly to abandon the concept of lower-class culture. A lower-class culture exists as a reality for most of the poor, together with a core culture.

Lower-class behavior. The concept of adaptive drift provides a perspective on lower-class behavior that indicates its situational variability and the retention of learned cultural modes during situational change, and leads to the prediction of a variety of personal and group adaptations in times of increasing affluence. It suggests that in static poverty the poor possess many bicultural traits which they retain in times of change, developing new subcultural forms from experience, much like Stonequist's "marginal man."[44] Thus a tension is established between the self-definition of the lower class and the definition of their behavior applied by the "moral entrepreneurs" of a predominantly middle-class society. The poor are "signified," but they also participate in their own definition.

This marginal status of the poor is clearly demonstrated by examining their dealings with the primary institutions of society outside the family which affect its critical functioning, particularly political, economic, welfare, and educational institutions.[45] These structures both provide the poor with mainstream values and limit them to opportunity structures that do not permit the realization of those values. Further, this gap is recognized by the creation of mainstream definitions that characterize the poor as lazy, undeserving, or subhuman. The poor react to this situation by seeking to adjust to the double bind in which they find themselves—proved inadequate by the denial of opportunity to achieve mainstream status, and confirmed inadequate by their signification as shiftless and undeserving. Thus, it is the interaction of their marginal opportunity with their uneven treatment that leads them to create self-images that are necessarily variable with situational opportunity and the definition of that situation by their peers. They learn the mainstream values, but at the same time learn to be distrustful and cynical, developing alternative values to deal with their marginal status. They remain ever ready to shift their definition of a situation, ever adapting to a world that proves itself mercurial, inconsistent, and usually intractable to purposes they set for themselves.

The Future of Inequality

THUS, as the situational model contends, the behavior of the poor is fettered by the limited nature of their opportunities. And, as the culture of poverty hypothesis contends, the poor do develop and adopt values and norms peculiar to their situation. But, as the culture of poverty model does not permit, the evidence is more than clear that the poor possess in their behavioral repertoires many mainstream values and normative orientations. And, as the situational model does not recognize, they also develop modes of evaluating reality that cannot be expected to disappear when opportunities change.

Thus, we suggest that there is little reason to believe that inequalities be reduced, the ex-poor will behave just as the present middle masses do, or will.[46] The behavior of the poor in the adaptive drift model does not simply reflect an inadequacy of income, nor the lack of opportunity, but rather is the consequence of their marginal position at the bottom of the stratification hierarchy. In the marketplace, they are unable to contribute sufficient net marginal productivity to make their labor worth buying at a decent wage. Furthermore, lacking any substantial claim to status or access to power, they are better able to perceive the importance of these factors in the everyday operation of the social order around them.[47] Unlike Glazer,[48] we are not surprised that the increasing level of welfare payments in New York City has failed to alter substantially the behavior of the poor. Even if we grant the unlikely assumption that these increased payments are adequate as subsistence income, they do not affect the basic conditions of life at the bottom. The poor still pay more for what they get; the housing market and the job market remain the same. The schools to which they send their children have not changed, and their access to good health care is as poor as always. They still face the capriciousness of the welfare department, manipulated by reactionary state legislators. Furthermore they have little power, as always, to effect any changes in these circumstances.

Income equalization as proposed by Rainwater is not sufficient, for equality must be achieved on the other dimensions of stratification as well.[49] The behavior of the poor which reflects their poverty, not their ethnicity, is unlikely to change unless a radically more equal society is created along all dimensions. Lower-class persons have learned, through bitter experience, to perceive privilege; the elimination of privilege in one dimension is not likely to blind them to its persistence in other dimensions. They will reserve their commitment to mainstream values and perserve their own designs for living until the larger society provides not just equality of opportunity but also equality of results.

FOOTNOTES

1. The present article is a revision of a paper presented at the 1971 meeting of the American Sociological Association in Denver. In making the revision, the authors were particularly helped by the suggestions made by Leon Bramson, S. M. Miller, Hans-Eberhard Mueller, and Martin Rein.
2. See Frederick D. Holliday, "Comments on 'The Culture of Poverty: The View from New York City,' " in *The Poor: A Culture of Poverty, or a Poverty of Culture?*, ed. J. Allen Winter (Grand Rapids, Mich.: Eerdmans, 1971), pp. 49-53.
3. CRM Books, *Society Today* (Del Mar, Calif.: CRM Books, 1971), p. 228.
4. Ibid., p. 230.
5. We hope we are able to heed George Homans' warning that to the classic peril of being impaled on the horns of a dilemma, we moderns should add the peril of "being split by a false dichotomy" (*The Human Group* [New York: Harcourt, Brace and Co., 1950], p. 319).
6. Louis Kriesberg, *Mothers in Poverty: A Study of Fatherless Families* (Chicago: Aldine Publishing Co., 1970).
7. Elliot Liebow, *Tally's Corner* (Boston: Little, Brown and Co., 1967), p. 223.
8. Ulf Hannerz, *Soulside: Inquiries into Ghetto Culture and Community* (New York: Columbia University Press, 1969).
9. CRM Books, *Anthropology Today* (Del Mar, Calif.: CRM Books, 1971), chap. 7.
10. John H. Burma, ed., *Mexican-Americans in the United States* (Cambridge, Mass.: Schenkman Publishing Co., 1970), p. 22.
11. Patricia Cayo Sexton, *Spanish Harlem: Anatomy of Poverty* (New York: Harper & Row, 1965), pp. 61-62.
12. Elena Padilla, *Up from Puerto Rico* (New York: Columbia University Press, 1958), pp. 260-64.
13. Oscar Lewis, *A Study of Slum Culture: Backgrounds for La Vida* (New York: Random House, 1968), p. 5.
14. Milton Rokeach and Seymour Parker, "Values and Social Indicators of Poverty and Race Relations in America," *The Annals* of the American Academy of Political and Social Science, vol. 388 (March 1970), pp. 110-11.
15. Peter H. Rossi and Zahava Blum, "Class, Status and Poverty," in *On Understanding Poverty: Perspectives from the Social Sciences*, ed. Daniel P. Moynihan (New York: Basic Books, 1968), p. 44.
16. Alvin L. Schorr, *Explorations in Social Policy* (New York: Basic Books, 1968). See also Richard Cloward and Lloyd Ohlin, *Delinquency and Opportunity* (New York: Free Press, 1960); Liebow, *Tally's Corner;* Hannerz, *Soulside;* and Kriesberg, *Mothers in Poverty.*
17. Oscar Lewis, *La Vida* (New York: Random House, 1966). See also Liebow, *Tally's Corner.*
18. Lee Rainwater, "The Problem of Lower Class Culture," *The Journal of Social Issues*, vol. 26, no. 2 (Spring 1970), p. 147.
19. Hannerz, *Soulside.*
20. Dennis H. Wrong, "The Oversocialized Conception of Man in Modern Sociology," *The American Sociological Review*, vol. 26, no. 2 (April 1961), pp. 184-95.

21. Claude Brown, *Manchild in the Promised Land* (New York: Macmillan Co., 1965), p. 387.

22. Studies of social mobility have tended to focus on the antecedents of mobility, and not on behavioral responses to mobility. Further, the process of group mobility, as opposed to individual mobility, has been largely neglected in its study in the American context. Nonetheless, the work of Robert A. Ellis and W. Clayton Lane ("Social Mobility and Social Isolation: A Test of Sorokin's Dissociative Hypothesis," *The American Sociological Review*, vol. 32, no. 2 [April 1967], pp. 237-53) indicates the marginal status of the upwardly mobile individual.

23. Hyman Rodman, "The Lower-Class Value Stretch," *Social Forces*, vol. 42, no. 2 (December 1963), p. 209.

24. *Lower-Class Families: The Culture of Poverty in Negro Trinidad* (New York: Oxford University Press, 1971), p. 196.

25. S. M. Miller, Frank Riessman, and Arthur Seagull, "Poverty and Self-Indulgence: A Critique of the Non-Deferred Gratification Pattern," in *Poverty in America*, ed. Lewis A. Ferman, Joyce L. Kornbluh, and Allen Haber (Ann Arbor: University of Michigan, 1965), pp. 285-302.

26. S. M. Miller and Martin Rein, "Poverty, Inequality, and Policy," in *Social Problems: A Modern Approach*, ed. Howard S. Becker (New York: John Wiley & Sons, 1966), pp. 492-93. See also S. M. Miller and Frank Riessman, *Social Class and Social Policy* (New York: Basic Books, 1968); S. M. Miller, Martin Rein, Pamela Roby, and Bertram W. Gross, "Poverty, Inequality, and Conflict," *The Annals* of the American Academy of Political and Social Science, vol. 373 (September 1967), pp. 16-52; and S. M. Miller and Pamela Roby, *The Future of Inequality* (New York: Basic Books, 1970). The simultaneous possession of middle-class organizational capacities and lower-class expressiveness also characterized the welfare rights organization studied by one of the present authors (Jon Van Til, "Becoming Participants: Dynamics of Access among the Welfare Poor" [Ph.D. diss., University of California, Berkeley, 1970]). This group of recipients advanced its interests with great skill, while also providing a setting in which members could engage in storytelling, bickering, and other behavior that might be predicted by the culture of poverty hypothesis.

27. Hannerz, *Soulside*, pp. 185-87.

28. Charles A. Valentine, *Culture and Poverty: Critique and Counter-Proposals* (Chicago: University of Chicago Press, 1968), p. 142.

29. CRM Books, *Anthropology Today*, p. 99. It should be noted that this finding regarding the relationship between ethnicity and class directly counters Herbert Gans' findings about working-class whites in *The Urban Villagers: Group and Class in the Life of Italian-Americans* (New York: Free Press, 1962), p. 229.

30. "Deficit, Difference, and Bicultural Models of Afro-American Behavior," *Harvard Educational Review*, vol. 41, no. 2 (May 1971), pp. 141, 143.

31. Burma, *Mexican-Americans*.

32. Padilla, *Up from Puerto Rico;* and Lewis, *A Study of Slum Culture*.

33. *Mexican-Americans*, p. 27.

34. Max Weber, "Class, Status, Party," in *From Max Weber: Essays in Sociology*, ed. H. H. Gerth and C. Wright Mills (New York: Oxford University Press, 1958), p. 189.

35. Ibid.

36. Lewis, *La Vida*, p. xliv.

37. Valentine, "Deficit, Difference, and Bicultural Models"; and Rodman, *Lower-Class Families*, p. 7.

38. Miller and Rein, "Poverty, Inequality, and Policy," p. 493.

39. Rodman, *Lower-Class Families*, pp. 195-97; Lee Rainwater, "The Problem of Lower Class Culture and Poverty-War Strategy," in Moynihan, *On Understanding Poverty*, p. 246; Lewis, *A Study of Slum Culture*, p. 5; and Hannerz, *Soulside*, p. 186.

40. David Matza, *Delinquency and Drift* (New York: John Wiley & Sons, 1964).

41. In contrast to Rodman, we do not read Matza as saying that the mainstream values have a necessarily stronger hold on the individual than do subcultural values. We believe that this interpretation rests on our greater reliance on his theory as expressed in *Delinquency and Drift*, whereas Rodman ("Controversies about Lower-Class Culture: Delinquency and Illegitimacy," *Canadian Review of Sociology and Anthropology*, vol. 5 [November 1968], pp. 254-62) pays greater attention to his essay with Sykes (Gresham M. Sykes and David Matza, "Techniques of Neutralization: A Theory of Delinquency," *The American Sociological Review*, vol. 22, no. 6 [December 1957], pp. 666-70). In his book, Matza notes that the "delinquent transiently exists in a limbo between convention and crime, responding in turn to the demands of each, flirting now with one, now the other, but postponing commitment, evading decision. Thus, he drifts between criminal and conventional action" (p. 28).

42. Rodman, "Controversies about Lower-Class Culture," p. 257.

43. "The Problem of Lower Class Culture and Poverty-War Strategy," p. 247.

44. E. V. Stonequist, *The Marginal Man* (New York: Charles Scribner's Sons, 1937).

45. See Marcia Guttentag, ed., *Professionals and the Poor*, The Journal of Social Issues, vol. 26, no. 3 (Summer 1970).

46. Indian experience with eliminating caste restrictions suggests that "the coming into existence of new opportunities, educational, economic, and political, brought about an increase in horizontal solidarity...." In traditional India, fission seems to have been the dominant process, whereas today the trend has been reversed and fusion has replaced fission. And as Beteille has pointed out, fusion does not take place arbitrarily but takes into account traditional alignments. (M. N. Srnivas, *Social Change in Modern India* [Berkeley: University of California Press, 1968], pp. 114-15.)

47. See William H. Form and Joan Huber, *Income, Race, and the Ideology of Political Efficacy*, University of Illinois, Institute of Labor and Industrial Relations Reprint 221 (Urbana, 1971); also Robert W. Miller, Frederick A. Zeller, and Harry R. Blaine, *Implications of Social Class Differences in Beliefs Concerning Causes of Unemployment*, West Virginia University, Office of Research and Development Research Series 2 (Morgantown, 1968).

48. Nathan Glazer, "The Culture of Poverty: The View from New York City," in Winter, *The Poor: A Culture of Poverty or a Poverty of Culture?*, pp. 29-48.

49. Miller, Rein, Roby, and Gross, "Poverty, Inequality, and Conflict."

5

James Simmons

CHANGING RESIDENCE IN THE CITY

ABOUT 20 percent of the population of the United States changes residence annually. Although many moves are made by a small number of highly mobile persons, 50 percent of the entire population moves within a five-year period. Given the extent of this movement, the distribution and characteristics of the population remain remarkably stable; the in-migrants to an area, for the most part, resemble the out-migrants in numbers and attributes. Over a sufficient period of time, however, migration is an important instrument in altering the spatial patterns of social and demographic variables, and under certain conditions it leads to dramatic short-run changes in small areas—for example, the rapid growth of a new subdivision or the expansion of a ghetto by "blockbusting."

The present study is concerned with an important, but relatively neglected, aspect of migration, namely changes in residence that take place within a city.[1] Measured in one-year intervals, the intracounty mobility rate is 12 to 13 percent, or about two-thirds of all moves (Table I).[2] Many of these relocations take place in the same neighborhood or on the same block, but longer moves determine most of the growth or decline of population in different parts of the city and virtually all the changes in relative income levels and ethnic or racial concentrations.

Migration has been widely studied and several excellent reviews of the subject are available,[3] but these have limited application to movement

---

[1] Henry S. Shryock, Jr.: Population Mobility within the United States (University of Chicago, Community and Family Study Center, 1964), p. 10. Shryock, following the practice of the Bureau of the Census, restricts the use of the term "migration" to movements across county lines. The present study, then, is primarily of mobility rather than of migration, though larger cities may include more than one county—if not within the city itself, at least as part of the Standard Metropolitan Statistical Area. Many census aggregations refer to intracounty movements, but data provided for individual census tracts data measure intrametropolitan moves.

[2] "Mobility of the Population of the United States, March 1964 to March 1965," Current Population Repts., Ser. P-20, Population Characteristics, No. 150, U. S. Bureau of the Census, Washington, D. C., 1966.

[3] The models available are reviewed by Walter Isard: Methods of Regional Analysis (New York and London, 1960, Chap. 3, Migration Estimates); Gunnar Olsson: Distance and Human Interaction: A Review and Bibliography, Regional Sci. Research Inst. Bibliogr. Ser. No. 2, Philadelphia, 1965; and E. G.

within urban areas because economic opportunity, the mainstay of migration theory at the interstate and international levels, is largely irrelevant to movement within a commuting area or to patterns of gross migration. As a result, the investigation of intraurban mobility has been primarily the realm of the sociologist rather than of the economist, but the many facets of the

TABLE I—MIGRATION IN URBANIZED AREAS IN THE UNITED STATES, 1955-1960
(*In percentages*)

RESIDENCE IN 1955	CENTRAL CITY	FRINGE	TOTAL
Same house as in 1960	48.5	47.5	47.8
Different house in United States	47.5	50.0	48.0
Same county	33.6	28.7	31.4
Different county	13.9	21.1	16.6
Same state	5.7	10.1	7.3
Different state	8.3	11.0	9.3
Abroad	1.8	1.4	1.6
Moved, residence in 1955 not reported	2.5	1.1	1.9

Source: United States Census of Population: 1960, Subject Reports: Size of Place, *Final Report PC (3)-1B* (Bureau of the Census, Washington, D. C., 1963), Table I.

topic cover the whole range of the behavioral sciences. This study attempts to synthesize the subject under three headings. First, *who moves?* What information do we have about the sociological and psychological characteristics of movers? Is it possible to predict the mobility rates for various categories of population? Second, *why do they move?* What sociopsychological and economic factors cause a given household to move? Here the emphasis is on the decision-making unit, the family. Finally, the almost completely neglected question, but the one of greatest concern to students of the urban spatial structure, *where do they move?* Are there spatial regularities in the relocation process? How does the household go about finding a new home? What is the relation between the supply of different kinds of housing and the demand by various consumer units?

WHO MOVES?

The spatial distribution of demographic characteristics is a major factor in differentiating mobility rates throughout the city, and the housing and access requirements of various life-cycle groups dominate the patterns of

Moore: Models of Migrations and the Intra-Urban Case, *Australian and New Zealand Journ. of Sociology*, Vol. 2, 1966, pp. 16–37. Shryock (*op. cit.* [see footnote 1 above], p. 435) discusses sources of data. Julian Wolpert (Behavioral Aspects of the Decision to Migrate, *Papers Regional Science Assn.*, Vol. 15, 1965, pp. 159–169) and Tosten Hägerstrand (Migration and Area, *in* Migration in Sweden, *Lund Studies in Geogr.*, Ser. B, Human Geography, No. 13, 1957, pp. 27–158) present important contributions to the theory.

flow. The large number of intraurban residential movements largely reflects the high rates of mobility of a few age groups.

Almost all the research on intraurban relocation before 1950 was concerned with the measurement of mobility rates. Sociologists in the 1920's and 1930's stressed mobility as a cause of urban social problems, but the absence of census data on rates of movement forced each investigator to develop his own measures. Caplow's detailed review of the early studies of intraurban mobility reveals the wide variations in mobility rates, derived at different times and from numerous sources of information.[4] A controversial point is whether mobility rates are increasing or decreasing over time. The measuring techniques are so imperfect and so dissimilar that it seems unlikely the question will be resolved. The general impression gained from the pre-World-War-II studies is that intraurban mobility in the first quarter of the century was greater than it is today. Albig,[5] using city directories, found a steady decline in intraurban mobility rates from more than 50 percent a year in 1903–1910 to 20 percent in 1930–1932, and Goldstein[6] also identified a decline, though not so marked. On the other hand, an unpublished study by Rossi,[7] based on the life histories of a sample population, indicates continuously increasing intraurban mobility.

Once the United States Bureau of the Census began to gather information

---

[4] Theodore Caplow: Incidence and Direction of Residential Mobility in a Minneapolis Sample, *Social Forces*, Vol. 27, 1948–1949, pp. 413–417. Other good bibliographies are found in Sidney Goldstein: Patterns of Mobility, 1910–1950 (Philadelphia, 1958), pp. 244–249, and in Peter H. Rossi: Why Families Move (Glencoe, Ill., 1955), pp. 185–195. See also Janet Abu-Lughod and Mary Mix Foley: Consumer Strategies, *in* Housing Choices and Housing Constraints (by Nelson N. Foote, Janet Abu-Lughod, Mary Mix Foley, and Louis Winnick; New York, 1960), pp. 71–271. Studies deriving mobility rates include Andrew W. Lind: A Study of the Mobility of Population in Seattle, *Univ. of Washington Publs. in the Social Sciences*, No. 3, 1925, pp. 1–64; T. Earl Sullenger: A Study in Intra-Urban Mobility, *Sociology and Social Research*, Vol. 17, 1932–1933, pp. 16–24; *idem:* The Social Significance of Mobility: An Omaha Study, *Amer. Journ. of Sociology*, Vol. 55, 1949–1950, pp. 559–564; William Albig: The Mobility of Urban Population, *Social Forces*, Vol. 11, 1932–1933, pp. 351–367; *idem:* A Method of Recording Trends in Urban Residential Mobility, *Sociology and Social Research*, Vol. 21, 1936–1937, pp. 120–127; *idem:* A Comparison of Methods for Recording Trends in Urban Residential Mobility, *ibid.*, Vol. 21, 1936–1937, pp. 226–233; Sidney Goldstein and Kurt B. Mayer: Residential Mobility, Migration and Commuting in Rhode Island, Rhode Island Development Council, *Planning Division Publ. No. 7*, Providence, 1963. An incredible amount of data (eight 321 x 321 flow matrices) was assembled in the 1930's, but remains largely unanalyzed (see Howard Whipple Green: Movements of Families within the Cleveland Metropolitan District, *Real Property Inventory of Metropolitan Cleveland, Repts. Nos. 3, 5, 7, 9, 11, 13, 15,* and *17;* Cleveland [issued annually, 1934–1942]). The data, however, stimulated the seminal paper by Samuel A. Stouffer: Intervening Opportunities: A Theory Relating Mobility and Distance, *Amer. Sociol. Rev.*, Vol 5, 1940, pp. 845–867.

[5] Albig, A Method of Recording Trends in Urban Residential Mobility [see footnote 4 above]. The decline is great enough to overcome errors in his sources.

[6] *Op. cit.* [see footnote 4 above], pp. 211 ff.

[7] Quoted in Abu-Lughod and Foley, *op. cit.* [see footnote 4 above], p. 161.

on mobility, researchers had the tool they needed to turn their attention to the study of process. The 1940 Census of Population asked about place of residence in 1935, though moves within areas smaller than a county were not aggregated. The 1950 census, however, provided information for the year 1949–1950 on intracounty moves, tabulating it for urban places and by

TABLE II—PERCENTAGE OF MALES MOVING WITHIN CITY ANNUALLY

	AGE				
	18–24	25–34	35–44	45–64	65+
EDUCATION (in years)					
0–8	—	24.1	14.2	8.5	6.6
9–11	—	26.2	10.7	7.8	5.2
12	—	18.9	11.1	7.0	5.4
13 or more	—	19.4	10.3	7.5	5.9
OCCUPATION					
White collar	27.2	19.9	9.4	6.3	3.0
Manual	30.4	22.9	12.0	8.2	5.9
Service	25.6	25.5	16.7	9.0	5.9
Farm	15.9	11.1	9.5	6.8	2.0
EMPLOYMENT					
Self-employed	15.9	14.1	8.1	4.8	2.5
Wage and salary	28.8	22.0	11.5	8.1	4.7
Unemployed	22.3	26.4	17.2	11.7	—

Source: "Mobility of the Population of the United States" [see text footnote 2].

census tracts.[8] The 1960 census broadened the categories (Table I) and extended the time period to five years, 1955–1960.[9] For comparisons over time, the Current Population Reports[10] have produced annual estimates of national and regional mobility rates since 1948, though no data are provided for specific cities or parts of cities. These reports indicate little fluctuation in intraurban mobility rates between 1948 and 1965.

The census materials make it possible to obtain information on gross migration rates for different subsets of the population, defined either on the basis of destination or on socioeconomic characteristics. The life cycle[11] causes

---

[8] United States Census of Population: 1950, Vol. 2, Characteristics of the Population. Based on a 20 percent sample of persons.

[9] United States Census of Population, 1960, Vol. 1, Characteristics of the Population. My headings in Table I differ slightly from those listed in the Census—that is, "Central City of SMSA," "Other Part of SMSA," "Outside SMSA." In addition, the Census of Housing, 1960, identifies the date of movement into the present residence: 1958 to mid-1960; 1954 to 1957; 1940–1953; 1939 or earlier.

[10] "Mobility of the Population of the United States" [see footnote 2 above], issued annually since 1948, uses a national sample of 30,000 families.

[11] John B. Lansing and Leslie Kish (Family Life Cycle as an Independent Variable, Amer. Sociol. Rev., Vol. 22, 1957, pp. 512–519) point out that the stage of family formation is more accurate than age alone in predicting expenditure, housing characteristics, and, undoubtedly, mobility. Most data, however, are tied to age, and the two variables are used interchangeably in this discussion.

many of the apparent variations in mobility rates for different areas and for different socioeconomic groups, since the differentials attributable to occupation, income, and so on are minor (Table II). The annual intracounty mobility

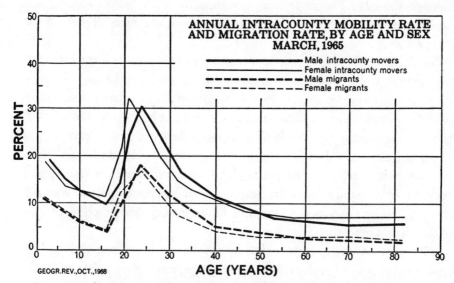

FIG. 1—Annual intracounty mobility rate. *Source:* "Mobility of the Population of the United States March 1964 to March 1965" [see text footnote 2 for reference].

rate for children under five is about 20 percent, then it declines to about 12 percent for teenagers, maximizes at more than 30 percent for persons in their twenties, and drops again to less than 10 percent for those over forty-five (Fig. 1).[11] A slight tendency toward greater mobility for lower-income groups complements their lower migration rates. Farmers, the self-employed and homeowners have lower mobility rates.[13] For these people investment creates a higher threshold to be overcome before moving, and ownership itself may indicate a psychological commitment to an area.

Mobility rates vary within the metropolitan area. Rates of in-movement (Figs. 2 and 3) are generally highest in the city center and in the most recently developed suburbs. The distribution of out-migration is more significant

---

[12] The concentration of movement in a short period in the life-span accounts for the phenomenon of repeated migration, in which a single person or household moves several times during the period of study. See Sidney Goldstein: The Extent of Repeated Migration, *Journ. Amer. Statist. Assn.*, Vol. 59, 1964, pp. 1121–1132, and also his "Repeated Migration as a Factor in High Mobility Rates," *Amer. Sociol. Rev.*, Vol. 19, 1954, pp. 536–541.

[13] Rossi, *op. cit.* [see footnote 4 above], p. 69.

because this measure is much less sensitive to the addition of new housing. Rates of out-migration from the city center are about double those of the suburban area, and Moore[14] explains about 60 percent of the variation as being a function of distance. Mobility rates are also slightly higher in low-income sectors of the city. The impression obtained from an examination of the spatial pattern of mobility is of the large number of moves in all parts of the metropolitan area.

The effect of the size of the observation unit, in this case the city, is a measurement problem common to all migration studies.[15] Large cities provide more migration opportunities than small cities, and a large observation unit allows people to move farther without crossing a boundary. The growth rate is another factor that tends to increase mobility within a city. Rapid growth stimulates new housing investment, creates a ready market for older properties, and accelerates the processes of suburbanization, invasion, and succession. In Canadian cities the percentage of intrametropolitan movers, 1956–1961, using 1956 as the base, can be expressed as a function of city population and growth:

$$\text{Percent movers} = -28.67 + 10.24 \log \text{population} + 0.45 \text{ growth rate.}$$

Population explains 52 percent, and growth 26 percent, of the variation in the intrametropolitan migration rate. The first is a systematic measurement error owing to the definition of mobility that is used; the second accelerates movements that take place for other reasons.

WHY DO THEY MOVE?

Housing needs generated by life-cycle changes cause the majority of moves and produce high rates of out-movement in all parts of the city, but the reasons for changing residence within the city vary with the characteristics of the mover. The large number of movers in the age group fifteen to twenty-

---

[14] Moore (*op. cit.* [see footnote 3 above], p. 26), using data from Brisbane, Australia. Lind (*op. cit.* [see footnote 4 above], Fig. 1) shows the pattern of out-migration in Seattle, where the highest rates in the central area are two or three times as great as in the suburbs. Albig (The Mobility of Urban Population [see footnote 4 above]) finds the same pattern, but with the central area about 50 percent higher. See also Elsa Schneider Longmoor and Erle Fiske Young: Ecological Interrelationships of Juvenile Delinquency, Dependency, and Population Mobility: A Cartographic Analysis of Data from Long Beach, California, *Amer. Journ. of Sociology*, Vol. 41, 1935–1936, pp. 598–610; and Green (*op. cit.* [see footnote 4 above]), in each of his Cleveland reports.

[15] The effect of size has been studied theoretically by Gunnar Kulldorff (Migration Probabilities, *Lund Studies in Geogr.*, Ser. B., Human Geography, No. 14, 1955), and empirically by Bertil Wendel (Regional Aspects of Internal Migration and Mobility in Sweden, 1946–1950, *in* Migration in Sweden [see footnote 3 above], pp. 7-26).

five weights the overall pattern toward their particular needs and dissatisfactions, but other subpopulations—for example, the aged or the residents of a particular part of the city—may have different reasons for moving. A great

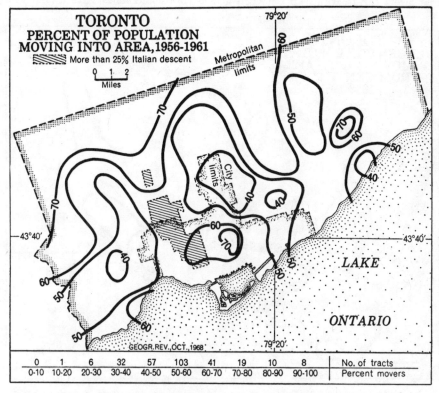

FIG. 2—Movement into the Toronto area, 1956–1961. *Source:* "Migration, Fertility, and Income by Census Tracts," Census of Canada, 1961 (CX-1, Ottawa, 1965).

deal of social change can take place without significantly altering the mobility rate, but a variety of social factors may modify the out-movement of subpopulations from certain areas.

The decision to move can be examined from several points of view. The social psychologist sees the household as acting under various kinds of stress; the economist views the move as maximizing satisfaction of the household requirements; and the human ecologist treats it as an element in a larger pattern of movements or as part of the processes of growth and succession. From any point of view, however, the decision to move is complex. It is concerned, on the one hand, with the needs and values of the household, which change over time, and, on the other, with the characteristics of the environment, which encompasses home, neighborhood, and alternative locations.

TYPES OF SOCIAL CHANGE

In order to overcome the time and money costs of moving, some attraction or dissatisfaction is required. The most obvious factor is social change that alters the relationship between a household and its environment. The

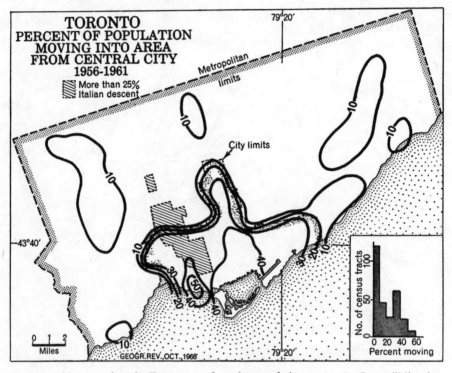

FIG. 3—Movement into the Toronto area from the central city, 1956–1961. *Source:* "Migration, Fertility, and Income by Census Tracts," Census of Canada, 1961 (CX-1, Ottawa, 1965).

size, age, or income of a household may change; the environment may be altered by such things as blight, invasion by other cultural groups, or increased land values. More likely, both the household and the environment change simultaneously, but at different rates. Three major clusters of social variables should be examined for their contributions to mobility: urbanization, including demographic characteristics and life-style; economic status, combining measures of income, occupation, and education; and segregation, identifying ethnic or racial origin and religion.[16]

The evidence indicates that the urbanization, or life-cycle, factor is the

[16] Theodore R. Anderson and J. A. Egeland: Spatial Aspects of Social Area Analysis, *Amer. Sociol. Rev.*, Vol. 26, 1961, pp. 392–398; Brian J. L. Berry: Cities as Systems within Systems of Cities, *Paper Regional Science Assn.*, Vol. 13, 1964, pp. 147–163; Robert A. Murdie: Ecological Structure and Chance in Metropolitan Toronto, *Univ. of Chicago, Dept. of Geogr. Research Papers* (forthcoming).

most powerful inducement to people to change their residence. Rossi,[17] after his intensive series of interviews and follow-up studies on residential relocation, concluded: "the major function of mobility [is] the process by which families adjust their housing to the housing needs that are generated by the shifts in family composition that accompany life cycle changes." The sharp variations in mobility rates shown in Figure 1 reinforce Rossi's statement. The life-cycle stages (Fig. 4) account for at least five of the eight or nine moves that

MOVES DURING THE LIFE CYCLE

AGE	STAGE	MOVES
0	Birth	
	Child	1
10		
	Adolescent	
20	Maturity	1
	Marriage	1
30	Children	1
40		
	Children mature	
50		
60		1
	Retirement	
70		
	Death	
80		

FIG. 4

might be expected in a lifetime, as an individual grows up, leaves home, marries, has children, and ages. The cluster of moves in quick succession in the fifteen-to-twenty-five age bracket is evident. Although some of the life-cycle adjustments occur through intercounty migrations, many people have far more complex life cycles, with several moves at certain stages, such as childhood, maturity, and marriage. Most movers are dependents, accompanying the head of the household; thus the family characteristics, rather than those of the individual, are the critical factor. Rossi[18] classified about one-third of the moves he studied as forced, coming as an aftermath of other major events such as eviction, marriage, death, or sudden loss of income. The

---

[17] Rossi, op. cit. [see footnote 4 above], p. 9. Rossi was able to predict a large proportion of mobility on the basis of a mobility index, based on age, household size, and tenure preference (p. 76). Similar results were obtained by R. Wilkinson and D. M. Merry: A Statistical Analysis of Attitudes to Moving, Urban Studies, Vol. 2, 1965, pp. 1–14. See also Abu-Lughod and Foley, op. cit. [see footnote 4 above), p. 155.

[18] Op. cit. [see footnote 4 above], p. 135.

most common reason for the voluntary moves is the need for more space for a growing family. Less frequently, there is the adjustment to a smaller unit when the family is grown, though often this move is not made until the household is broken up by illness or death.

Often in combination with the housing adjustment, the family may choose, or be compelled, to change its neighborhood. Several studies of the adjustment of low-income families to new neighborhoods indicate that the loss of kinship and other contacts creates severe problems, which can lead to return movements.[19] But the variety of life-styles already experienced by middle-class households give them more flexibility. For instance, a young man may flee the suburbs for a mildly bohemian area in the city, exchange it for a more respectable town-house district on his marriage, and later seek a low-density suburb for his children. New low-density housing and, particularly, the opportunity to own rather than to rent attract the young family. On the basis of research to date, it is difficult to determine which comes first: do people change their way of life and then seek a more suitable environment, or do the physical surroundings modify the way of life?[20]

In general, any alteration in the demographic characteristics of a neighborhood—most frequently the overall aging of the population—coincides with the changes taking place in the households. Even if a family were out of phase with the age structure of the neighborhood, it seems unlikely that this form of stress would be sufficiently severe to lead to a move. One generator of mobility is the demographic change associated with the redevelopment cycle in the central city. Old houses are converted to rooming houses or are replaced by high-rise apartments, thereby increasing the neighborhood density. These areas, however, constitute only a small part of the city and generally undergo gradual adjustment in the wake of out-movements for other reasons.

ECONOMIC AND SOCIAL STATUS

Economic status includes income, occupation, and certain housing variables. Since urban areas are strongly differentiated with respect to class, a

---

[19] See, for example, Michael D. Young and Peter Willmott: Family and Kinship in East London (Chicago and London, 1957); Marc Fried: Grieving for a Lost Home, in The Urban Condition (edited by Leonard J. Duhl; New York, 1963), pp. 151–171.

[20] A continuing investigation into the effect of physical environment and way of life is being undertaken by William Michelson: An Empirical Analysis of Urban Environmental Preferences, *Journ. Amer. Inst. of Planners*, Vol. 32, 1966, pp. 355–360. See also the review of the adjustment process by Robert Gutman: Population Mobility in the American Middle Class, in The Urban Condition [see footnote 19 above], pp. 172–183, and by Herbert J. Gans: The Effects of the Move from City to Suburbs, *ibid.*, pp. 184–198; *idem*: The Levittowners (New York, 1967).

person who changes his social status might be expected to change the location of his residence. However, Lipset and Bendix,[21] using two class categories, found that only 30 percent of North Americans leave the social class in which they were raised, and hence residential relocation is required only once in the lifetime of a third of the population. Even if a more complex set of social-class categories were used, so that almost everyone changed categories, only one move in a lifetime would be explained by social mobility. More effective, perhaps, are the income changes that take place without altering relative social class. Each household reaps the advantage of the annual 2–3 percent increase in the standard of living, and while working in the same job a man's disposable income may increase as he gains seniority and shifts expenditures from children and appliances to housing and other goods. The effect is to remove the cost constraint that may have restricted the adjustment of housing needs. During the same period, of course, the original housing, even if adequate in size and location, becomes less attractive relative to the total housing stock. In this way, housing "filters down" to lower-income groups while people "filter up" to better housing.[22]

The majority of moves adjust housing within neighborhoods of similar characteristics (Table III). About 80 percent of intracity movement takes place within census tracts of the same class or adjacent classes.[23] The economic status of a neighborhood changes as one social class replaces another; the rich buy out the poor or the poor make life uncomfortable for the rich. The tendency for higher-income people to move outside the city limits accelerates the filtering down of housing opportunities and the net movement of lower-income groups into higher-income areas. In most instances these movements are gradual, and do not increase the rate of migration. Even urban renewal projects, which may relocate thousands from a given area during a period of two or three years, account for only a small part of the total mobility in a city.[24]

[21] Seymour M. Lipset and Reinhard Bendix: Social Mobility in Industrial Society (Berkeley and Los Angeles, 1959), Table 2-1. Goldstein (Patterns of Mobility [see footnote 4 above], p. 185), using six categories, found that less than 50 percent of those he studied shifted during a ten-year period.

[22] For a detailed discussion of the filtering process, see William G. Grigsby: Housing Markets and Public Policy (Philadelphia, 1963), Chap. 3.

[23] Sidney Goldstein and Kurt B. Mayer: Metropolitanization and Population Change in Rhode Island, Rhode Island Development Council, Planning Division Publ. No. 3, Providence, 1961, p. 51 Table 18). Green (op. cit. [see footnote 4 above], Rept. No. 11, p. 63) obtained similar results in Cleveland.

[24] For instance, of a total of more than 1,200,000 moves in Chicago (1955–1960) only about 80,000 persons were relocated because of public demolition activities, including urban renewal, public housing, and expressways ("Housing and Urban Renewal Progress Report" [Chicago Community Renewal Program, December 31, 1964], Fig. 7; and United States Censuses of Population and Housing, 1960, Final Rept. PHC (1)–26, "Census Tracts, Chicago, Illinois").

Studies of ethnic and racial groups have generated a complex, and often contradictory, body of theory about their intraurban movements.[25] The assimilation processes that European minorities underwent in the nineteenth century and the early twentieth are less relevant to present-day groups, who have different problems and who live in cities with dissimilar patterns of inter-

TABLE III—MOVES AMONG SOCIAL AREAS
(*In percentages*)

SOCIAL CLASS	SOCIAL CLASS OF DESTINATION TRACT				
	I (high)	II	III	IV	V (low)
I (high)	63.8	12.0	11.3	8.2	4.8
II	8.2	51.0	20.6	13.3	6.8
III	6.1	18.8	50.4	16.7	8.1
IV	5.1	13.0	21.0	52.7	8.1
V (low)	4.1	13.2	17.3	17.4	48.1

Source: Goldstein and Mayer, Metropolitanization and Population Change in Rhode Island [see text footnote 23], p. 51.

action and opportunity. The Negro ghetto is larger and more permanent than the enclaves of the earlier minority groups, and many recent European immigrants have avoided the ghetto stage entirely.

The traditional ethnic community had a core area where much of the assimilation took place, and from which the successful immigrants, either as individuals or as groups, moved out socially and spatially. If the flow of inmigration slackened, the core area itself might be relocated, particularly if spatial assimilation had been a group process. The net effect was a decline in the concentration of such ethnic groups, but their movements have not had an appreciable effect on mobility rates. Members of ethnic groups move for the usual reasons—for example, the need for better housing—and the communities expand gradually.[26] The ethnic factor acts as a constraint only on the number of possible alternatives, explaining "where" people move rather than "why" they move.

---

[25] Patterns of residential segregation are discussed in Davis McEntire: Residence and Race (Berkeley and Los Angeles, 1960), pp. 9–101, and in Stanley Lieberson: Ethnic Patterns in American Cities (New York, 1963). For particular cities, see Paul Frederick Cressey: Population Succession in Chicago: 1898–1930, *Amer. Journ. of Sociology*, Vol. 44, 1938–1939, pp. 59–69; Richard G. Ford: Population Succession in Chicago, *ibid.*, Vol. 56, 1950–1951, pp. 156–160; Christen T. Jonassen: Cultural Variables in the Ecology of an Ethnic Group, *Amer. Sociol. Rev.*, Vol. 14, 1949, pp. 32–41; John Kosa: Hungarian Immigrants in North America: Their Residential Mobility and Ecology, *Canadian Journ. of Econ. and Polit. Sci.*, Vol. 22, 1956, pp. 358–370.

[26] When the mobility rates for Metropolitan Toronto were plotted the large Italian area (more than 100,000 persons) of recent origin and its surroundings showed slightly greater mobility on one map (Fig. 2).

The expansion of the Negro ghettos in northern cities increases mobility more dramatically. Typically, the highly segregated and rapidly growing Negro areas can expand only into nearby white neighborhoods.[27] If the whites panic, the turnover takes place rapidly, affecting as many as 75 percent of the dwellings in two or three years. The mobility rate for Negroes increases as the normal rate of white out-migration (about 50 percent in five years) is accelerated by racial and economic fears. The crucial aspect in the changeover is not the accelerated white out-migration but the almost total cessation of white in-migration.[28] Negro in-migrants of the same socioeconomic level as the whites fill the vacuum.[29] Even in a city the size of Chicago, with a large and rapidly growing Negro population, the number of moves stimulated by racial shifts is small in proportion to total moves. An examination of the 1960 data for the south side of the city reveals that about 10 percent of the census tracts had high mobility rates, but even these high rates were less than 50 percent above the normal rate. Racial shifts generated from 3 to 5 percent of all movements in that part of the city.[30]

INDIVIDUAL DECISIONS

The final set of factors that induces a change of residence reflects personal problems in adjusting to the environment, beyond the effects of physical needs and the constraints of class and culture outlined above. Evidence for these personal aspects of mobility is provided by Rossi,[31] who found it necessary to evaluate the complaints about dwellings along with life-cycle and tenure information in order to predict mobility. The complaints generated by the differences between expectation and reality as perceived by the household are not predictable from any socioeconomic measures; neither are conflicts with neighbors, which may make an area untenable. Some persons are chronically restless and dissatisfied; others blunder in their evaluation of alternative neighborhoods or are unable to adjust their life-style to a particular environment. All these things affect an individual's perception of the cost, of

---

[27] For a discussion of the process in Northern cities, see Otis Dudley Duncan and Beverly Duncan: The Negro Population of Chicago (Chicago, 1957); Chester Rapkin and William G. Grigsby: The Demand for Housing in Racially Mixed Areas (Berkeley and Los Angeles, 1960); Richard L. Morrill (The Negro Ghetto: Problems and Alternatives, *Geogr. Rev.*, Vol. 55, 1965, pp. 339–361) and Karl E. Taeuber and Alma F. Taeuber: Negroes in Cities (Chicago, 1965). These writers have shown that the ghetto in southern cities expands differently because access to the urban fringe allows Negroes to move directly into new housing.

[28] This has been documented by Rapkin and Grigsby, *op. cit.* [see footnote 27 above], pp. 52–72.

[29] Taeuber and Taeuber, *op. cit.* [see footnote 27 above], pp. 156 and 180.

[30] "Census Tracts, Chicago, Illinois" [see footnote 24 above], Table 1.

[31] *Op. cit.* [see footnote 4 above], p. 92–94.

the characteristics of the dwelling unit, and of the immediate social and economic environment. Rossi's comparison of the perception of housing by residents and by an "objective observer" (Table IV) sheds some light on the source of complaints. Agreement is best for the most significant variable, the

TABLE IV—AREA CHARACTERISTICS AND THEIR PERCEPTION BY RESIDENTS

ATTRIBUTE	RANKING			
	Oak Lane	West Philadelphia	Kensington	Central City
LOCATION				
Observed	4	1	3	2
Perceived	3	2	1	4
PHYSICAL FACILITIES				
Observed	1	2	3	4
Perceived	2	3	1	4
DWELLING-UNIT SIZE				
Observed	1	3	2	4
Perceived	2	3	1	4

Source: Rossi, Why People Move [see text footnote 4], pp. 26–30.

dwelling-unit size. Only a few complaints concerned location, in the sense of access, and these had little effect on mobility.

In order to explain expectations of movement, Lansing and Barth[32] combined two social variables (age of household head and crowding) with three attitude variables (satisfaction with housing, neighborhood, distance from city center) and obtained results that confirmed Rossi's work. Rossi has also associated mobility with the perceived difference in social class between residents and their neighbors.[33]

The role of the goals and knowledge of the individual household in the decision to move is difficult to evaluate, though recent studies of environmental perception may be of some assistance.[34] A theoretical structure has been provided by Wolpert's behavioral model of migration.[35] Each social

[32] John B. Lansing and Nancy Barth: Residential Location and Urban Mobility: A Multivariate Analysis (Inst. for Social Research, Ann Arbor, Mich., 1964), p. 18.

[33] Rossi, op. cit. [see footnote 4 above], p. 34.

[34] Studies of individual perception of the environment are presented in two collections of papers: R. W. Kates and J. F. Wohlwill, edits.: Man's Response to the Physical Environment, Journ. of Social Issues, Vol. 22, No. 4, 1966; and David Lowenthal, edit.: Environmental Perception and Behavior, Univ. of Chicago, Dept. of Geogr., Research Paper No. 109, 1967. Significant studies of urban phenomena include Kevin Lynch: The Image of the City (Cambridge, Mass., 1960); Robert L. Wilson: The Livability of the City, in Urban Growth Dynamics (edited by F. Stuart Chapin, Jr., and Shirley F. Weiss, New York, 1962), pp. 359–399; and George L. Peterson: A Model of Preference: Quantitative Analysis of the Perception of the Visual Appearance of Residential Neighborhoods, Journ. of Regional Science, Vol. 7, 1967, pp. 19–31. So far urban studies relate to the selection of neighborhood rather than to motivations for moving.

[35] Wolpert, op. cit. [see footnote 3 above].

group has a constant propensity to move, which is related to its *threshold of utility*—that is, the degree of differentiation of place utility between where people are living and alternative locations necessary to make them move. Place utility is the measure of attractiveness or unattractiveness of an area relative to alternative locations, as perceived by the individual decision maker, and as evaluated according to his particular needs.[36] For instance, elderly working-class people have a very high threshold of utility: only an earthquake could make them move. Elderly middle-class people have a slightly lower threshold: they can be lured away by Florida sunshine. Young people, on the other hand, require little incentive to leave home.

Thus place utility both initiates relocation and determines the new location. But the theory of search behavior also explains location. The individual evaluates the alternatives with which he is familiar: nearby places, communities where friends and relatives live, areas visited in travel, places described by mass media. Generally these alternatives are clustered around one or two locations. The decision process, however, is complicated by the possibility of time lags after changes in the household–environment relationship, the tendency to minimize uncertainty, and the option of adjusting to the existing situation. In a later paper Wolpert[37] enlarges the threshold-of-utility concept into a strain-stress model in which an individual migrates as a form of adaptation to stress exerted by his environment. The two elements—the change in the individual over time and the stress exerted by the environment—are modified by the susceptibility of the individual.

To summarize, then, within a moderately growing city more than 50 percent of the intraurban mobility results from the changing housing needs generated by the life cycle. Abu-Lughod and Foley[38] estimate that about 30 percent of intraurban moves are involuntary, with 10 percent following the creation of new households and 20 percent resulting from demolition, destruction by fire, or eviction. Perhaps another 10 percent reflect changes outside the life cycle, such as social mobility, ethnic assimilation, and neighborhood invasion. The most meaningful aspects of the housing adjustments are the size and facilities of the dwelling unit, followed by the social environment

[36] Further evidence is provided by Peter Gould: (On Mental Maps, *Michigan Inter-University Community of Mathematical Geographers Discussion Paper No. 9*, 1966), who obtained consistent structures of location preferences for individuals.

[37] Julian Wolpert: Migration as an Adjustment to Environment Stress, *in* "Man's Response to the Physical Environment [see footnote 34 above], pp. 92–102.

[38] Abu-Lughod and Foley, *op. cit.* [see footnote 4 above], p. 135. Peter H. Rossi (Why Families Move, *in* The Language of Social Research [edited by Paul F. Lazarsfeld and Morris Rosenberg; Glencoe, Ill., 1955], pp. 457–468; reference on p. 459) suggests slightly smaller values.

of the neighborhood. The physical site and access to other parts of the city are relatively insignificant. All studies reject job location as an important reason for moving.[39] Given the high rate of mobility generated by the life cycle, changes in the numbers and characteristics of the population within an area generally reflect a change in the pattern of in-migration.

WHERE DO THEY MOVE?

Knowing why a family moves tells us little about its final destination. This is apparent when maps of intraurban migration are studied.[40] Flows and counterflows crisscross the urban area, and these major regularities, such as the tendencies to move nearby and within the same sector, are determined by the procedure for seeking a new home rather than the reason for leaving the old. Once the decision to move has been made, the family takes another set of factors into consideration. The selection of a new home depends not only on demand conditions (the priorities that the family assigns to different housing characteristics) but also on supply constraints (the cost and quantity of different types of housing in different parts of the city). Then, too, the search procedure used by a family to examine and evaluate alternative locations is significant.

Both the supply and demand sides of the housing market strongly influence the choice of a place to live.[41] The supply of housing is differentiated by such variables as tenure, number of rooms, age, and location; the demand for housing is a function of such characteristics of the urban population as income, point in the life cycle, family size, and place of employment. The demand submarkets have varying degrees of independence from other submarkets; often a family will find it difficult to choose between quite different alterna-

---

[39] Rossi, Why Families Move [see footnote 4 above], p. 85; Howard S. Lapin: Structuring the Journey to Work (Philadelphia, 1964), p. 163.

[40] Maps of mobility-desire lines are found in Lind (op. cit. [see footnote 4 above], p. 28), in Albig (The Mobility of Urban Population, [see footnote 4 above], pp. 352–353) and in Green (op. cit. [see footnote 4 above], Rept. No. 9, p. 52, and Rept. No. 11, pp. 54–55). Caplow (op. cit. [see footnote 4 above] p. 416) tabulated his data by rings from the city center, in order to examine the degree of decentralization. No one has yet produced an urban counterpart to the remarkable work by C. Warren Thornthwaite: Internal Migration in the United States (Philadelphia, 1934), in which flow lines summarize the whole pattern of interstate migration, or the study by Daniel O. Price: Distance and Direction as Vectors of Internal Migration, 1935–40, Social Forces, Vol. 27, 1948–1949, pp. 48–53.

[41] One of the most stimulating discussions of the housing market is found in Grigsby (op. cit. [see footnote 22 above], Chap. 11). Other studies that approach the city's housing market from the point of view of supply and demand are Chester Rapkin and William G. Grigsby: The Demand for Housing in Eastwick (Redevelopment Authority of the City of Philadelphia, 1960), and their Residential Renewal in the Urban Core (Philadelphia, 1960); and Beverly Duncan and Philip M. Hauser: Housing a Metropolis —Chicago (Glencoe, Ill., 1961).

tives—for example, an aging duplex in a central location or a suburban bunga-
low. Housing surveys and the economics of the construction industry provide
the supply schedules for each submarket, and knowledge of past behavior
patterns and surveys of consumer preference permit the construction of
housing-demand curves for each subpopulation.[42] Grisgby[43] has constructed
matrices that show movements of households between demand submarkets
and relationships between supply and demand categories. Because of the large
number of variables differentiating housing submarkets and household
characteristics, matrices relating supply and demand are complex. However,
the number of housing alternatives is lessened by the fixed supply of housing
in the short run and the correlations among housing characteristics. For instance, the majority of the smaller dwelling units are for rent, and older
housing is found near the city center.

Each family chooses from the housing available at any one time,[44] but
relatively little is known about the complex selection process. Some data are
available, but the survey methods—the form of questionnaire, the location
of the sample, the timing—vary so much that the data are almost useless. The
hierarchy of criteria is still hypothetical,[45] but cost undoubtedly plays a major
role. Each household has a housing budget, which is a function of its "normal" income, defined as the long-run expected income of the family.[46] A
crucial option is whether to own or to rent, a decision related both to income

[42] The San Francisco Community Renewal Program has undertaken a project that will measure and
predict the present and future supplies of housing stock and housing demand as a policy aid in renewal
planning (Ira M. Robinson, Harry B. Wolfe, and Robert L. Barringer: A Simulation Model for Renewal
Programming, *Journ. Amer. Inst. of Planners*, Vol. 31, 1965, pp. 126–133. Michelson analyzes the demand
by one set of consumers, those likely to prefer downtown high-rise apartments (William Michelson:
Potential Candidates for the Designer's Paradise: A Social Analysis from a Nationwide Survey, *Social
Forces*, Vol. 46, 1967–1968, pp. 190–196.

[43] *Op. cit.* [see footnote 22 above], pp. 64–69, 51, and 54, respectively.

[44] Grigsby differentiates between the total stock of housing and the amount on the market at one
time. Certain submarkets, such as owner-occupied single-family dwellings, have a lower turnover than
others, and the supply of this type of housing for rent or sale is disproportionately low at any one time,
(*ibid.*, p. 83).

[45] The best information to date in this area is the national sample of interviews carried out by the
Survey Research Center, Institute for Social Research, University of Michigan, Ann Arbor: John B.
Lansing and Eva Mueller: Residential Location and Urban Mobility (1964); Lansing and Barth, *op. cit.*
[see footnote 32 above]; John B. Lansing: Residential Location and Urban Mobility: The Second Wave
of Interviews (1966). An interesting gaming approach developed by Wilson (*op. cit.* [see footnote 34
above]) asks people to spend a given amount of money on various housing features.

[46] Margaret G. Reid (Housing and Income [Chicago, 1962]) finds that housing expenditures are tied
more closely to average incomes than to actual incomes because of the short-term fluctuation in the
latter. Housing expenditures form a higher proportion of income as income increases, and as tenure
shifts from renting to owning (p. 378). See also Louis Winnick: Economic Constraints, *in* Housing
Choices and Housing Constraints [see footnote 4 above], pp. 3–67.

and to life-cycle characteristics. The other important consideration is the amount of space required. Social factors (access to downtown, familiarity of the neighborhood, ethnic groupings) further complicate the decision.

SPATIAL ASPECTS OF THE HOUSING MARKET

The division of the housing stock into locational submarkets does not, in itself, severely reduce the supply of available dwelling units. Mobility rates are high enough that some housing units are available in virtually every area. Generally, a wide range of cost alternatives also exists throughout the city, if one is willing to trade size for cost. Only in a few instances (the eighteenth-century home, the $300,000 mansion, the 50-cent flophouse) would availability and cost alone define the location. The location constraint operates in conjunction with other variables, and the requirement of living in a certain neighborhood becomes difficult to fulfill only when housing of a certain size or standard is specified. More often location comes so far down on the hierarchy of criteria that the location of a dwelling results from decisions about other factors.

Submarkets may be defined at all levels of the decision-making process. One can consider in turn the submarket of cheap housing, cheap apartments, cheap suburban apartments, and so on, each of which has spatial implications because of the distribution of that phenomenon. But a submarket at any level need not be confined to one location, since cheap housing, for instance, can be found in several areas of a city. In general, as the submarket is defined more precisely, the housing characteristics restrict the number of possible locations until the final decision focuses on a single house.

The distribution of various kinds of housing will affect the direction of flow. Although the variety of housing found in the central city is increasing, as old houses are subdivided and new apartments are erected, the range of choice in that area is restricted in two ways. Housing in the central part of the city, particularly the single-family dwelling, is old, lacks many amenities, and is therefore rejected by some families. Also, densities are much higher in the central areas, following the variations in land costs. It should be remembered that the relative importance placed on access, space, and other criteria varies with the household and with the neighborhood. People who live downtown have already opted for access; suburban dwellers have placed more importance on space and quiet. But the selection of an appropriate population density by a family is seldom explicit; it emerges from such decisions as whether to seek a single-family house or how big a lot to look for.

The best factor for predicting the location of a new residence is the location of the former house. All the evidence indicates that most moves are short, within familiar territory, and reflect both satisfaction with the neighborhood and location with respect to the urban structure. For example, a number of studies show that about a quarter of all moves take place within a

TABLE V—FAMILY MIGRATION, PROVIDENCE, 1950–1959
(*In percentages*)

| DESTINATION | SOCIAL CLASS OF ORIGIN TRACT | | | | | |
	I (high)	II	III	IV	V (low)	Total
Within tract	18.3	20.0	22.5	28.1	29.1	24.2
Within city	35.1	38.3	46.0	48.3	45.6	43.9
Outside city	46.8	40.7	31.5	24.6	25.2	31.9

Source: Goldstein and Mayer, Metropolitanization and Population Change in Rhode Island [see text footnote 23], p. 51 (Table 18).

census tract (Table V).[47] The short moves may produce a net spatial change in one direction (as suggested by the process of decentralization)[48] or they may ust be at random. The high rate of local movement provides a large number of opportunities for in-migrants throughout the metropolitan area and indicates that a household should be able to satisfy its housing requirements relatively easily.

The large number of local moves, adjusting housing needs within the same social area, overshadow longer moves that may involve a change in the social environment of the mover. The decline of moves with distance becomes more irregular when other factors, such as the location of housing alternatives, come into play. However, it is possible to describe the probability of relocation of a migrant as a function of distance, and several formulas have been suggested, with various theoretical bases and empirical demonstrations.[49] In

[47] For the years 1933 to 1937, Green (*op. cit.* [see footnote 4 above]) obtained values of 31, 28, 30, 26, and 24 percent of moves within the same tract in Cleveland. Caplow (*op. cit.* [see footnote 4 above], p. 417) gives 25 percent for Minneapolis, 1940–1948; Albig (The Mobility of Urban Population, [see footnote 4 above], Table 6) indicates in Danville, Rock Island, and Moline, Illinois, 1929–1930, that 25 to 30 percent of the moves were less than 1200 feet.

[48] Richard Dewey: Peripheral Expansion in Milwaukee County, *Amer. Journ. of Sociology*, Vol 54, 1948–1949, pp. 118–125; reference on p. 120. Dewey states that most out-movement occurs by a succession of short moves, but provides no substantiating data.

[49] See Kulldorff, *op. cit.* [see footnote 15 above], and Hägerstrand, *op. cit.* [see footnote 3 above] pp. 112–126. See also Richard L. Morrill: The Distribution of Migration Distances, *Papers Regional Science Assn.*, Vol. 11, 1963, pp. 75–84.

each case the models posit a sharp initial decline in the relocation rate, which then levels off.[50] Although few curves have been fitted to urban areas, the general relationship seems to hold, despite the distortions introduced by the patterns of social variation in the city. For the simplest expression of distance decay, the Pareto equation,

$$\text{in-migration/population} = a/\,(\text{distance})^b,$$

several estimates have been made of the parameter b:[51] Åsby, Sweden (1950), $b = 1.6$; Cleveland (1933–1936), $b = 2.5$; a group of small Midwestern cities (1930), $b = 1.8$.

The tendency of movers to choose destinations nearby has two possible reasons. The household may deliberately select a nearby location in order to maintain spatial familiarity, social contacts, institutional links or to maintain its access to the city as a whole, while adjusting housing size or tenure. The decline in the number of destinations with distance, however, suggests that short moves may also reflect imperfections in the housing market, especially since location is relatively unimportant and nearby alternatives are more likely to be evaluated than distant ones. Rossi found that almost 50 percent of all housing units were obtained through personal contact.[52]

CULTURAL CONSTRAINTS

The tendency to relocate in the same neighborhood may reflect the requirements, voluntary or involuntary, of being near people of similar origin or interest or of access to certain institutions. The effect of the cultural constraints is to emphasize movements within sectors as demonstrated by Caplow[53] and by Green.[54] Households are able to adjust their housing and access costs without crossing the sectoral boundaries, defined by nonresidential land use or by the location of other income and cultural groups. The tendency for high-income movers to relocate in the same sector forms a central part of

[50] See the discussion of the migration field in Olsson, op. cit. [see footnote 3 above], pp. 43–73. See also Richard L. Morrill and Forrest R. Pitts: Marriage, Migration, and the Mean Information Field, Annals Assn. of Amer. Geogrs., Vol. 57, 1967, pp. 401–422.

[51] The Åsby and Cleveland parameters are given by Duane F. Marble and John D. Nystuen: An Approach to the Direct Measurement of Community Mean Information Fields, Papers Regional Science Assn., Vol. 11, 1963, pp. 99–109, reference on pp. 103–106; the parameter for small Midwestern cities is derived from Albig, The Mobility of Urban Population [see footnote 4 above], Table 6.

[52] Op. cit. [see footnote 4 above], p. 161.

[53] Caplow (op. cit. [see footnote 4 above]), p. 415 (Table 2). Dewey (op. cit. [see footnote 48 above], p. 120) claims to have observed the same phenomena on the outskirts of Milwaukee.

[54] Green, op. cit. [see footnote 4 above], Rept. No. 9, p. 52, and Rept. No. 11, p. 54. Stouffer (op. cit. [see footnote 4 above]), using the same data, found that directional variations and moves by ethnic groups distorted his explanatory model, which was based on housing opportunities.

Hoyt's theory of the residential structure.[55] Hoyt suggests a number of reasons for this, among them the attraction of site characteristics, such as shorelines, and of fast transportation, both of which are essentially sectoral phenomena. However, the most prized residential sites in the city often are not intrinsically different from less desirable sites, but they represent the cumulative effect of high-income areas attracting prestige commercial establishments and community leaders, which in turn attract high-income residents. Minority groups are also sensitive to linkages. Entire Jewish communities have been transplanted from the old urban core to the suburbs as they climb the economic ladder; Negroes find tremendous internal and external forces opposing their movement out of the ghetto.

Families in higher social classes tend to move farther (Table V). More of them move outside the census tract, outside the central city, and outside the metropolitan area. Their evaluation procedures are apt to be more thorough and to embrace a more complex set of constraints. For these families, the cost of moving, estimated to be at least 10 percent of house value,[56] requires a substantial change in dwelling or environment to make it worthwhile. At the lowest end of the income scale, however, the slightest financial crisis may prevent the payment of rent and require relocation, and any change in the family structure creates pressures for adjustment.

We have assumed here that people tend to remain in the same income or ethnic environment when they move. Moves by the upwardly mobile or by ethnic families who are rapidly assimilating are less easy to predict, but these form only a small part of total moves. The time lag may be of considerable importance: movers select a neighborhood according to their perception of its characteristics in the near future, characteristics which may resemble the neighborhood they are leaving as it was five, ten, or twenty years ago. The degree of contiguity of income and culture areas will also have an effect. A city may have only one high-income area or it may have half a dozen, providing alternative locations.

ACCESS TO THE REST OF THE CITY

As we have seen, the consensus of studies of consumer preference is that the location of the house is generally less important than the characteristics of

---

[55] [Homer Hoyt:] The Structure and Growth of Residential Neighborhoods in American Cities (Federal Housing Administration, Washington, D. C., 1939), pp. 114–118. Hoyt's conclusions are evaluated for Boston by Lloyd Rodwin: Housing and Economic Progress (Cambridge, Mass., 1961), Chap. 6.

[56] Grigsby, op. cit. [see footnote 22 above] p. 79.

the dwelling unit. For most people the three aspects of location that have the most importance are the social environment (nearness of friends and institutional amenities); the physical environment (quiet, maintenance, and design); and access to the city as a whole or to places of work. After trying unsuccessfully to explain differences in stated access preference by measures of income, life cycle, and family activity, Lansing and Barth[57] concluded that access was relatively unimportant to most people and that location decisions reflect other kinds of preference, such as privacy, cost, and type of dwelling. Yet access becomes an important factor in the decision if only because of the constraints it imposes on the supply side. The supply and demand for access have generated consistently declining housing costs along the continuum of submarkets moving outward from the city center to the suburbs, as Alonso and Wingo have shown theoretically, and Brigham, Muth, and Seyfried have demonstrated empirically.[58] This pattern reflects the differential access to the rest of the city. Housing costs also vary sectorally with changing access to higher social-class amenities and sometimes with certain site characteristics such as water frontage or elevation. Although Yeates[59] has demonstrated a steady decline in the effect of access over time as the reduction of transport costs lessens the importance of centrality and man-made amenities outweigh natural advantages, strong radial variations in housing costs remain.

Considerable evidence indicates that the majority prefer to live farther from, rather than closer to, the CBD; they find the quiet, the spaciousness, and the general suburban image more attractive than downtown.[60] Most of the demand for residences in the city center is generated by a relatively few families. For instance, the white middle-to-high income group is older and has a family structure and employment characteristics that differ from those

---

[57] Lansing and Barth, *op. cit* [see footnote 32 above], p. 21.

[58] William Alonso: Location and Land Use (Cambridge, Mass., 1964); Lowdon Wingo, Jr.: Transportation and Urban Land (Resources for the Future, Washington, D. C., 1961); E. F. Brigham: A Model of Residential Land Values (Rand Corporation, Santa Monica, Calif., 1964); Richard F. Muth: The Variation of Population Density and Its Components in South Chicago, *Papers Regional Science Assn.*, Vol. 15, 1965, pp. 173–183; Warren R. Seyfried: The Centrality of Urban Land Values, *Land Economics*, Vol. 39, 1963, pp. 275–284. See also John D. Herbert and Benjamin H. Stevens: A Model for the Distribution of Residential Activity in Urban Areas, *Journ. of Regional Science*, Vol. 2, No. 2, 1960, pp. 21–36. Bernard J. Frieden discusses in detail the demand for access and the cost of access in "The Future of Old Neighborhoods" ([Cambridge, Mass., 1964], Chap. 3 and Appendix C).

[59] Maurice H. Yeates: Some Factors Affecting the Spatial Distribution of Chicago Land Values, 1910–1960, *Econ. Geography*, Vol. 41, 1965, pp. 57–70.

[60] Lansing and Mueller (*op. cit.* [see footnote 45 above], p. 26) and Lansing (*op. cit.* [see footnote 45 above], p. 35) found three times as many people preferring to live farther from the city center than closer to it. Similar results were found by Theodore Caplow: Home Ownership and Location Preferences in a Minneapolis Sample, *Amer. Sociol.* Rev., Vol. 13, 1948, pp. 725–730.

of their counterparts in the suburbs. The most significant difference is the almost total absence of school-age children.[61] Although access is important to this group, they are concerned with the availability of social amenities rather than with employment.[62]

The high cost of housing near the city center is not a response to over-whelming demand but a result of competition from other land uses and of a slowly increasing demand for residences, while the supply of housing is fixed or decreasing. Almost all the net addition to the city's housing occurs in the outer, suburban, parts of the metropolitan area. The dwelling units added by increasing the housing density in the central area are counterbalanced by the removal of other residential units to accommodate other land uses. The result of this imbalance is a continuous increase in housing costs in the city center, which is amplified by the perception of future urban development as seen by investors. The constant-cost isopleth moves steadily outward, re-quiring outward movement for families with fixed income and housing needs. Different types of housing vary in response to access costs, depending on supply and demand. Single-family homes, requiring a minimum lot size, cannot support population densities above a certain level.

The movement away from the city center because of personal preference and cost is encouraged by the proportion of housing opportunities found on the outskirts. A city growing at the rate of 10 percent a year, with an overall annual mobility rate of 20 percent, will generate one-third of all housing opportunities on the periphery. It can be shown, using simple assumptions and calculus, that a large majority of the population will have a higher propor-tion of their housing opportunities farther from the city center than their present residence. The result is a persistent net movement outward as the city grows (Table VI). For instance, about 10 percent of the 1956 population of the central city (Toronto) moved beyond the city limit, but many other moves within the city and the fringe had the same decentralizing effect. A similar outward bias shows up in Caplow's table[63] and on Green's maps,[64] and is an important assumption in Burgess' discussion of city structure.[65]

---

[61] Janet Abu-Lughod: A Survey of Center-City Residents, in Housing Choices and Housing Con-straints [see footnote 4 above], pp. 462–465; Michelson, op. cit. [see footnote 42 above], p. 193.

[62] Rapkin and Grigsby (Residential Renewal in the Urban Core [see footnote 41 above], pp. 40–52) found that 50 percent of residents in sample areas near the city centers gave access to social activities as the major factor in moving to the area. See also Lansing and Mueller, op. cit. [see footnote 45 above], p. 28.

[63] Caplow, Incidence and Direction of Residential Mobility in a Minneapolis Sample [see footnote 4 above], p. 416.

[64] Green, op. cit. [see footnote 4 above], Rept. No. 9, p. 53, and Rept. No. 11, p. 54.

[65] Ernest W. Burgess: The Growth of the City, in The City (Robert E. Park, Ernest W. Burgess, and Roderick D. McKenzie; Chicago, 1925), pp. 47–62.

Certain groups are much more likely to move outward—households with young children, renters wanting to own, and people with preferences for low-density areas. Alonso and Kain have tried to explain these location decisions from economic theory, given different preferences for space.[66] Caplow notes that there is also a countercurrent, with young people forming new

TABLE VI—GROSS MOVEMENT PATTERNS IN THE TORONTO METROPOLITAN AREA

ORIGIN	DESTINATION		
	Fringe	Central City	Total
Fringe	343,500	17,900	361,400
Central City	63,000	197,800	260,800
TOTAL	406,500	215,700	622,200
Population (1961)	1,152,100	672,400	1,824,500
(1956)	834,400	667,700	1,502,100

households at the city center and older households ready to trade space for access.[67] There is no evidence of a greater propensity toward decentralization on the part of higher-income groups,[68] but this may have been true in the past. Rodwin[69] points out that the constraints of income, transportation, and cultural values used to prevent low-income people from moving to the suburbs.

Access plays an important role in the development of new suburban areas. Virtually every model of urban growth introduces the effect of access, generally to the CBD, but frequently to the areas of employment, and to shopping centers, schools, and highways as well. Several studies have developed empirical relationships. Hansen[70] used density and access to the city center, to other residential areas, and to jobs to predict 87 percent of the variation in a measure of development (new dwellings divided by possible sites). All his variables correlated strongly with the dependent variable and with one

[66] Alonso, op. cit. [see footnote 58 above], pp. 107–109; John F. Kain: The Journey-to-Work as a Determinant of Residential Location, Papers Regional Science Assn., Vol. 9, 1962, pp. 137–160.

[67] Caplow, Incidence and Direction of Residential Mobility in a Minneapolis Sample [see footnote 4 above], p. 416.

[68] This hypothesis has been examined by Sidney Goldstein and Kurt B. Mayer (The Impact of Migration on the Socio-Economic Structure of Cities and Suburbs, Sociology and Social Research, Vol. 50, 1965, pp. 5–23, and Population Decline and the Social and Demographic Structure of an American City, Amer. Sociol. Rev., Vol. 29, 1964, pp. 718–729) and by Karl E. Taeuber and Alma F. Taeuber: White Migration and Socio-Economic Differences between Cities and Suburbs, ibid., Vol. 29, 1964, pp. 718–729.

[69] Rodwin, op. cit. [see footnote 55 above], p. 103.

[70] Willard B. Hansen: An Approach to the Analysis of Metropolitan Residential Expansion, Journ. of Regional Science, Vol. 3, No. 1, 1961, pp. 37–55. T. R. Lakshmanan (An Approach to the Analysis of Intraurban Location Applied to the Baltimore Region, Econ. Geography, Vol. 40, 1964, pp. 348–370) obtained similar results.

another. In a series of multiple regressions Chapin and Weiss[71] evaluate the effect of a number of growth factors, and find that 60 percent of the urban development in a given area could be explained by eight factors: poor land, access to employment, assessed value, distance to major street, residential amenities, distance to school, sewers, and zoning, in that order. A study by Kaiser,[72] which develops the Chapin-Weiss model further, indicates that the contributions to development are, in order of importance, socioeconomic rank, contiguous residential subdivision, public utilities, zoning protection, and access to employment. The change in order, together with the propinquity effect noted earlier, suggests that urban growth may be related primarily to access to older residential areas which serve as sources of migrants and that access to the city center is meaningful only to the extent that it acts as a surrogate.

THE JOURNEY TO WORK

The relationship between job and residence is a particular form of access, which is defined for each employment location. All families are concerned to some extent with their location relative to the CBD, but only a few hundred may care about their relationship with a specific industrial area. Although few people move in order to be closer to their jobs, the place of employment may act as a constraint when it comes to selecting a dwelling. Several studies show a weak but consistent decline in the employment field with distance.[73] Lansing[74] notes that only 36 percent of movers explicitly defined a maximum time for the journey-to-work in searching for a new home, though 92 percent of those who did, kept within the limit.

A number of factors offset the apparent attraction of reduced travel time. Many drivers enjoy the journey to work;[75] many more don't mind it. When

---

[71] F. Stuart Chapin, Jr., and Shirley F. Weiss: Factors Influencing Land Development (Institute for Research in Social Science, Univ. of North Carolina, Chapel Hill, 1962), p. 17.

[72] Edward J. Kaiser: Locational Decision Factors in a Producer Model of Residential Development (paper presented to the Regional Science Association, Philadelphia, 1965).

[73] Edward J. Taaffe, Barry J. Garner, and Maurice H. Yeates: The Peripheral Journey to Work (Evanston, Ill., 1963), p. 34, explain 46 percent of variations in commuter location by a function of population and distance. See also Lapin, op. cit. [see footnote 39 above], pp. 123–140; Ira S. Lowry: Location Parameters in the Pittsburgh Model, Papers Regional Science Assn., Vol. 11, 1963, pp. 146–165; Beverly Duncan and Otis Dudley Duncan: The Measurement of Intra-City Locational and Residential Patterns, Journ. of Regional Science, Vol. 2, No. 2, 1960, pp. 37–54; John R. Wolforth: Residential Location and the Place of Work, B. C. Geogr. Ser. No. 4, Vancouver, 1965; and J. R. Meyer, J. F. Kain, and M. Wohl: The Urban Transportation Problem (Cambridge, Mass., 1965), Chap. 6, "The Interrelationship of Housing and Urban Transportation." This last demonstrates the interaction of job location and type of housing structure in determining location.

[74] Lansing, op. cit. [see footnote 45 above], p. 74.

[75] Of the drivers, 53 percent enjoyed the journey to work; 34 percent didn't care; and 13 percent disliked it (ibid., p. 99).

Goldstein and Mayer analyzed the interactions between commuting and migration in Providence, Rhode Island (Fig. 5), they found that more than 25 percent of those who worked in the central city moved out of the city. They

PLACE OF WORK AND MIGRATION

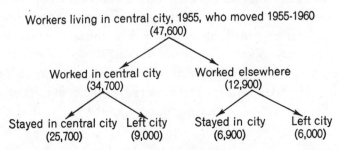

Workers living in central city, 1955, who moved 1955-1960
(47,600)

Worked in central city
(34,700)

Worked elsewhere
(12,900)

Stayed in central city   Left city
(25,700)   (9,000)

Stayed in city   Left city
(6,900)   (6,000)

FIG. 5—Place of work and migration. *Source:* Goldstein and Mayer: Residential Mobility, Migration and Commuting in Rhode Island [see text footnote 4 for reference], p. 58.

outnumbered (9000 to 6000) those who worked elsewhere and moved, presumably to reduce the journey to work. However, the probability of outward movement is much higher for persons working outside the central city. When these and similar data are examined for all towns in Rhode Island, the pattern of employment location is found to be closer to the pattern of mover origins than of destinations. Apparently the majority prefer to live farther from, rather than closer to, downtown. However, many members of the labor force do not make the location decision, but follow the head of the household; others, such as retail clerks or handymen, can find local employment wherever they live. For the population as a whole, the journey to work tends to increase with each move, reflecting the residential decentralization process.[76] The only workers who consistently relocate closer to their jobs are those employed in the suburbs. Thus continuing decentralization of employment may lead to the increased importance of job location in predicting residence location. Job changes and residence changes have approximately the same frequency of occurrence.[77]

Information on the effects of the journey-to-work constraint on different income groups is inconsistent. Lansing finds few differences; Lapin indicates a longer work trip for middle-income clerical, sales, and blue-collar workers;

[76] Goldstein and Mayer, Residential Mobility, Migration and Commuting in Rhode Island [see footnote 4 above], p. 24; Lapin, *op. cit.* [see footnote 42 above], p. 153; Beverly Duncan: Intra-Urban Population Movement, *in* Paul K. Hatt and Albert J. Reiss: Cities and Sociology (rev. edit.; New York, 1957), p. 307.

[77] Gladys L. Palmer: Labor Mobility in Six Cities (Social Science Research Council; New York, 1954).

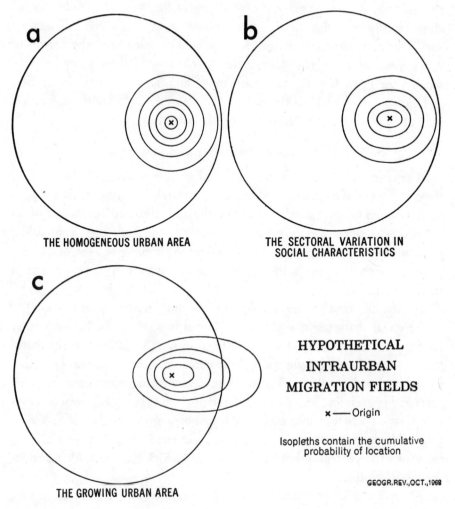

THE HOMOGENEOUS URBAN AREA

THE SECTORAL VARIATION IN
SOCIAL CHARACTERISTICS

**HYPOTHETICAL
INTRAURBAN
MIGRATION FIELDS**

x—Origin

Isopleths contain the cumulative
probability of location

GEOGR. REV., OCT., 1968

THE GROWING URBAN AREA

Fig. 6

and Lowry and Duncan show higher-income persons to be farther away from job locations.[78]

To summarize, then, the destination of an intracity move is determined by the interaction of a series of constraints. Some are imposed by the needs and preferences of the household, and others by the distribution of different kinds of housing. Despite the complexity of the decision process, it is possible to make some generalizations about the shapes of the migration field around a point of origin in a hypothetical city (Fig. 6). The most powerful regularity is

[78] Lansing, *op. cit.* [see footnote 45 above], p. 90; Lapin, *op. cit.* [see footnote 39 above], p. 100; Lowry, *op. cit.* [see footnote 73 above], p. 150. See also Beverly Duncan: Factors in Work-Residence Separation: Wage and Salary Workers, Chicago, 1951, *Amer. Sociol. Rev.*, Vol. 21, 1956, pp. 48–56.

the tendency to relocate near the origin, producing a migration field that declines equally in all directions. Superimposed on this is the effect of sectoral variations in income and ethnic characteristics coupled with the barrier of downtown, which together distort the migration field along a sectoral axis. Finally, the growth of the city, increase of housing costs in the inner city, and expansion of housing alternatives on the outskirts skew the migration field away from the city center toward the suburbs.

FUTURE RESEARCH: PROBLEMS AND IMPLICATIONS

The spatial differentiation of residential attributes is largely the result of the cumulation of intraurban moves. Unfortunately, the type of data available has caused urban research to focus on the static distributions instead of on the processes that generate urban patterns. Yet so many significant urban phenomena—for example, social segregation, the housing market, and urban growth—operate through the mechanism of intraurban mobility that it merits systematic study.

Perhaps the most remarkable aspect of intraurban mobility is the stability of the social characteristics of neighborhoods in spite of the high mobility rates throughout the city. The tendency of movers to relocate nearby maintains the spatial equilibrium, but the occasional dramatic social change within a neighborhood is a reminder of the complexity of the adjustments between form and process that lead to social differentiation. The equilibrium between in-migration and out-migration encompasses a great variety of factors—physical characteristics of the city, economic conditions, and, particularly, the values and perceptions of the population—which may contradict or reinforce one another.

Regular, consistent measures of area-to-area flows are critically needed for a better understanding of intraurban location. Current census data that give mobility rates for in-movers identify only a limited number of origins; these are useful, but not sufficient. The development of models that will explain and predict patterns of flow, and hence spatial change, within the city will require a full matrix, identifying flows from every subdivision of the city to every other subdivision. The problems of filing and storing such information become enormous, since n areas generate n^2 possible flows, and one metropolitan area might comprise twenty to thirty communities (10^3 flow dyads) or several hundred census tracts (10^5 flow dyads). Recent technological advances make possible the use of such data.[79] The problem of gathering an adequate

---

[79] The census has published data on intermetropolitan flows between SMSA's of more than 250,000 population (101^2 flow cells) ("Mobility for Metropolitan Areas," U. S. Census of Population, 1960:

sample from interviews or city directories overwhelms the private researcher, particularly when it is desirable to obtain socioeconomic information at the same time.[80] The most promising avenue is the compilation of change-of-address data gathered for other purposes but capable of modification to provide the necessary variables. Public-utilities data, transportation studies, and various kinds of government files have also been used.

The other necessary set of variables is housing measures, based on many small areas and classified by the critical aspects of location, cost, tenure, number of rooms, and quality. These measures of opportunity, when combined with existing data on the social characteristics of the population, can be used to predict the volume of in-movers and out-movers.

Although the accumulation of pertinent data should lead to better models of intraurban migration in the short run, the prospects over a longer period are more uncertain. The housing needs of the population under thirty-five dominate the mobility pattern, but a large hazy area of perception, preference, and institutional effects is also concerned. The attitudes toward a given neighborhood can shift more rapidly than the physical characteristics of the area, and the actions of planning boards, real-estate associations, and mortgage brokers are capricious.

It is increasingly apparent that virtually all the elements that enter into location decisions reflect individual perception and evaluation of needs and opportunities, which are shaped in turn by the values and habits of various subcultures. Households with similar social characteristics but different life styles prefer widely different housing and neighborhood conditions. Even such a basic element as size of house is perceived differently; some households prefer large units and others, even the more affluent, prefer a smaller number of rooms.[81] Location preferences are more obviously tied to the background or to the role aspirations of the household. The problem of planners, who try to design urban environments on the basis of such a tenuous structure of likes and dislikes, is brought out forcefully in "Environment for Man,"[82] a

---

Subject Repts., *Final Rept.* PC (2), Part 2C, 1963, Table 2); and Berry has analyzed a 43,000 × 4300 matrix of commuter movements from census data (Brian J. L. Berry: Metropolitan Area Definition: A Re-Evaluation of Concept and Statistical Practice, U. S. Bureau of the Census, Working Paper 28, 1968, p. 11. Long before electronic data processing Green (*op. cit.* [see footnote 4 above]) annually produced flow matrices among 321 census tracts (approximately 100,000 cells), using public-utilities data.

[80] See Sidney Goldstein: City Directories as Sources of Migration Data, *Amer. Journ. of Sociology,* Vol. 60, 1954–1955, pp. 169–176.

[81] Abu-Lughod and Foley, *op. cit.* [see footnote 4 above], Chap. 7, "Consumer Preferences: The Dwelling."

[82] William R. Ewald, Jr., edit.: Environment for Man (Bloomington, Ind., and London, 1967). This is the report of a symposium sponsored by the American Institute of Planners.

collection of papers that demonstrates clearly the uncertainties and conflicting interpretations of human needs as seen by professional planners. In the absence of rigid functional requirements for urban residential areas, the alternatives seem to be either the esthetics of the professional planner or the preference of the man in the street as interpreted in the market place. The returns to planners in understanding and modifying preferences are enormous. A shift in middle-class norms regarding the value of access to downtown could be more significant than all the urban renewal to date; changing attitudes toward land tenure could modify the suburban landscape; and a desire for a greater variety of social contacts could alter the social-spatial distribution of the entire city.

III

Siting of Industry
and Commercial Activity

6

William Applebaum

SHOPPING CENTER STRATEGY

A critical analysis of the Del Monte Center experience was made in mid-1969 by seven experienced, successful shopping center developers [1] who met for two days at Carmel, California, under the auspices of the International Council of Shopping Centers.

The group interviewed the developer, Jerome C. Draper, Jr., at the Del Monte Center, toured the project, visited competitive centers and retail business districts in the trade area as well as alternative shopping center sites, and interviewed E. P. Anderson, president of six Draper companies in which title to the

[1] Robert L. Bermant, National Shopping Centers, Inc., Rye, New York; Ralph Biernbaum, Stamford, Connecticut; Ernest W. Hahn, Ernst W. Hahn, Inc., Hawthorne, California; Morris A. Kravitz, The M. A. Kravitz Company, Inc., Philadelphia, Pennsylvania; Jerome S. McDermott, The Rouse Company, Baltimore, Maryland; Harry Newman, Jr., Newman Properties, Long Beach, California; and Neil R. Wood, Fairview Corporation, Limited, Toronto, Canada.

In preparation for the meeting, the panelists studied the manuscript of the first six chapters. During the course of the meeting, they made several sugges-

center was vested at the time, and John Egan, regional vice president of R. H. Macy & Co., the key retailer in the Del Monte Center.

The objective of the group was to evaluate this case in terms of the lessons that might be learned from it by practitioners in the shopping center industry. Their approach was to construct a series of "decision points" at which significant alternative actions had been possible, and to explore the consequences of what was in fact done compared with what might have been done at each of the critical junctures.

To set the stage for the panel's critical analysis of the Del Monte Center case, Harry Newman, Jr., panel moderator, explained:

"What we're trying to do is to take a critical look at the case and determine, at various moments of decision, what we might have done had we been in the position of the developer.

"The object of the case is to take a shopping center from its inception through all the stages to completion. The object of the panel discussion, based on the case, is to illustrate how experienced developers engage in clinical analysis as an aid in making future decisions concerning shopping center development."

"We are not here to find fault with anyone," Mr. Newman said, "nor to prove that we might have developed a more profitable center.

"We are here to find the lessons that can be learned and the

---

tions for amplifying the manuscript in the light of new information that developed from their interviews with several of the principals in the development and operation of the Del Monte Center.

Critical comment by the panel was extracted by ICSC from the stenographic record of the panel's discussion. In general, the comment quoted represents the consensus of the panel. In some cases, comment by more than one individual is quoted as if it were said by a single person. This was done particularly where one panel member finished a thought expressed by another panel member. Although the panelists did not disagree on most essential questions, nuances of opinion were expressed, and they are reflected in the quotations presented in the text. The entire chapter was reviewed by all panlists who agreed that it fairly presents their joint analysis of the Del Monte Center experience.

pitfalls that can be avoided in developing any shopping center."

Although the circumstances of the Del Monte Center are unique, the method of analysis of the case in this chapter may be applied to any set of circumstances in the shopping center field. In the course of analyzing the Del Monte Center experience, the seven practitioners demonstrated how they themselves arrive at business decisions concerning shopping center development and revealed, to a remarkable degree, how complex a shopping center venture can be.

Decision Point No. 1

Should a shopping center (of any size) have been planned for the Monterey property owned by Del Monte Properties Company?

Background: Del Monte Properties owned a large amount of land in the Monterey area, of which the site of what eventually became the Del Monte Center formed a part. Del Monte Properties appears to have concluded that a shopping center should be built on that site, without having first performed necessary basic research and without having considered alternative plots in the general trade area.

Analysis by the Panel:

(a) "Del Monte Properties had a piece of property that they owned and wanted to develop it in some manner. . . . This is not a shopping center developer who found a need for a community center in a given area and went out to find a proper piece of land."

(b) "Had they been shopping center developers, objectively they might even have moved to another location . . . but they were not shopping center developers. They owned thousands of acres and were trying to find good use for the ground closest to the City of Monterey."

(c) "The issue at that point was not whether a regional or a community center should be built but whether a shopping center should be built on that site at all."

(d) "A report in 1957 (Appendix B) for Del Monte Properties assumed a community center might be built on the site. A report prepared in 1961 (Appendix C) for the Monterey Peninsula Area Planning Commission was intended to guide planners of a downtown renewal project and, to the extent that it measured projected requirements for a shopping center outside of the downtown area, it assumed a regional center might be built. Neither report was adequate for the purpose of planning a center, community or regional, for the site."

(e) "Del Monte Properties, believing there was a need for a community center, but not having a really full market analysis, picked out this piece of property; it is the closest-in piece of property which they owned in the City of Monterey. They felt the site would have adequate access and that from this site they could serve the area with a community center. They hired architects and started drafting a plan for the development of a community center. . . . This is not the way an experienced developer would start to develop any type of center, community or regional. . . . He wouldn't start with the architects and the planning commission . . . being inexperienced developers Del Monte Properties did it that way."

Conclusions:

The decision of Del Monte Properties to arrange to build a shopping center on the site in question was unduly influenced by the fact that it owned the land.

An experienced developer would have approached the proposition differently, *viz:* (i) by determining whether the trade area could support a shopping center; (ii) by determining the size and character of a shopping center required to serve the trade area most effectively; (iii) by evaluating all available plots of ground suitable for such a development; and (iv) by selecting the land that most nearly conformed to the requirements for the development of a center of the size and character indicated by the research and that most nearly fulfilled the criteria of economic feasibility. The research performed for Del Monte Properties and for the Monterey Peninsula Planning Commission did not provide sufficient guidelines for determining how the site should best be used.

Del Monte Properties in effect made an *a priori* decision to develop the site as a shopping center.

Decision Point No. 2

Should Jerome C. Draper, Jr., have accepted Del Monte Properties' proposal that he develop the site as a shopping center?

Background: Realizing that it was not equipped by experience to develop a shopping center, Del Monte Properties negotiated with Draper, who had built a number of community centers, to assume the role of developer of the Monterey site.

Analysis by the Panel:

(a) "We're dealing with the particular land Del Monte Properties wanted to use. The experienced developer should have asked, 'Is the site close enough to the population and is it well located for a community center to be successful?' Instead, they asked, 'Can we put a community center on our land?' and they apparently answered the question in the affirmative. That's the situation Draper walked into."

(b) "If he accepted the site, Draper would be saddled with the John Carl Warnecke and Associates architectural plan, which Warnecke had introduced to the Monterey City Council

and toward which the City Council was favorably disposed; and he would be saddled with the Monterey Planning Commission and 'the hearts and flowers' group which insisted on giving priority to oak trees and the esthetics of the project. He would also be saddled with the preconceived ideas of Del Monte Properties and the Monterey Planning Commission about the size of the center. These factors all militated against the developer's success in undertaking a shopping center project on that site."

(c) "We don't know Draper's original dealings with Del Monte Properties. Draper was trying to develop a team and a reputation as a big center developer and syndicator. That might have influenced his decision to take the site. . . . He was involved in many other projects at that time and several years later encountered severe financial difficulties."

(d) "If I had been the developer I would have looked over the territory completely to determine whether there were better locations for what was proposed to be built. I would have compared the site with others in the area which might be suitable for a shopping center. Apparently this was not done at the time Draper accepted Del Monte Properties' proposal that he develop the center."

(e) "At this decision point, the developer could have stopped. Abandoning the project prior to the signing of the ground lease with Del Monte Properties would not have been costly. Abandonment subsequently would have cost the developer $57,458 paid on execution of the ground lease, prior to approval of plans by the Monterey Planning Commission."

Conclusions:

Draper accepted the Del Monte Properties site somewhat uncritically. More research should have been performed before the proposal was acted upon. Research was required on both the location and the optimum size of the center. A preliminary *pro forma* economic analysis relating to the land cost and the building design being contemplated was also necessary before accepting the proposal.

Decision Point No. 3

A decision to build a shopping center on the Monterey site having been taken, what type and size of shopping center would have been most appropriate?

Background: Although a community center of approximately 150,000 square feet had been planned, the advent of Draper and the interest shown by department stores in the site in 1962 resulted in a change in concept from that of a community center to a regional center of about 400,000 square feet. The basic decision to increase the size of the center and to change its essential character was taken prior to the undertaking of market research by Draper.

Analysis by the Panel:

(a) "A community center was needed in Monterey. There was an old downtown section with very little parking. A community center was needed and would have survived, provided that the site in question was the right location for it. There was nothing in the way of that kind of development, and population was there to support a community center."

(b) "In 1958, Monterey had what it has now, only it was probably in a worse state of repair. The downtown had not been rejuvenated at all. Monterey had no outlying shopping. It did not have a major drug or grocery store chain. It did not have any of the ancillary-type stores usually connected with community centers. Greater Monterey had a population of perhaps 50,000 people. Based on these factors a community center with

100,000 square feet, if not 150,000 square feet, could thrive at the site."

(c) "At that point Draper had a community center plan. Del Monte Properties expected him to develop a community center. The ground lease offered by Del Monte Properties had some severe drawbacks to the development of a community center. Draper did not explore other possible locations for a community center."

(d) "I haven't seen one survey that said there should be a 400,000 square foot center. . . . I think the area would have supported a community-type center plus Macy's, but no more."

(e) "I cannot build a 400,000 square foot center unless I have at least one major space user in addition to the anchor department store. In the Del Monte Center case, a second major tenant taking 60,000 or 70,000 square feet, in addition to Macy's 150,000 square feet, would have left about 180,000 square feet to be rented to others in order to achieve a 400,000 square foot center.[2] As it was, however, the developer agreed to 400,000 square feet and, in effect, had to fit the size of the center to the Macy's deal without knowing how he would come out. If you overbuild, you immediately bring down your average square foot rental because you must 'reach' for tenants."

(f) The panel considered some possibilities that might have been explored:

(i) "A community center of 100,000 or 150,000 square feet.

---

[2] The Macy's ground lease transaction with The Draper Companies called for a simultaneous building program under which the Macy's store and at least 200,000 square feet of additional floor area for other stores would be constructed. No more than 50,000 square feet additional could be built subsequently during the first five years of the center's existence. Macy's cotenancy provision required the landlord to obtain at least 12 leases by a certain date, with seven of such leases to be in each of seven specific categories, as spelled out in an exhibit attached to the lease. Each of the 12 leases was to be for a term of at least 15 years. There was no requirement as to the total floor area that had to be under lease in order for Macy's to be required to go forward. When the landlord advised Macy's that he had obtained leases in only six of the seven categories, Macy's waived the seventh category.

(ii) "A community center plus a Macy's store—an augmented free-standing location for Macy's.

(iii) "A two-department-store regional center with enough pulling power to bring customers in from a wide-spread market area embracing six or seven separated communities. The developer did not explore this possibility adequately. He had what he thought was a very severe and immovable zoning restriction, as well as a Macy's limitation of 100,000 square feet on the size of a second department store. He adjusted to these restrictions." [3]

(g) "Confronted subsequently with market studies at variance with one another, the developer should have questioned whether he could build a successful center of 400,000 square feet."

(h) "Instead of agreeing in December, 1964 to provide 200,000 square feet of space in addition to the Macy's store, the developer could have said to Macy's representatives: 'We don't know whether a 400,000 square foot center can be leased and financed in a satisfactory manner. We want adequate time to go into a leasing program and to determine how many square feet can properly be leased to the right tenants at this location.' Since that arrangement would have worked to the benefit of Macy's as well as Del Monte Properties, it seems to have been a logical one. But Draper didn't do that. He signed an agreement with Macy's and then started to grade the property. If Draper had taken the other approach and subsequently found that 200,000 square feet could not be leased at the rental structure necessary to support the costs at that time, he could have pursued other possibilities."

(i) "The critical point was that the developer did not know what the site could support. His research and analysis were not sufficient to give him the answer to this question."

[3] The limitation of 100,000 square feet on the size of a second department store was not onerous at the time as the store under consideration would not require more than 100,000 square feet. A possible second department store such as Penney was discussed and Macy's did not object. However, the Monterey Planning Commission and the limited buildable land created obstacles.

(j) "Once Macy's conditions were accepted, a large center became inevitable if it were to be built with Macy's in it. Macy's construction requirements called for 200,000 square feet of space in addition to Macy's, including a major women's wear store such as Joseph Magnin. At the end, Macy's waived that requirement, after the shell of such a store was built and it was found that it could not, for various reasons, be rented to that type of tenant. The main point, however, was that acceptance of Macy's requirements made it necessary for the developer to build too large a center in relation to the number and types of tenants desirable and available at rentals sufficient for profitable operation of the center."

(k) "Knowing that Macy's pressure for 'incentive tenants' was on him, the developer had good reason to drop the deal if he chose to do so."

(1) "Experience has shown that in that kind of limited market area it would be most difficult to lease to the right tenants 200,000 square feet in addition to the Macy's store. That's more satellite store space than there is in many mall centers with two or three department stores."

(m) "The developer was seemingly impressed by the Macy's name. He felt this gave him the opportunity to create something outstanding that would give him prestige."

(n) "Without a second department store the developer built too much. Part of the 'too much' was a convenience center handicapped by its position in a corner; it could not carry the arithmetic of the high development and building costs."

(o) "The interchange of traffic was only 19 per cent between the convenience center (within the large center) and Macy's, as the later study indicated. That shows that the convenience center was not integrated into the regional center. A more compact plan was needed."

(p) "This case study brings out clearly that when a regional shopping center is being built one should beware of pitfalls inherent in building a convenience center into it. High quality construction and high quality stores can bear the construction cost for a regional center. The construction of the supermarket and drug store and service shops cost $4 or $5 a square foot more than they should, by reason of the very nature of the design of the center, and there is no commensurate increase in rental income from the convenience stores."

Conclusions:

Having decided to build a shopping center on the Monterey site, the developer committed himself to a ground lease with Macy's which required him to produce 200,000 square feet of space to be rented to additional tenants. He did this at a time when he had insufficient evidence that the trade area could support that large a center and that he could properly rent that much space in order to produce sufficient rentals.

After considering the nature of the trade area, the nature of the site, the traffic patterns and the competitive retail facilities in and beyond the primary trade area, the panel concluded that the Del Monte site in Monterey would have supported a convenience shopping center of about 60,000 square feet in addition to a 150,000 square foot Macy's-type department store. (Macy's states, however, that neither Macy's nor any other department store chain would consider being a tenant in such a center unless there were very unusual circumstances, which did not obtain.) In a shopping center of that kind, the panel felt, the department store's sales volume would be about the same level as it is now—a level that a Macy's representative has said is satisfactory—and a group of carefully selected convenience goods store in limited space would have enjoyed equally satisfactory sales.

The high quality of the existing stores in Carmel, and their unusually great appeal to and acceptance by consumers, should have cautioned the developer not to install competitive facilities.

The panel questioned whether the convenience portion of the center had been correctly planned with respect to both location within the body of the center and type of construction. Construction cost was too high to support the marginal rents available from the convenience stores and the location of the convenience stores does not permit them to achieve maximum interchange of traffic with Macy's.

Had the developer been able to limit the center to Macy's plus a small, physically integrated, low-construction-cost convenience center, he would probably have obtained rentals high enough to pay all his obligations and yield a profit and the center itself would have been a readily salable property.

The panel also gave serious consideration to what might have happened had the developer succeeded in renting space to a second department store or junior department store. The Macy's lease permitted him to rent as much as 100,000 square feet to a second department store. Had he done so, the leasing problem for the center as a whole would have been simplified and a center would have been created which would have drawn shoppers from a wider trade area than it now does.[4]

The panel concluded that the type and size of center built on the Monterey site did not offer the best available solution to the problem posed at Decision Point No. 3.

Decision Point No. 4

Was the research adequate to permit correct decisions to be made concerning the use of the Del Monte site for a shopping center? [5]

Background: Several research studies, commissioned for different purposes, produced substantially different conclusions concern-

---

[4] Generally developers feel that two good department stores draw trade to a shopping center from a wider area than does one department store, even if the one store is as large as the two combined.

[5] The several Appendixes which form a part of the *Del Monte Shopping Center* case are precise, accurate statements of all the significant information in the market research studies that were made, and which I have assumed were taken fully into consideration in the decision-making processes of Del Monte Properties Company, The Draper Companies, the City Council of Monterey, and presumably also by R. H. Macy and some of the other tenants. I have not investigated whether the lending institutions have availed themselves of any of these research studies.

ing the probable retail sales that could be generated by a department store on the site as a part of a shopping center. They also produced substantially different conclusions concerning the total sales that a shopping center on the site could produce. The studies were not well documented as to methodology and sources of information. In two of the studies, the trade area assumed to be available to stores on the Del Monte site covered a territory much wider than later proved to be the case. The research studies did not consider the type and character of the stores contemplated for the site. None of the studies delineated the type of merchandising needed to achieve the projected sales levels.

Analysis by the Panel:

(a) "With all market research studies for shopping centers, the point is to catalog purchasing power in relation to the type of merchandise the people will buy. In the case of the Del Monte Center, to sell the quantity of merchandise that the market surveys projected could be sold it would have been necessary to build a downgraded type of center—one that would sell low-priced goods with mass appeal to lower-income consumers. But the actual center developed (and the basic concept of the center all along) was a medium-to-high-line center."

(b) "It is axiomatic that a center built to appeal to higher-

---

Pages 118 to 126 in this book present my subsequent evaluation of the market research studies, and my interpolations of the projections and sales estimates which they contain. I have scaled these estimates to the actual size of the shopping center and department store that were built. As best as I could determine, the combined sales of the stores in the Del Monte Center fall within a reasonable margin of error, on the basis of my interpolations, compared with the projections in the research reports.

However, the several market research studies are at variance in many respects, and none of the studies specifically recommended a regional shopping center of 400,000 square feet store space with one department store of 150,000 square feet. The feelings of the members of the International Council of Shopping Centers panel, whose views constitute Chapter 7, that the size of the Del Monte Center is more in compliance with the R. H. Macy lease than with precise guidlines provided by market research findings, are valid, in my opinion.—W.A.

income consumers, tenanted by stores selling prestige merchandise, costs more to construct than a center tenanted by low-end stores appealing to low-income shoppers. Thus, one reason for the high cost of building the center was the planned nature of the center's appeal and its type of tenancies."

(c) "The market surveys relate to the dollar volume of merchandise that could be sold but say nothing about types of merchandise. The overall dollar sales projected by the market surveys were not based on an assessment of the quality of merchandise required for the center. This suggests an assumption that whatever kind of stores, selling whatever kind of merchandise, put into the center would develop the kind of volume projected."

(d) "One thing missing in several of the surveys (except Reports C and E) is the residual purchasing power: *i.e.,* money which could be spent in the area but which is not being spent there. This kind of analysis takes into consideration the GLA available, in the projected trade area, based on the type of tenancy and merchandise. The figure on residual purchasing power in the area, if documented and favorable, would give me confidence.

"Carmel probably has five times as much space as Del Monte Center in high-lines merchandise. Information about Carmel was available at the time the center was being planned. If I had been the developer I would have asked: 'Is there a need for 400,000 square feet of additional space, much of which would compete for trade with Carmel?' The research should show what free dollars are available in addition to what was being spent in Carmel."

(e) "It is one thing to say that $12,000,000 is available for a department store in the general area; it is quite another thing to say it is available at the Del Monte Properties site. . . . If I had been the developer I would have given more specific instructions to the research organization as to the kind of survey that would be most helpful to me. I would have been concerned especially about competition."

(f) "The market studies differed greatly. The developer went ahead with his plans for a regional center to include a large Macy's store. Macy's letter of intent undoubtedly reinforced this decision."

(g) "We learned that when Montgomery Ward inquired about the possibility of coming into the center, the developer had already decided that he preferred Macy's. Ward, in his opinion, devoted too high a percentage of space to storage. In addition, he was convinced that Macy's was the preferred store for the area. When Ward indicated it would seek another site in the area, the developer sent an associate out to look at other possible sites, but he had already made a commitment to Del Monte Properties and probably to Macy's."

(h) "Basically, none of the market surveys described in detail what stores existed at the time, especially in Carmel. This site presented an odd geographic problem which involved putting a center not in the middle of one city, but at a location which could serve seven or eight distinct pockets of population separated by miles. One survey said, without specifying the kind of department store, that there was $12,000,000 available in annual purchasing power for a department store in the center. The survey did not specify what proportion of the $12,000,000 would be residual and what proportion would be taken from the sales of competitive stores in the trade area. In any case, to arrive at $12,000,000, the survey assumed a trade area well beyond Salinas. Two studies went to, or almost to, King City, halfway to Paso Robles—and the way to King City is through Salinas. In Salinas, Sears operated a very high-volume store in one of the early regional shopping centers with parking behind the stores. Both studies projected that customers would pass Sears, as well as Penney's, in Salinas, to come to Monterey."

Conclusions:

The research was not adequate to permit correct decisions to be made concerning the use of the Del Monte site for a shopping center, the panel concluded. Furthermore, the research did not indicate how large a center the site could support, and the type of merchandise and the level of price lines that should be emphasized. Some of the research erred, the panel said, in that it assumed that the boundaries of the trade area were much farther from the site than should have been assumed. In fact, the effective trade area turned out to be much smaller than that delineated by two research reports.

The surveys had wide variations in estimated sales volume available at the site.

For all these reasons, the panel concluded, the developer should have attempted by additional means, including perhaps new studies based on a revised set of instructions, to determine what use, if any, should be made of the site as a shopping center.

Apparently studies made were to support *a priori* conclusions, although it is clear that the research organizations involved acted in good faith. In any case, the developer had signed a ground lease with Del Monte Properties well before he had conducted or commissioned market surveys.

Decision Point No. 5

Should the developer have signed a ground lease with Del Monte Properties to commence April 2, 1962, in which he agreed to certain spectific terms and conditions?

Background: Acting for The Draper Companies, Jerome C. Draper, Jr., president, signed a ground lease for the Monterey property with Richard Osborne, president, and Paul S. Winslow, secretary, acting for Del Monte Properties Company, to commence April 2, 1962 and to terminate 30 years following completion of the shopping center. Significant provisions of the ground lease include:

1. The lease would terminate automatically if the center were not completed by April 2, 1969. The center would be deemed completed when 70 per cent of its GLA was occupied and open for business.

2. Ground rental prior to completion of the center would be 12 per cent of any gross rentals. After occupancy date it would be $2,400 per acre per year, or $112,300, against 12 per cent of gross rentals received; gross rentals not to include common area maintenance payments, dues paid for merchants association, real property taxes paid and assessments or insurance paid. On execution of the ground lease, $57,468 would be paid to Del Monte Properties.

3. John Carl Warnecke and Associates were to prepare plans and specifications which, after approval by lessor, were to be submitted to the Monterey Planning Commission. Upon approval of the plans and specifications by the commission, lessee was to pay lessor $63,365.88 as reimbursement for architectural services.

4. Lessee was to invest at least $1,000,000 toward the cost of construction prior to using any borrowed funds. Lessor would subordinate ground to a mortgage not to exceed 75 per cent of construction cost plus 75 per cent of 62½ per cent of the value of the demised premises. It was agreed that the property had a present value of $1,880,000, making the land subject to subordination to the extent of $881,250.

5. The lessor had the right of first refusal to buy improvements from the lessee within 60 days of notification that actual sale was to be made. Lessee had six months to consummate sale if first refusal right were not exercised.

6. Lessor was to construct and pay for certain improvements off the site.

Following the signing of the ground lease, zoning was applied for in September, 1962 and was obtained in March, 1963. In September, 1963 a letter of intent was signed with Macy's and in December, 1964 a lease was signed with Macy's.

Analysis by the Panel:

(a) "The original agreement to make a ground lease was based on the concept of a community center rather than a regional center. Although the formal letter of intent from Macy's was obtained in September, 1963, and the Macy's lease was signed in December, 1964, it is clear that Macy's had exhibited interest at a considerably earlier date. In fact, Macy's and Del Monte Properties had held conversations about the property some years before Draper entered the picture, and Macy's, as well as other department stores, showed interest in 1962, prior to the signing of the ground lease by Draper and Del Monte Properties. Terms suggested for the ground lease kept changing, particularly with respect to total dollars, as the amount of land contemplated for a center increased."

(b) "Del Monte Properties wanted to protect itself from inflation; hence it insisted on a percentage of gross revenue with a minimum rental as a base. If everything looked good, and it must have looked good to Draper at the time, would we, as developers, have walked away from the deal simply because Del Monte Properties was going to get a bit of the action? Most likely no. The developer, it appears, entered the deal without having made market surveys and without having prepared detailed *pro forma* statements to determine the implications of the terms of the ground lease in relation to the total economics of the development."

(c) "The ground lease's provision giving Del Monte Properties the right of first refusal to buy the center, in the event that it was offered for sale, became a thorn in the side of the developer. Draper tried to sell the center and get out whole, but in every case there was tremendous resistance because Del Monte Properties held the right of first refusal. It's not a good provision for the lessee because it does inhibit the possibility of sale.

However, because Del Monte Properties had subordinated the land to the first mortgage it was therefore entitled to the right of first refusal. If it had not subordinated the land it would probably not have been entitled to first refusal."

(d) "With such a condition of the right of first refusal in a ground lease, it becomes somewhat difficult to sell the property, but not impossible. The right of first refusal on simple property with nothing on it is not much of a handicap to a sale. The buyer doesn't have to go through a great deal of effort before he decides whether to buy at the price. If it's a shopping center, however, a great deal of analysis is required before an offer can be made. A potential buyer may not be willing to put in the effort that's necessary if he knows there is a possibility that he won't get the property even if he makes an attractive offer. However, a potential buyer can protect himself to some extent by arranging for some compensation in the event that he does not become the successful buyer based on his having made an acceptable offer. In any case, the land owner's right of first refusal does act as a deterrent with respect to a sale of a shopping center."

(e) "The developer's liability under the ground lease started only when the center was complete—apart from his initial payment of $57,468 and the Warnecke fee of $63,365.88. He was not making payments under the lease until the center was occupied and open for business. So that his gamble was minimized by the fact that he might never have built the center."

(f) "Del Monte Properties agreed to make off-site improvements and in fact did so at a cost of about $10,000 per acre, or almost $500,000. That amount was necessarily reflected in the ground rent paid by Draper. In addition, Del Monte Properties made certain on-site improvements related to drainage. Because of Del Monte Properties' contribution, Draper's cost for the common area was relatively low despite the topographic and drainage problems."

Conclusion:

Although the terms and conditions of the ground lease appeared to the panel to be onerous to the developer, and although the developer signed the ground lease well in advance of having made a firm agreement with Macy's, or having performed necessary market survey work, or having set up careful estimates of probable income and expense, the panel also cited considerations in extenuation of the developer's having signed the ground lease when he did.

The developer's liability was limited. If he had been unable to lease enough space in the center or had been unable to obtain financing he could have withdrawn from the project and the lease would have been terminated. It is true that he would have been liable for total payments of approximately $120,000 on execution of the lease and in reimbursement of the architect. It is by no means clear, however, whether he would have been unable to recover all or part of that sum, and he may well have been able to do so had a third party taken over the project or had Del Monte Properties proceeded to develop the center itself. In any case, even after having signed the ground leases, Draper could have withdrawn.

Secondly, although no formal agreement with Macy's had been made when the ground lease was signed, enough interest had apparently been exhibited in the site by Macy's to give Draper confidence that a formal agreement could be made soon thereafter. The fact that a letter of intent was received from Macy's one year and one-half after the ground lease was signed does not necessarily mean that Draper could not have reasonably anticipated that Macy's would have given him the letter earlier.

Because of the developer's shopping center interest that ranged far beyond the Del Monte Center, Draper may have felt that Macy's strong interest in the site obviated the need for a formal survey which might have otherwise been needed to justify a developer's confidence in the site.

The panel agreed that the base ground rent of $112,300 a year was not necessarily excessive and that the developer had no way of determining whether it was excessive at the time that he signed the ground lease. Later, when Macy's agreed to pay a ground rent in excess of an average of $38,000 a year, the developer's net annual ground rent was reduced to $74,300 or approximately 30 cents per square foot of GLA for 250,000 square feet of shopping center space (exclusive of the Macy's store). That amount, in and of itself, was not deemed excessive by the panel, especially after giving weight to Del Monte Properties' contribution in the form of off-site and on-site improvements.

The requirement that the developer pay Del Monte Properties 12 per cent of gross rentals or $112,300 per year, whichever was greater, was not regarded as an impossible condition. The imposition of a percentage arrangement, presumably as a hedge against inflation, is more common today than it was in 1962 when the ground lease was signed. However, in this case both the minimum dollar rental and the percentage were agreed upon before the developer could have had a reasonable idea of his expectations in relation to both expenses and income.

Decision Point No. 6

Was the tri-party agreement among Del Monte, Dillingham and Draper the best available procedure to assure interim financing and construction of the shopping center?

Background: Draper was experiencing financial difficulties with his various properties. Del Monte Properties Company was pressuring Draper to demonstrate that the project was going forward, so Draper decided to begin rough grading and simultaneously to retain a contractor who would, in effect, assume responsibility for financing the building. Draper was able to induce the Dillingham Construction Corporation to agree to a tri-party agreement which called for Dillingham to arrange for construction financing and to build the center, and for Del Monte Properties to assume the obligation to pay Dillingham and to repay loans in the event that Draper was unable to do so.

Analysis by the Panel:

(a) "Many developers get trapped into ground breaking and ribbon-cutting ceremonies, with subsequent premature site grading, in the belief that this impresses people. However, it is almost axiomatic that one should not start work on the ground before there is assured ultimate and construction financing and the program is ready to go through."

(b) "At that point, Draper could again have walked away from the deal."

(c) "Assuming Draper's decision to go ahead at this point, he made a very sound deal with Dillingham, with one exception. The tri-party agreement did not specify with sufficient clarity what the maximum cost of each major component of the construction would be. But, all things considered, it bought the necessary time for Draper and it gave him the option to come back into the picture if he could raise money through syndication, as he visualized he could."

(d) "In addition, Del Monte Properties agreed to pay for the cost of building the entire center. At the end of the tri-party agreement they had to repay Dillingham for all costs and to take possession, if Draper could not do so. Del Monte Properties had no choice. They had to do it, although it took the form of lending Draper the money to pay Dillingham— $1,500,000 at 8 per cent. Otherwise, Draper would have borrowed the money from the Sixty Trust at 10 per cent."

Conclusion:

The decision to begin rough grading was premature, in the panel's opinion. However, considering the entire situation at the time—the heavy investment Draper investor companies had made, the pressure to begin construction of the center, and Draper's ability to make a deal ensuring repayment of Dillingham by Del Monte Properties—the idea of going ahead with grading and construction under the tri-party agreement was probably the best decision that could have been made. Draper bought one essential asset—time; time in which to raise money through syndication or borrowing, or time in which to sell the center, possibly at a profit. Del Monte Properties achieved its objective of having a center built on its site so that within some reasonable time the property would begin to throw off income. Dillingham achieved its objective of launching its Dilco operation at a highly profitable level.

Decision Point No. 7

Should Del Monte Properties, with no experience in shopping center management, have taken over the management of the center for a nine-month period, as it did?

Background: Del Monte Properties' second mortgage loan agreement for $1,500,000 contained a provision that Del Monte Properties could take over management of the center under certain conditions. It did so, from the end of May, 1968 to the end of February, 1969. No new leases were written by Del Monte Properties during that period.

Analysis by the Panel:

(a) "The center is now open. We have a situation in which Del Monte Properties ran the center for nine months with no center-oriented advertising."

(b) "Del Monte Properties leased 600 square feet of expansion space to the pet and fish store operator, but no additional space, and it is reasonable to ask whether it intended to do so until it attained full control of the center."

(c) "Is Del Monte Properties capable of properly managing a center? Probably not. If they should take over the center's management in the future, they should hire a manager to do the job properly."

Conclusion:

Del Monte Properties' decision to take over the center's management was apparently made with the idea that the arrangement would be temporary. Had Del Monte Properties used the nine-month period to make additional leases at terms advantageous to the center, the center's value would have been enhanced and the possibility of a sale increased.[6]

Had the center's attraction to potential buyers been increased, Draper might have sold the center and conceivably salvaged his stockholders' equity investment.

Additional leases resulting in actual occupancy by more ten-

---

[6] According to Jerome C. Draper, Jr., unleased space in the Del Monte Center from July 1, 1967, through April 1, 1969, was:

July 1, 1967: 29,581 square feet
October 1, 1967: 28,726 square feet
January 10, 1968: 28,601 square feet
January 10, 1969: 33,450 square feet
May 1, 1969: 33,450 square feet

According to Mr. Draper, the Andersons were in charge of leasing from June, 1967 to June, 1968, and Del Monte Properties Company was in charge of leasing from June, 1968 to June, 1969.

ants would have developed an increased cash flow and mortgage payments would have been somewhat easier to make.

Disregarding what Del Monte Properties did or did not do when it managed the center for nine months, from Del Monte Properties' viewpoint apparently nothing useful had happened under Draper's management, and the situation was not made worse under the new management.

The panel felt that no clear-cut case could be made, on the facts, for Del Monte Properties to have taken over the center's management or to have refrained from doing so.

Decision Point No. 8

Del Monte Properties having sold its second mortgage interest to Bernard Osher, what actions should be taken at that juncture? [7]

Background: With approximately 19 per cent of total GLA (other than Macy's) unrented, the center's first urgent need is to obtain occupancy of vacant spaces in accordance with some economic rental structure. To do this, qualified management is needed. Only after the rent has stabilized will it be possible to set a value on the center for purposes of selling it or holding it as an investment. One large space of 19,000 square feet, originally intended for a women's specialty store, is still in an unfinished condition. One plan calls for it to be subdivided into small shops arranged in bazaar fashion, of the type associated with the City of Carmel—handicrafts, fine specialty items,

---

[7] The panel met in mid-1969, several weeks after Bernard Osher purchased Del Monte Properties' second mortgage interest. At that time, Mr. Osher had started foreclosure proceedings which, under California law, required a total of four months to be completed. Mr. Osher had made a cash offer of $40,000 over the loan for a deed in lieu of foreclosure and that offer had been accepted by the board of directors of the six Draper corporations. Jerome C. Draper, J., solicited proxies to block the sale. Subsequent events are described in the Epilogue.

tourist-type merchandise. That plan has apparently been abandoned.

Analysis by the Panel:

(a) "What must be done is to lease out the rest of the center —and to promote; to concentrate on improving the tenant mix to the point of moving out tenants who aren't making it and putting in tenants on percentage leases, even to the extent of requiring no minimum rentals for very good merchants."

(b) "Del Monte Properties has such a large stake that it is worth-while for them to invest two or three years in trying to rectify the situation. Even after selling its second mortgage interest, Del Monte Properties of course still owns the land."

(c) "Our recommendation is that they improve tenant mix and sales volume. That means getting rid of some of the tenants who do poorly, who would be happy to leave. Change the complexion of the center. Try to get some downtown Carmel people to come in with no minimum rental. That's a constructive thing to do. Minimums don't mean a thing at this point. Get the common area paid for, and the taxes. Increase the traffic."

Conclusion:

The probability is that Del Monte Properties or Bernard Osher will control the center and will operate it. The equity base will probably be reduced to the extent that the original Draper investment will be lost.

Under those circumstances, the panel recommends that:

1. Professional management be retained to operate the center.

2. Vacant space be rented to tenants who are carefully selected for their ability to draw traffic.

3. If necessary, new tenants be given leases calling for percentage rentals without minimums.

4. Current tenants who are doing poorly be moved out of the center or into smaller spaces.

5. A consistent, large-scale promotional effort be launched to increase traffic and sales, including review of the hours during which the center is open for business.

The panel is mindful of the fact that its recommended program will take time to implement. It is also aware that the landlord's investment in finishing store space for new tenants may be somewhat speculative if minimum rental guarantees are not obtained.

The fact that Macy's expresses itself as satisfied with its present level of sales in the center and is optimistic about the future sets a positive tone for the entire enterprise. The panel believes that the landlord should enlist Macy's active assistance, in their mutual interest, in revising the tenant mix, obtaining new tenants and promoting the center as a whole.

7

Brian J. L. Berry

THE BLIGHT OF RETAIL NUCLEATIONS

BLIGHT

The Webster's definition of blight is "any disease . . .
resulting in withering, cessation of growth, and death of parts"
or "that which impairs or destroys." As such, blight constitutes
an abnormality--a malignant deviation from the healthy state of
an organism. The healthy state is one of equilibrium; blight
therefore involves disequilibrium.

If all other things remained equal, demands and supplies
would settle down in a state of balance, according to the principles of conservation of energy. Things never remain equal,
however. Short run changes in the environment (demands) require
readjustments in commercial systems (supplies). Increasing demands can be met by construction of new plant . Decreasing demands are not so readily counterbalanced by demolition to reduce
capacity, though. Operating units diminish, but the excess plant
remains, often unused and vacant. An equilibrium between demands
and actual operating units may exist, but inertia leads to a
coterminous disequilibrium between demands and total capacity.
Longer term changes within both system and environment engender
further changes. These include the inexorable process of aging
of buildings, which actually makes them less desirable places to
do business, and increasing obsolescence of plant in the face of
changing technology.

Types of Commercial Blight

Since there are many possible reasons for disequilibrium
to exist, it is obvious why no single definition has ever been
provided for the term "commercial blight." At least four types
of blight have been identified, each reflecting a different reason for a decline in the desirability of areas as places to do
business: economic, physical, functional, and frictional.[1]

Economic blight

Economic blight exists when changes on the demand side
lead to losses of markets. Among such changes are reductions in

[1]Brian J. L. Berry, Commercial Blight. A Review, Report
to the Community Renewal Program of the City of Chicago, February,
1962.

numbers of people supported, lowering of the socio-economic level of the area served, and reduction of demands because of the development of new sources of competition. Outward manifestations of economic blight may include: excessive vacancy rates, generally due to the failure of the more specialized stores; a change in character of use from higher-order specialization towards duplication of smaller establishments, or the inward movement of uses which previously occupied the ribbons; changes in the kinds of goods carried by the stores which remain, reflecting their readjustment to reduced demands and resignation to reduced volumes.

Physical blight

Physical blight occurs when the structure occupied by a business deteriorates. In part, deterioration may be a function of use and maintenance--many older buildings can be maintained in excellent condition by proper care--but this form of blight is usually a fairly simple function of age. The older the structure, the more likely it is to suffer from physical blight. Careful building-to-building surveys provide the best measures of physical blight[1] but quicker windshield surveys can pick out at least the most serious examples.[2]

Functional blight

Functional blight (or technological obsolescence) results from changes on either the demand or the supply side. On the supply side, changing technology has moved in the direction of increases in store size, resulting in many older buildings that are no longer adequate for efficient operations, as for example the widely-scattered streetcorner stores that used to house "ma and pa" groceries. Demand side changes towards increasing mobility of consumers have the same effects. Many retail location experts consider functional blight to be the major problem facing American cities. They argue that new forms of establishments and types of business and centers are evolving so rapidly that all present commercial plant will be obsolete within two decades if it is not obsolete already.

Frictional blight

Frictional blight (environmental blight) exists when a

---

[1]City Plan Commission, St. Louis, Missouri, Measuring Deterioration in Commercial and Industrial Areas. The Development of a Method (1957).

[2]See the discussion below of the Department of City Planning, City of Chicago's Commercial Blight Survey of 1959.

business has a deleterious effect upon surrounding areas or uses,
including transportation arteries, or conversely when these surrounding things have an adverse effect upon the operations of the
business. Examples include creation of traffic congestion because
of uncontrolled or poorly designed access and egress, reduction
of land values of adjacent residential properties, creation of
litter, attraction of undesirable persons, or creation of excessive
policing and fire hazards.

Composite forms

At different times each of the four proposed forms of
blight--economic, physical, functional, and frictional--has been
put forward either singly or in combination with one or more of
the others as constituting a serious urban problem calling for
remedial treatment through public action. Tables 76 and 77 attempt
to summarize the relevant literature. Table 76 recognizes several
grades of each form of blight, and possible forms of renewal treatment proposed by planners and others.[1] Table 77 lists combinations
of blight forms, classifying them according to the postulated categories of renewal treatment.

TABLE 76

POSSIBLE FORMS OF COMMERCIAL BLIGHT[a]

Physical   I   Major--renewal required
              II   Minor--conservation?
              III   None

Economic   A   Present--demands for business reduced
              B   None

Functional   1   Serious--physical realignment impossible, not
                      suitable for changed use
              2   Minor--realignment or changed use possible in
                      conservation program
              3   None

Frictional   a   Serious--no effective realignment, or controls
              b   Minor--possible to realign
              c   None

Combined: 3 physical x2 economic x3 functional x3 frictional gives
           54 possible combinations (for example, the desirable
           IIIB3c)

[a]As proposed in the literature, but debated in this study.

_____

[1]No attempt will be made to list the literature in which
these proposals are found, but one has only to read any general
plan document to find them in some form or other.

TABLE 77

RENEWAL TREATMENT FOR BLIGHT COMBINATIONS[a]

Reconstruction and replanning	IA, IB
Reconstruction or conservation	IIA, IIB1, IIB2a, IIb3a IIIA1, IIIA2a, IIIA3a IIIB1, IIIB2a, IIIB3a
Conservation	IIB2b, IIB2c, IIB3b, IIB3c IIIA2b, (IIIA3b)
No public action needed	IIIB3c

[a]As proposed in the literature, but subject to considerable debate.

A simple scanning of these two tables will reveal clearly enough the inadequacies of existing discussions. One could argue, for example, about the ways in which each form of blight has been graded, the types of renewal treatment proposed, and the assignment of combinations to particular treatment categories. But such discussions, in the absence of empirical experience concerning blight, would be specious. Hence, we now turn to an evaluation of the forms of blight and underlying causative processes in the City of Chicago. To accomplish this, it is first necessary to review some of the salient features of equilibrium and change that have been presented in the previous three chapters.

Equilibrium and Change in Chicago

Chicago's commercial structure evidences two equilibrium situations, one a four-level hierarchy of centers, well-stocked ribbons, and many specialized functional areas in the higher income zones of the city, and the other a two-level hierarchy with less specialized ribbons in lower income communities. The latter occupy the older inner city, where most of the retail facilities grew during the first phase of outlying commercial expansion in the early twentieth century. The former is found in the outer city and occupies more modern plant, not a little of which has been built since the end of the Second World War.

During the last decade the inner city has lost 10 per cent of its population, whereas the outer city has gained 9 per cent. We have already seen how a 1 per cent change in population engender a 1 per cent change in demands for retail establishments (Table 73) so that these population change figures for the last decade can be directly translated into changes in retail business.

There is an ongoing process of residential change such
that higher income groups are being replaced in the city's neighborhoods by those with lower incomes. If we let the median income
for the city be 100, the income level of the higher income communities contiguous to lower income neighborhoods is 110. During
the first decade of change this drops to 82 as higher income families leave and are replaced by families with lower income levels.
Stability of the lower income type is reached during the second
decade at a level of 62-65 as initial social changes are followed
by succession and consolidation of the lower income community.
These relative income data are detailed in Table 75. During a
period of some twenty years the income drop relative to the city
median (set to 100) amounts to 35 points, or 1.75 points per
annum. Each one point drop occasions a 1.25 per cent drop in demands for retail establishments (Table 73), so that the impact of
social change amounts to a 2.2 per cent decline in demands for
retail establishments per annum.

However, these declines are offset by secular increases in
real income of 3.2 per cent per annum, which are in their turn
counterbalanced in the opposite direction by technological changes
in retailing and increasing consumer mobility leading to declines
in numbers of retail establishments amounting to 5.8 per cent per
annum.

These different rates may be drawn together. Consider
first an average high income community. Over the past decade population increased by 1 per cent per annum, calling forth a 1 per
cent increase in retail stores (Table 73). The real income increase
was 3.2 per cent, implying an additional 2.71 per cent per annum
increase in demands for retail stores (Table 74). The 3.7 per
cent increase was, however, offset by the 5.8 per cent secular
change (Table 74), resulting in a net decline in establishments
of 2.0 per cent per annum in high income zones. Conversely, a
1 per cent population loss in lower income communities under similar real income and technological trends meant that the central
areas of the city experienced a net decline in establishments of
4.0 per cent per annum. Areas in transition from higher to lower
income status present a more complicated picture. The impact of
technology remains at -5.8 per cent, offset by the +2.71 per cent
shift induced by real income. Population and overcrowding increase,
but the relative income shift occasions a 2.2 per cent annual decline in establishments (see above). On balance, then areas in
transition experience a 5.0 per cent per annum decline in demands
for retail establishments during the period of change.[1]

---

[1]An approximate translation of these rates for establish-

Note that the actual 1950-1960 rates for the higher income zones of the city included: Far North -1.67 per cent; North -2.78 per cent. In lower income zones the rates included: West -4.18 per cent; Near South West -3.10 per cent. Rates in the most marked transitional area, the Central South zone amounted to -5.34 per cent. Thus the actual rate data accord well with predictions based upon rates of socio-economic, population, and technological change reconstructed in the previous chapter from a variety of equations. The reason for the +2.15 per cent rate in the Far South West is to be found in the large population and income increases in this last area of the city to become fully developed (population shifts were +3.9 per cent and income shifts +7.63 per cent, see Table 72).

Vacancies and Economic Blight

The change data indicate that real income shifts have been unable to offset the effects of technological change, so that all except the developing areas of the city in the Far South West have experienced declining demands for retail establishments in the last decade. These declines are compounded by relative income shifts in areas in transition from higher to lower level equilibrium, and by population losses in lower income communities located in the older inner city.

If an equilibrium between demands and supplies existed prior to invasion, then the effects of invasion and eventual replacement of the higher by a lower level equilibrium must be the creation of a large pool of unused stores (compare the equations in Table 49 with those in Table 50). Commercial vacancies, then, are the reflection of declining demands. Economic blight is caused by technological change in all areas of the city, and socio-economic turnover as higher income communities are invaded by lower income groups.

Vacancies in centers

Table 78 lists quantities and percentages of establishments, front footage, ground and upper floor area vacant in Chicago's outlying business centers.[1] As Figure 28 shows, the different percentage scales are collinear, and so we will use percentage of establishments vacant as our index of economic blight in the succeeding discussion. The vacancies are mapped in

---

ments into rates for space demanded will be found in the summary to this chapter.

[1] The upper floor figures refer only to separate establishments performed entirely from upper floor locations, and ignore upper floor operations of stores also operating from ground floors.

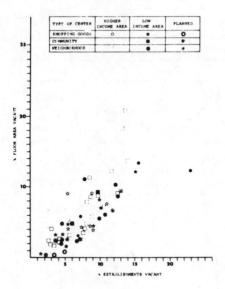

TYPE OF CENTER	HIGHER INCOME AREA	LOW INCOME AREA	PLANNED
SHOPPING GOODS	☆	★	○
COMMUNITY		■	◕
NEIGHBORHOOD		●	◔

Figure 28

Figure 29. If this figure is compared with Figure 27 it will be
seen that there is an extremely high correlation between high
vacancy rates in centers and the communities with high relative
income declines in the decade 1950-1960. This bears out the previous discussion. Areas with high relative income losses are
those which experienced social change during the decade--high
vacancy rates in centers are thus a function of the socio-economic
changes taking place in Chicago's neighborhoods. Declining demands for establishments are a direct result of declining relative income levels and the passage from one equilibrium pattern
to another.

     That this is no idle generalization is well illustrated
by a contrast. Table 79 presents the vacancy rates for Chicago's
major outlying centers in 1933, right after the wave of failures
due to the great depression. The low prevailing income levels
are reflected in the very high vacancy rates--far higher than obtain now. Table 80 presents similar data for Cincinnati for both
1933 and 1955. Note the downward shift in vacancy rates as relative incomes have risen, and the somewhat higher rates remaining
in the older centers vis-a-vis those which have developed since
1933.

TABLE 78

VACANCY RATES IN CHICAGO'S OUTLYING BUSINESS CENTERS

Center	Establishments		Front Feet		Floor Area		Upper Floor	
	No.	%	Amount	%	Amount	%	No.	%
A*1	33	13.0	875	10.9	72,045	9.0	15	32.6
A*2	8	4.3	195	3.2	14,275	2.6	9	11.2
A*3	11	5.3	330	4.7	52,500	9.1	14	15.2
A*4	15	8.5	300	5.8	17,560	4.4	22	9.0
A5	15	11.0	320	8.8	25,325	7.6	-	-
A6	13	7.3	245	4.7	18,625	4.2	6	33.3
A7	14	9.0	240	5.3	16,575	3.8	5	19.2
A8	5	5.3	170	6.7	10,275	4.2	8	18.6
A9	9	8.8	240	9.1	19,500	9.1	10	20.0
A10-	4	3.7	105	3.0	11,975	3.1	24	16.1
A11-	8	9.1	180	6.1	14,435	4.5	11	45.8
A12-	4	4.6	80	2.7	8,200	3.3	-	-
A13-	5	5.2	110	4.0	11,350	4.6	33	80.5
A14-	9	6.8	190	4.9	10,600	3.1	15	28.3
A15-	2	1.5	25	0.7	1,550	0.5	-	-
A16-	9	9.9	220	9.0	16,900	8.2	2	22.2
A17-	18	15.1	505	13.4	50,500	12.2	-	-
A18-	9	10.1	235	8.6	20,775	7.0	-	-
A19P	1	3.3	15	1.0	450	0.3	-	-
A20P	2	4.9	30	2.2	1,200	0.8	-	-
B1	1	2.4	40	2.6	4,800	2.6	-	-
B2	3	4.1	65	3.3	5,175	3.0	-	-
B3	7	11.3	130	9.2	8,350	8.4	-	-
B4	4	4.9	105	4.4	10,025	4.7	2	9.1
B5	2	3.0	40	2.5	2,200	1.8	-	-
B6	12	13.5	260	12.4	22,125	13.6	8	33.3
B7	7	12.5	205	11.7	11,725	9.0	-	-
B8	7	7.5	115	5.6	5,275	3.5	7	43.8
B9	5	8.6	120	7.4	9,100	8.6	-	-
B10	8	11.6	185	11.6	13,500	12.2	11	35.5
B11	8	10.4	170	7.4	13,725	7.1	-	-
B12	9	9.7	280	7.4	28,125	8.8	-	-
B13	4	5.5	80	4.1	4,750	3.1	-	-
B14	4	7.7	95	6.0	4,775	4.1	-	-
B15	12	8.8	290	7.3	20,775	5.8	-	-
B16	9	8.0	195	7.2	10,325	4.8	3	3.7
B17	14	13.6	465	18.4	37,725	20.8	-	-
B18	7	8.1	165	7.7	11,075	7.9	-	-
B19	4	4.1	85	3.3	4,375	2.6	8	40.0
B20	3	4.1	115	4.7	4,375	2.3	2	33.3
B21	2	3.1	35	1.9	2,525	1.7	-	-
B22	8	13.3	400	18.1	21,625	18.2	-	-
B23-	9	9.6	250	9.2	18,950	9.2	-	-
B24-	0	0.0	0	0.0	0	0.0	-	-
B25-	3	5.9	65	4.8	6,150	4.9	-	-
B26P	0	0.0	0	0.0	0	0.0	-	-
B27P	4	13.0	140	12.2	16,350	9.3	-	-
B28P	1	3.7	75	6.1	2,475	2.5	-	-
C1	1	2.5	50	4.7	5,750	6.4	16	59.2
C2	0	0.0	0	0.0	0	0.0	1	6.7
C3	2	5.1	55	5.4	4,950	6.7	-	-
C4	3	7.5	50	3.3	2,200	2.5	-	-
C5	3	5.3	95	6.3	5,275	5.3	-	-
C6	0	0.0	0	0.0	0	0.0	-	-
C7	0	0.0	0	0.0	0	0.0	-	-

TABLE 78--Continued

Center	Establishments		Front Feet		Floor Area		Upper Floor	
	No.	%	Amount	%	Amount	%	No.	%
C8-	3	4.3	50	2.7	2,825	2.5	-	-
C9-	6	10.7	110	8.4	6,925	5.9	-	-
C10-	1	2.2	10	0.7	250	0.2	-	-
C11-	4	7.8	120	10.3	9,700	11.0	-	-
C12-	2	7.1	45	5.5	2,800	5.7	4	20.0
C13-	2	4.7	35	3.2	3,750	4.7	2	14.3
C14-	6	12.2	170	10.3	15,175	10.2	-	-
C15-	3	5.2	55	2.8	2,500	1.5	12	38.8
C16-	-	-	-	-	-	-	-	-
C17-	2	4.4	40	4.0	2,200	2.0	-	-
C18-	10	15.6	200	11.9	13,000	13.2	-	-
C19-	5	12.5	120	9.0	9.375	8.9	-	-
C20-	8	22.9	125	12.4	6.000	12.1	-	-
C21-	4	9.8	105	8.8	5,050	5.5	-	-
C22P	1	7.1	15	3.2	1,200	2.6	-	-
C23P	1	5.3	20	3.1	1,200	2.5	-	-
C24P	1	6.7	20	2.9	1,400	2.4	-	-
C25P	2	11.8	50	7.2	4,800	6.7	-	-
C26P	0	0.0	0	0.0	0	0.0	-	-

TABLE 79

VACANCY RATES IN CHICAGO'S OUTLYING BUSINESS
CENTERS IN 1933[a]

Center	Per Cent of Property Vacant
67th and Stony	5.2
Lawrence and Kedzie	8.7
47th and South Park	9.0
63rd and Halsted	10.2
47th and Ashland	10.9
North and Crawford	11.6
111th and Michigan	13.9
92nd and Commercial	14.6
Roosevelt and Halsted	15.3
Lincoln, Belmont, Ashland	16.6
Average of Major Centers	17.0
Broadway and Wilson	18.4
63rd and Cottage Grove	18.5
Madison and Kedzie	20.0
Madison and Crawford	20.4
Milwaukee and Logan Square	20.7
79th and Halsted	20.9
North, California to Western	22.2
Milwaukee, Irving Park and Cicero	24.4
Roosevelt and Kedzie	25.3
Milwaukee and Paulina	34.0

[a]Source: M. J. Proudfoot, The Major Outlying Business
Centers of Chicago (Chicago: University of Chicago Libraries,
1938).

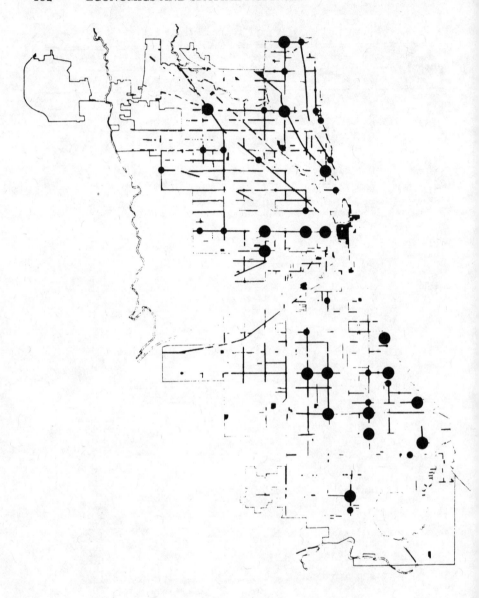

Figure 29: VACANCIES IN STUDY CENTERS

Centers with vacancy rates exceeding 10 per cent are indicated as
follows ●. Rates of 6-10 per cent are denoted: ● , and low rates
of less than 6 per cent:• .

TABLE 80

VACANCY RATES OF CINCINNATI'S OUTLYING CENTERS,
1931-33 AND 1954-55[a]

Per Cent of Stores Vacant by Center	All Centers in 1931-33	All 1933 Centers in 1954-55	Centers Established Since 1933 in 1954-55	All Centers 1955
0- 1	39	33	54	87
1- 2	1	7	1	8
2- 3	2		3	3
3- 4	7	9	3 average 4.4%	12 average 4.4%
4- 5	1	6 average 5.6%	4	10
5- 6	5	4	2	6
6- 7	1	5	3	8
7- 8	2 average 8.7%	7	2	9
8- 9	2	2		2
9-10	5	8	5	13
10-11	2	2		2
11-12	3	1	2	3
12-13	2	3	1	4
13-14	5	1		1
14-15			1	1
15-16	2	1	1	2
16-17	4	2	3	5
17-18	1	1	1	2
18-19	1			
19-20	4	3	2	5
20-21				
21-22				
22-23			2	2
23-24				
24-25	3	2	2	4
25-26				
26-27	1			
27-28				
28-29				
29-30	4			
30-31				
31-32				
32-33				
33-34		2		2
41-42	1			
49-50	1		1	1
54-55				
57-58	1	1		1
59-60			1	1
67-68			1	1
Total	100	100	95	195

[a]Source: W. Applebaum and B. L. Schapker, Atlas of Business Centers. Cincinnati-Hamilton County, Ohio (Cincinnati: The American Marketing Association, 1955).

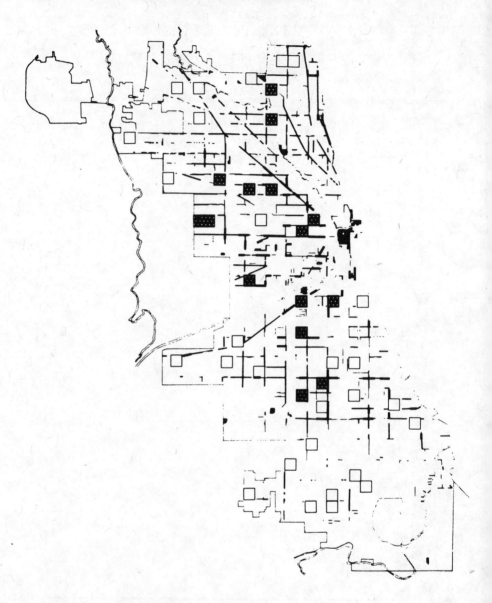

Figure 30:   RIBBON VACANCIES

The sample cells which have been shaded have more than 16 per cent of all stores in them vacant.   The 1959 Commercial Blight Survey provides data which indicates how the sample can be generalized to larger areas of the city.   All business streets shaded heavily had a similar 16 per cent or more vacancy rate at the time of that survey.

Vacancies in ribbons

Tables 81-87 record various facets of ribbon vacancies, again including both quantities and percentages of number of establishments, front footage, ground and upper floor area vacant. The data are listed separately for the various ribbon samples, for adjacent and isolated samples, for contiguous ribbons, scattered developments, and small isolated nucleations. The ribbon and scattered data are also listed by zones of analysis. Figure 30 shows where the ribbon vacancies occur within the city.

TABLE 81

VACANCIES IN RIBBONS BY ZONE OF ANALYSIS, 1961

Zone	Establishments	Front Feet	Ground Floor Area
Far North	453	8,655	572,863
North	808	13,717	753,997
North West	499	10,780	562,100
Far West	742	14,820	957,060
West	1,165	20,553	1,271,685
Near South West	746	13,090	740,575
Far South West	804	16,356	1,134,580
Central South	927	19,549	1,289,895
South	430	7,500	416,000
Far South	119	2,310	121,200
Totals	6,693	127,330	7,819,955

TABLE 82

RIBBON VACANCIES: SAMPLES ADJACENT TO CENTERS

Number	Establishments		Front Feet		Floor Area		Upper Floor	
	No.	%	Amount	%	Amount	%	No.	%
4	12	18.5	330	14.5	24,200	17.8	0	0.0
8	23	16.5	415	10.7	22,525	7.4	7	50.0
12	1	3.4	10	0.8	500	0.3	0	0.0
13	17	18.1	445	15.7	29,375	14.2	3	30.0
14	16	21.3	350	17.1	27,775	17.5	0	0.0
15	26	20.7	530	16.7	26,250	11.8	1	20.0
16	25	19.1	515	15.5	30,325	13.1	4	18.2
17	14	24.1	385	21.4	25,225	21.4	0	0.0
19	24	19.7	530	16.6	32,300	13.9	2	22.2
20	9	10.2	195	8.8	13,200	8.2	4	44.4
21	21	26.3	410	21.1	25,150	18.9	5	67.5
24	16	17.6	315	11.4	16,550	8.2	0	0.0
25	21	18.1	475	14.8	28,350	13.0	5	45.5
29	21	20.1	465	19.7	33,200	19.1	3	50.0
34	11	14.3	210	11.2	12,575	10.3	0	0.0
35	14	16.1	370	16.3	25,675	15.0	1	11.1
39	11	9.2	195	5.4	11,125	4.0	0	0.0
42	4	8.3	260	10.8	23,000	10.2	0	0.0

TABLE 83

RIBBON VACANCIES: SAMPLES ISOLATED FROM CENTERS

Number	Establishments		Front Feet		Floor Area		Upper Floor	
	No.	%	Amount	%	Amount	%	No.	%
1	5	8.8	70	3.3	3,950	1.9	1	25.0
2	9	9.8	190	5.5	10,900	4.0	1	20.0
5	0	0.0	0	0.0	0	0.0	0	0.0
6	6	6.5	200	5.4	11,000	4.0	2	100.0
7	9	11.4	185	9.3	9,075	6.2	0	0.0
9	3	12.0	70	9.5	6,600	12.4	0	0.0
18	0	0.0	0	0.0	0	0.0	0	0.0
27	18	22.2	380	15.7	21,425	12.7	0	0.0
28	2	4.6	20	2.1	1,000	1.8	0	0.0
30	4	4.4	65	2.2	3,650	2.1	0	0.0
32	6	9.1	285	14.1	28,750	17.8	1	16.7
33	16	11.5	355	11.6	20,300	8.3	0	0.0
36	12	17.2	265	14.0	17,050	13.6	4	100.0
37	10	8.1	215	6.4	11,675	5.4	3	60.0
38	11	14.9	240	8.4	10,700	4.6	0	0.0
40	7	13.2	180	12.4	9,675	9.9	0	0.0
41	1	2.8	15	0.8	975	1.0	0	0.0
43	2	4.9	35	1.9	2,625	1.5	0	0.0
44	1	5.9	20	3.2	1,400	2.4	0	0.0
45	2	11.8	35	4.6	2,100	3.0	0	0.0
47	2	7.7	45	7.3	2,550	10.2	1	100.0
48	3	9.4	65	5.9	2,725	3.2	0	0.0

TABLE 84

VACANCIES AMONG SCATTERED USES
BY ZONE OF ANALYSIS, 1961

Zone	Establishments	Front Feet	Ground Floor Area
Far North	-	-	-
North	84	2,000	119,040
North West	-	-	-
Far West	10	208	9,360
West	112	2,856	159,630
Near South West	77	1,595	75,350
Far South West	17	412	28,875
Central South	108	2,244	141,100
South	40	1,000	55,000
Far South	-	-	-
Totals	364	8,315	469,315

Note how ribbon vacancies are concentrated in the West,
Near South West, and adjacent parts of the Far West and North
West. If Figure 13 is consulted, it will be found that these
areas of high ribbon vacancies are Chicago's "blue collar" neighborhoods. High vacancy rates in ribbons are related to the socio-
economic level of the areas served. The tables show, as a corol-
lary, that the vacancy rates also are greater in those ribbons
adjacent to centers--in the area called in Chapter II the "frame"
of the business centers.

<u>Vacancies and the Process of
Socio-Economic Change</u>

The geography of vacancies differs for centers and ribbons.
Vacancies in centers are highest in areas of social change. Ribbon
vacancies reach their peak in lower income neighborhoods, and
there particularly in the "frame" of business centers. Why should
there be these correlations? Why should centers and ribbons
differ?

Apparently the reason is to be found in the process of
socio-economic change. Consider first a high income area adjacent
to zones undergoing change. In this area there is an equilibrium
between demands and supplies, or as close an approximation to
equilibrium as is possible given the rate at which the equilibrium
is moving under the impact of technological change. Since commercial activities are oriented to local consumers, the demands which
are being satisfied are those of higher income families.

Social changes now begin in the area, and incomes drop.
Some stores can exist on reduced volumes. Others can survive by
changing the lines of goods offered, particularly convenience
goods stores. The activities which are hardest hit are small
specialty shops that cater to higher income groups. In due course
many of these go out of business. Since such specialty shops
locate in centers, vacancies in the centers shoot up.

After initial changes have taken place, the area consoli-
dates at lower income levels. With reductions in sales, land
values and rents drop in the business centers, and stores previously located in the "frame" move inwards to fill the vacant
spaces left by the specialty shops. They can afford it because
the spaces are now being offered at lower rents. Other kinds of
stores catering specifically to the lower income groups also enter
the centers. Thus, the centers fill up, and as far as the centers
are concerned an approximation to equilibrium conditions of the
lower income type is once again achieved.

Inward movement of activities from the ribbons leads to an

TABLE 85

VACANCIES: SCATTERED USES IN RIBBON SAMPLES ADJACENT TO CENTERS

Number	Establishments		Front Feet		Floor Area		Upper Floor	
	No.	%	Amount	%	Amount	%	No.	%
13	1	14.3	20	13.3	900	6.2	0	0.0
14	0	0.0	0	0.0	0	0.0	0	0.0
15	4	14.8	100	17.1	5,625	18.0	0	0.0
16	0	0.0	0	0.0	0	0.0	0	0.0
19	5	14.7	115	9.7	7,175	7.6	0	0.0
20	0	0.0	0	0.0	0	0.0	0	0.0
21	1	12.5	40	13.6	1,600	6.7	0	0.0
24	4	19.0	75	14.7	3,725	16.0	0	0.0
25	3	15.8	70	16.1	3,125	10.8	0	0.0
29	13	16.1	285	14.6	14,225	11.4	2	66.7
34	0	0.0	0	0.0	0	0.0	0	0.0
35	4	10.3	90	10.2	6,200	14.1	0	0.0

TABLE 86

VACANCIES: SCATTERED USES IN RIBBON SAMPLES ISOLATED FROM CENTERS

Number	Establishments		Front Feet		Floor Area		Upper Floor	
	No.	%	Amount	%	Amount	%	No.	%
5	0	0.0	0	0.0	0	0.0	0	0.0
18	1	9.1	25	8.8	1,250	6.2	0	0.0
32	0	0.0	0	0.0	0	0.0	0	0.0
33	2	8.7	25	4.4	1,225	2.7	2	100.0
36	1	6.2	25	3.9	1,750	2.9	0	0.0
38	1	25.0	25	26.3	1,250	26.4	0	0.0
40	2	22.2	50	23.6	2,750	24.8	0	0.0
44	0	0.0	0	0.0	0	0.0	0	0.0
45	0	0.0	0	0.0	0	0.0	0	0.0
48	0	0.0	0	0.0	0	0.0	0	0.0

TABLE 87

VACANCIES: SMALL ISOLATED NUCLEATIONS IN RIBBON SAMPLE ZONES

Number	Establishments		Front Feet		Floor Area		Upper Floor	
	No.	%	Amount	%	Amount	%	No.	%
8	3	30.0	50	23.3	2,900	22.3	0	0.0
33	2	3.3	30	2.2	1,500	2.1	0	0.0
41	6	10.2	120	9.9	6,850	8.1	1	50.0

increase of vacancy rates in the ribbons, however. This is compounded by a reduction in demands for services as incomes drop,
and abandonment of older smaller ribbon establishments in the
face of technological change. A chronic surplus of commercial
facilities emerges in the ribbons of low income areas, and persists.

Loss of the specialty shops, accompanied by greater local
shopping orientation, results in two levels of centers in the low
income areas, one convenience and the other shopping, rather than
the four that previously existed under the higher income conditions.
Similarly, decline in services and movement of "frame" activities
inwards to the centers, results in a decline in numbers and varieties of specialized functional areas within the ribbons. Vacancies
therefore also reflect another facet of economic blight--increasing
localism.

Structural Faults and Physical Blight

Structural deterioration is a relative thing--a continuous
process which begins as soon as a building has been completed and
increases as the building ages. The rate of deterioration depends
upon many things. Among these are the mode and type of construction, materials used in building, and the way in which the building has been used. Whatever the combination of these factors,
however, the probability that a structure will display signs of
deterioration increases with the age of the building.

If deterioration is progressive, it becomes a highly subjective matter to label buildings with such appellations as "good,"
"deteriorating," and "deteriorated." Whether or not a building
falls into one of these classes depends upon the way in which
they have been defined and the criteria selected as bases for the
classification.

It is a time-consuming and expensive process to rate buildings in a detailed manner using careful building-to-building surveys, whatever criteria for evaluating deterioration may be selected.
Skilled surveyors are needed, and each building must be examined
with a toothcomb. Only in such a manner can a proper quantitative
scale of physical deterioration be selected.[1] The alternative is
to select one or two criteria, define "deteriorated" conditions in
terms of these criteria, and make a quicker qualitative survey of
the "worst" cases of blight. The analyst is thus faced with a
dilemma: incur the time and costs of extremely detailed surveys
to produce a truly quantitative scale, or make a quicker survey

---

[1]City Plan Commission, St. Louis, Measuring Deterioration
in Commercial and Industrial Areas, op. cit.

which searches out those cases with obvious qualitative manifestations of serious problems of physical deterioration.

The Commercial Blight Survey

The latter approach is the one upon which the following
discussion is based. Data were collected in the summer of 1959,
prior to the initiation of the present study, by the then urban
renewal programming staff of the City of Chicago's Department of
City Planning, and so this study adhered to the qualitative ratings
of that study. A report summarizing the findings of this survey
has never been prepared, although a survey manual[1] and three maps[2]
are on file with Chicago's Community Renewal Program.

The manual shows the survey to have been a general one,
intended to cover the entire City of Chicago in a brief period of
time to provide a rapid picture of the extent of deteriorating
commercial areas. Windshield observations were taken of a series
of factors relating both to individual buildings and to entire
areas. Since many of the ratings were "good," "fair," "bad," and
the like, considerable judgment on the part of the field observers
was involved, although steps were taken to ensure standardization
of judgments, and by checking reports, to control as much as possible the individual observer bias.

"Blight factors" recorded in the field survey for each
commercial block of the city studied included:

    (a) Vacancies--numbers of establishments vacant.

    (b) Obsolescence--whether or not buildings were adjudged
        to be obsolete in terms of age, "lack of adherence to
        modern design principles," need for modernization,
        cramped window displays, etc.

    (c) Condition of Building--whether or not the building re-
        quired maintenance, minor repair, or either major
        rehabilitation (extreme settlement, etc.) or was unfit
        for rehabilitation (jerry-built, out of line, and the
        like).

    (d) Character of Area--whether the area within which the
        business frontage was located showed signs of deteriora-
        tion, litter, etc.

Of these, only the windshield evidence relating to condition of
building will be used, and we will focus on those blocks in which

---

[1] Department of City Planning, City of Chicago, Commercial
Blight Survey. Manual for Field Evaluators, July 14, 1959.

[2] These deal with "Excessive Ground Floor Vacancy" "Major
Structural Faults" and "Obsolete Structures." Only the second is
used here, because our surveys provided more useful materials on
vacancies, and because the work dealing with obsolescence is of
questionable value. See Brian J. L. Berry, Commercial Blight. A
Revue, Report to the Community Renewal Program of the City of
Chicago, February, 1962.

at least one in five establishments were recorded as requiring major rehabilitation or as being unfit for rehabilitation.

Figure 31 depicts the resulting pattern. The sections of ribbon which have been shaded with the solid black line are those in which two or more contiguous blocks have at least a third of their establishments located in buildings which display major structural faults. Clearly, long stretches of deteriorating ribbons are to be found.

Note how major structural faults are associated with the city's lower income neighborhoods (compare Figures 31 and 13). This is not unexpected, since the lower income groups live in the older and/or more centrally located sections of the city. There is, as B. Duncan has shown, a strong negative correlation between the age of buildings in an area and the incomes of the persons residing in that area.[1] Locational concentrations are, further, confined to the major arterials radiating from the central business district, and adjacent to industrial land uses, within these lower income neighborhoods. (B. Duncan records that the spatial distribution of lower income "workingmen's" neighborhoods is "explainable" in terms of proximity to city center, industrial workplaces, and age of buildings.)

Correlations of vacancies and physical blight

Note the coincidence of ribbon vacancies and major structural faults within the city. Evidently, as areas settle down into a low income equilibrium pattern, the vacancies not only settle down in the ribbons, but those establishments which become vacant and remain vacant are those which are in the worst physical condition. Lack of use accelerates the natural processes of decay, and so it becomes less and less likely that these buildings will be reoccupied, and until they are demolished they remain vacant and crumbling.

Obsolescence and Functional Blight

There is no doubt that there has been an increasing specificity in the kinds of space demanded by retail and service establishments. During the first phase of commercial growth in Chicago, most retail activities required very simple structures, and were satisfied with ground floor locations in three or four story buildings located on very narrow lots with offices and apartments on

---

[1] B. Duncan, "Variables in Urban Morphology," in E. W. Burgess and D. J. Bogue (eds.), Research Contributions to Urban Sociology (Chicago: University of Chicago Press, in press).

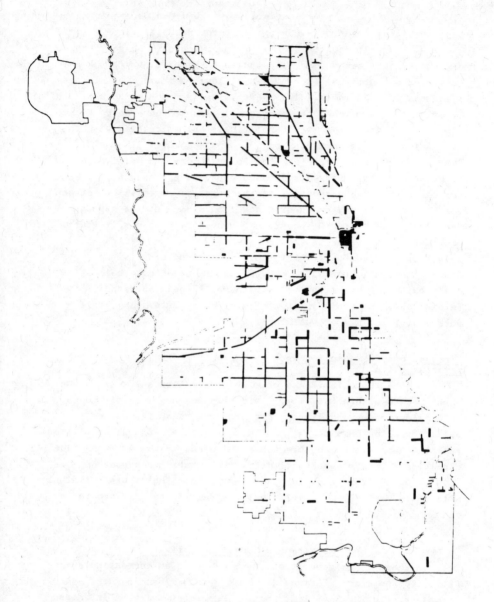

Figure 31:   MAJOR STRUCTURAL FAULTS

The business streets with the darker shading comprise those groups
of two or more contiguous blocks for which the 1959 Commercial
Blight Survey recorded at least a third of the commercial buildings
as displaying major structural faults.

the upper floors. Few types of establishments had any substantial
degree of specialized space requirements. As business has developed, however, an increasing array of demands for retail and
service space of a variety of sizes and shapes has emerged. Less
stores fit so readily into the space which developed in the first
phase of commercial expansion.

The shift in scale of establishments is particularly important. Whereas large scale structures can be subdivided if
needed, small spaces confined by load-bearing masonry walls are
not easily adaptable or enlarged. Further contributing to the
obsolescence of older commercial buildings is the decreasing demand for upper floor business space in the older larger centers.[1]

Parking as a major factor

Delivery and loading services in most older shopping centers are inadequate. Trucks deliver goods from the street front
and alleys, and these trucks must drive through already congested
streets to their destinations. To this must be added the totally
inadequate supply of parking space for private automobiles. Although
in the older more central areas of the city many customers still
arrive at business centers by public transit, the proportion is
declining through time. There is an increasing tendency throughout
the city to make all shopping trips by automobile, except the walk
to the local streetcorner store which is open at all hours for the
person residing in the most densely populated parts of the city.

Physico-economic blight and obsolescence

There is a paradox when the physico-economic forms of
blight (vacancy settling down in the oldest buildings in low income areas of the city) are compared with obsolescence, however.
To be sure, the most obsolete structures are bound to be found in
the older areas of the city. These were the areas of earliest
growth--those which experienced rapid development of commercial
facilities during the first explosive phase of growth in the early
twentieth century. The paradox is this: in the lower income areas
there is a proportionately greater demand for small stores of the
older less specialized kind, to serve local neighborhood shopping
needs in a very local manner. Moreover, with greater local orientation, demands for parking diminish, since the automobile is not
used on the quick trip to the store at the street corner. Physico-

---

[1]Thomas P. Melone, Business and Commerce Chapter, Comprehensive Policies Plan, City of Chicago, Department of City Planning, July, 1962. First draft.

economic blight thus eliminates many of the problems of functional
blight. Since there are no demands for the space, the space
cannot, in turn, be inadequate for the operations of anyone. It
generates neither truck nor automobile traffic; hence congestion
and parking problems are not relevant. As the areas which experienced commercial growth during its first phase stabilize in the
lower income equilibrium, then, spreading physico-economic blight
largely eliminates problems of obsolescence.

Frictional Blight

Two main threads run through the discussions of frictional
blight. First, inadequate loading and parking facilities in older
business developments, plus excessive cross street movement by
pedestrians at business centers located athwart intersections and
the resulting intermixture of pedestrian and vehicular traffic
lead to traffic congestion and high accident rates. Second,
deteriorating business streets lead to the spread of blight into
surrounding residential neighborhoods. The former is well-
documented. The latter, in spite of such quotations as the following (from a well-known planning textbook) is not:

> There is little to support the retention of commercial develop-
> ment along the highways. Consolidation of urban facilities
> is urgently needed to restore stability to property values and
> convenience for the daily multitude who daily patronize the
> variety of business enterprise in our cities. It is also
> needed to stem the insidious spread of blight which is gnawing
> at the core of our cities. This consolidation will come by
> recreation of "centers" of business and the rejection of
> "strip" or "shoestring" zoning along the highways which retain
> the horse and buggy tempo of the village.[1]

Correlations of frictions and other blight forms

Such frictions as do exist are again a function of age,
and are thus most likely to be concentrated in the older areas of
the city. But again, the problems of frictional blight appear to
be largely self-correcting. As an area settles down to lower income
status, excessive vacancies appear in the ribbons where the greatest
problems of traffic congestion existed. Decline in demands implies
decline in traffic generation and decline in use of the street for
business purposes, and this in turn means an increase in the desirability of the street as a through traffic artery. To be sure,
certain frictions may increase, such as increased fire hazard, and
perhaps policing problems associated with the use of otherwise
vacant stores by undesirables, but frictional blights are largely

---

[1]A. B. Gallion, The Urban Pattern (New York: D. Van Nostrand
and Company, 1950).

eliminated, or are reduced to the extent that increasing vacancies reduce use of the street for shopping purposes.

Summary and Implications

Several kinds of change are affecting the commercial structure of Chicago. Long run changes in scale and mobility are causing an average annual (geometric) rate of decline of establishments of 5.8 per cent. Conversely, real income increases of 3.2 per cent per annum are calling forth a 2.7 per cent average annual growth in demands. A process of population redistribution is also taking place, with thinning out of the inner city and increasing densities in the outer city at rates of about 1.0 per cent per annum in each case. Further, high income groups are being replaced by lower-income families in many neighborhoods. The effect of this socio-economic process is a 1.75 point average annual drop in relative income, or a 2.2 per cent decline in demands for establishments. Summing all these plus and minus terms, the net effects are for demands for retail establishments to decline at a rate of 2.0 per cent per annum in stable high income communities, 4.0 per cent per annum in stable low income communities, and 5.0 per cent per annum in zones of transition.

These rates refer only to numbers of establishments, of course, and not to actual space demands. Declines in numbers of establishments because of increasing scale of operation are presumably offset to some extent by the greater space demands of the fewer but larger stores. The only data available on changing space demands are those for Cincinnati (Table 71), which indicate that in a twenty year period average store frontages increased by 50 per cent, or with standard lot depths, lot areas increased by about 40 per cent. This translates into an average annual rate of increase in lot sizes of 2.0 per cent. If this rate is transferred to the Chicago scene and applied literally, it means that the 2.0 per cent decline in establishments in higher income areas was probably balanced by the increasing space requirements of the fewer larger stores replacing the smaller less efficient ones. The net decline in space demands may, similarly be conjectured to be 2.0 per cent per annum in lower income communities and 3.0 per cent per annum in the zone of transition.

These declines imply increasing vacancy rates, if not offset by reductions in the supply of space. Some reductions are, of course, being made. In urban renewal projects, for example, the supply of retail establishments has been reduced drastically. Similarly, expressway construction has meant considerable demolition. Since many operating tenants in the demolition areas are

relocated to otherwise vacant property elsewhere, the net result
is to reduce vacancy rates (a good example of this is the filling
of 53rd Street in Hyde Park as business along 55th Street is
eliminated). In other parts of the city private initiative has
had similar effects, although on a more limited scale--for example,
a row of old small shops may be knocked down to make way for a
new supermarket.

The present geographic pattern of vacancies correlates well
with the rate differentials noted above, but with some interesting
variations. Rates are relatively low in higher income areas.
They rise sharply in centers in zones of transition as income
changes result in loss of markets by the smaller specialty shops,
then drop in centers once again as areas stabilize at a lower income level and less specialized uses centralize. But the centralization of less specialized uses takes place at the expense
of the ribbons, and the resulting hard core of residual vacancies
at present exceeds 16.0 per cent of the available supply of establishments in the lower income areas. This is "hard core" vacancy--
economic blight--the result of reduced demands.

Lower income areas are characteristically also the oldest
areas of the city, and much of the commercial property was built
during the pre-depression expansion phase. As buildings age, the
probability that they will display structural deterioration--
physical blight--increases, and the city's problems of physical
blight are also therefore largely confined to the lower income
areas. It appears that physical and economic blight coincide--
hard core vacancies settle down in the most deteriorated structures,
and idleness accelerates the process of deterioration.

Buildings constructed before the depression are also increasingly obsolete because of the increasing specificity and scale
of space demands and lack of parking space, and the latter in turn,
combined with locational patterns at main intersections on the
city's arterial street system, lead to frictions with streets as
traffic arteries, high accident rates, congestion, and the like.
Both of these latter forms of blight are functions of use, however--
obsolescence is obsolescence for certain uses--but if the demands
are not there, the question of functional or frictional blight is
irrelevant. If demands are absent, buildings are not used, traffic
is not generated, and congestion and related frictions are removed.
Thus, increasing physico-economic blight in the city largely
corrects problems of a functional and frictional kind. Traffic
in the city benefits from increasing vacancies in the commercial
ribbons, especially in the older areas where traffic problems are
the most acute.

Commercial blight reexamined

It appears, therefore, that there is a single composite form of "commercial blight" caused by the union of economic and physical conditions. Economics provides the motive power for spread and general localization in ribbons of lower income areas. Physical conditions provide the "hard core" sites in the most deteriorated buildings. The joining of economic and physical blight largely eliminates any functional or frictional problems in the blighted areas, however.

Such is our understanding of the "extent, location, nature and trends of (commercial) blight and deterioration" in the City of Chicago today.

8

Management and Economics Research, Inc.

PLANT LOCATION DECISION-MAKING

Characteristics of Location Decisions

Decisions with respect to the location of manufacturing establishments are, in the United States, almost uniformly made in the private sector, and generally on the basis of market and other economic factors. There have been cases, such as plants built in wartime, where the government has influenced location because of national security considerations. There have also been cases where subsidies of one kind or another have influenced the pattern of location. However, even these decisions were made with an eye to the market forces and cost factors likely to prevail in the long term.

To those concerned with economic development planning, the nature of the plant location decision and the process by which it is made in private industry is an important subject, since the promotion of private investment in the area involved is a major function of most development agencies.

While there are no precise data on the number of manufacturing plant location decisions made in the course of a year, fragmentary data presented earlier suggest that it is on the order of 3,000 to 4,000, with a substantial percentage of these being new companies. In view of the large number of existing manufacturing companies, it appears that a plant location decision is one that arises but seldom in the life of most manufacturing enterprises. Furthermore, the short average tenure of men in such positions as president or chairman of the board suggests that a particular management might face this problem only once or twice in its years of leadership. Thus this is a type of problem in which experience plays a minor role.

Three basic types of plant location decisions can be identified. They are: the relocation of an existing plant, the establishment of a branch plant, and the establishment of the first plant of a new company. The economic factors that enter into the location analysis, as well as the process of decision-making in the case of relocations and branch plants, are very

much the same. The circumstances surrounding the location of a new enterprise, however, are quite different.

While the frequency of relocations is not known, it is presumed to be
small, relatively speaking. Many of the relocations that have occurred have
received a great deal of attention because of their impact on the areas they
vacated. In such cases, there is, of course, a loss of payroll, a loss of
volume to local suppliers of goods and services, and, perhaps worst of all,
a depressing effect on the industrial development prospects of the area.
This negative economic impact imposes upon management important public relations considerations.[1]

In addition to these public relations problems, relocations have certain
other distinguishing features. One of these is the balance between market
considerations and considerations related to costs of production. While the
factors important in a relocation and those important in the location of a
branch plant, in a particular industry, are much the same, there is some evidence that their relative importance will vary. One study states:

> "Yet the data suggest that plans to relocate are strongly influ-
> enced by changes affecting costs of production, while plans to
> expand through new plants at locations different from the
> original plant or plants are dominated by considerations of
> demand and efficient marketing."[2]

Still another factor unique to the relocation problem is that of timing.
There is an element of inertia that affects the decision to relocate that is
not present in a branch plant decision. This is likely to result in a time
lag in the decision-making as management faces up to the difficulties involved in departing from a long-established location. Subjective and even
emotional factors are likely to override for a time what may be compelling
economic forces.

----

[1] For detailed analysis of a specific case in relocation, see Whitman
and Schmidt, Plant Relocation (Ref. 103).

[2] Mueller et al., Location Decisions and Industrial Mobility in Michigan
(Ref. 77), p. 55.

A more common case in plant location decision-making is that to establish a branch plant. Such a decision usually arises as the result of company
growth. As long as the capacity of a firm remains in balance with the share-
of-market it commands, expansion is not necessary. When sales growth and
future prospects indicate the need for substantial additional production, management has at least two alternatives: to expand in the existing location, or
to establish a branch in some other location.

There have been significant geographical shifts in U.S. population and
markets in the past two decades. Accordingly, most companies have found that
the geographical distribution of their markets varies significantly from that
existing at the time the original plant was established. When this market
factor is combined with the changes in costs occasioned by shifts in such
factors as raw material, labor, transportation, etc., an entirely new optimal
location is likely to appear. These circumstances have given rise to extensive branching of companies in most manufacturing industries.

The location of the first plant of a newly established manufacturing
firm is a special case. Most such firms start small, depend on a local or
regional market, and are located where the founder and his associates live.
The cases of new industries in which there is a careful analysis of the economic factors of location to select an optimum point are probably the exception and not the rule. Thus, the question as to whether the domicile of the
entrepreneur is an economic location for the firm becomes one of the elements
that determines survival rather than a pre-established element. Many small
firms probably survive in spite of a less-than-optimal location by means of
sacrifices in returns to management and capital; some grow up and later correct the initial error; and many fail. Some find they are well located as a
fortunate happenstance.

The location of new enterprises is not as random as the above discussion
might imply. In manufacturing, many new firms are started by men who learned
the business working in an established company. If the employee then starts
a competitive firm in the same location, the success of his former company
would argue that the location must, at least, be adequate.

The analysis of all three types of locational decisions involves a common set of locational factors. In the case of relocations and branches these are generally applied at two or even three levels of analysis. These levels may be defined as the regional analysis, the community analysis, and the site analysis. These three are often discussed as one locational problem; and while it is true that the same locational factors are often involved, in any specific case they may vary widely in their relative importance and impact on the decision from one level of analysis to another.

For instance, in the location of a branch plant, the first step is generally to decide in which region of the country it is to be located. This requires a study of the size, nature, and geographical configuration and future prospects of regional markets. It also involves a study of the supply pattern to determine where additional capacity is needed. Once the decision is made on the region, the market factor declines in importance as alternative communities at the center of the market to be served are studied. Now community facilities, land, transportation, and labor supply become more important although markets may continue to be a factor, in combination with transportation.[1] Finally, at the site level of analysis, markets are no longer an important consideration. Access streets, the size of water and sewer mains, and the bearing strength of the soil emerge as major factors, along with the cost of the alternative parcels of available land.

As important as all three of these levels are in locating a particular industrial plant, this paper is concerned primarily with the regional analysis, and only secondarily with community and site considerations.

Plant Location Factors

The analysis of plant location problems is generally made in terms of a number of plant location factors. Their number and definition vary in the literature from author to author, each author presenting his own list. Some

---

[1] For an analysis at this level see Dunn, "The Market Potential Concept and the Analysis of Location" (Ref. 30).

of these lists are quite short, while others are very long and detailed. One
student of the subject is reported to have developed a list of over 600 factors that should be taken into account in analyzing a locational problem. As
a guide for this discussion, the following summary list is suggested as including those considerations that appear in virtually every list:

> Markets
> Labor
> Transportation
> Raw materials
> Power, fuels, and water
> Community factors
> Site factors

The relative significance of these factors in the location analysis will
vary widely from one industry to another. Since the industrial environment
is highly dynamic, their importance will also vary within a particular industry from one time to another.

Certain general trends have been identified in the changing impact of
these factors on locational decisions, which are important both to indus-
trialists and to area developers. These trends will be examined in two
interrelated groups: first, trends in locational factors that affect the
comparative advantages of areas, and second, trends that affect the locational
determinants of various industries or industry groups.

Differences among Areas

Early industrialization patterns in the United States reflected a match-
ing of the dominant locational factors of certain industries with the areas
that were most favored by that factor. Thus, market-oriented industries
were highly concentrated in the Northeast and particularly on the Atlantic
seaboard and around Chicago. Raw-material-oriented industries were located
at the best source of those raw materials, which in many cases was the West.
Many of the labor-intensive industries sought location in the South, where
labor was abundant, cheap, and not affected by union activity.

Over time these factor-area relationships have been changing. Slowly at first, but accelerating since World War II, these changes are lessening the comparative advantage that certain regions have traditionally enjoyed. Nevertheless, there are still important differences in most location factors, and these are likely to persist.

Turning first to what is perhaps the dominant factor in most industries-- markets--some definition is necessary at the outset. It is important to differentiate between consumer markets, which are generally a function of population and income patterns, and industrial markets, which are a function of manufacturing concentrations. There are important differences in the geographical distribution of consumer and industrial markets, although these differences are not as great as formerly.[1] Markets, in this context, refer to regional markets rather than district or local markets.

Consumer markets are still highly concentrated. As Harris has pointed out, half the retail sales in the United States are in the Northeast, from Boston to St. Louis.[2] Some states in this area have a density of market several hundred times as high as some states in the West. Densities in most of the Mountain and Plains states are also very low.

That this situation is slowly changing is obvious from the higher population growth rates of Western and Southern states. However, much of this growth has, up to now, been concentrated in oasis-like areas in the West and in the South, such as Southern California, Phoenix, and parts of Texas. In between, there are vast areas of very sparse consumer market, which affects the market pull of these growth areas. While, in general, there is a trend toward the development of significant markets in regions other than the Northeast, the differences in regional market densities remain very sizable.

---

[1] Chinitz and Vernon, "Changing Forces in Industrial Location" (Ref. 23).

[2] Harris, "The Market as a Factor in the Location of Industry in the United States" (Ref. 51).

Industrial markets are even more highly concentrated. About two-thirds of all manufacturing employment is still in the Northeast. These markets have traditionally been concentrated, according to industry, in certain regions or even cities. For instance, the automobile industry market has been concentrated in Detroit, the rubber industry market in Akron, and the steel industry market in Pittsburgh and Chicago.

The tendency of consumer markets to disperse has been followed by a similar, but less extensive, tendency for industry to broaden its locational patterns. This is reflected statistically in a "marked convergence in the ratio of manufacturing employment to population among the different regions of the country toward some common national ratio."[1] At present rates of decentralization, however, traditional concentrations will persist for a long period into the future.

Another factor that varies significantly among regions is wages. Wage differences as high as 25 percent between developed urban areas are not uncommon. Differences between urban and rural areas are even more striking.

There are forces, however, that are tending to narrow these differences. They include union organization and collective bargaining, particularly at the national level, federal minimum wage laws, and the migration of industry itself. When industry moves into an area of low wages, it increases employment. If other plants later locate close by, demand may put an upward pressure on wages and tend to reduce the differential that previously existed.

This is, of course, an imperfect mechanism. Not every industry is free to seek low wages, and many that could do so might hesitate for fear the advantage will disappear with time. Thus, equalization does not occur as readily and completely as theory might suggest. Chinitz and Vernon quote a study by Martin Segal, which concludes that while differences in wage levels have tended to narrow in recent decades, the narrowing has been quite slow and spotty.[1]

1/ Chinitz and Vernon, "Changing Forces in Industrial Location" (Ref. 23).

This trend toward equalization of regional differences is also true to some degree in labor availability. Skills that at one time were highly concentrated in the Northeast have become available in many other areas as the result of population migration. So strong has been the pull of amenities toward the Southern and Western coasts that significant numbers of highly skilled people have been willing to work at lower skilled jobs to earn a living, pending the opportunity to use their specialty in the area.

In the field of transportation, too, new technology and changing cost patterns have tended to reduce the disadvantage of certain areas. The development of truck transportation, which has had a revolutionary impact on transport costs, has tended to promote the decentralization of industry. For instance, the relative decline in the cost of short hauls and of small lots, as compared with the cost of long hauls and large lots, has helped the Southeast and the West in their industrialization.[1]

In addition to cost differentials, trucks are able to offer a speed and service not available from railroads. Furthermore, they can offer it at origins and destinations that have no rail service at all.

Other developments in transportation may tend to open more distant markets to producers. These include the development of "piggy-back" services, the growth of air freight, and the prospective reorientation of the railroad rate structure. These developments will tend to reduce the cost or improve the service on long hauls as against short hauls, countering the advantages of the truck. While they may not permit the New York producer to compete with the Los Angeles producer for the California market, they might permit him to compete with the Texas producer for that market. Thus, these changes too tend in some instances, to reduce the differences between regions or, stated another way, broaden the locational choice of a producer to serve stated markets.

---

[1] Perloff and Dodds, How a Region Grows (Ref. 82), p. 105.

An examination of the raw material supply patterns of industry indicates that in this factor, too, there is a declining impact of geography. In the first place, the raw materials of more and more industries are now drawn from manufactured sources rather than natural ones. The former are more widely distributed than the latter, tending to locate in the various industrial areas of the country. Second, the reduction of tariffs and the gradual freeing of foreign trade have opened up foreign sources that can provide materials at all major ports at comparable costs. Such availability has permitted, for instance, the location of the Fairless Works of U.S. Steel Corporation on the basis of market factors, within an industry that has traditionally been resource-based.

Finally, technology has permitted the development of resources in areas where those resources were previously uneconomic. Where the best deposits of ore or stands of timber have already been used, remaining sources are more widespread and do not have as strong a location pull as the prime sources had. Furthermore, through the use of improved processing methods, the economics of remaining sources have tended to be equalized.

Similar comments can be made with reference to power and fuels. The widespread distribution of natural gas, new technologies in coal utilization, and the development of high-voltage distribution systems have changed the energy picture. Many more areas can now offer energy, even in alternative forms, at more reasonable rates than ever before. The development of economically competitive atomic energy will contribute further to the reduction of area differences.

Progress in water supply has not been as notable. Industries that are heavy users of water are still restricted in their location, although water reuse and even saline conversion have, in some cases, helped to overcome area disadvantages. It is expected that important area differences in water supply will continue for a long time, but such differences affect a relatively small segment of industry.

Of particular interest has been the change in community and site factors. Good community environments among populations that welcome industry are much more widely available than ever before. Some of the external economies, which have traditionally been available only in the established industrial centers, have become available in many other areas. The availability of special skills was mentioned earlier. Developed industrial sites are now readily available in many medium- and small-sized towns and at much lower prices than in the major cities.

Many of the elements included as community and site factors are subject to local improvement. Area development agencies and community development groups are working diligently, particularly in the less industrialized areas, to reduce the relative disadvantages of their communities or states. A review of these efforts cannot but lead to the conclusion that, in such factors, the area differences are also declining.

Partly as a result of these trends and partly reinforcing them is the slowly declining degree of specialization among areas. Ashby has shown, through an analysis of employment shifts, that the economic structure of the various regions is tending to become less specialized and more alike over time.[1]

It should be made clear that while there is evidence to support the hypothesis that area differences in major plant location factors are declining, this decline, in many cases, is slow. There remain important regional and area differences in most location factors, which are likely to continue for a long time.

Differences by Industry

While almost all major location factors enter into most locational decisions, one factor often appears to dominate the locational decision in a particular industry. Thus, some studies have classified industry as "market-oriented," "labor-oriented," or "raw-material-oriented."[2] In this classification scheme, those not fitting into one of the three groups have often been described as "footloose."[3]

1/ Ashby, "The Geographical Redistribution of Employment. An Examination of the Elements of Change" (Ref. 6).

2/ McLaughlin and Robock, Why Industry Moves South (Ref. 78), p. 25.

3/ Hoover, The Location of Economic Activity (Ref.60), p. 36.

Later studies, notably that of the New York Metropolitan Region, have developed other classifications that are more definitive and that recognize the shifts taking place in the characteristics of American industry. In his part of the study referred to, Lichtenberg developed a set of seven classifications that he used in studying the industry of the region.[1] In this system, markets to be served were differentiated as local or regional and had their impact in terms of transportation costs; labor costs were differentiated between skilled and unskilled; external economies and inertial forces were considered explicitly as separate locational factors.

This classification scheme emphasizes factors that are of growing importance and that are pertinent to so many of the fast-growing, high-technology industries. It also eliminates the "footloose" classification, which was often a misnomer when used as an "all other" class for industries not fitting the three traditional classes.[2]

Lichtenberg's approach will be further refined in the work currently in progress at the National Industrial Conference Board (NICB). In this study, Creamer will examine the locational patterns of 400 four-digit industries on the basis of nine locational classifications.[3] These nine are a modification of the system developed by Lichtenberg.

As useful as these classifications are for the purpose of overall analysis, much more detail is needed to get a thorough understanding of the relative importance of plant location factors by industry. There is a need for additional studies of the relative impact of location factors within individual industries at the four-digit level. The aggregation at the two- and three-digit levels tends to be so great as to hide wide variation among the component industries.

---

[1] Lichtenberg et al., <u>One Tenth of a Nation</u> (Ref. 68), p. 35.

[2] See Spiegelman, "A Method for Determining the Location Characteristics of Footloose Industries" (Ref. 94).

[3] See Chapter VIII, "Research in Progress."

Some studies of this kind were started by the Office of Area Development in the Department of Commerce about 1960. Six industries, including instruments and electronics, were analyzed in terms of their locational patterns.[1] Additionally, within the individual states and regions a great many separate industry location studies have been made. However, most of these are of limited usefulness because of their orientation to a specific geographical area. For example, see the publications of Industrial Research and Extension Center, University of Arkansas, Little Rock, or of the Industrial Development Division, Georgia Institute of Technology, Atlanta.

A new study has recently been started that should throw some light on this problem. This study is being made by Fantus Factory Locating Service under contract with the Appalachian Regional Commission. It is described in Chapter VIII.

Such studies will permit a better understanding of the relative importance of the various location factors as they apply to particular industries. They should also make it possible to define more precisely the shifts that are taking place in the relative impact of these factors over time. This should be useful not only to business management but also to regional development agencies in their effort to match the comparative advantages of their area against the needs of industrial prospects.

Location Decision-Making in Industry

Studies of the process of plant location decision-making in industry indicate that this process varies widely from case to case. The nature of the industry and its products, the characteristics and history of the company, and even the attitudes of the executives involved, all influence the process. Thus, the number, identity, and weight accorded the economic and non-economic factors vary widely. Also, the nature and extent of analysis, the number of alternatives considered, and the role of outside agencies must vary from case to case.

---

[1] See Spiegelman, "A Method for Determining the Location Characteristics of Footloose Industries" (Ref. 94).

Reference was made earlier to the way in which location decisions usually arise. Of the major locational decisions, the greatest number are those made with respect to branch plants; these arise as the result of company growth. Two further aspects of location decision-making are common to almost all cases. The first of these is that industry intends to locate its plants at the point of greatest potential profit. Attaining this objective is not a simple matter. While in some cases all relevant locational factors can be quantified with hard, comparative numbers, this is not always so. In many cases such quantification is not possible, either because of lack of data or because there are important factors that cannot be expressed numerically.

The second aspect of location decision-making that seems clear is that this decision is almost always made by top management, usually by one man. One study reported that in 51 cases out of 69 examined, the decision was that of a single individual.[1] Since locational decisions arise very infrequently, and since they are of such importance that they can significantly affect the long-term profitability of the company, they are properly the concern of the chief executive officer.

A number of studies have been made in recent years to determine the relative importance of the various plant location factors from the viewpoint of industry. These studies differ considerably in their purpose. Some have sought to determine the importance of a particular factor, such as taxes or financial inducements. Others have sought data to guide community development efforts. Still others have been concerned with solving the development problems of specific areas. However, the characteristics these studies have in common are, first, that all approached their problem by surveying industrial executives; and, second, they all asked for a ranking of plant location factors.[2]

1/ Wallace, "Factors Affecting Industrial Location in Southern Indiana" (Ref. 100), p. 8.

2/ For an example of such studies see: McLaughlin and Roboch, Why Industry Moves South (Ref. 78); Mueller et al., Location Decisions and Industrial Mobility in Michigan (Ref. 77); Bergin and Eagin, "Economic Growth and Community Facilities" (Ref. 11); Mace, Industry and City Government (Ref. 71); Wallace, "Factors Affecting Industrial Location in Southern Indiana" (Ref. 100).

These studies are fairly consistent in their general findings. They confirm the importance of markets, labor, and raw materials as major locational
factors, with markets usually leading the list. Beyond such a general conclusion, however, it is not possible to learn much from these studies about the
decision-making process, except where special questions, dealing with some
particular aspect of the locational problem, were included. Furthermore, the
significance of the studies for present purposes is impaired because in most
cases the samples were small and confined geographically; there was usually
no stratification of the responses by industry or by level of decision; and,
of course, the objectives of the studies were themselves specific rather than
general.

The survey technique is a difficult one through which to gain a true picture of the locational process. This is because of the attitudes and behavior
of the business executive when confronted with questions about a decision
after the fact. In many cases, unless the questioning is very skillful, the
decision may be rationalized in terms now useful to the company as a resident
of the area, rather than in terms helpful to a prospective industry. Some
executives will reply with a story useful to the enhancement of the company's
image in the community. In other cases, the replies will cite factors that,
at the time of location, may have been minor ones. Taxes are a prime example.
Taxes appear repeatedly as a minor factor in location decision-making, but in
interviews after the fact, taxes are often cited as very important.

The Michigan study (Ref. 77) is notable for its effort to circumvent
these problems. One interesting approach used was to ask the respondents
about the locational characteristics of planned expansions. The emphasis was
thus placed on a future, rather than a past, decision and yielded some interesting insights.

It is well recognized that many non-economic, and even personal, factors
enter into the actual decision-making process. A common case is that in which
the initiation of expansion of a company takes place where the owner-manager
lives. In some cases this may, of course, be a good location. If the economic disadvantages are not so serious as to threaten survival, the business
may continue and grow until the occasion arises to examine the locational problem on a more rational basis.

Even in more complex situations, where considerable staff work is done in examining alternatives, there is a possibility that the prejudices and personal preferences of top executives will influence the decision.

Partly as a means to protect the objectivity of a locational analysis and partly because of a lack of skilled staff, outside consultants are sometimes used. In other cases, state development agencies, utilities, railroads, or chambers of commerce are used as sources of data and guidance. However, because of the need for confidentiality, many firms do the necessary staff work quietly and do not reveal their plans to anyone. One study of about 70 location decisions (an admittedly small sample) reported only 6 firms as using professional help and 16 others as having used data sources like those mentioned above. In all other cases, the analysis was made entirely by company personnel.

To the degree that the economic constraints on location are moderating in some industries, it is expected that personal wishes and non-economic factors related to community living and working environments will become increasingly important. In those industries where management, professional, and technical personnel are an important factor in the success of the enterprise, locational decisions are likely to be significantly influenced by the recreational, educational, and cultural characteristics of communities. This factor can be important to community development groups because these are factors that local groups and agencies can influence.

Concurrent with, but in a sense counter to this concern over non-economic factors, is the development of new computer-associated mathematical techniques for analyzing locational alternatives in those cases where the factors of location can be quantified. In industries where investment is high in relation to labor and competition is strong, the selection of an optimum location is vital to profitability. In such cases, there has been an increasing use of the operations research and linear programming techniques. Where transportation is a major factor, some companies have used freight costs on inbound and outbound materials and products to develop a mathematical model and then have employed this model to examine alternative locations.

A few companies are experimenting with more comprehensive models that include all the quantifiable factors affecting alternative locations. For instance, one company has built its own analog computer, which will simulate the entire product flow of the company. Estimates of future markets are fed into the computer, on the basis of which the computer assigns the product flow to various processing plants, warehouses, and other facilities to obtain the lowest-cost combination. The usefulness of this kind of system in making expansion decisions is obvious.

While such firms certainly are exceptions, a wider and more extensive use of mathematical techniques in locational analysis is certain to develop. Their application will demand more accurate and more complete data from many sources. Their use will set standards within the applicable industries, which through the force of competition, will have to be adopted by others. To the degree that these methods optimize locational decisions, the industry and the entire economy will gain.

The decision-making processes of industry with respect to location, varying as they do from no explicit analysis at all in some cases, to highly sophisticated analyses in others, do not lend themselves to generalization. There is a need to differentiate these decisions, both by level of decision and by detailed industrial classification. Within industrial classifications, there is an opportunity for worthwhile research on both the economics and the process of locational decisions.

New Industrial Companies

The industrial development of an area has, in general, the three sources mentioned earlier: the growth of established enterprises, the establishment of branch plants of firms headquartered outside the area, and the formation of new manufacturing businesses in the area. Most of the interest and concern of area developers, particularly those in the non-industrialized regions of the United States, has been focused on branch plants.

The reasons for this are obvious. There is usually little that a development agency can do to help an existing industry grow, unless a special program is set up for the purpose. Such a program is costly, and its results are often disappointing. While there are individual cases where such programs have been productive, most agencies give only lip service to assisting existing industry.

On the other hand, branch plants offer an attractive opportunity to the developer. There are a great many such plants established each year. They are generally sizable, so that a new plant means substantial investment and a significant payroll. Moreover, the construction of such a plant offers dramatic evidence of the industrialization of the area.

The establishment of a new manufacturing enterprise is a special case. Such industrial growth has no institutional framework within which it occurs. No particular agency, public or private, is concerned with the process. Although the development agencies generally list the encouragement of new industry among their functions, most do very little about it. The formation and building of a new company is a long, slow, and often painful process. It is a difficult route to industrial development; and yet, in a free enterprise economy, new business formation is an important element in the total growth process.

As discussed earlier, little is known of the number, kind, or location of new manufacturing firms established in the United States in a year or a decade. Fragmentary information suggests the following general propositions, which cannot, however, be proved. They are:

1. That new manufacturing firms constitute a substantial portion of the new plant locations in the United States.

2. That the manufacturing corporate birth rate is probably higher in the new and in the high-growth-rate industries than it is in the mature, well-established ones.

3. That the birth rate of new manufacturing firms is higher in the faster growing areas and in urban environments.

One guide to the proportion of the total new establishments that represents new firms is the number of small establishments. The detailed data on new locations available from certain of the state development agencies provides

helpful information. These states report the number of new establishments
with fewer than 20 employees included in the total number of new establishments. Analysis of data for these states yields percentages ranging from a
low of 50 percent to a high of 80 percent. It is believed that these small
establishments are predominantly the new firms. If this is so, then these
new firms account for a significant percentage of the total of new locations.

The formation of a new manufacturing firm is presumed to be motivated by
the opportunity for profit. Such a firm is usually based on either a new
product or a new process, on the one hand, or an effort to capitalize on a
local or regional market opportunity, on the other. Certainly, these are the
factors most likely to provide the basis of a successful business. If neither
of these elements is present, the chances of success are poor, although,
through miscalculation, a number of businesses are established when these elements do not exist.

Assuming, however, that the great majority of businessmen able to raise
the capital necessary to start a business have a sound basis to justify that
business, one would expect the concentration to occur in the faster-growing
industries. It is these industries that are characterized by either a new
and expanding technology or a rapidly growing market demand, or both.

Of particular interest to the subject of plant location are those new
companies that successfully capitalize on shifts in the optimum location
from which a particular industry should serve a particular market. In
rapidly growing industries the optimum location can shift significantly over
time. Existing firms are slow to adjust to such changes precisely because
they are established. Although they may ultimately meet the problem through
relocation or branching, new firms can often get started during the resulting
time lag.

There are no available data to show the geographical distribution of new
manufacturing business formations. Theory, cited earlier, suggests that the
industrialized urban area is the logical location for new enterprises, particularly those concerned with new technology. This is further supported by the
clustering of the R & D and associated "intellect-oriented" industries into
a few large urban complexes. Even in market-oriented industry the local market

is larger and denser in urban areas than in outlying areas, even though the
competition is also more severe. In many cases, the importance to a new firm
of the external economies of the environment can be overriding.

Of particular importance to the formation of new enterprises is the
entrepreneur himself. From a location standpoint, he may appear anywhere.
This is the reason that every area is presumed to have a potential for the development of homegrown industry. While some evidence seems to indicate that
the entrepreneur is more numerous in the high-technology and high-growth industries than in others, there is no proof of this. However, he tends to start
his business where he lives. He may fail for the reason that this was a poor
place in which to start such a business, but this will probably not inhibit
him. The fact that more businesses are started in urban areas is probably because more entrepreneurs live there, rather than because of any conscious relocation of such people to what is a better seedbed for new firms.

The manner in which this works out in the newer industries is interesting. The scientist-entrepreneur is attracted to the R & D complexes either
in his graduate study period or to obtain his first job. If he is later
motivated to start a business, he is already in the kind of area needed to
support the activity he wants to undertake.

The importance of entrepreneurship in new business formation cannot be
overestimated. The energy and enthusiasm required to get a business "off the
ground" is a rare and essential ingredient that is not as well understood as
it should be. An area of industrial development activity that has been neglected and that deserves study, understanding, and active support, is what
might be described as the "care and feeding" of the innovator and the entrepreneur.

The importance of this element is particularly notable where the application of new technology is involved. As Bright has pointed out:

> "Many radical innovations, if not most, do not progress until a
> zealot takes over. Stubbornness, persistence, aggressiveness,
> and blind belief are needed to upset traditional concepts. The
> zealot frequently has a personality that makes him a good inno-
> vator but a poor manager."[1]

1/ Bright, Management and Technological Innovation--Technological Change and
Economic Growth (Ref. 16).

The encouragement of manufacturing business births, as well as their survival as successful business enterprises, is an attractive area for research
activity. Over the years, a number of public and private agencies have concerned themselves with this problem, and some interesting experimental programs have been launched. The cumulative experience of these many agencies
could reveal much concerning what can effectively be accomplished in this field.

9

Charles M. Christian and Sari J. Bennett

INDUSTRIAL RELOCATIONS
FROM THE BLACK COMMUNITY OF CHICAGO

SINCE World War II, industrial enterprises have been moving away from core areas of the nation's metropolitan regions in increasing numbers.[1] In the wake of this exodus, large blocks of once highly productive land have been left to less intensive uses, multistory industrial structures have been left to urban blight, and aspiring in-migrants have been left without job opportunities at traditional receiving sites.[2] As a result, burgeoning problems of unemployment, financing the city and its public service functions, weakening of the city's tax base, and problems resulting from the increasing growth of low income populations within the central city have resulted in both city and federal governments' giving high priority to their solution. Furthermore, industrial decentralization is making job sites more inaccessible to residents of the black community and has resulted in lengthened journeys-to-work for a population that can least afford it.[3] Manufacturing firms have traditionally been major employers of central city residents, and numerous problems result from their leaving the city. This preliminary research will describe and analyze the relocation of manufacturing firms and employment opportunities within and from the black community of Chicago. The results confirm earlier findings about industrial relocation in Chicago. In addition, they offer new evidence that some types of relocations can be predicted in terms of direction and distance.

The city of Chicago has experienced an absolute decline in manufacturing employment.[4] From 1947 to 1963, approximately 147,900 jobs in manufacturing were lost from the central city, with the greatest and most consistent decline found within highly concentrated black residential and adjacent areas.[5] The black areas still are losing the major portion of the job opportunities, as is substantiated by Figure 1. The areas that suffered the worst losses during the period 1957-69 were the outer business ring, the south side, the west central area, and the southwest inner city. These areas, with the

exception of the southwest, are predominantly black (see Figure 2). In contrast, areas which gained manufacturing employment during the same period had small proportions of black population.

Our analysis reports only moves of businesses which existed in 1969. We did not analyze businesses which began operations or moved into the black areas after 1969. Any inferences drawn from our data can apply only to the population examined. The reader should note that these are intended only as results of an exploratory study.

The black community is defined here as those postal zip code zones[6] which have populations composed of 30 percent or more black residents.[7] Postal zones rather than smaller areal units such as census tracts were used in our analysis because most published listings of Chicago industry are recorded by such zones; in addition, they are sensitive to population density, generally stable, and territorially inclusive.[8]

Movement Trends

A questionnaire was constructed and mailed to approximately 2,000 firms listed in the *1969 Illinois Manufacturers Directory* for postal zones of the black community. An "address correction requested, return postage guaranteed" stamp was affixed to each envelope to identify firms which had moved. Six hundred twenty-six questionnaires were returned either by firms or by the post office, of which 73.2 percent (458 firms) indicated a change of address or change in business status, such as closure.

Movements and changes of status were classified into six categories: (1) in-zone movements, that is, within the same zip zone; (2) between-zone movements within the black area; (3) between-zone movements to zones outside the black area; (4) movements to suburbs and other areas within the state; (5) out-of-state; and (6) unclassified (movements based on the postal department's responses of "moved—left no address," "addressee unknown," or "out of business"). Table 1 summarizes these movements.

The authors are Ph.D. candidates in the Department of Geography, University of Illinois, Urbana-Champaign.

FIGURE 1. GAINS AND LOSSES OF
MANUFACTURING EMPLOYMENT
BY DISTRICT, CHICAGO, 1957-69

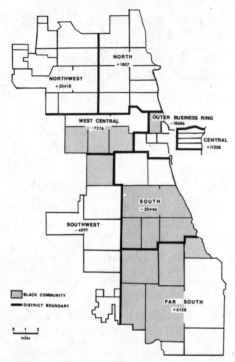

Source: Chicago Area Labor Market Analysis Unit,
"Employment Covered under the Illinois Unemploy-
ment Compensation Act: 1957-1969," (Springfield:
State of Illinois, Department of Labor, 1971).

In-zone movements. Almost 2 percent of the industrial movements affecting the black community were
in-zone. Most of these movements were found on the
outer margin of the black area, particularly in zones 20
and 28. Because these movements involved short distances, it is hypothesized that they are responses to the
need for better site facilities and space, while maintaining labor and market advantages.

Between-zone movements within the black area.
These movements comprised 5.6 percent of the total

TABLE 1. INDUSTRIAL RELOCATIONS
BY TYPE OF MOVEMENT

Type of Movement	Number of Firms
In-zone	9
Between zones within black area	26
Between zones to outside study area	71
To suburban and other areas in Illinois	105
Out of state	26
Unclassified	221
Total	458

movements (see Figure 3). No specific pattern either in
direction or distance emerged in the analysis. In general,
a greater proportion of these movements occurred in the
southern part of the black area. Zone 43 received approximately one-quarter of all between-zone movements
within the black area. Interestingly, zone 43 received all
of its relocated industries from contiguous zones 20 and
28. These industrial relocations involved a movement of
308 jobs and an estimated capitalization of $1.4 mil-
lion.[9] Zone 43 received the bulk of each—22 percent of
the job opportunities and 22 percent of the estimated
capitalization relocating between zones within the black
area.

Between-zone movements from black area. Movements to sites in zones outside the black area comprised
15.8 percent of all moves. These relocations involved
1,705 job opportunities and approximately $8.4 million
in capitalization.

Destinations for these relocated industries were
divided into two general categories: (1) relocations near
or to the central business district (CBD), and (2) relocations to the northern postal zip code zones of the city
(see Figure 4). Twenty-three of the relocations near and
to the CBD were directed to zones 1, 3, 4, 6, 7, and 16.
Origin zones for these relocated firms were primarily
zones 20, 23, and 24.

Outer zones 41, 51, 26, and 34 made up the second
large category of industrial relocation destinations.
These zones received twenty relocations. Origin areas of
these movements were mostly zones 12, 24, and 44,
which supplied sixteen of the relocating firms. Few
industrial firms from the southern portion of the black
area relocated in the northern postal zones of the city.
Further, of the twenty-eight industrial firms which relocated from the southern zones of the black area, only six
chose new locations in northern zones, while the remaining twenty-two relocated in adjacent zones and the CBD
zones. Industrial firms from the western zones of the
black area relocated almost totally in northern zones and
the CBD zones; only two firms relocated in southern
zones.

On the basis of these findings, between-zone industrial
relocations to zones outside the black area tend not only
to be short distance, but also directionally biased; southern firms do not generally move to northern zones, and
western firms show no tendency toward moving to
southern zones within the city. These observations suggest that a firm's distance and direction biases are the
results of the entrepreneur's information field, which
decreases with distance and varies with direction. In
other words, site selection is influenced by knowledge of
adjacent zones rather than by lack of knowledge of more
distant zones within the city.

Movements to suburbs and within the state. Movements to the suburbs and to other cities within the state
were 23 percent of all movements; 93.3 percent of these
moves were to suburban locations and involved a loss of
3,379 jobs and capitalization of approximately $17.8
million from the black community of Chicago.

FIGURE 2. PERCENTAGE BLACK POPULATION
BY POSTAL ZONES, CHICAGO, 1970

Source: U.S. Department of Commerce, Bureau of the
Census, *Census of Population and Housing, 1970, Chicago and Northwestern Indiana Standard Consolidated
Area.* Reproduced by Chicago Association of Commerce
and Industry, 1971.

FIGURE 3. BETWEEN-ZONE MOVEMENTS
WITHIN BLACK AREA, CHICAGO,
1969-71

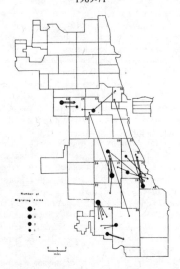

FIGURE 4. BETWEEN-ZONE MOVEMENTS
OUTSIDE BLACK AREA, CHICAGO,
1969-71

FIGURE 5. INDUSTRIAL RELOCATIONS
TO CHICAGO SUBURBS FROM BLACK
AREA, 1969-71

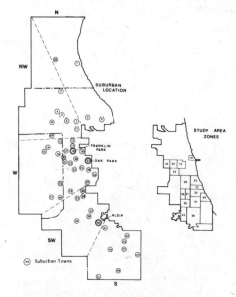

Table 2 and Figure 5 summarize the pattern of relocation to suburban Chicago. Outward movements were
mainly to the western suburbs. This trend does not
coincide with observations by Reinemann, who analyzed

industrial development and movement trends for the
entire Chicago standard metropolitan statistical area
(SMSA) from 1947 to 1954.[10] He concluded, using
similar movement classifications, that the major direc-

FIGURE 6. INDUSTRIAL RELOCATIONS FROM BLACK COMMUNITY OF CHICAGO TO OUT-OF-STATE DESTINATIONS, 1969-71

FIGURE 7. INDUSTRIAL RELOCATIONS, CHICAGO, 1969-71

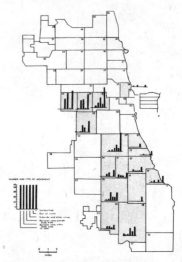

TABLE 2. INDUSTRIAL RELOCATIONS TO THE SUBURBS FROM BLACK AREA OF CHICAGO, 1969-71

	Key [a]	Number of Relocations		Key [a]	Number of Relocations
West			**Southwest**		
Franklin Park	18	7	Alsip	40	10
Oak Park	23	7	Chicago Ridge	38	2
Cicero	26	4	Justice	35	1
Elmhurst	16	3	LaGrange	33	1
Oak Brook	52	3	Oaklawn	37	1
Bellwood	22	3	Palos Hills	39	1
Downers Grove	31	2	Summit	34	1
Hinsdale	46	2	Total		17
Northlake	27	2	**South**		
River Forest	19	2	Hazelcrest	44	3
Rosemont	12	2	South Chicago	48	3
Addison	14	2	Heights	51	2
Berkeley	20	1	Park Forest	41	1
Berwyn	28	1	Blue Island	42	1
Broadview	25	1	Dolton	53	1
Bensenville	13	1	Glenwood	47	1
Forest Park	24	1	Lansing	43	1
Hillside	21	1	South Holland		
Lombard	15	1	Total		13
Melrose Park	30	1	**Northwest**	10	4
Roselle	49	1	Elk Grove Village	7	2
Schiller Park	17	1	Des Plaines	11	2
Lyons	29	1	Park Ridge	5	1
Total		51	Arlington Heights	2	1
North			Barrington	6	1
Skokie	9	2	Mt. Prospect	4	1
Morton Grove	8	1	Palatine		
Lake Forest	1	1	Total		12
Mundelein	50	1			
Total		5			

[a]Refer to Figure 5 for location of suburb.

Source: Based on responses to survey questionnaire mailed to Chicago firms located within the black community. Directional locations of suburbs based on those used by the Bureau of Employment Security, Illinois Department of Labor.

tion of all industrial relocations and new industrial development had been toward the northern and northwestern suburbs immediately adjacent to the city of Chicago. However, in the present analysis of the relocations from the black community, the western suburbs, most particularly Oak Park and Franklin Park, received the highest number of firms. The latter two received about 15 percent of all industrial relocations from the black area. A distance bias is again noted as most firms relocated in suburbs adjacent to the city boundary.

Oak Park received seven of the suburban relocations, four of which were from the adjacent zone 44. The remaining two moves also had their origins in the western portion of the black area, zones 12 and 24. These relocations to Oak Park involved 123 jobs and an estimated capitalization of more than $0.5 million. Franklin Park, also a western suburb, received seven industrial relocations. Three of the seven originated in the proximate zone 44, and four originated in zones 12 and 24. Approximately 743 jobs and a capitalization of $1.55 million were relocated from black areas to Franklin Park. Alsip, a southwestern suburb, received 9.5 percent of the total suburban movements. Total employment opportunities moving to Alsip were 241 and the estimated capitalization was $1.15 million. Four of these moves were from zones 20, 28, and 43, zones within the southern portion of the black area.

The ninety-eight suburban relocations involved fifty suburbs within the Chicago metropolitan area. Other cities in the state that received relocated firms were Joliet, Peoria, Fox River Grove, Benton, Champaign, and Urbana. These movements represented a loss of 478 job opportunities and a capitalization of approximately $0.8 million from the black area.

Out-of-state movements. Approximately 6 percent of the total industrial movements involved relocation from the black area of Chicago to out-of-state locations from 1969 through 1971 (see Figure 6). A total of 1,078 job opportunities and an approximate capitalization of $5.1 million were lost from the black community. Over half (57 percent) of these industrial relocations were to northeastern states. One-third relocated within two neighboring states—Indiana and Ohio—each receiving four relocated firms.

Ohio received 389 jobs, while Indiana received only 15. The estimated capitalization relocating to Ohio from the black community of Chicago was $1.66 million and to Indiana, $0.25 million. Ohio received three firms from zone 9 and one from zone 38 while the origin

TABLE 3. INDUSTRIAL RELOCATIONS BY TYPE OF MOVEMENT AND SIC CLASSIFICATION

Type of Industry	SIC Code	In-Zone	Between Zones within Black Area	Between Zones to Outside Study Area	To Suburban and Other Areas in Illinois	Out of State	Unclassified	Total
Fabricated metals	34	2	1	13	23	5	41	85
Wholesaling	50	2	4	7	16	3	31	63
Chemicals	28	1	8	2	4	1	21	37
Printing and publishing	27	2	8	7	7	1	9	34
Food	20	0	0	6	3	2	18	29
Primary metals	33	0	1	4	6	0	14	25
Electrical machinery	36	1	2	6	7	2	6	24
Personal services	72	0	0	3	2	0	12	17
Miscellaneous	39	0	0	4	0	2	9	15
Lumber and wood	24	0	0	2	2	0	9	13
Rubber and miscellaneous plastics	30	0	0	6	2	0	5	13
Machinery, except electrical	35	0	1	1	7	0	4	13
Scientific instruments	38	0	0	2	3	2	6	13
Furniture	25	0	1	2	1	3	5	12
Apparel	23	0	0	0	4	1	5	10
Miscellaneous repair services	76	0	0	0	0	1	8	9
Paper	26	0	0	0	3	0	5	8
Stone, clay, and glass	32	0	0	3	2	1	2	8
Motor freight transport and warehousing	42	0	0	1	5	0	2	8
Construction	17	0	0	0	1	1	2	4
Petroleum refining	29	1	0	0	3	0	0	4
Textiles	22	0	0	0	1	1	1	3
Leather goods	31	0	0	0	2	0	1	3
Transportation equipment	37	0	0	0	1	0	1	2
Transportation services	47	0	0	2	0	0	0	2
Hotels and lodging	70	0	0	0	0	0	2	2
Educational services	82	0	0	0	0	0	2	2
Total		9	26	71	105	26	221	458

zones for firms moving to Indiana were 28, 20, and 43. Two relocations were made to each of the states of California, North Carolina, Pennsylvania, Tennessee, and Wisconsin; and Florida, Louisiana, Michigan, Minnesota, New Jersey, New York, Oklahoma, and the Virgin Islands received one relocation each.

Unclassified movements. The existence of many unclassified movements tends to reinforce many of the notions presented earlier, specifically the perceived undesirability of the black community for industry. Of the 458 movements, approximately 48 percent were unclassified. Certain zones of the black area tended to have predominant numbers of unclassified movements—zones 12, 9, 44, 24, and 23 (see Figure 7). These zones were characterized as zones of rapid transition from white to black population and at present have a relatively high percentage of black residential population concentration (refer to Figure 3).[11]

Types of Relocating Firms

Industrial relocations, by standard industrial classification (SIC) codes, appear to be predominantly in the lines of fabricated metals, wholesaling, chemicals, and printing and publishing. Because of insufficient data representing the composition of industry existing within each of the zones of the black area, it is difficult to generalize the results of this analysis to all types of potential movers.

An industrial relocation matrix is presented in Table 3. Overall, fabricated metals, wholesaling, chemicals, and printing and publishing appeared to dominate the types of industries relocating within and from the black community. In a previous study of industrial movements it was found that the fabricated metals and electrical and nonelectrical machinery industries displayed the highest number of relocations from the city during the period

1947-57.[1][2] The present analysis suggests that these firms are indeed active in relocating.

Industrial Exodus

Industry and employment opportunities are moving out of the black community in great numbers. Although industrial movements within and from the city of Chicago have been many, industrial firms located in black areas before 1969 have avoided relocations within the zones of high black population, seeming to prefer other zones within the city. The western and southwestern postal zones, from which a majority of the moves were made, may have lost industry because of the influence of riots in 1968. The riots and fires damaged and destroyed many commerical buildings in the areas, and the areas are generally regarded as high risk sections with poor access to transportation. Other forces negative to industry are spreading urban blight, high taxes, and general deterioration of the black community itself.

In the intra-black-community moves which did occur, little order was to be found. In moves to nonblack areas, however, relocation tended to be short distance and in a specific and consistent direction. Firms previously located in western and southern Chicago most often moved to western and southern suburbs; those in the northern and inner city areas tended to favor the northern suburbs and the central business district as their new homes.

. Approximately seven thousand jobs and millions of dollars of capitalization have been lost from black inner city areas as a result of industrial movements during the period 1969-71. This research has been exploratory; a more detailed and complete analysis would likely reveal a larger number of industrial relocations, a larger number of lost job opportunities, and a greatly increased capitalization loss from the black community of Chicago.

FOOTNOTES

1. John F. Kain, "The Distribution and Movement of Jobs and Industry," in *The Metropolitan Enigma,* ed. James Q. Wilson (New York: Doubleday, 1970).

2. Mayor's Committee for Economic and Cultural Development, *Mid-Chicago Economic Study,* vol. 2, *Technical Analysis and Findings* (Chicago: Mayor's Committee, 1966).

3. See John F. Kain, "Housing Segregation, Negro Employment and Metropolitan Decentralization," *Quarterly Journal of Economics,* vol. 82 (May 1968), pp. 175-97; Donald R. Deskins, Jr., "Residence-Workplace Interaction Vectors for the Detroit Metropolitan Area: 1953-1965," *Inter-action Patterns and the Spatial Form of the Ghetto,* Special Publication No. 3 (Evanston, Ill.: Northwestern University, Department of Geography, 1970); and James O. Wheeler, "The Spatial Interaction of Blacks in Metropolitan Areas," *Southeastern Geographer,* vol. 11, no. 2 (November 1971), pp. 101-12.

4. Northeastern Illinois Planning Commission, *Industrial Employment Study* (Chicago: NIPC, 1964).

5. Mayor's Committee for Economic and Cultural Development, *Mid-Chicago Economic Study.*

6. Postal zip code zones were superimposed over census tracts, and the total black-white populations were computed for all census tracts enclosed to derive a percentage black population for each zone.

7. Calculations were based on U.S. Department of Commerce, Bureau of the Census, *Chicago and Northwestern Indiana Standard Consolidated Area: Statistics for Census Tracts,* reproduced by Chicago Association of Commerce and Industry, Research and Statistical Division (Chicago: Chicago Association of Commerce and Industry, 1971). Postal zones of 30 percent or more black residents were used in defining the black community for the following reasons. (1) When black occupancy within an area attains a level of approximately 30 percent, whites discontinue seeking housing in close physical proximity (Harold Rose, "The Development of an Urban Subsystem: The Case of the Negro Ghetto," *Annals of the Association of American Geographers,* vol. 60, no. 1 [March 1970], pp. 1-17). (2) Chicago has the highest racial segregation index of any major U.S. metropolitan city. Over 96 percent of the black population in Chicago live in census tracts of 30 percent or more blacks (Pierre DeVise, "Chicago, 1971: Ready for Another Fire?" in *Geographical Perspectives on American Poverty,* ed. Richard Peet [Worcester, Mass.: Antipode, 1972], pp. 47-66).

8. Ronald Abler, "Zip Code Areas as Statistical Regions," *Professional Geographer,* vol. 22, no. 5 (September 1970), pp. 270-74.

9. Capitalization is the estimated financial appraisal of a firm's capital outlay. This appraisal was estimated by each firm entered in the *Illinois Manufacturers Directory.*

10. Martin W. Reinemann, "The Pattern and Distribution of Manufacturing in the Chicago Area," *Economic Geography,* vol. 36, no. 2 (April 1960), pp. 139-44.

11. Mayor's Committee for Economic and Cultural Development, *Mid-Chicago Economic Study.*

12. City of Chicago, Department of City Planning, *Industrial Movements and Expansions, 1947-1957, City of Chicago and Chicago Metropolitan Area,* Study No. 3 (Chicago: City of Chicago, January 1961).

IV

Metropolitan
Economic Development

10

Niles M. Hansen

DEVELOPMENT POLE THEORY
IN A REGIONAL CONTEXT

I. Introduction

Economic analysis generally has tended to emphasize how much of
a given resource should be allocated to a given end while neglecting
the related issue of where the activity in question shall be located.
Nevertheless, as FRIEDMANN and ALONSO have pointed out, 'the decision of *where* to locate a new project is as important as the decision
to invest in it. The questions of social justice in the distributions of
the fruits of economic development are as important and as difficult
in terms of regions as in terms of social classes[1].

One of the principal difficulties in applying economic analysis to
spatial aspects of public policy has been the highly simplified and
abstract nature of the purely deductive models of classical location
theory[2]. For example, the classical framework assumes that all activities are located on a smooth undifferentiated surface; all considerations of geographic terrain are eliminated. It is further assumed
that a transport surface exists, such that costs of moving a good are
constant for any given distance in any direction. Transport facilities
in all directions, distribution of agricultural population, tastes and
scales of preferences, industrial raw materials, technical knowledge,
and availability of production opportunities are uniform over the
surface. Within this framework activities are allocated by means of
purely market forces. Unfortunately, most contemporary problems
of resource allocation in space necessarily involve complex urban-
industrial growth patterns which are not amenable to treatment in
terms of analysis which make such assumptions and which abstract
from external effects. Thus, RODWIN finds that turning to the traditional theorists for guidance in regional resource allocation problems

1. JOHN FRIEDMANN and WILLIAM ALONSO, 'Introduction', in *Regional Development and Planning*, edited by J. FRIEDMANN and W. ALONSO (Cambridge, The MIT
Press, 1964), p. 1.

2. See, for example, JOHANN H. VON THÜNEN, *Der isolierte Staat in Beziehung
auf Landwirtschaft und Nationalökonomie* (Hamburg, Fr. Derthes, 1826); AUGUST
LÖSCH, *The Economics of Location*, translated by WILLIAM WOLGOM and W. F.
STOLPER (New Haven, Yale University Press, 1954).

'is a disappointing experience since the assistance furnished by them on this topic is relatively meager whereas one might have expected them to be the most helpful'[3]. Similarly, BAUCHET has remarked that the classical approach to location 'has remained liberal; it has not proposed guidelines for action'[4].

As a result of inadequacies in the traditional approach to location problems a new body of thought has emerged in recent years which centers on the notion of development poles *(pôles de croissance)*. This concept was first put forth systematically in a well-known article by PERROUX, who argued that the fundamental fact of spatial, as well as sectoral, development is that 'growth does not appear everywhere and all at once; it appears in points or development poles, with variable intensities; it spreads along diverse channels and with varying terminal effects for the whole of the economy'[5]. Following PERROUX, HIRSCHMAN finds that for an economy to attain higher income levels it 'must and will first develop within itself one or several regional centers of economic strength. This need for the emergence of "growing points" or "growth poles" in the course of the development process means that international and interregional inequality of growth is an inevitable concomitant and condition of growth itself'[6]. This approach likewise is reflected in a recent British study if European regional policies:

> at any one time there will be some industries, firms or regions which, acting as 'poles' of growth, are developing rapidly while others are at a standstill or declining. Conditions of decline—in an industry or in a region—may give rise to... a demand for state intervention. The question as to whether the state should intervene in such circumstances cannot be resolved in purely economic terms; but economic analysis can evaluate the nature of the choice[7].

---

3. LLOYD RODWIN, 'Choosing Regions for Development', in C.J. FRIEDRICH and S. HARRIS, editors, *Public Policy*, XII (1963), p. 149.

4. PIERRE BAUCHET, 'La comptabilité économique régionale et son usage', *Economie appliquée*, XIV (January, 1961), p. 69.

5. FRANÇOIS PERROUX, 'La notion de pôle de croissance', *L'économie du XXème siècle*, second edition (Paris, Presses Universitaires de France, 1964), p. 143. This article originally appeared in *Economie appliquée*, Nos. 1–2 (1955).

6. ALBERT O. HIRSCHMAN, *The Strategy of Economic Development* (New Haven: Yale University Press, 1958), pp. 183–4.

7. POLITICAL AND ECONOMIC PLANNING, *Regional Development in the European Economic Community* (London: Political and Economic Planning, 1962), p. 13.

Although the development pole concept has now come into use in many countries, its relevance as an analytic device and a tool for guiding public policy decisions has continued to receive greatest attention in France. This phenomenon is no doubt largely a consequence of France's unique efforts to create a comprehensive and coherent set of regional planning institutions (including the 21 'program regions' and their respective *préfets* and Regional Economic Development Commissions) and to regionalize the annual budget of the central government. In fact, 'up to the present France is the only European state which has undertaken to create regional institutions on an economic base'[8]. It is now generally accepted in France, as elsewhere, that the central government has the possibility 'to create the bases for equilibrium growth throughout the country... by means of public intervention', as well as the means to bring about 'a balanced division of economic activity among regions'[9]. Unfortunately, these very general aims are not in themselves adequate as policy guidelines since one must specify more carefully what is meant by 'equilibrium growth' throughout a country and a 'balanced distribution of economic activity'. Of course, value judgments concerning more specific variables such as regional income, migration and public investment patterns must to a great extent be taken by the economist as given. Nevertheless, consideration of these issues requires considerable refinement of the highly general notion of a development pole. It is the purpose of this article, therefore, to examine the often ambiguous uses which have been made of this concept, and to evaluate its strengths and weaknesses as a tool of economic analysis.

The development pole concept is also prominent in relevant policy studies of the European Economic Community. See, for example, *La politique régionale dans la Communauté Economique Européenne* (Brussels, Communauté Economique Européenne, 1964), pp. 46, 73.

8. J. F. GRAVIER, *L'aménagement du territoire et l'avenir des régions françaises* (Paris: Flammarion, 1964), p. 127. Unfortunately, detailed consideration of these institutions is beyond the scope of the present article. In this regard, however, there exist a number of good sources. See, for example: JACQUES DE LANVERSIN, *L'aménagement du territoire* (Paris: Librairies Techniques, 1965), and OLIVIER GUICHARD, *Aménager la France* (Paris, Laffont-Gonthier, 1965).

9. P. POTTIER, 'Axes de communication et théorie de développement', *Revue économique*, XIV (January, 1963), p. 128.

II. Development Poles and Economic Space

Although the theory of development poles may be useful in examining and comparing differing consequences of alternative choices of location, it is not in itself strictly speaking a theory of location. Thus, a development pole is not equivalent to a key industry, an economic base, an industrial zone, or even some geographically concentrated phenomenon. Rather, it should be interpreted in its essentially economic and functional sense[10]. To fully appreciate this perspective it is necessary to place PERROUX's original article on development poles in the context of his somewhat earlier work on economic space.

PERROUX's concept of economic space should not be confused with simple location as defined by geographical or political divisions. 'A banal sense of space location creates the illusion of the coincidence of political space with economic and human space'; but by distinguishing between Euclidean and abstract space 'we may distinguish in our discipline as many economic spaces as there are constituent structures of abstract relations which define each object of economic science.' For PERROUX, there are three types of economic space: economic space as defined by a plan, economic space as a field of forces, and economic space as a homogeneous aggregate. Moreover, in each case it is quite clear that PERROUX's analysis centers on complex economic relations rather than on specifically geographical considerations. In particular, the second type, that which is most relevant in the present context, 'consists of centres (or poles or foci) from which centrifugal forces emanate and to which centripetal forces are attracted. Each centre being a centre of attraction and repulsion, has its proper field, which is set in the field of other centres'[11].

In contrast to PERROUX's non-geographical orientation is BOUDEVILLE's emphasis on the regional character of economic space. Following PERROUX, BOUDEVILLE maintains that from an economic viewpoint there are three types of space: homogeneous, polarized, and program, or planning, space. Thus, in the first instance a region

10. JEAN PAELINCK, 'La théorie du développement régional polarisé'. *Cahiers de l'Institut de Science Economique Appliquée*, Série L, No. 15 (March, 1965), pp. 10–11.

11. FRANÇOIS PERROUX, 'Economic Space: Theory and Applications', *Quarterly Journal of Economics*, LXIV (February, 1950), pp. 90–7.

can be characterized by its degree of uniformity; the notion of a homogeneous region corresponds to a continuous space wherein each of the constituent parts or zones has relevant characteristics as close as possible to those of the others. In the second case a region can be studied in the light of the degree of interdependence of its diverse parts. Polarized space is closely related to the notion of a hierarchy of urban centers ranked according to the functions they perform; a polarized region is a heterogeneous space whose different parts complement and support one another and where they have more exchange of goods and services with a dominant intraregional urban center, or pole, than with neighboring regions. Finally, a region can be envisaged from the point of view of the aims which it pursues. Thus, the planning, or program, region is a space whose various parts depend upon the same decision; in addition, it is an instrument placed in the hands of an authority, not necessarily localized in the region, to attain a given economic goal[12]. The fact that the twenty-one geographic units which have been created in France for regional planning purposes are termed *régions de programme* is no mere coincidence, since government policy in this regard is generally associated with the corresponding theoretical concept. BOUDEVILLE himself has explicitly made this connection[13]. In general, then, although BOUDEVILLE (and others) adopts PERROUX's terminology he gives it a more concrete usage by maintaining that the theory of economic space 'is the application of a mathematical space on or in a geographic space'[14]. However, any evaluation of this approach first requires consideration of another aspect of development pole theory, namely, the concept of dominance.

III. Economic Dominance and the Process of Polarization

The concept of dominance, like the related concept of development poles, marks a key element in PERROUX's general effort to provide a

12. JACQUES BOUDEVILLE, *Les espaces économiques* (Paris: Presses Universitaires de France, 1961), pp. 8–16.
13. *Ibid.*, p. 16.
14. JACQUES BOUDEVILLE, 'Les notions d'espace et d'intégration', Paper given at the International Congress for Town and Regional Planning, Basle, Switzerland, September 22–25, 1965, p. 2.

dynamic interpretation of economic activity. For PERROUX, the effect of domination 'consists of an irreversible or partially reversible influence exercised by one unit upon another. An economic unit exercises this effect by reason of its dimension, its negociating strength, the nature of its activity, or because it belongs to a zone of dominant activity.' The effect of domination has both a purely economic dimension, abstracted from considerations of geographic space, and a spatial dimension. At the level of the firm this effect may exist between production and consumption units, or between differing production units. Domination occurs when 'a firm controls an abstract economic space, the market for a product or a service or a group of products or services'. Moreover, a firm 'exercising its control in one economic space exercises its influence on another economic space, either in a permanent and structural manner (a commercial bank), or in an accidental fashion (a firm becomes dominant by the presence of temporary bottlenecks)[15]. In addition, 'as soon as any inequality among firms appears, the breach is opened by which the cumulative effect of domination insinuates itself'[16]. Given these phenomena, it follows that the dominant, or propulsive, firm generally will be oligopolistic and large, and will exert an important influence on the activities of suppliers and clients. Moreover, in terms of geographic space dominant and propulsive industries make the agglomerations where they are located the poles of their regions[17].

The concept of dominance does in fact have a corresponding empirical counterpart. AUJAC, for example, has developed a model which orders French sectors in input-output form in such a manner that relatively large intermediate demands are situated below the principal diagonal, whereas those which are relatively weak are situated above it. This triangularization of the matrix is carried out by the criterion of the best customer. If A_{ij} represents sales from industry i to industry j and A_{ji} the converse, then j is said to dominate i if $(A_{ij}/P_i) > (A_{ji}/P_j)$, where P_i and P_j are, respectively, the total sales of i and j. On the basis of such calculations a hierarchy is established in which each sector dominates the one which follows[18].

15. PERROUX, *L'économie du XXe siècle*, *op.cit.*, pp. 85–7.
16. *Ibid.*, p. 40.
17. *Ibid.*, p. 152.

However, the difficulties involved in any straight-forward application of the national pattern of flows on a regional level would be
considerable. Depending on the number and magnitude of interregional linkages, which are certain to be very great for areas such
as those of the French program regions, many interindustry linkages will pass to the 'rest of the world'. Links between local production and local consumption, as well as the effects of investment
on employment, would require a great deal of special attention.
Moreover, the prospects for effectively utilizing interregional matrices are not bright. As RODWIN has aptly remarked, 'the neglect
of price effects, the difficulty of getting data for these models, the
vastly increased computational problems which regional break-
downs entail coupled with the egregious simplifications of industry
categories and the unrealistic linearity assumptions makes one skepti-
cal of the immediate, not to mention the long term usefulness of this
instrument'[19]. In general, then, while the notion of dominance has
been given empirical verification for the structure of industry in a
nation as a whole, it is not now operationally feasible to regionalize
or otherwise give spatial content to the national model.

Nevertheless, the problem of analyzing the role of dominant sectors as localized development poles need not be limited to input-
output techniques. Indeed, it can be argued that these would not
be sufficient in any event, even if the purely technical difficulties involved in their preparation and utilization could be overcome. Input-output data are incapable in themselves of explaining the process of economic development, though they may aid in giving insights into its manifestations. Therefore, if it may be assumed that
the economic development of a region generally is related to its degree of industrialization, it is necessary to examine more carefully
the process of change in industrial interdependencies. Systematic

18. H. AUJAC, 'La hiérarchie des industries dans un tableau des échanges
interindustriels, et ses conséquences dans la mise en œuvre d'un plan national
décentralisé', *Revue économique*, XI (May, 1960), pp. 169–238.
19. RODWIN, *op. cit.* pp. 150–1. Even on a national level, 'the precision of the
input-output table in a medium sized economy like France, more and more open
to foreign markets, actually seems questionable'. SYLVAN WICKHAM, 'French
Planning: Retrospect and Prospect', *Review of Economics and Statistics*, XLV (November, 1963), p. 340.

study of these linkages and their evolution under different conditions is required if regional policy is to have the means for initiating and reinforcing optimal growth patterns. As PAELINCK has stated, it is not enough for the economist working on regional development problems to limit analysis to 'the classical interdependencies (of either the Walras- or Leontief-type) of economic flux, whether in quantity or in value terms. He must be able, in addition, to recognize the *technical origin* of this interdependence, which explains its ever-increasing complexity'[20].

It will be recalled that the concepts of economic space and development poles have been defined in terms of abstraction from concrete spatial location and in terms of geographical areas. The dominance of a propulsive industry has been treated similarly. PERROUX's view of the growth process is consistent with his theory of economic space in that the industry remains his point of departure and the essential element in subsequent development. AYDALOT has correctly maintained that while PERROUX sometimes 'seems to study the localization of the growth process, in fact this localization seems secondary to him' since 'the primary phenomenon is "the appearance and disappearance of industries", "the diffusion of the growth of an industry"[21]'.

The effects generated by a propulsive industry which qualify it as a development pole have been explored in theory by a number of writers. Some of these effects are internal to the industry itself; that is, its own growth generates increased investment, employment, and distribution of factor payments, including profits which may be retained and reinvested. The internal growth of an industry also generates numerous external effects; vertically and horizontally induced effects of course may be dealt with in the framework of input-output matrices. The effects of polarization may be further examined theoretically by the application of appropriate matrices or vectors to the initial Leontief-type matrix. Among the phenomena which have been explored in this context are the classic Keynesian multiplier based on marginal propensities to consume applied to income increases, the accelerator principle in connection with change in

20. PAELINCK, *op. cit.*, p. 8.

21. PHILIPPE AYDALOT, 'Note sur les économies externes et quelques notions connexes', *Revue économique*, XVI (November, 1965), p. 962.

final demand, and the interplay of prices among related sectors and enterprises[22].

Despite some differences of emphasis, three basic characteristics of a propulsive industry (or firm) emerge from the relevant literature. First, it must be relatively large in order to assume that it will generate sufficient direct and potentially indirect effects to have a significant impact on the economy; second, it must be a relatively fast growing sector; and third, the quantity and intensity of its interrelations with other sectors should be important so that a large number of induced effects will in fact be transmitted.

The importance of bigness, first emphasized by PERROUX, has been equally stressed in subsequent writings of other scholars. BAUCHET, for example, writes that the growth of an underdeveloped region depends upon the actions of large economic units. 'Their mass alone is capable of starting the region on the path to economic growth[23].' Similarly, DAVIN maintains that 'the principal poles are found in heavy, highly capitalized industry, and are the domain of large firms; it is essentially a matter of metallurgy involving special types of steel, metal manufacturing industries using the most evolved possible products, chemistry, and activities destined to furnish products for which the demand is in fundamental expansion'[24]. Thus, 'the multiplicity of small firms of small dimension, working in dispersed fashion, without relying on a few large firms, is not of a nature to set in motion a truly dynamic regional economy'[25]. Nevertheless, as will be discussed shortly, the notion of industrial bigness is not without difficulties in this regard. On the other hand, it is reasonable to assume that a propulsive firm or industry should be rapidly grow-

---

22. See, for example, JACQUES BOUDEVILLE, 'La région plan', *Cahiers de l'Institut des Science Economique Appliquée*, Série L, No. 9 (October, 1961); FRANÇOIS PERROUX, 'La firme motrice dans une région, et la région motrice', *Ibid.*, pp. 192–241; JEAN PAELINCK, *op.cit.;* and LOUIS DAVIN, *Economie régionale et croissance* (Paris, Editions Génin, 1964), pp. 54–72.

23. PIERRE BAUCHET, *Les tableaux économiques, analyse de la région lorraine* (Paris, Génin, 1955), p. 10. Another discussion of development poles maintains that in the initiation of growth in a region the role of large industrial ensembles is capital'. L. E. DAVIN, L. DEGEER and J. PAELINCK, *Dynamique économique de la région liègoise* (Paris, Presses Universitaires de France, 1959), p. 156.

24. DAVIN, *op.cit.*, p. 56.

25. *Ibid.*, p. 64.

ing. However, when it comes to the third criterion, that of inter-relations with other sectors, several problems may be raised.

AYDALOT has argued that all things considered, the most simple definition which may be given of a propulsive industry is that it is a producer of external economies[26]. Here again, though, the question must be posed as to what kind of economic space is involved. AYDA-LOT is quite correct in pointing out that *a priori* the concept of polari-zation does not imply geographic concentration. Polarization 'is the process by which the growth of an economic activity termed pro-pulsive sets in motion that of other economic activities by the chan-nel of external economies'[27]. But this process takes place in abstract economic space. Thus, although a propulsive industry certainly must have a location in geographic space, the *process* of polarization is not amenable to unambiguous geographic location.

Proceeding from his definition of the polarization process, AYDA-LOT points out that the automobile industry is an example of a pro-pulsive industry, and that the Régie Renault provides an example of a propulsive firm. In view of its world-wide affiliates on both input and output sides, one can say that Renault is a pole whose center is Paris and whose periphery embraces most of the world. However, this denies an autonomous spatial existence to the pole. Thus, al-though one may understand why Renault is an industrial pole, it is not apparent that this makes Paris a geographic pole[28]. Moreover, contrary to the approach taken by many writers, the propulsive industry is not necessarily the causal agent in the polarization pro-cess. To say that a given area constitutes a growth pole because of the agglomerating power of its propulsive industries does not explain why these industries are themselves located in this area; the spatial pole also has a causal role in the location of propulsive industries. In other words, even if propulsive industries do induce other activi-ties, they constitute only one link in the process of industrial-geo-graphic polarization since they too are induced. Therefore any ade-quate treatment of this phenomenon should take account of the pronounced tendency for industrial growth to be oriented primarily toward already industrialized areas because of the external econo-

26. AYDALOT, op. cit., p. 963.
27. *Ibid.*, p. 964.
28. *Ibid.*

mies which the latter generate, including a wide range of tertiary services, close proximity to buyers and suppliers, labor with necessary skills and training, and plentiful public overhead capital. Of course, this also implies that insofar as a central government has a regional policy, external economies which it provides directly (public overhead capital) or indirectly (tax and credit policy) can be used to modify economic growth along lines consistent with policy objectives[29].

IV. A Critique of Development Pole Theory

One of the basic common denominators in the development pole literature is the idea that the process of economic growth has its origin and continuing stimulus as a result of big industrial undertakings, a notion which derives from the theory of dominance. Some of the more naively enthusiastic interpretations of the theory would maintain that to generate economic growth in a region it is merely necessary to establish a large firm or several large firms, preferably in a relatively fast growing industry. The fact that bigness alone is not sufficient in this regard is well illustrated by the case of the steel industry in Lorraine. The development of this industry was not accompanied by a corresponding development of industries consuming steel. As a result, Lorraine became highly dependent upon exterior sources of supply for machinery and other equipment. Despite the existence of coal mines, energy sources, transportation facilities and markets in close proximity to the steel complex, it would appear on the basis of input-output data that only a very small part of regional steel output was consumed in the region. Thus, there exists the paradox of relatively weakly developed industry existing side by side with conditions highly favorable to industrial location[30].

29. For more detailed evidence and discussion concerning these issues see the following articles by the present author: 'Regional Planning in a Mixed Economy', *Southern Economic Journal*, XXXII (October, 1965), pp. 176–90; 'The Structure and Determinants of Local Public Investment Expenditures', *Review of Economics and Statistics*, XLVII (May, 1965), pp. 150–62; 'Unbalanced Growth and Regional Development', *Western Economic Journal*, IV (Fall, 1965), pp. 3–14; 'Some Neglected Factors in American Regional Development Policy: The Case of Appalachia', *Land Economics*, LXII (February, 1966), pp. 1–9.

30. PAELINCK, *op. cit.*, pp. 12–13; BAUCHET, *Les tableaux économiques, op. cit.*, pp. 58–59.

As PAELINCK has emphasized, 'the facts do not indicate that one may consider any isolated industrial implantation as a necessarily efficient development pole, by which effective polarization relations, technical or otherwise, are produced'[31].

The type of development which characterized the Lyon region provides a striking contrast to the experience in Lorraine:

> Parting from an economy based essentially on textiles, the Lyon region progressively developed the construction of machines for the textile industry (a derived pole) and, by induction, specialized mechanical and foundry sectors (lateral pole). At the same time, there developed an industry producing chemical products for the textile industry, which in turn stimulated the chemical sector in general; the latter became a lateral development pole of the greatest importance for the region[32].

It should be pointed out, however, that even where the complexity of the functional conditions for successful implantation of a potentially propulsive industry are fully appreciated, there may still be a tendency to be overoptimistic about the chances for success. For example, HIRSCHMAN's growth theory is quite similar to development pole theory as it has been elaborated in France and Belgium, especially in its emphasis on unbalanced growth in relation to the polarization process. HIRSCHMAN remarks that public investment policies 'can be counted upon to stage at least an attempt to heal the split' between regional economic levels. One approach would be to give poorer regions as good an infrastructure system as exists in more advanced areas; however, according to HIRSCHMAN, this may not be the most efficient way of inducing growth because lack of sufficient entrepreneurship may well mean that the purely permissive nature of this approach will not be exploited. Therefore, although some infrastructure investment may be required, the 'essential task' is to endow poorer regions 'with some ongoing and actively inducing economic activity' of their own. Among the government development moves which he believes may be effective in this respect are the building of a steel mill in Columbia's Oriente and the founding of Brazil's new capital in that nation's interior[33]. Nevertheless, although such activities have considerable potential as development

31. PAELINCK, *op. cit.*, p. 13.
32. *Ibid.*
33. HIRSCHMAN, *op. cit.*, pp. 194–5.

poles, their induced effects only will become active in the presence of already existing external economies. Of course, HIRSCHMAN would maintain that a pronounced need for the latter, made evident by the introduction of a propulsive activity, is in fact just what is needed to generate their appearance. However, the evidence thus far in this regard is not impressive. AYDALOT has pointed out correctly that 'development theory has tried to integrate the theory of development poles, but without great success. Indeed, the great complexes of "propulsive industries" which have been set up in certain African countries have not, in most cases, fulfilled this role'[34]. The difficulties confronting newly developing countries in this regard also apply to problems of regional development in more developed countries, even though the latter have external economies not found to the same degree in the former. The case of Lorraine already has been cited. An even better illustration of this point is provided by the case of Lacq, in Southwestern France.

The discovery of large natural gas deposits at Lacq aroused great hopes that industrialization of the relatively undeveloped Southwest would be assured by the presence of this energy source. In fact, 'the Lacq complex corresponds perfectly well to the definition that F. PERROUX has given of propulsive industries (assymetric effects, rate of growth superior to the national average)'[35]. A British study stressed not only the potential opportunities presented by the Lacq discovery, but also treated its regional significance as a development pole as an accomplished fact[36]. In reality, however, the Lacq complex has been essentially a local phenomenon which has done little to modify the general economic situation of the Southwest. Because of the presence of vastly greater external economies in other regions it generally has been more economical to transport the gas to already industrialized areas than to create new industry around Lacq. Thus, GUGLIELMO is correct in remarking that:

It remains to be seen if the indicative planning of liberal economies is capable of resolving the problem of the industrialization of depressed rural regions. The 'Cassa di Mezzogiorno' has not succeeded in creating the basis for regional

34. AYDALOT, op. cit., pp. 967–8.

35. AYDALOT, 'Etude sur le processus de polarisation et sur les réactions des industries anciennes à la lumière de l'expérience de Lacq', Cahiers de l'Institut de Science Economique Appliquée, Série L, No. 15 (March, 1965), p. 111.

36. POLITICAL AND ECONOMIC PLANNING, op. cit., p. 51.

industrial development in southern Italy. Indeed, the only new industries which have located in these regions are extractive industries or highly automated basic industries (petroleum refineries, chemical plants) which employ few persons and are scarcely capable of producing the multiplier effect which people sometimes expect, as is illustrated by the example of Lacq, whose complex remains isolated in the countryside[37].

If the stimulating effects on general regional growth resulting from the location of 'propulsive' industries often have been over-estimated, so have the importance of both bigness and industry. BOUDEVILLE, for example, considers that on a European scale Denmark just fulfills the minimum requirements with respect to area, population and income in order to qualify as an 'independent' region[38]. Yet the prosperity of this region was not initiated and has not been sustained by a big, propulsive industry, but rather by scattered (through cooperating) and relatively small agricultural units.

Moreover, even if a propulsive industry is considered as being as much an effect of the polarization process as a cause of it, it is clear that development pole theory has not given a satisfactory general explanation of the agglomerating process. As VERNON has shown, the industries which are most attracted by the external economies generated by large urban areas are not characterized by a highly oligopolistic structure, but are rather industries with numerous small and medium sized firms which are highly dependent upon auxiliary business services and which need frequent direct personal contacts with buyers and sellers[39].

Another difficulty with development pole theory is that its regional policy criteria have not been explicitly related to the goals which are often sought in practice. For example, DAVIN poses the following question: From the viewpoint of political economy, what is the nature of the principal polarizing activities (active or potential), and how can the flux among these poles be created or increased? In response, he maintains that the industries or industrial sectors which are most favorable to regional growth (defined as a

37. RAYMOND GUGLIELMO, 'Géographie active de l'industrie', in: *La géographie active* (Paris, Presses Universitaires de France, 1964), pp. 223–4.

38. JACQUES BOUDEVILLE, *Les programmes économiques* (Paris, Presses Universitaires de France, 1963), pp. 80–2.

39. RAYMOND VERNON, *The Changing Economic Function of the Central City* (New York, Committee for Economic Development, 1959), pp. 28–37.

significant increase in the flux of products and of revenues) are those where: (1) the value-added per worker is the highest or most likely to increase; (2) the foreseeable increase in production indicates an accelerated rate of expansion, and where technological progress is the most rapid and the most probable; (3) the process of automation or semi-automation can be most easily applied; (4) the flux of products and of services with the development poles are most intense; and (5) the constitution of large production units is achieved most easily, since these units are capable of releasing a maximum of induced reactions and of realizing a maximum of technical and commercial productivity[40].

However, these criteria are not related to specific policy objectives. Is the 'increase in flux of products and of revenues' supposed to increase hourly earnings of workers, annual income per employed inhabitant, the number of persons employed, or some other possible regional variables? The emphasis which is put upon automation and high worker productivity would conflict with what is perhaps the most generally sought after goal of regional policies, namely, increased employment opportunities. Even if one adds, for example, the goal of increased earning power per employed inhabitant, it is not clear that these criteria would guarantee success. The outcome in this regard would depend in large measure upon the extent to which induced effects actually are localized in the region in question. If regional policy is to aim for increased flux in economic activity, then opportunity cost considerations would lead to implanting firms or industries characterized by DAVIN's criteria in already advanced regions, where they could benefit from relatively large external economies. On the other hand, if these firms or industries are established in lagging regions the flux may be dissipated as a result of linkages with other regions. A particular difficulty in this regard would be income flows to owners of capital who reside outside of the region; lagging regions generally would not be the type to furnish the savings required for investment in the big, capital intensive undertakings described by DAVIN.

Finally, it should be emphasized that development pole theory is badly in need of a thorough semantic reworking; the concepts and the language which characterize it need more precise definition and

40. DAVIN, *op. cit.*, p. 57.

more consistent usage. The very notion of a development pole is still used in contradictory ways. Thus, DAVIN states that 'the idea of a development pole is made more precise by that of a propulsive industry *(industrie motrice)* and a key industry *(industrie clef)*. The first engenders activities in other industries, either suppliers or clients for merchandise or services; the second determines the increase of maximum activity[41].' PAELINCK, on the other hand, states that:

> The development pole concept often has been misunderstood. It has been confused with the notions of key industry, basic industry, and industrial ensemble; from this follows the erroneous conception according to which the development pole would be an industrial monument raised to the glory of future regional industrialization, a guarantee of certain economic growth. Or again... some would have as a development pole any important establishment of firms, preferably industrial, which would exercise beneficial effects on the geographic area where it is located[42].

A great deal of semantic confusion arises because the same nominal concepts are employed in the context of abstract, non-geographic space, at other times in the context of certain more or less well defined geographic areas, and at yet other times in a fashion which indiscriminately mingles abstract and geographic space in the same context. Of course, a scholar should be free to define his terms of discourse provided that he then proceeds to employ them in a systematic and consistent manner. Too often, however, articles in the development pole literature define (no matter how vaguely) essential concepts and then bring in references to nominally identical concepts from other articles which, unfortunately, have been defined or used in a different manner. Even this would not be objectionable if the various definitions or usages were contrasted critically or otherwise differentiated, but this is rarely the case. In general, then, greater emphasis on conceptual clarity is needed if development pole theory is to provide tools for more operationally feasible regional development models.

On the positive side, it may be said that development pole theory still represents a potentially promising effort to come to grips with the complexity of the process by which economic growth is initiated and sustained, a process which too frequently has been treated in oversimplified terms. In particular, the theory's main concepts—

41. *Ibid.*, p. 56.
42. PAELINCK, *op. cit.*, pp. 10–11.

development poles, propulsive firms and industries, dominance, etc. —are correctly posited on the assumption that economic growth is basically unbalanced. Moreover, even if the emphasis which has been given to heavy industry and to bigness has been overdrawn, these factors undoubtedly are relevant to many situations involving the stimulation of economic growth.

Perhaps the best approach to development pole theory as applied to regional problems is that given by PAELINCK, who proposes that it be regarded as 'a *conditional* theory of regional growth; it is valuable chiefly to the extent that it clearly indicates the conditions under which accelerated regional development can occur'[43]. Of course, this conditional approach implies that the relevance of the theory to concrete regional cases must be judged on the basis of the nature and prospects of the particular regions, or types of regions, in question. Thus, the policy implications of the disequilibria involved in the growth process, and the various and complex ways in which growth may be transmitted (or inhibited) may vary from place to place and over time for any given place. Further progress in relevant theoretical refinements and classifications therefore will probably depend upon the extent to which they are associated with systematic empirical studies of growth at the regional level. France's new system of regional planning institutions and the regionalization of the government's budget should provide unique opportunities in this regard. For example, French regional policy is now giving priority to eight 'métropoles d'équilibre', primarily in the form of increased promotion of infrastructure and tertiary activities, in order to balance the growth of the Paris region and to create provincial development poles. This means, of course, that the polarization process is being treated increasingly in terms of external economies rather than more direct means to attract industry, e.g., investment subsidies, and that industrial growth is being regarded increasingly as an effect, as well as a cause, of economic development. Thus, French regional planning experience should provide valuable data in the near future for refining the theory of rational spatial resource allocation to which French economists have so largely contributed.

University of Kentucky   NILES M. HANSEN

43. *Ibid.*, p. 47, The emphasis is PAELINCK's.

11

Edward L. Ullman

THE NATURE OF CITIES RECONSIDERED

ARE CITIES REALLY NECESSARY?...or even farms, for that matter? Recent trends prompt one almost to raise this question or at the least to ask what kind. This does not necessarily mean that most people will live nowhere and do nothing (but it might help!). Cities have been growing in size, expanding even more in area, and declining in overall density. Analysis of these developments will bring up to date some of "The Nature of Cities" written in 1944[1], which emphasized, among other facets, that "The support of a city depends on the services it performs not for itself but for a tributary area. Many activities merely serve the population of the city itself." In this presentation the degree to which a city actually is "supported" by performing services for itself will be measured and related to the size and growth of cities. The second and larger part of this study will analyze the expansion of urban areas and bring up to date the increasing importance of the "Multiple Nuclei" concept of urban structure first suggested in the earlier study.

THE GROWTH OF CITIES

Not only is rural and much small town population declining absolutely, but the very largest cities appear to be increasing more rapidly than any others. Actual figures for relative growth of metropolitan areas in the U.S. between 1950 and 1960, however, indicate that small and large have all grown about the same in terms of percentage increase. Rates are: over 3,000,000, 23% increase; 1,000,000 to 3,000,000, 25%; 500,000 to 1,000,000, 36% increase (the largest); 100,000 to 500,000, 26%. Still other groupings indicate about the same.

---

[1] Chauncy D. Harris and Edward L. Ullman, "The Nature of Cities", *Annals of the American Academy of Political and Social Sciences*, Nov. 1945, pp. 7–17.

However, if the absolute amount of growth is allocated by groups still another interpretation can be made. For example, the five cities over 3,000,000 had an absolute increase of about 5,000,000. The second group also had an increase of about 5,000,000, but this was spread out over 16 cities. The next smaller groups had about 5,000,000 increase but the increase was distributed over still more cities. Thus an increasing quantity of U. S. population was concentrated on the average in each of the largest cities. This, then, is presumably the justification for emphasizing metropolitan growth.

If, in general, each of the largest cities on the average have been growing somewhat more, what is the explanation? No pat answer is possible but the following three factors may be involved: (1) Mere size attracts size—a mass, gravity effect; the larger the center the more innovators, the more persons who have relatives and friends who are attracted as in-migrants, etc. (2) The external economies of larger centers provide a greater range of interdependent specialities and facilities. (3) A relative improvement in internal, urban transit has occurred, primarily because of the short haul advantages of the auto and truck; this latter factor has been particularly significant in the expansion of urban area. Leon Moses suggests that the truck allows suburban factories to develop and thus enables the metropolitan area now to compete with outlying regions by providing not only relatively cheap land, but also urban nearness and access to the scale economies just noted.

All three of these forces presumably are given greater scope to influence growth because of the well known shift from primary, to secondary, and particularly to tertiary activities—toward more processing and consequent lesser orientation of production to resource locations.

SCALE ECONOMIES

What is the evidence for the scale economy factor, which has been mentioned so much recently by Vernon, Hoover, and others? In this connection some new findings will be advanced, indicating the degree to which a city is self-contained—takes in its own washing, if you please—which varies according to size and other particulars.

According to studies which Michael Dacey and I, and others, have made using what we call the "Minimum Requirements" method, there is, on the average, a definite relationship between size of a city and its degree of self-containment.[2] (Figure 1) Thus, towns of 10,000 have about one-third of their employment serving internal needs and two-thirds external, for an Export-Internal or Basic-Service ratio of about 1:.5; cities of 500,000 are about evenly divided, one-half internal, one-half external, etc.

This exponential relationship also fits approximately other logical relationships. When extended downward it crosses 0% at about four persons, where it should according to logic, since a family unit can sell nothing to itself;

---

[2] Edward L. Ullman and Michael F. Dacey, "The Minimum Requirements Approach to the Urban Economic Base," *Papers and Proceedings of the Regional Science Association*, Vol. 6, 1960, pp. 175-94.

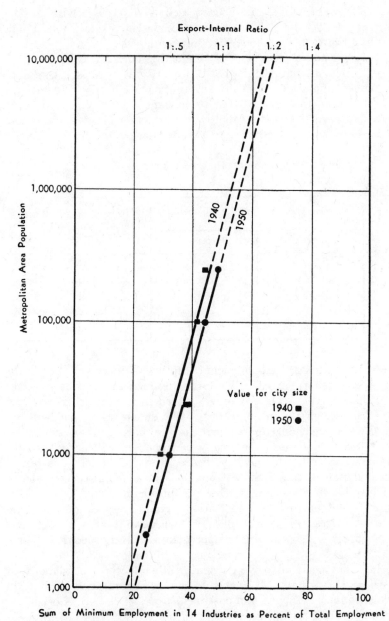

FIGURE 1. Association of Internal (Service or non-Basic) Employment with City Size. based on Minimum Requirements Method.

when extrapolated upward, a more dubious procedure, it crosses within about 10% of the expected for the United States population, as a whole, if one assumes the United States to be about 90% self-contained.

If this relationship holds, then the only deduction one can make about the optimum size of cities is that the larger cities are, the more self-contained they are. By extension, on the basis of this measure *alone*, we tentatively conclude that the larger the city, the more efficient it is, since it can trade more with itself and save transport costs to and from other places. We cannot say there is an optimum size, other than that the larger the better, by this measure.

The following table indicates some other measures of the gain:

City Size	Approximate % Total Employment		Approximate % of "Remaining" External Employment "Captured" by Increasing City Size Ten-Fold
	Internal	External	
1,000	21	79	—
10,000	32	68	14
100,000	43	57	16
1,000,000	54	46	19
10,000,000	65	35	24

Thus the amount of "external" employment "captured" increases, but is the increase really proportionate in effective terms to increase in size of city? For example, is there more "scale economy" gained in increasing from 10,000 to 100,000 than from 1,000,000 to 10,000,000? We do not know and will not know until we know a great deal more about the workings of urban economies.

In any event it does not mean that many metropolises will become multi-million population centers in the next 50 years, first for the obvious reason that the total population of the U. S. will not be large enough to accommodate many, and secondly because many activities are top hierarchical, one-of-a-kind functions—national headquarters, United Nations, etc. They cannot pyramid in numerous cities. Does the latter consideration mean that one city, New York, (or two or three) will become the super giants, as Haig speculated some years ago?[3]

In considering this possibility we encounter other factors—persistence of some resource orientation, whether it be the old ones of minerals and agriculture or the newer role of resort climate, and possible *diseconomies* of scale, or simple lack of scale economies in a significant number of activities, as in government. Foremost among the diseconomies today *may* be environmental limitations—increasing cost of controlling air, and secondly water pollution from large

---

[3] R. M. Haig, Toward an Understanding of the Metropolis: "Some Speculations Regarding the Economic Basis of Urban Concentration," *Quarterly Journal of Economics*, XL (1926), 179–208.

concentrations, although future technology may alter this in unknown ways.[4]

Still other forces are at work in individual cities, as the rapid growth of aviation and electronics centered in the attractive climate of Los Angeles which in turn grows as a second center of the U. S. in its own, somewhat protected, western territory. With the small number of giant cities over 5,000,000 (3 in the U. S.) it is impossible to single out one common force more important than the individual influences at work on each of the cities. To a lesser degree this is true also of the 19 cities from 1,000,000 to 5,000,000, which range from Dallas to Seattle to Philadelphia. The individual differences outweigh the similarities, but the scale economy factor would appear to be an underlying force of varying magnitude. Just how this operates and the magnitude of the effect of increasing size, now and in the future, is an explicit question needing further research.

THE INTERNAL EXPANSION OF URBAN AREAS

As our cities grow in size paradoxically their overall densities appear to decline. Suburbs and satellites boom, some fringe areas are by-passed, blight produces a gray area around most of the closer-in parts of central cities, and downtowns decline. This unsettles land values and existing tax bases and alarms powerful groups. The central cities are particularly hit because most of them are unable to expand their city limits. Some conclude that cities are therefore suffering from some unknown disease. There is, however, a logical explanation, already alluded to, related to improved circulation and communication, and particularly to the nature and wide-spread use of the automobile. Improvements in transportation and communication have benefited short hauls and especially self-loading and unloading commodities like passengers or telephone messages dialed by the individual. These are improvements at metropolitan scale distances.

Before analyzing the forces promoting change, let us attempt to establish what actually has been happening in our cities, a somewhat difficult task both for statistical reasons and because of the recency of the change.

For the country as a whole the census bureau indicates that SMSA's (all central cities and their counties over 50,000) have increased 26 per cent in population, but the central cities alone, based on holding city limits constant to 1950, increased only 1.5 per cent as compared to 62 per cent in the remainder of the metropolitan areas. This is natural; as cities grow, they might be expected to expand in all directions. However, even within the 1950 city limits there is vacant land, especially on the edges, so that actually the innermost portions of cities have declined. In some areas increase in other activities has pushed out residences, but, as will be seen, on an overall basis, probably not

---

[4] A highly urbanized region may also have scale economies. *Cf.* Chauncy D. Harris, "The Market as a Factor in the Localization of Industry in the U. S.", *Annals of the Association of American Geographers*, Vol. 44, 1954, pp. 315–48, and Edward L. Ullman, "Regional Development and the Geography of Concentration", *Papers and Proceedings of the Regional Science Association*, Vol. 4, 1958, pp 179–98. See also references to Gottmann and others in footnote six.

even this has compensated for the loss.   A net, although unevenly distributed, decline is evident.

For other measures beyond population, it is difficult to obtain data from the census, except for retail trade, and for the office function on a consistent basis it is impossible.   To obtain as much consistency as possible a representative group of cities, of all size classes has been chosen and changes in the central city have been compared to the whole metropolitan area. (Tables I and II) The measures were limited to eighteen cities which from 1947 to 1958 had virtually no change in boundaries. Percentage calculations for the average of these cities are given on Table I.

These eighteen metropolitan areas and their central cities grew slightly faster than all U. S. metropolitan areas, with the central cities showing a six per cent increase compared to one and one-half per cent nationally.   This probably means, therefore, that the other measures of decline of central city proportion of all metropolitan activity are slightly understated in Table I. Also, as noted for population, the measures used probably actually understate the degree of inner decline since the city limits themselves are drawn fairly far out.   Finally, the figures are for 1958; later data would show still more relative decline.

Even with these qualifications, relative decline of the central city is apparent.   The decrease from 1948 to 1958 in the degree of central city concentration as a percentage of the metropolitan area is shown in the last four figures (28, 29, 30, 31) where Manufacturing in 1958 is eighty-eight per cent of 1947, Wholesale Trade ninety-one per cent of 1948, Selected Services ninety-three per cent, and Retail Trade ninety-one per cent, as compared to eighty-four per cent for Population.

The actual per cents of population or employment in the central city in 1958 were as follows: Population about fifty-four per cent, Manufacturing sixty per cent, Wholesale Trade eighty-two per cent, Selected Services eighty per cent, Retail Trade seventy-two per cent.

It is clear that population leads the way to the suburbs, but jobs are not far behind, especially in manufacturing.   Factories appreciate the roominess of the suburb just as much as ranch houses.   One-story structures with ample parking are the rule.   Walk-up or elevator factories in town are abandoned as soon as conditions permit by most industries, save some with high labor requirements and production processes not sensitive to poor layout or with light weight raw materials and end products.   Wholesaling, especially warehousing, should increasingly join manufacturing in low density structures, although its traditional nature, and especially greater market within the city, in contrast to manufacturing, probably explains the greater urban concentration up to now.

The number of individual establishments in manufacturing are more concentrated in the city than is employment, indicating that the larger, more self-contained industries, requiring more space, have led the way to the suburbs. In wholesale trade the reverse appears, indicating probably relatively more warehouse, low labor activity in suburbs.

TABLE I. Changes in Proportion of Selected Activities for 18 U.S. Central Cities and Metropolitan Areas, Various Dates 1929–1960[a]

#		Unweighted Mean Percent
1	*Population*: proportion of SMSA located in central city, 1948	64
2	〃　　〃　　〃　　〃　　〃　　〃　　〃　 1960	52
3	change in SMSA/Central City concentration, 1960/1948 (1948/1958:84)	81
4	change, SMSA 1960/1948	133
5	change, central city 1960/48	106
6	*Manufacturing*: production workers in central city, 1929	74
7	〃　　　　　　〃　　〃　　〃　　〃　　〃　 1939	71
8	〃　　　　　　〃　　〃　　〃　　〃　　〃　 1947	70
9	〃　　　　　　〃　　〃　　〃　　〃　　〃　 1954	64
10	〃　　　　　　〃　　〃　　〃　　〃　　〃　 1958	60
11	establishments in central city, 1947	75
12	〃　　　　　　〃　　〃　　〃　 1954	69
13	〃　　　　　　〃　　〃　　〃　 1958	67
14	*Wholesale trade*: paid employees in central city, 1948	89
15	〃　　　　〃　　〃　　〃　　〃　　〃　 1954	88
16	〃　　　　〃　　〃　　〃　　〃　　〃　 1958	82
17	establishments in central city, 1948	86
18	〃　　　　　　〃　　〃　　〃　 1954	83
19	〃　　　　　　〃　　〃　　〃　 1958	80
20	*Selected services*: paid employees in central city, 1948	86
21	〃　　　　〃　　〃　　〃　　〃　　〃　 1954	82
22	〃　　　　〃　　〃　　〃　　〃　　〃　 1958	80
23	establishments in central city, 1954	72
24	〃　　　　　　〃　　〃　　〃　 1958	69
25	*Retail trade*: paid employees in central city, 1948	79
26	〃　　　〃　　〃　　〃　　〃　　〃　 1954	77
27	〃　　　〃　　〃　　〃　　〃　　〃　 1958	72
28	*Manufacturing*: change in concentration of prod. workers, 1958/1947	88
29	*Wholesale Trade*: 〃　　〃　　　　〃　　　　〃 paid employees, 1958/1948	91
30	*Selected services*: 〃　　〃　　　　〃　　　　〃　　〃　　　　〃 1958/1948	93
31	*Retail trade*: 〃　　〃　　〃　　　　〃　　〃　　　　〃 1958/1948	91

[a] Central cities chosen were those with virtually no boundary change 1947–58: metropolitan area (SMSA) figures adjusted to 1958 area.
\# Numbers refer to numbers of columns in following table for individual cities.
Sources:　U.S. Census of Manufactures 1947, 1954, 1958; Census of Business 1948, 1954, 1958; Census of Population 1960.
D. J. Bogue, "A Technique for Making Extensive Population Estimates," *Journal of the American Statistical Association*, 45 (June, 1950), pp. 149–163.

TABLE II. Ratios of Activities of Selected Central Cities to SMSA's

	#1	2	3	4	5	6	7	8	9	10	11	12	13	14	15	16	17	18	19	20	21	22	23	24	25	26	27	28	29	30	31
Buffalo	56	41	73	124	93	60	50	48	43	42	69	62	61	87	85	80	84	80	75	81	72	70	60	55	70	65	59	88	92	86	84
Chicago	66	57	86	115	99	74	72	70	65	59	83	75	71	88	87	79	88	83	77	85	81	76	71	63	70	70	64	84	90	89	91
Cleveland	65	49	75	123	93	89	86	83	70	68	87	80	76	93	93	87	92	87	81	88	84	83	70	69	78	74	69	82	94	94	88
Detroit	61	44	72	129	94	75	58	60	53	49	69	56	52	86	77	74	87	77	73	86	78	75	66	59	71	65	56	82	86	87	79
Philadelphia	57	46	81	122	98	66	61	61	56	55	71	65	62	89	82	77	85	75	70	75	75	72	62	57	69	63	58	90	87	96	84
St. Louis	52	36	69	126	88	70	71	71	63	56	78	71	68	—	86	80	80	73	70	77	76	73	58	55	70	62	59	79	80	95	84
Akron	68	57	84	125	103	89	82	82	81	67	71	64	59	87	92	85	88	86	82	91	88	82	74	69	81	78	74	82	98	90	91
Miami	53	31	58	209	124	79	77	74	70	50	72	66	57	94	79	72	93	77	70	73	46	45	60	54	66	63	55	68	77	62	83
New Orleans	85	72	85	131	111	78	77	77	68	61	89	83	79	95	91	88	93	90	87	96	90	90	86	82	93	90	86	79	93	94	92
Portland	54	45	83	126	107	68	63	63	60	58	68	56	59	81	91	89	78	85	84	89	84	85	73	68	79	79	77	92	110	96	97
Rochester	69	54	78	123	97	92	94	95	94	92	90	87	84	95	95	92	93	92	91	97	93	87	88	84	85	90	82	97	97	90	96
Syracuse	64	51	80	131	105	76	71	47	43	40	55	49	49	84	79	71	76	74	71	82	78	69	54	51	67	65	60	85	85	84	90
Baton Rouge	79	66	84	145	121	18	17	28	23	37	57	77	83	87	94	92	88	95	93	89	98	95	97	89	91	96	94	132	106	107	103
Des Moines	79	78	99	122	121	91	95	86	77	69	93	84	85	—	96	94	91	93	92	98	96	95	92	90	92	95	92	80	94	97	100
Erie	62	55	89	121	107	67	69	54	56	57	70	67	64	90	90	87	83	82	79	89	85	83	72	67	82	81	77	106	97	93	94
Flint	62	53	85	147	125	96	99	98	80	68	62	56	65	—	89	54	82	83	79	89	90	89	69	71	85	83	79	69	54	100	93
Salt Lake City	67	49	73	150	111	70	61	70	71	72	84	80	77	92	95	93	91	90	90	89	90	91	78	81	85	87	85	103	101	102	100
South Bend	59	56	95	122	115	82	81	80	81	73	74	66	66	83	77	81	81	79	78	77	81	83	73	71	81	79	75	91	98	108	93
Average	64	52	81*	133	106	74	71	70	64	60	75	69	67	89	88	82	86	83	80	86	82	80	72	69	79	77	72	88	91	93	91

* Adjusted to 84 for 1958

\# Numbers at top of columns are identified on Table I.

These general trends in themselves are not conclusive evidence of expansion and lower density, but several studies of individual cities, among them New York, Chicago, Boston[5] indicate the dispersal as well as the classic example of Los Angeles, a city which has grown up in the recent period.

REASONS FOR THE PRESENT AND FUTURE REARRANGEMENT OF CITIES

Before citing other evidence of the expansion and rearrangement of cities, let us examine the fundamental changes in background which have made this possible. As is well known, improvement in transportation and circulation has changed the nature of urban space, allowing greater distances to be covered[6] and particularly the development of *favored sites*—parts of the city more on

---

[5] Perhaps the most significant finding along these lines of the New York Regional Study is buried in a footnote added after the study was completed and using last minute, 1960 census returns: "....the tendency to fill up the previously by-passed land of the inlying counties does not appear to be quite as strong as our projection assumes....In general the dispersive population forces in the region seem even stronger than those built into our model." Raymond Vernon, *Metropolis 1985*, Harvard University Press, Cambridge, 1960, footnote, p. 222.

Examples of two earlier but recent quantitative studies proving the shift in urban structures are: John R. Hamburg and Robert Sharkey, "Chicago's Changing Land Use and Population Structures," *Journal American Institute of Planners*, Vol. XXVI, Nov. 1960, pp. 317-323, and, *A Report on Downtown Boston*, Greater Boston Economic Study Committee, 1959.

[6] *Cf.* the prophetic statement of H. G. Wells in "The Probable Diffusion of Great Cities" in *Anticipations* (London, 1901) where, in discussing urban growth promoted by improved methods of transport he says, "It is not too much to say that before [2000]-the vast stretch of country from Washington to Albany will be all of it available to the active citizen of New York and Philadelphia—This does not for the moment imply that cities of the density of our existing great cities will spread to these limits" (quoted by K. C. Edwards, "Trends in Urban Expansion," *Advancement of Science*, No. 62, Sept. 1959, p. 60.)

Jean Gottmann (*Megalopolis*, New York, Twentieth Century Fund, 1960) eloquently describes the human geography of the whole area from Boston to Washington as one unit. Norton S. Ginsburg, "The Dispersed Metropolis: The Case of Okayama", *Toshi Mondai*, (Municipal Problems, in Japanese), June 1961, pp. 67-76, equally eloquently proposes a new type of city based on several centers and improved transportation.

Some less careful enthusiasts have overplayed the urban explosion however, partly sparked by a change in definition of metropolitan areas in 1950 by the U.S. Bureau of the Census from a minor civil division basis to a county basis. When mapped it appeared as though urbanization had taken a gigantic leap into the countryside. Actually open country still surrounds all major metropolises even on the eastern seaboard of the U.S., even though the built-up area and ribbon development, much of it low density, has spread greatly. *Cf.* Lester E. Klimm, "The Empty Areas of the Northeastern U.S.", *Geographical Review*, Vol. XLIV, 1954, pp. 25-45. What has happened is more to be measured by invisible indicators in the landscape: commuting, shopping and other trips, telephone calls, TV, etc., spreading out and beyond suburbia and exurbia. (For an example of quantitative indicators of this see: Edward L. Ullman, Ronald R. Boyce and Donald J. Volk, *The Meramec Basin*, Washington University Press, St. Louis, Mo., 1962, Chapter 1.

the basis of their intrinsic natural and cultural characteristics, and less because of their location or situation. For example, before the automobile, some poor water recreation areas reached by streetcar or train on the edges of cities were very popular. Since the automobile has taken over, these nearby areas, if of poor quality, have declined drastically and visitors travel up to 100 or 200 miles to new impoundments or natural water bodies with better water and scenery, or build swimming pools. In this case, both the opportunity to travel and the ability to pay for something better in our increasingly affluent society have created a change.

Thus the stage is set for urban areas. First, as is well known, provision of street cars and mass transit enabled cities to expand especially out along radial corridors; the volume required for this type of transport tended to focus on one large center—downtown. With the widespread use of the automobile, not dependent on large volume, the interstices could also be served which provided access to enormous additional amounts of land on the expanding circumference. The area of a circle increases by πr^2, which means, for example, that doubling the distance from the center increases the area four times.

Most of the inventions in communication also seem to favor a more open pattern. The telephone with its postage stamp rate over wide areas freed dependence on messengers, the movie made it possible to bring entertainment into the communities and neighborhoods from downtown, and the TV now brings it into the individual house and makes the home even more independent of other localities in the city.

What is happening in cities can be compared to what happened to world land use in the 19th and 20th centuries when improved transport enabled distant fertile lands to produce for the world market and in the process compete with less fertile lands nearer the market. Thus, the steamship and railway brought agricultural products to Europe from fertile prairies in America, Argentina, or Australia and either forced abandonment or drastic alteration of agriculture in many less fertile lands in the European market. Thus the present subsidy to European agriculture might be compared to the subsidy to cities through redevelopment programs, although no value judgment is implied.

Cities might thus initially be compared to the Von Thünen model of land use around a city, with intensity generally decreasing as distance increased from the central market. Urban transportation, especially the automobile, removes much of the handicap of distance just as the steamship and railway did for the world's regions.[7]

One might thus paraphrase and add to some well known economic principles by coining a new law of *urban expansion* and *specialization* as follows:

As urban transport improves cities not only can expand in area, but the range of location choice is widened; the more desirable sites within a city can be reached and developed according to their intrinsic advantages.

The second part of the generalization, relating to *site* qualities rather than *situation* qualities, as geographers would define them, is just as important as

---

[7] Homer Hoyt anticipates me somewhat in this interpretation (as he constantly does) in "Changing Patterns of Land Values," *Land Economics*, Vol. XXXVI, 1960, p. 114.

the first, or expansion part of the law. The monopoly quality of close-in urban locations is weakened.

Even in parts of Europe the same phenomenon is occurring as witness a statement in 1960 by Dr. Aage Aagesen of the Geography Department of the University of Copenhagen:[8]

The Intensive urbanization which has developed in proximity to the railway stations seems to have been transformed into a more general, less pronounced urbanization of more extensive areas; this is a natural result of the fact that the importance exercised by motor-cars and other motor-vehicles on the daily transport is constantly increasing. Another consequence is that there are almost no limits to the choice of residence; this allows preference to be given to *esthetic* considerations by choosing the site in costal regions, in undulating land, at the edge of a wood or of a lake. A combination of these factors has caused the expansion of the Copenhagen district toward the north, in the sub-glacial stream-trenches of North Zealand filled with lakes and woods. To the west and to the southwest of Copenhagen, in a flat and fertile moraine-land, the relief of the landscape is far from being as attractive and, therefore, has not invited an expansion of the same dimensions.

The same occurs in American cities where waterfront property, as on Lake Michigan in Chicago or Lake Washington in Seattle, is sought, or attractive wooded hill lands in part draw high class residence as in western St. Louis or north-western Washington, D. C. Likewise, close in hilly sites are by-passed by factories in favor of out-lying, level lands.

Thus specialization on the basis of natural site qualities occurs, whereas 100 years ago, before the street car or auto, close-in Back Bay in Boston was filled in for high class residential use, or centrally located Nob Hill in San Francisco was built up in mansions and Leland Stanford reportedly got cable car service, an invention of the time uniquely fitted to serve hills. Today many, if not most, of these residents have moved to more spacious sites in the suburbs. Thus different natural factors may apply to urban sites than to rural areas, such as scenically attractive land for high grade housing or level land for factories rather than fertile land for crops.

Urban sites, however, for various reasons, probably cannot be rated so much on their natural characteristics as rural lands, but rather more because of certain man-made or *cultural* attributes. The result is a *push-pull* relationship.

First, close-in locations generally are relatively unattractive because of smoke, noise, traffic, crime, and other well known attributes of crowding.

Secondly, closer in lands may be by-passed by new building for two principal reasons: 1) the generally smaller size of parcels close-in compared to large outlying tracts suitable for large subdivisions and the lower cost mass building techniques of today, and 2) the greater cost of acquiring old structures

---

[8] Aage Aagesen, "The Copenhagen District and its Population," (paper presented to 1960 Symposium on Urban Geography, Lund, Sweden, August, 1960), published in *Geografisk Tidsskrift*, Vol. 59, 1960, pp. 204-13, (citation on p. 210).

and paying high land prices near the center as opposed to using raw land farther out.

The cost of acquiring close-in sites may run from $100,000 to $200,000 and more per acre[9] as compared to $10,000 to $25,000 per acre for outlying land. As a result, few one story or even two story structures can afford costs of close-in sites, whether for house or factory; at the same time the demand for multi-story apartments or other intensive uses is simply not great enough to cover all the gray areas. As a further result the government must subsidize redevelopment, contributing two-thirds or more and the local government the remainder to get site costs down to competitive levels. Even so, the temptation is to build to high densities, which in the past has produced high rise, low income housing, in many cases of dubious attractiveness.

Furthermore, anywhere in the city it appears that low density—that is two story group houses—are the cheapest way to house people because of lower construction costs, lack of elevators, etc. Even in England this is claimed.[10] As Hans Blumenfeld notes the cheapest cost building in a country is apt to be the type which is built most.[11] The higher standard buildings may last somewhat longer, but even the average annual payments do not appear to be significantly less.

It is argued that cost of utilities—sewers, water, electricity, is higher if dispersed building is allowed on the fringes. As Lovelace remarks, "The underground system of sewers and water mains is about all that is holding [the city] together.[12] Even this is questionable, as Lovelace also notes.

Cheaper methods of lagoon sewage treatment or small package plants have been developed for small subdivisions, septic tanks at low densities are suitable on many soils, and even farmhouses have electricity and telephone at not excessive rates. It is true that new schools and other community facilities may have to be built, but these may replace similar facilities close-in which have outlived their usefulness. One story schools, requiring more land, are preferred to the old urban two, or three story structures with inadequate playgrounds.

As a concrete example, Lovelace points out that much of southwestern Michigan outside the cities is developed for low density, non-farm uses in an area of sandy soils with high water table so that sewers and water mains are not required.[13] This illustrates graphically a natural site advantage which can now play a role with cheap transportation. Areas unsuitable for septic tanks can be skipped over.

---

[9] Raymond Vernon, "The Economics of the Large Metropolis," in "The Future Metropolis," *Daedalus,* Winter, 1961, Vol. 90, *Proceedings of the American Academy of Arts and Sciences,* p. 44.

[10] *Cf.* "The two story house on new land is still the cheapest form of development in Britain," Myles Wright, "Further Progress" in *Land Use in an Urban Environment,* Liverpool, 1961, p. 251.

[11] Hans Blumenfeld, *Urban Land,* Vol. 21, No. 7, Aug. 1962.

[12] Eldridge Lovelace, "Urban Sprawl Need not be a Tragedy," *Landscape Architecture,* Vol. 51, 1961, pp. 230-1.

[13] Lovelace, *op. cit.*

Furthermore, low density, sprawl on the fringes of a city is not unattractive simply because it is low-density, but rather because of the way it is done with ribbon development, removal of trees, growth of junk yards and the like. It is not the low density itself that is to blame. Restraining cities to dense, contiguous settlement is not the only answer, nor even the best answer to unsightly sprawl. Sprawl does however produce some obvious inefficiencies.

THE CENTRAL BUSINESS DISTRICT

The core of the city is generally declining relatively and in many cases absolutely. The best data indicating these trends are for retail sales. The top part of Table III shows change in CBD sales and SMSA sales in terms of constant value dollars from 1948 to 1958. The decreases for CBD's range from sixteen per cent for cities over 1,000,000 down to about 10 per cent for those from 100,000 to 250,000. At the same time the remainder of the SMSA's outside the CBD's were increasing from thirty-three to sixty-four per cent. The lower portion of Table III shows what percentage CBD sales are of total SMSA's. Note the decline from sixteen per cent to ten per cent for those over 3,000,000, from twenty-six to fifteen per cent for 1,000,000 to 3,000,000 etc. Note also the lower percentage of total SMSA sales in the CBD in the larger cities, as would be expected, ranging from 9.6 per cent in the largest group to 32 per cent in the smallest. Pre-war, the only firm figure we had, was the special census under Proudfoot for Philadelphia which reported 37.5 per cent in 1937.

These figures show the effect of the construction of large branch department stores and shopping centers and the general movement of shopping to customers. If much of the retail trade leaves downtowns what will replace it?

Before attempting to answer this question, two fundamental points about downtowns should be noted:

1) Most large cities have developed on water and have grown more in one direction than another so that the central business district is not now centrally located in many cities. As a result it loses sales and economic activities as cities grow away from it.[14] Street grids and mass transport focussing on the CBD mitigated this handicap in the past and the construction of radial superhighways to downtown will probably help overcome it to some extent in the future, especially if the parking problem can be solved.

2) Even more serious than the off-center location, in many cases, is the surrounding of the CBD by the low income, blighted, "gray area" of cities. Redevelopment, therefore, in many cases is pushed in part as a means of providing customers. In addition, a market for high and medium income apartments can be developed around downtowns, especially as older people

---

[14] *Cf.* Ronald R. Boyce's forthcoming study suggested this point of the relation of CBD retail sales to CBD centrality. Also note William Weismantel, "A Multicenter Transportation Plan," *Washington University Law Quarterly*, June, 1962, pp. 310–37, for an excellent discussion of St. Louis' growth patterns in relation to transportation.

TABLE III. Central Business District Sales Data.

I. *Changes in Retail Sales CBD and Metropolitan Areas, 1948-58 Adjusted to 1948 Dollars and for 1960 SMSA's.*

SMSA Population (1960)	All Retail Sales						Women's Specialty Stores (Clothing)					
	Changes in CBD Sales			Changes in SMSA Sales (Less CBD Sales)			Changes in CBD Sales			Changes in SMSA Sales (Less CBD Sales)		
	1948-54	1954-58	1948-58	1948-54	1954-58	1948-58	1948-54	1954-58	1948-58	1948-54	1954-58	1948-58
3,000,000 or more (5 cities)	−11.6%	−5%	−16%	+21%	+11%	+33%	−2.1%	+11.5%	+9.3%	+13%	+4%	+17%
1,000,000 to 3,000,000 (14 cities)	−7.8%	−7.8%	−16.3%	+31%	+17%	+50%	−16.8%	−5%	−21%	+12%	+32%	+48%
500,000 to 1,000,000 (25 cities)	−7%	−8%	−14.4%	+38%	+23%	+64%	−11.7%	−6.7%	−17.5%	+16%	+29%	+49%
250,000 to 500,000 (32 cities)	−4.3%	−6.7%	−10.6%	+35%	+18%	+55%	−10.3%	−13.7%	−23%	+60%	−3%	+55%
100,000 to 250,000 (14 cities)	−2.3%	−7.1%	−9.7%	+30%	+18%	+50%	−10%	−10%	−20%	+101%	+13%	+118%
U.S. Average	−6.6%	−7%	−13.4%	+30.4%	+16.8%	+51%	−10%	−4.8%	−14.4%	+40.2%	+15%	+57%

Source: Calculated from U. S. Census of Business, 1958, 1954, *Central Business District Statistics.*

II. *CBD Retail Sales as Percentage of SMSA Sales, 1948-58.*

SMSA Population (1960)	All Retail Sales			Women's Specialty Stores (Clothing)		
	% of SMSA Sales in CBD			% of SMSA Sales in CBD		
	1948	1954	1958	1948	1954	1958
3,000,000 or more (5 cities)	15.6%	11.4%	9.6%	33.8%	27.4%	26.8%
1,000,000 to 3,000,000 (14 cities)	26%	18.8%	15.4%	58.8%	47.5%	41.1%
500,000 to 1,000,000 (25 cities)	34.3%	24.3%	19.7%	78.3%	65%	55.3%
250,000 to 500,000 (32 cities)	38.7%	28.5%	24.4%	84.8%	75.6%	70.8%
100,000 to 250,000 (14 cities)	44.5%	37.2%	32.1%	91.7%	81.8%	77.8%
U.S. Average	31.8%	24%	20%	69.5%	59.5%	54.4%

Source: Calculated from U. S. Census of Business, 1958, 1954, *Central Business District Statistics.*

with grown children come onto the market, as well as a new wave of post-high school and young college graduates.   This market in most cities, however, does not appear large enough to affect a significant change.   Probably a larger natural apartment market for retired persons exists in suburbs and other centers.

The remaining large activity for CBD's is the office function.   This is growing, and growing particularly in New York which has witnessed a boom in central office and other activities locating there for national control, in part made possible by the airplane.   To a degree the same is happening in Washington.   For most cities this does not appear so likely.   Even Chicago's recent expansion and planned new construction will only result in the same per capita office space as in 1930, although it will help the Loop.[15]   Most other cities are worse off.

The unknown question is how much is face-to-face contact—linkages of various kinds—necessary for various functions, especially outside New York City.   Many activities apparently do not require it, particularly in insurance and in single-function office buildings.

In some cities, even beside Los Angeles, notably St. Louis, outlying office centers are now starting to develop.   Clayton, seven miles west of the CBD and more centrally located in reference to the high income area, has many modern, city-wide or nation-wide office buildings, with rents as much as three times higher than downtown, but with land values only about 1/3; Clayton illustrates a location nearer the geographic center of a city as well as closer to executives' homes.   Ancillary businesses and social services, including luncheon clubs, have sprung up, although the center is not as large as downtown St. Louis.   Executives, however, can still go downtown for luncheon club conferences.   They drive to their offices in Clayton, then drive downtown for lunch and return in the afternoon, avoiding all rush hour traffic.

Many activities are downtown just because they are there, or in response to linkages which disappeared years ago.   Many could be served better elsewhere.   In any case, the average downtown should be greatly improved in order to compete with the greater number of sites now accessible by modern transportation.   This will be increasingly difficult in view of the outward movement of housing, retail trade, manufacturing, and other activities which now begin to reinforce each other elsewhere in the city.

It looks as though the CBD may become one of the many centers in a city, in many cases the most important, but a center of much less relative importance than in the past.   A logical development would make it the shopping center for the large, low income area around it and an office center on a reduced scale for older activities or smaller concerns needing poor, vacant space or using large amounts of cheap labor.   The high grade activities characteristic of the top hierarchical position of the CBD will abandon it for centers better located to serve the high income areas.[16]

Other centers elsewhere will develop on a regional or specialized basis,

---

[15] *Urban Land*, April, 1961, p. 8.

strengthening the multiple nuclei generalization suggested in the earlier "Nature of Cities." Conventions and out of town visitors will find it increasingly more convenient to locate near the airport which, because of its own space needs locates on the periphery; outlying shopping centers will handle retail trade; large factories and employment centers will be on the outskirts on large tracts of land; special entertainment, educational, cultural, and recreational centers will be scattered all over the city to serve the whole population.

Many have said that a city cannot exist without a heart, the CBD. The metropolis of today and increasingly in the future is not only one city, but a federation of general and special centers. As such it is likely to have several hearts better located than one, and basically will be better off because of reduction in travel time, congestion, and utilization of better sites.

CONCLUSION

The generalizations about urban growth and re-arrangement will vary with individual cities because individual natural environments, economic bases, and civic actions vary. Many of the location changes in cities hinge on small margins with inertia and tradition holding many activities in uneconomical, old areas. Identical offices and industries can thrive in CBD's, suburbs, and small towns. They adjust accordingly.

If we were to start over, however, we would not build our cities as they are today. If we were to apply private enterprise depreciation principles to the inner portions of cities we would write them off—just as machinery is scrapped, and throw them away, but where would we throw them?

As a citizen I recognize that the major problem of cities—slums and the gray area—cannot be tolerated. We may well have to eliminate them before we eliminate all the causes, including poverty, ignorance, and racial discrimination against the new arrivals, or the orther manifold ills of our society both old and new.

Some might say that the new pattern of our cities is the result of a plot hatched by Detroit, the sub-dividers, and land speculators. Inflated land values are a part of the "pernicious" process of urban sprawl.[17] The auto does not pay its fair share for use of the city and hidden costs are passed on to the public in urban expansion. This may be true, but three points seem germane: 1) the magnitude of the underpayment is probably not enough to result in anything more than a slowing down in the process, even if corrected. 2) Countervailing forces are already deployed on the other side, sparked in part by the threatened decline in land values in the center. Urban redevelopment is subsidized, and priority is given a radial pattern for the interstate highway system focussing on downtown, reflecting old flow patterns, with generally

---

[16] This will eliminate some of the cross hauling now occurring as executives travel from the residential suburbs into the center and workers travel from the center outward to suburban industrial sites.

[17] Cf. the thoughtful article by Mason Gaffney "Urban Expansion-Will it even Stop?," 1958 Yearbook of Agriculture (Washington, Govt. Printing Office, 1959), pp. 503-22.

only one circumferential, when some inner or intermediate belts are also required. 3) Even if the whole process is a plot, it is our foreseeable institutional arrangement and as a geographer I see it producing the future expansion—specialization—federation patterns sketched above.

A key question then will be the inerrelations between the centers and parts. How much will they benefit from being adjacent, or would separate cities of 100,000 to 500,000 be as good or better? The latter seems unlikely since there are still some specialized services, such as jet aircraft flights, that are better performed for millions than thousands. The problem remains to design cities to take advantage of scale economies and the other advantages of concentration, and at the same time to provide optimum livability.

12

Richard Morrill

ON THE SIZE AND
SPACING OF GROWTH CENTERS

FREQUENTLY raised in the growth center literature is the issue of size.[1] Defined as a city whose
growth is the result of forces in the private economy,
which seems capable of sustaining further growth with
governmental assistance, and which is located in an economically disadvantaged region, a growth center seemingly could be a city of any number of residents. An
important question is one of minimally efficient size. We
know that there are thousands of economically and
socially viable places with from ten to ten million inhabitants, all with some role to play in the economy. We also
know that larger places tend to have higher median
family incomes and a higher degree of self-sufficiency,
probably as a consequence of economies of scale and
agglomeration.

To be useful in regional development, a growth center
should provide employment opportunities and urban
amenities sufficient to absorb rural migration and to
spread economic and cultural benefits to the surrounding hinterland.[2] Since existing places may be presumed
to provide as many goods and services as are demanded
by their surrounding areas, the success of a growth
center presumably depends, at least initially, on the
attraction of export activities. Generally these desired
activities involve manufacturing, but increasingly they
include professional, administrative, and other services
destined for large regional or national markets. Several
recent studies have suggested that a minimum population of about two hundred fifty thousand is necessary
for a growth center to be capable of self-sustained
growth.[3] The objective of this paper is to explore
whether this minimum is reasonable and necessary and
to see if some wider range of sizes may be as acceptable.
A second objective is to consider the implications of size
of growth centers on their spacing.

*Richard Morrill is Professor of Geography at the Uni-
versity of Washington.*

How Small?

The Economic Development Administration (EDA) in
administering the Appalachian Regional Development
Program, conceived of growth centers as cities of between ten thousand and two hundred thousand persons.
The median size of growth centers chosen was 24,145 in
1965.[4] Program efforts and expenditures were concentrated on social and economic overhead capital such as
roads, schools, post offices, and training programs in the
hope of attracting industry. Although necessary, these
efforts were not sufficient to induce growth in many
designated growth centers. Partly because of this failure,
but also on economic principle, the smallness of these
growth centers has been criticized. Such authors as
Hansen, Berry, and Alonso have argued that the minimum size of a growth center should approach two
hundred thousand, which is the maximum size for
original EDA eligibility.[5] A city of two hundred thousand to two hundred fifty thousand is considered large
enough to constitute at least a partial market, is able to
offer a variety of professional and business services, and
has superior transport connections. In addition, such a
city can be expected to have a varied and flexible labor
force, educational and cultural services that encourage
and accompany economic innovation, and some industrial diversification and, therefore, employment
stability, which together tend to guarantee self-
sustaining growth. According to Berry, the regional
influence of smaller centers is too limited to justify
putting public resources into them.[6] Frequently, the
income transfer from commuting, the local agricultural
markets, and other economic factors are considered
insufficient to improve the welfare of the hinterland
significantly.

On the other hand, Sweden, which depends much
more than the United States on efficient export industries, and West Germany sustain an amazing industrial

vitality and competitiveness in scores of smaller cities and villages with as few as a thousand persons. Metropolitan labor shortages are an important factor in inducing industrial development in nonmetropolitan areas in these countries.[7] Similarly, in the United States we can identify scores of prosperous, industrially stable, growing cities with from ten thousand to two hundred thousand population.

Certainly places over two hundred fifty thousand will, on the average, find it easier to attract and innovate industries and to achieve self-sustaining growth, and such places are likely to have a greater effect on the hinterland. Yet size does not guarantee employment diversification and stability (Seattle is a case in point), nor is new industry in a city or region necessarily a product of local innovation.

Contrary to the generally held notion, many industries and services do not require large metropolitan locations in order to be competitive, as many have demonstrated in their location behavior.[8] Much metropolitan location may be more in the nature of self-fulfilling prophecy (because futurists stress how metropolises are growing) than because of necessity. The search, then, should be directed not at finding cities of a particular minimum size, but at finding firms that can utilize local labor and compete successfully in regional and national markets.

Indiscriminate pouring of overhead capital into either smaller or larger cities is not recommended, since such indirect investments are no guarantee of expansion of employment opportunities.[9] That industry does not rush in to take advantage of a new road or school is in itself no indication of a place's inherent unattractiveness to industry. The failure of growth-center-oriented development programs should not be interpreted as evidence that only metropolises over two hundred fifty thousand can be successful, but that we have not concentrated on what really matters—employment in export activities.[10] Merely hoping that public investment in infrastructure will induce private corporations to locate in less successful regions is hardly sufficient impetus for development.

If we are serious about helping weaker regions, many of which contain no cities as large as two hundred thousand persons (for example, Idaho, Montana, and Wyoming), then we should consider places on their inherent merit, promise, need, and location, regardless of present population. In small or sparsely populated regions, developing growth centers of a hundred thousand might well be sufficient to stem excess out-migration and raise levels of hinterland income.

How Large?

The concept of growth centers as derived from the development literature stresses the gradual, private trickle-down or spillover of industry from growth centers of a million or more persons to the hinterlands.[11] Presumably external economies in the metropolis are so

overwhelming that it is inefficient to try to spread investment initially; later, owing to eventual metropolitan diseconomies such as high wage rates or increased demand for products by persons at the periphery, we might expect industrial spillover into the larger towns of the periphery.[12] Empirical evidence in the United States indicates vast suburban decentralization of industry, but very little industrial trickle-down to the hinterland; concentration of investment in the metropolis tends to polarize growth and aggravate peripheral weakness. It seems clear from the evidence reported by Berry and others that favorable effects of metropolitan growth on regional welfare are limited to the commuter zone.[13] In the United States most metropolises over two hundred fifty thousand and their commuting areas are already fairly prosperous and growing and are hardly in need of development help.

One-quarter of the population and the most depressed regions lie beyond the commuter zones of places of over a quarter of a million.[14] Therefore it is both unnecessary and insufficient to designate as growth centers metropolises over two hundred fifty thousand, except for the few that have been unable to adapt to sectoral decline (as in certain mining and heavy industrial centers) and the few which have demonstrated excessive dependence on low wage industries and therefore have only marginal economic effects on their hinterlands.

Growing Centers in the Past

Continuing metropolitanization of the population was apparent in the 1960s when metropolitan counties gained 5.3 million new residents through net in-migration, while nonmetropolitan counties lost 2.3 million. (Net U.S. immigration was 3 million.) Yet the more metropolitan North experienced net out-migration (-438,000), while the South (+590,000) and West (+2,850,000) gained. Further, as we shall see, more rapid and successful growth evidenced by in-migration was not confined to the larger metropolitan areas. Sixty-four of eighty-seven SMSAs whose urbanized areas exceeded two hundred thousand persons in 1960 gained in the decade, while twenty-three lost. These areas losing population included such giants as Chicago, Detroit, Pittsburgh, Cleveland, Buffalo, Milwaukee, and Cincinnati.

Of the 169 smaller urban agglomerations between fifty thousand and two hundred thousand in 1960, 88 gained and 81 lost through migration. (See Figure 1.) Twenty-three of the gaining areas were within commuting distance of very large metropolises, 13 were in rapidly growing California and Florida areas, but 52 were located far from larger SMSAs or in generally less metropolitan regions. In aggregate they gained seven hundred forty thousand through net in-migration in the 1960s. Some of these grew because of increased spending in the defense industry (Huntsville, Alabama and Fayetteville, North Carolina) or increasing investment in education (Champaign, Illinois; Lafayette, Indiana; and

Bloomington, Indiana) but most experienced significant industrial growth.

Many smaller urban centers across the nation managed respectable growth in the 1960s. Slightly over half (111 of 218) of the counties containing urban agglomerations between twenty-five thousand and fifty thousand in either 1960 or 1970 received net in-migration in the 1960s. The aggregate gain was 1,007,000, although

FIGURE 1. SMALLER CITIES WITH ABOVE
AVERAGE GROWTH, 1960-70

● SMSAs of 50,000-200,000 population in 1960 with net
   in-migration, 1960-70

○ Cities of 25,000-50,000 population in either 1960 or
   1970 with net in-migration, 1960-70

Source: U.S. Department of Commerce, Bureau of the Census, *Census of Population: 1960*, and *1970 Census of Population* (Washington, D.C.: Government Printing Office, 1962 and 1971); and "Components of Population Change by County—1960 to 1970," *Current Population Report*, P-25, no. 461 (Washington, D.C.: Government Printing Office, 1971).

305,000 of this number went to California and Florida. Clearly, these cities in nonmetropolitan regions cannot absorb all the population entering the labor force, and a great amount of out-migration is necessary from many regions. Still their growth and widespread distribution attest that they are growth centers, and that they have the potential to absorb some regional population.

Spacing

Regular spacing of growth centers would be of basic importance if the national objective were to assure the development and prosperity of the entire nation. An alternative strategy to locate growth centers only in the most promising regions would be much cheaper and more efficient in the short run, but long-term population decentralization may have advantages.[15] As Berry has demonstrated, where metropolitan areas are closely spaced (less than 100 miles) their commuting fields overlap, and income levels and other indices are often more favorable in the countryside between the metropolises than in the central cities themselves.[16] But where metropolises are farther apart and constitute less than a

majority of the regional population, the favorable effects gradually give way to net unfavorable effects, such as out-migration of highly trained people, loss of economic activities, and declining opportunities and relative income.[17] An important reason for this weakness of the nonmetropolitan periphery is the unwillingness of much of the surplus population to move to the urban areas. Too great a separation of cities leads to the probable decline of the periphery and lack of access to metropolitan benefits.

Closer spacing obviously requires a larger number of centers at a proportionally higher cost of investment to bring all areas and people into metropolitan commuting range. In the United States, at least, access to metropolitan centers is extremely important because of the marked concentration of employment and services (for example, medical and cultural). Because many people hesitate to move to the metropolis, the possibility of commuting is vital, especially in the absence of industrial trickle-down, to improving income and opportunities in declining rural hinterlands.

The city size necessary to inspire the critical level of commuting (10 to 20 percent of the labor force) which seems to assure an income transfer sufficient to bring an area to acceptable levels of welfare depends on the severity of conditions in the hinterland and such factors as population density and quality of transportation facilities.[18] In low density and/or relatively prosperous regions, as in much of the Great Plains region and the West, somewhat smaller centers of fifty thousand to one hundred thousand spaced widely (over 100 miles apart) are often able to bring metropolitan benefits to the hinterland and permit commuting to the centers. In higher density and/or relatively poorer regions, as in parts of Appalachia and the South, somewhat larger centers (over one hundred thousand) at closer intervals appear to be necessary. Detailed investigation of income transfers, employment, and population impacts with respect to distance from centers of differing sizes is currently underway.[19]

The essential point of this discussion, however, is to illustrate that flexibility is possible in planning the location of growth centers, that it is not necessary to insist upon either a particular size or spacing, but that these can vary, reflecting area conditions. In addition, except for very small poverty pockets, it may well be most efficient to encourage a mix of sizes and spacings of centers rather than to depend on one very large center or to spread resources among too many too-small places. If only centers of two hundred thousand or more are aided, the areas and people of greatest need will not have been helped. On the other hand, it is not necessary to bear the risk of utilizing very small places (under ten thousand) since in almost all regions there are places between twenty-five thousand and two hundred thousand which show some promise of becoming growth centers and to which about 95 percent of the population is within commuting distance.

FOOTNOTES

1. Pertinent references include Niles M. Hansen, *Rural Poverty and the Urban Crisis* (Bloomington: Indiana University Press, 1970); A. O. Hirschman, *The Strategy of Economic Development* (New Haven, Conn.: Yale University Press, 1958); D. F. Darwent, "Growth Poles and Growth Centers in Regional Planning," *Environment and Planning*, vol. 1 (1969), pp. 5-32; and J. R. Lasuén, "On Growth Poles," *Urban Studies*, vol. 6 (1969), pp. 137-61. See also comment and reply on Lasuén in *Urban Studies*, vol. 7 (1970), pp. 82-88. In this discussion, we are explicitly treating growth centers as conglomerations of people and economic activities at specific geographic locations, *not* in the earlier "growth pole" sense of an expanding and dominant firm.

2. Gordon Cameron, "Growth Areas, Growth Centers, and Regional Conversion," *Scottish Journal of Political Economy*, vol. 17 (1970), pp. 19-38; and Vida Nichols, "Growth Poles: An Evaluation of Their Propulsive Effects," *Environment and Planning*, vol. 1 (1969), pp. 193-208.

3. See references, note 1, and Brian J. L. Berry, "Commuting Patterns: Labor Market Participation and Regional Potential," *Growth and Change*, vol. 1 (October 1970), pp. 3-11.

4. Hansen, op. cit., p. 153.

5. Ibid.; William Alonso, "What Are New Towns For?" *Urban Studies*, vol. 7 (1970), pp. 37-56; and Brian J. L. Berry, *Growth Centers and Their Potential in the Upper Great Lakes Region* (Washington, D.C.: Upper Great Lakes Regional Commission, May 1969).

6. Berry, "Commuting Patterns," p. 10.

7. Gunter Krumme, "Development Centers and Central Places in West German Regional Planning Schemes," *Review of Regional Studies*, vol. 2 (1972), pp. 215-34.

8. For example, Darwent, op. cit. and Lasuén, op. cit.

9. Brian J. L. Berry and Frank Horton, *Geographic Perspectives on Urban Systems* (Englewood Cliffs, N.J.: Prentice-Hall, 1970).

10. Richard L. Morrill, "Fundamental Issues Concerning Future Settlement in American," in *Geographic Perspectives and Urban Problems*, ed. Frank Horton (Washington, D.C.: National Academy of Science, 1973).

11. Trickle-down is discussed in Carl W. Hale, "Mechanism of the Spread Effect in Regional Development," *Land Economics*, vol. 43 (1967), pp. 433-44; L. H. Klaasen, "Growth Poles in Economic Theory and Policy," in *Review of Concepts and Theories of Growth Poles and Growth Centers*, ed. A. Kuklinski (Geneva: UNRISD, 1970); and Barbara M. D. Smith, "Industrial Overspill in Theory and Practice," *Urban Studies*, vol. 7 (1970), pp. 189-204.

12. See Nichols, op. cit.

13. Berry, "Commuting Patterns"; and Berry and Horton, op. cit.

14. Richard L. Morrill and Ernest Wohlenberg, *Geography of Poverty in the United States* (New York: McGraw-Hill, 1972).

15. John Friedmann, "The Feasibility of a National Settlement Policy," *Growth and Change*, vol. 2 (April 1971), pp. 18-21.

16. Berry, "Growth Centers."

17. See Gunnar Myrdal, *Economic Theory and Underdeveloped Regions* (London: Gerald Duckworth, 1957); Morrill and Wohlenberg, op. cit.; and Hansen, op. cit.

18. The more depressed the hinterland and the lower the metropolitan wage levels, the higher the critical level of commuting. Where conditions are unusually severe, urban growth and commuting may not suffice to raise levels of regional welfare adequately.

19. Some preliminary results are reported in Richard L. Morrill, "Growth Center-Hinterland Relations," in *Proceedings, Symposium on Transmission of Regional Growth*, ed. Walter Stohr (London, Ontario: International Geographical Union, 1973).

13

U. S. Bureau of Labor Statistics

MODELING U. S. ECONOMIC GROWTH

Assumptions

The estimates of 1980 demand, output and employment presented in this report are not forecasts but projections of what the economy might be like under a given set of assumptions. One assumption is that the Viet Nam conflict will have been resolved and that defense expenditures will have been reduced somewhat, although the level will be still somewhat higher than just before the Viet Nam build-up. Another assumption is that the economy will continue to grow at approximately its potential growth rate based on continued high resource utilization.

Four alternative 1980 models are presented in this report. These four models are grouped into two sets of models—one set is called the basic models and the other the high durable goods models. Each of the sets has two models with identical characteristics throughout except for the unemployment rate which is varied: one of the models in each set has a 3 percent rate and the other has a 4 percent rate.

Most of the discussion throughout the text of the 1980 report will present the basic models. These are used because they represent what is believed to be the more likely projection to 1980 than the high durable models. The basic models reflect the long-term shift towards services and away from goods. In order to evaluate the difference it would make to the structure of employment if this shift were slowed down considerably, an alternative set of estimates were prepared that emphasize expenditures on durable goods. The high durable models are discussed in detail in chapter V and are summarized later in this chapter.

The basic models have the following characteristics: a 3 or 4 percent unemployment rate and a distribution of GNP that primarily reflects a continuation of past trends modified to take account of specific anticipated developments. As a proportion of gross national product, it shows personal consumption expenditures somewhat higher than in the past. State and local government purchases are also projected as an increasing proportion of GNP. Federal Government purchases on the other hand, show a sizable drop as a proportion of GNP, particularly when compared with current levels which include a large amount of Viet Nam related expenditures. However, Federal nondefense purchases are projected to increase relative to GNP so that total government purchases for nondefense functions, Federal as well as State and local, are projected to increase faster than the over-all growth rate and as a proportion of GNP. The Armed Forces in the basic models return to 2.7 million —about their pre-Viet Nam level. Investment, both nonresidential and residential, are projected to take a slightly larger proportion of GNP than at the present time.

In the high durable models the major assumptions are: a 3 or 4 percent unemployment rate and the major areas of demand related to durable goods a higher proportion of GNP than in the basic models. Therefore, Federal Government expenditures, particularly defense, do not drop as much as a proportion of GNP as in the basic models. Investment, both residential and nonresidential, are higher as a proportion of GNP than currently or than found in the basic models, and consumer expenditures for durable goods are higher in the high durable models. The other elements of demand—State and local government expenditures and consumer nondurables and services expenditures—are lower proportions than in the basic models.

Approach

The 1980 projections are made in a series of distinct but closely inter-related steps. First, the potential gross national product is developed based on a projection of the labor force, assumptions regarding the rate of unemployment and the level of the Armed Forces, and by projecting trends in average hours and output per man-hour. Given the potential gross national product, projections are developed of the composition of GNP among demand components—government, consumption, business investment and net foreign demand. Once the composition of GNP is determined, the detailed distribution of each of these final demand components is projected. In order to translate projections of industry demand into industry output requirements, input-output relationships which have been projected to 1980 are used. After the calculation of industry growth rate is completed, the final step is to derive the projected level of employment, by industry, by using projections of changes in output per man-hour by industry.[1]

Highlights

Gross national product in the basic models is projected to grow at an annual rate of 4.3 percent a year in real terms between 1965 and 1980.[2] This growth rate results in a 1980 gross national product of $1,165 billion in constant 1958 dollars under the 3-percent unemployment assumption and $1,155 billion under the assumption of a 4-percent unemployment rate.[3] The projected rate of growth in GNP of 4.3 percent a year is lower than the 4.9 percent recent rate of increase in aggregate output but higher than the long-run growth rate of 4.0 percent a year for the 1947–68 postwar period.

The overall growth rate in GNP is projected by taking into consideration changes in the labor force, hours of work, and output per man-hour. (See table 1.)

The labor force (1965–80) is expected to grow faster than in the 1957–65 period, 1.8 percent a year compared with 1.3 percent. The total number of jobs is projected to increase at a somewhat faster rate, 1.8 or 1.9 percent per year, compared with 1.1 percent.

In the 1957–65 period annual hours declined at a rate of 0.2 a year. During the projected period they are expected to decline also at a 0.2 a year rate. The projected decline in hours, however, will result to a considerable extent from the expected increase in part-time employment.

Output per man-hour is expected to grow at a somewhat lower rate than it has over the postwar period 1947–65 and particularly over the last decade. The slight decline in the projected rate of increase is due to the fact that the long-term favorable influence on overall productivity of the manpower shift from the low productivity farm sector to other higher productivity sectors had largely run its course

towards the end of the sixties and would contribute less in the future than in the past.

To summarize: the 4.3 growth rate in GNP reflects a higher projected labor force growth, slightly higher projected growth in total jobs, greater growth in projected private jobs, continuation of past rate of decline of average hours and a somewhat smaller rate of increase of output per man-hour.

Composition of gross national product. Gross national product and its major components for selected years and projections to 1980 for the basic models are shown in table 2. In comparing the 1980 projections with the historical data, several observations can be made about GNP and its components. The ratio of consumption to GNP is higher (65.1 percent) in the 1980 projections than it has been in the past. While no clear historical trend in the proportion of GNP going to consumption is evident the slight proportionate increase for this category does not substantially depart from past relationships. The increase for consumption in the basic models reflects the underlying assumption that part of the declining Federal defense share of GNP is distributed to consumers either by transfer payments or a cut in personal taxes.

The relationship of investment to GNP for 1980 differs with respect to continuation of past trends for its two major components—nonresidential fixed expenditures and residential structures. Nonresidential fixed investment has shown considerable fluctuations in past years between 10.7 and 11.2 percent of total

[1] A detailed description of the techniques used in developing the 1980 projections is contained in appendix A.

[2] All projections throughout this report are for 1965-80. This is because the period 1965-68 has been substantially affected in many cases by the Viet Nam war. The data for the 1965-68 period are shown wherever available for use by those who desire more recent benchmarks. The growth rate between 1968 and 1980 is about the same as for the 1965-80 period—4.3 percent.

[3] All calculations in the 1980 projections were made in 1958 constant dollars. If a translation is made to 1968 dollars, the 1980 GNP would be something over $1,400 billion.

Table 1. Factors determining gross national product, 1957, 1965, 1968, and projected 1980

Item	1957	1965	1968	Projected 1980 Basic models		1957-65	1965-80 Basic models	
				3-percent unemployment	4-percent unemployment		3-percent unemployment	4-percent unemployment
Total labor force (thousands)	69,729	77,177	82,817	100,727	100,727	1.3	1.8	1.8
Unemployed	2,859	3,366	2,817	2,940	3,918	2.1	—.9	1.0
Employed: jobs concept¹ (thousands)	70,953	77,689	84,688	102,896	101,867	1.1	1.9	1.8
Total private	61,197	65,695	70,274	84,396	83,552	.9	1.7	1.6
Annual man-hours (per job) private	2,085	2,052	2,000	1,977	1,977	—.2	—.2	—.2
Total man-hours (millions) private	127.6	134.8	140.5	166.9	165.2	.7	1.4	1.4
GNP per man-hour private² (1958 dollars)	3.22	4.21	4.61	6.54	6.54	3.4	3.0	3.0
Total GNP (1958 dollars)	452.6	617.8	707.6	³1,168.6	³1,156.9	4.0	4.3	4.3
Private GNP (1958 dollars)	410.6	567.0	647.9	1,091.9	1,081.0	4.1	4.5	4.4
Total GNP (1968 dollars)	553.8	754.3	865.7	1,427.8	1,415.7	3.9	4.3	4.3

¹ The estimates of 1980 employment start with an estimate of labor force which is a count of people and is converted to a jobs concept which is a count of jobs. This is more fully discussed in chapter II.

² The GNP per man-hour is private since by national income conventions government productivity is set at zero.
³ This is GNP as was derived, in all other calculations it is rounded to 1,165 and 1,155.

GNP. Most of these years have been years of relatively high growth. The projections for 1980 reflects a constant relationship to private GNP based on these past few years of high resource utilization. The projections of the residential structures component of gross national product, on the other hand, represents a break with the past trend. As can be seen clearly from table 2, during the 1957 to 1967 period residential structure fell from 4.5 percent of GNP to only 3.0 percent with a slight recovery in 1968. The projections for 1980 do not continue this downtrend but show some increase from the recent ratio and a return to a proportion of GNP only slightly lower than prevailed in 1965. This turn around in the residential structures component of GNP reflects a reservoir of demand for housing resulting from the increase in household formations, from the growth in the elderly population who increasingly maintain their own residences, and from a backlog of substandard housing. The 1980 projected level of housing is consistent with meeting the levels called for in the national housing goals.

The 7.3 percent of GNP for Federal Government purchases for goods and services ' in the 1980 projections is a drop from the 1965 level

' Expenditures by the Federal government for grants-in-aid to State and local governments and transfer payments to individuals such as social security are not counted as Federal expenditures on the expenditure or demand side of the national income and product accounts.

of 9.4 percent. The 1980 Federal purchases component of GNP reflect to a considerable extent a continuation of the downtrend of the 1957–65 period. Another way of looking at the decline in Federal expenditures as a proportion of GNP is to consider that expenditures by the Federal Government currently used for Viet Nam as well as any future fiscal dividends which may accrue, will largely be distributed in these models to Federal nondefense purchases and State and local governments through grants-in-aid and to business and consumers either through transfer payments or direct tax cuts. Although total Federal expenditures is projected to decline as a portion of GNP, Federal nondefense expenditures will be an increasing proportion of the total.

State and local government purchases had increased as a proportion of GNP from 8.3 in 1957 to 9.2 percent by 1965 and to 9.8 percent in 1968. The 1980 projections reflect a continuation of high rates of growth for State and local government purchases, but they do constitute some slow down from the very high rates of the most recent period. This slow down in the rate of increase results from an expected deceleration in school enrollment: an absolute decline at the primary school level and a slow down in the rate of increase for secondary schools and colleges. Though a slowing down of State and local expenditures is projected, they will still grow faster than GNP and are projected in 1980 to make up 10.8 percent of the total gross national product.

Projected industry output. In making the 1980 projections, for each of the components of gross national product discussed in the previous section, a projection of the detailed industry structure of demand is developed. These detailed bills of goods are translated into output for each industry by use of a projected input-output table.

In order to examine the sector composition of output a distribution of gross output originating is used.[5] An examination of table 3 reveals that sector composition of gross product originating is changing. The decline in the agricultural and mining proportions, for instance, is readily discernible.

The manufacturing sector has shown, for the historical period, a slight upward trend. However, the projections show that manufacturing's share will return to about the same proportions.

The proportions of gross product originating in trade and services have been rather stable in the past and the projections retain these proportions. Transportation, communication, and public utilities, and finance, insurance, and real estate have increased their proportion in the historical period and are projected to continue this relative growth.

Individual sectors. Table 4 shows those industries which are projected to grow most rapidly

[5] Gross output originating is a measure of the contribution of each sector in terms of payments to the factors of production. These payments, sometimes referred to as value added, when summed for all sectors, equal total gross national product. It differs from a sales or production value of an industry's output in that it excludes cost of materials, supplies, and services used in the course of production.

Table 2. Gross national product by major component selected years and projected 1980

[1958 dollars]

Component	1957	1965	1967	1968	Projected 1980 Basic models	
					3-percent unemployment	4-percent unemployment
Gross National Product	452.5	617.8	674.6	707.6	1,165.0	1,155.0
Personal consumption expenditures	288.2	397.7	430.3	452.6	758.3	751.9
Gross private domestic investment	68.8	99.2	100.8	105.7	186.3	184.7
Nonresidential	47.4	66.3	73.6	75.8	130.4	129.3
Residential structures	20.2	23.8	20.3	23.3	40.9	40.5
Net inventory change	1.2	9.0	6.9	6.6	15.1	15.0
Net exports	6.2	6.2	3.6	0.9	9.6	9.5
Government	89.3	114.7	140.0	148.4	210.8	208.9
Federal	51.7	57.9	74.8	78.9	85.0	84.3
State and local	37.6	56.8	65.2	69.5	125.8	124.6
				Percent distribution		
Gross National Product	100.0	100.0	100.0	100.0	100.0	100.0
Personal consumption expenditures	63.7	64.4	63.8	64.0	65.1	65.1
Gross private domestic investment	15.2	16.1	14.9	14.9	16.0	16.0
Nonresidential	10.5	10.7	10.9	10.7	11.2	11.2
Residential structures	4.5	3.9	3.0	3.3	3.5	3.5
Net inventory change	.3	1.5	1.0	.9	1.3	1.3
Net exports	1.4	1.0	.5	.1	.8	.8
Government	19.7	18.6	20.8	21.0	18.1	18.1
Federal	11.4	9.4	11.1	11.2	7.3	7.3
State and local	8.3	9.2	9.7	9.8	10.8	10.8

	Gross National Product by Major Component Selected Periods and Projected 1965–80 (Average annual rate of change) [1]			
	1957–65	1965–68	1965–80 Basic models	
			3-percent unemployment	4-percent unemployment
Gross National Product	4.0	4.6	4.3	4.3
Personal consumption expenditures	4.1	4.4	4.4	4.3
Gross private domestic investment	4.7	2.1	4.3	4.2
Nonresidential	4.3	4.6	4.6	4.6
Residential structures	2.1	—0.7	3.7	3.6
Change in business inventories			3.5	3.5
Net exports of goods and services			3.0	2.9
Government purchases of goods and services				
Federal	3.2	9.0	4.1	4.1
State and local	1.4	10.9	2.6	2.5
	5.3	7.0	5.4	5.4

[1] Compound interest rates between the terminal year.
SOURCE: Historical data are from the Office of Business Economics, U.S. Department of Commerce. The projections are by the Bureau of Labor Statistics.

Table 3. Sector composition of gross output originating [1] selected years and projected 1980

[Percent distribution based on 1958 dollars]

Sector	Selected Years						Projected 1980	
							Basic models	
	1950	1957	1963	1965	1967	1968	3-percent unemployment	4-percent unemployment
Total	100.0	100.0	100.0	100.0	100.0	100.0	100.0	100.0
Agriculture, forestry and fisheries	5.7	4.8	4.4	4.0	3.7	3.5	3.2	3.2
Mining	3.0	3.0	2.5	2.4	2.4	2.3	2.0	2.0
Construction	4.6	4.7	4.0	3.8	3.4	3.4	3.5	3.5
Manufacturing	29.7	29.7	29.5	30.8	30.5	31.2	30.3	30.3
Transportation, communication and public utilities	8.7	9.1	9.4	9.6	9.9	9.9	11.2	11.2
Wholesale and retail trade	17.0	16.6	16.8	17.0	16.9	16.9	17.4	17.4
Finance, insurance, and real estate	11.5	12.6	13.5	13.5	13.5	13.5	14.8	14.8
Services	9.3	9.2	9.5	9.3	9.4	9.3	9.6	9.6
Government and government enterprises	10.1	10.4	9.8	9.4	9.7	9.7	7.9	7.9
Other [2]	.4	—.1	.6	.2	.6	.2	.2	.2

[1] Gross output originating is the contribution of value added by each of the sectors to total gross national product.
[2] Includes rest of the world and statistical residual.

Source: Historical data are from U.S. Department of Commerce, Office of Business Economics. Projections are by the Bureau of Labor Statistics.

from 1965 to 1980. The ten sectors shown have projected growth rates ranging from about 6.0 percent a year (in real terms) for research and development to over 10.0 percent a year for office, computing, and accounting machines. Most of these industries have had high growth rates in the recent past so that the projections are a continuation of high growth rates for these sectors.

Projected Changes in the Structure of Employment. One of the primary objectives of the 1980 projections is to determine the effect of projected changes in the level and structure of demand on the employment structure by industry.

Total employment is projected to increase from 74.6 million in 1965 to 98.6–99.6 million by 1980, an annual rate of increase of 1.9 percent a year, which is considerably faster than the 1.2 percent a year rate which prevailed during the 1957–65 period.

The changes in the structure of employment between 1965 and 1980 as shown in table 5 generally are expected to be similar in many ways to those shifts experienced during the 1957–65 period. These changes—past or projected—are the net result of two basic forces: the rate of change in the output of the sector and the rate of productivity change within the sector. Increased output tends to require more employees; productivity increases mean that fewer employees are required for a given output. Thus, the service sector—which has experienced a high rate of increase in output and a relatively low productivity change—has had

large increases in employment. This sector—including personal, business, and private educational and medical services, has the second highest rate of growth in projected employment of the major sectors and the largest relative increases as a proportion to total employment—up by over 3 percent from 1965 to over 18 percent of the total in 1980. Concomitantly, the 7 million new jobs projected in the service sector are the most for any of the sectors. These projections reflect a continuing shift in demand for services and lower than average increases in productivity for the service industries.

Agriculture—with moderately increasing output but a very substantial productivity change—has had absolute declines in employment. Agriculture is projected to continue to have large increases in productivity accompanied by small gains in output that will result in further declines in employment.

Mining employment also has been declining for many years. This is attributable largely to

Table 4. Industries projected to grow most rapidly in output,[1] 1965–80

Sector number	Sector name
51	Office, computing and accounting machines
63	Optical, ophthalmic and photographic equipment
57	Electronic components and accessories
66	Communications; except radio and TV broadcasting
28	Plastics and synthetic materials
68	Electric, gas, water, and sanitary services
52	Service industry machines
32	Rubber and miscellaneous plastics products
73	Business services
56	Radio, television and communication equipment
10	Chemical and fertilizer mineral mining
29	Drugs, cleaning, and toilet preparations
74	Research and development

[1] Output growth is change in real terms of gross duplicated output. This differs from gross output originating in that it counts in the output of each industry its cost of materials as well as the products primary to its output which are made in other sectors as secondary products.

above average gains in productivity and decreased demand for mining products, particularly for coal. This sector is projected to continue to decline in employment, although at a reduced rate, because of some resurgence of coal demand.

Contract construction is one of the major sectors to show a substantially faster rate of growth in employment from 1965 to 1980 than from 1957 to 1965. Nearly 1.5 million new jobs are projected to be available in this sector by 1980. The projected increase in employment results from rising State and local government

needs, sharply increased housing requirements, and expanding investment by business.

The manufacturing sector historically has had, and is projected to continue to have, the largest single share of total employment. It is, however, a declining share—from 25 percent in 1965 to just over 22 percent in 1980. This is a consequence of the sector's slightly lower-than-average rate of growth in output, particularly from 1965 to 1980, along with its somewhat higher than average productivity gain. Still, manufacturing is projected to provide between 3.5 and 4.0 million new jobs between

Table 5. Civilian employment [1] by major sector, selected years and projected 1980

[Thousands of jobs]

Sector	1957	1965	1967	1968	Projected 1980 Basic models 3-percent unemployment	4-percent unemployment
Total	67,842	74,568	78,906	80,788	[2] 99,600	98,600
Agriculture, forestry, and fisheries	6,233	4,671	4,196	4,154	3,188	3,156
Mining	868	667	649	646	590	584
Construction	3,701	3,994	3,981	4,050	5,482	5,427
Manufacturing	17,586	18,454	19,805	20,125	22,358	22,133
Durable	10,098	10,644	11,670	11,854	13,274	13,141
Nondurable	7,488	7,810	8,135	8,271	9,084	8,992
Transportation, communications, and public utilities	4,453	4,250	4,470	4,524	4,976	4,926
Trade	13,709	15,352	16,160	16,604	20,487	20,282
Finance, insurance, and real estate	2,786	3,367	3,569	3,726	4,639	4,593
Services	8,446	11,118	12,194	12,678	18,280	18,097
Government	7,616	10,091	11,398	11,846	16,800	16,632
Households	2,444	2,604	2,484	2,435	2,800	2,770
			Percent distribution			
Total	100.0	100.0	100.0	100.0	100.0	100.0
Agriculture, forestry, and fisheries	9.2	6.3	5.3	5.1	3.2	3.2
Mining	1.3	0.9	0.8	0.8	0.6	0.6
Construction	5.5	5.4	5.0	5.0	5.5	5.5
Manufacturing	25.9	24.7	25.1	24.9	22.4	22.4
Durable	14.9	14.3	14.8	14.7	13.3	13.3
Nondurable	11.0	10.5	10.3	10.2	9.1	9.1
Transportation, communications, and public utilities	6.6	5.7	5.7	5.6	5.0	5.0
Trade	20.2	20.6	20.5	20.6	20.6	20.6
Finance, insurance, and real estate	4.1	4.5	4.5	4.6	4.7	4.7
Services	12.4	14.9	15.5	15.7	18.4	18.4
Government	11.2	13.5	14.4	14.7	16.9	16.9
Households	3.6	3.5	3.2	3.0	2.8	2.8

Sector		1957-65	1965-68	Projected 1965-80 Basic models 3-percent unemployment	4-percent unemployment
			Average annual rates of change [3]		
Total		1.2	2.7	1.9	1.9
Agriculture, forestry, and fisheries		3.6	3.8	2.5	2.5
Mining		3.2	1.1	0.8	0.9
Construction		1.0	.5	2.1	2.1
Manufacturing		.6	2.9	1.3	1.2
Durable		.7	3.7	1.5	1.4
Nondurable		.5	1.9	1.0	.9
Transportation, communications, and public utilities		.6	2.1	1.1	1.0
Trade		1.4	2.6	1.9	1.9
Finance, insurance, and real estate		2.4	3.4	2.2	2.1
Services		3.5	4.5	3.4	3.3
Government		3.6	5.5	3.5	3.4
Household		.8	-2.2	.5	.4

[1] Includes wage and salary workers, self employed and unpaid family workers.
[2] See chapter II for conversion from 102.5 million 1980 employ-ment shown earlier to the 99.6 million shown in this table.
[3] Compound interest rates between the terminal years.

1965 and 1980.

Total transportation employment has declined gradually throughout much of the postwar period, primarily because of a reduction in railroad employment. Recent increases in trucking and air transportation, however, have reversed this trend and total employment is projected to increase slowly through 1980. However, transportation's relative share of total employment is expected to decline further.

Communications and public utilities are characterized by higher than average productivity. The result is that, although services provided by these industries may increase sharply, employment will increase only moderately and decline as a proportion of total employment. On the other hand, employment in finance, insurance, and real estate is projected to increase at a faster rate than the overall average and to be a slightly larger share of total employment in 1980 than in the most recent period.

Because the trade function is interwoven so thoroughly with the economy, particularly the goods portion, changes in employment in this sector usually parallel those of the economy. Trade employment in the 1980 projections maintained exactly the same relative share of total employment as it held in 1965—20.6 percent. Given the very substantial size of the sector, trade is expected to contribute about 5 million new jobs between 1965 and 1980—ranking third among the major sectors as a source of new employment.

As a projected source of new jobs, State and local government ranks second with over 6 million jobs. In contrast, Federal Government civilian employment is projected to increase only moderately by 1980. However, since State and local government employment is much larger than Federal Government, the share of total employment attributable to government is expected to increase from 13.5 percent in 1965 to 16.9 by 1980.

Many of the Federal Government programs which may be expanded substantially by 1980 involve expenditures which are considered, in the national income and product accounts, as either transfers of funds to individuals and nonprofit organizations or grants to State and local governments. Examples of such programs

are aid to education, manpower training and retraining, and antipoverty programs, medicare, and area development. From the view point of demand for final goods and services, expenditures resulting from these programs appear as purchases of goods and services by consumers and State and local governments rather than as purchases by the Federal Government.

Employment by the household sector, which has virtually stabilized in the past decade, is projected to increase very slowly to 1980. If the projections are realized, household employment in 1980 will equal that of agriculture at about 2.8 million.

Industries with the highest rates of growth in employment are shown in table 6. Most of the sectors which have rapid growth in projected employment also will be among the most rapidly growing sectors in terms of output; in fact, of all industries on the list of highest output growth only three—communication; electric, gas, water, and sanitary services; and, chemical and fertilizer mineral mining—do not appear among the rapidly growing employment sectors. (See table 4.) The reason these sectors are not among the rapidly growing in terms of employment is that each has a high projected rate of growth in productivity.

Alternative models. In making and presenting the 1980 projections, the emphasis has been on the basic models. Because a number of crucial variables enter into the projections, another set of models also was developed in order to analyze what effect, if any, a significant change in some of these variables would have

Table 6. Industries projected to grow most rapidly in employment, 1965–80

Sector number	Sector name
51	Office, computing and accounting machines
73, 74	Business services
	State and local government
57	Electronic components and accessories
23	Other furniture and fixtures
32	Rubber and miscellaneous plastics products
46	Materials handling machinery and equipment
52	Service industry machines
67	Radio and TV broadcasting
50	Machine shop products
29	Drugs, cleaning, and toilet preparations
28	Plastics and synthetic materials
62	Scientific and controlling instruments
70	Finance and insurance
55	Electric lighting and wiring equipment
76	Amusements
56	Radio, television, and communication equipment
63	Optical, ophthalmic and photographic equipment
11, 12	Construction

Table 7. Projected 1980 labor force, hours and gross national product

Item	Projected 1980				Average annual rate of change [1] 1965-80			
	3-percent unemployment		4-percent unemployment		3-percent unemployment		4-percent unemployment	
	Basic	High durables	Basic	High durables	Basic	High durables	Basic	High durables
Total labor force (thousands)	100,727	100,727	100,727	100,727	1.8	1.8	1.8	1.8
Unemployed	2,940	2,940	3,918	3,918	.9	.9	1.0	1.0
Employment (jobs concept)	102,896	102,896	101,867	101,867	1.9	1.6	1.8	1.8
Government [2]	18,500	18,100	18,315	17,918	2.9	2.8	2.8	2.7
Federal	4,900	5,100	4,851	5,049	0.5	0.7	0.4	0.7
State and local	13,600	13,000	13,464	12,869	4.1	3.8	4.0	3.7
Private	84,396	84,796	83,552	83,962	1.7	1.7	1.6	1.6
Hours paid for (annual average)								
Private	1,977	1,977	1,977	1,977	-.2	.2	-.2	-.2
Total man-hour (millions)								
Private [3]	166,858	167,642	165,189	165,996	1.4	1.5	1.4	1.4
GNP per man-hour (1958 dollars)								
Private	6.54	6.54	6.54	6.54	3.0	3.0	3.0	3.0
Total GNP (billions of 1958 dollars)	[4] 1,168.6	[4] 1,172.1	[4] 1,156.9	[4] 1,160.3	4.3	4.4	4.3	4.3
Government	76.7	75.0	75.9	74.2	2.8	2.6	2.7	2.6
Federal	23.6	24.4	23.4	24.2	0.5	0.8	0.5	0.7
State and local	53.1	50.6	52.6	50.0	4.1	3.8	4.0	3.7
Private	1,091.9	1,097.1	1,081.0	1,086.1	4.5	4.5	4.4	4.4

[1] Compound interest rate between terminal years.
[2] The government employment to be consistent with the government product is from national income accounts. Government employment shown elsewhere in this report is from the Bureau of Labor Statistics establishment reports.
[3] Man-hours are estimated for the private sector only since the assumption is made of no change in hours of the government sector.
[4] The 1980 GNP is as calculated using the factors shown above. All calculations using the total GNP elsewhere in the report use 1,165.0 and 1,170.0 for these two models.

on the structure of industry employment in 1980.

The second set of alternative models for 1980 explored the effects of a different composition of GNP on the industry structure of output and employment. This second set of models also has a 3-percent unemployment and a 4-percent unemployment model. The factors determining the 1980 GNP are similar to those in the basic models except that the employment distribution in this model has lower government employment. The resulting higher private employment with its higher productivity results in a 1980 GNP about 5 billion higher than the respective basic models. Table 7 shows the factors which determine GNP in the high durable models and compares them with the same factors in the basic model with similar unemployment rates.

The composition of GNP in the second set of models is more heavily weighed toward durable goods than in the basic models. This change in the distribution was selected to provide a reasonable alternative since all aspects of durable goods are subject to a high degree of variability and are consequently more difficult to project. Therefore, it is important to analyze their effect on the structure of employment. The elements that are increased as a proportion of GNP in the alternative models are consumer durables, business investment (particularly producer durable goods) and defense expenditures (with emphasis on military hard goods). Table 8 highlights the change in the distribution of GNP in the 1980 high durable models compared with the 1980 basic models.

The change in assumptions has resulted in a quite different distribution of gross national product. The Federal Government proportion is higher because of the assumption about increased defense expenditures. State and local government is lower by approximately the same proportion. The demand of the private sector is characterized by a larger proportion devoted to fixed investment. In personal consumption expenditures, although a smaller part of GNP in the high durable models, a larger portion has been devoted to durable goods expenditures.

With the distribution of demand changed in the high durable models, it should follow that the distribution of employment will be affected. Table 9 shows a comparison of projected employment for 1980 in the basic models and the high durable models.

The distribution of employment in the 1980 high durable models is noticeably different from the basic models. Construction, and durable goods manufacturing have a larger share of total employment than in the basic model. Although manufacturing has a larger share in the high durable models than in the basic models, it is still a declining share. Services and government on the other hand, both have a lower share of employment than in the basic models but these sectors still have an increasing share of employment relative to the current distribution.

The alternative models, therefore, have shown that changing the distribution of GNP in the high durable models do not affect appreciably the overall level of employment but do have considerable effect on the distribution of total employment. Further, they clearly show that changes in the distribution of demand of the magnitude introduced in the alternative models are sufficient to change the rate at which employment shifts away from goods-producing sectors to services and government but do not alter the direction of that shift.

Implications. Important implications result from the projections because of the projected shift toward services and government employment. These sectors have generally experienced lower increases in output per man-hour than the goods-producing sectors. Since it can be expected that pressure for larger wages will also be experienced in these sectors, the implications for prices are important. If wage increases exceed gains in output per man-hour, pressure on costs will increase because of the rise in unit labor costs, which ultimately must effect prices. Therefore, unless price declines

are prevalent among goods-producing industries, the effort to hold down inflation will be increasingly difficult.

In addition to the implications the shift toward services has important implications for the efforts to control inflation, it has a further effect in that the economy will be less prone to severe swings in employment. Services and government employment is usually less volatile than employment in the goods-producing sectors. As employment shifts toward services and State and local government, the Nation should experience much smaller and less severe swings in employment, when business downturns are experienced.

Another implication raised by these projections is the continuing decline in farm employment opportunities. As employment shifts away from the farm more problems will occur in urban areas that have under-funded public services, inadequate housing, and out moded transportation systems.

The 1980 projections show services and government employment increases of about 7 million each. A large number of these workers will be in areas such as the medical sector, which includes occupational groups already in critically short supply. Increased employment requirements in the medical or education fields as well as other sectors which require high skills or a significant amount of training have implications for educational planning. Expansion must be planned for professional schools

Table 8. Projected 1980 gross national product by major component.

[Billions of 1958 dollars]

Sector	Projected 1980				Percent Distribution Projected 1980				Average annual rate of change 1965-80 [1]			
	3-percent unemployment		4-percent unemployment		3-percent unemployment		4-percent unemployment		3-percent unemployment		4-percent unemployment	
	Basic model	High durables	Basic model	High durables	Basic model	High durables	Basic model	High durables	Basic model	High durables	Basic model	High durables
Gross National Product	1,165.0	1,170.0	1,155.0	1,160.0	100.0	100.0	100.0	100.0	4.3	4.4	4.3	4.3
Personal consumption expenditures	758.3	748.0	751.9	741.6	65.1	63.9	65.1	63.9	4.4	4.3	4.3	4.2
Durable goods	133.2	142.1	132.1	140.9	11.4	12.1	11.4	12.1	4.7	5.2	4.7	5.1
Gross private domestic investment	186.3	200.2	184.7	198.5	16.0	17.1	16.0	17.1	4.3	4.8	4.2	4.7
Fixed investment	171.2	184.1	169.7	182.5	14.7	15.7	14.7	15.7	4.4	4.9	4.3	4.8
Nonresidential	130.4	137.3	129.3	136.1	11.2	11.7	11.2	11.7	4.6	5.0	4.6	4.9
Residential	40.9	46.8	40.5	46.4	3.3	4.0	3.3	4.0	3.7	4.6	3.6	4.6
Net exports	9.6	9.6	9.5	9.5	.8	.8	.8	.8	3.0	3.0	2.9	2.9
Government	210.8	212.2	208.9	210.4	18.1	18.1	18.1	18.1	4.1	4.2	4.1	4.1
Federal	85.0	99.8	84.3	99.0	7.3	8.5	7.3	8.5	2.6	3.7	2.5	3.6
State and local	125.8	112.4	124.6	111.4	10.8	9.6	10.8	9.6	5.4	4.7	5.4	4.6

[1] Compound interest based between terminal years.
SOURCE: Historical data are from the Office of Business Economics, U.S. Department of Commerce. Projections are by the Bureau of Labor Statistics.

Table 9. Projected 1980 civilian employment [1] by major sector

Sector	Projected 1980				Percent distribution				Average annual rate of growth [3]			
	3-percent unemployment		4 percent unemployment		Projected 1980				1965 80			
					3 percent unemployment		4 percent unemployment		3 percent unemployment		4 percent unemployment	
	Basic	High durables	Basic	High durables	Basic	High durables	Basic	High durables	Basic	High durables	Basic	High durables
Total	99,600	[2] 99,400	98,600	[2] 98,400	100.0	100.0	100.0	100.0	1.9	1.9	1.9	1.9
Agriculture, forestry, and fisheries	3,188	3,192	3,156	3,160	3.2	3.2	3.2	3.2	2.5	2.5	2.5	2.5
Mining	590	588	584	582	.6	.6	.6	.6	.8	-.8	.9	-.9
Construction	5,482	5,595	5,427	5,539	5.5	5.6	5.5	5.6	2.1	2.3	2.1	2.2
Manufacturing	22,358	23,240	22,133	23,005	22.4	23.4	22.4	23.4	1.3	1.5	1.2	1.5
Durable	13,274	14,322	13,141	14,176	13.3	14.4	13.3	14.4	1.5	2.0	1.4	1.9
Nondurable	9,084	8,918	8,992	8,829	9.1	9.0	9.1	9.0	1.0	.9	.9	.8
Transportation, communications and public utilities	4,976	4,961	4,926	4,911	5.0	5.0	5.0	5.0	1.1	1.0	1.0	1.0
Wholesale and retail trade	20,487	20,501	20,282	20,296	20.6	20.6	20.6	20.6	1.9	1.9	1.9	1.9
Finance, insurance and real estate	4,639	4,538	4,593	4,593	4.7	4.6	4.7	4.6	2.2	2.0	2.1	1.9
Services	18,280	17,785	18,097	17,606	18.4	17.9	18.4	17.9	3.4	3.2	3.3	3.1
Government	16,800	16,200	16,632	16,038	16.9	16.3	16.9	16.3	3.5	3.2	3.4	3.1
Households	2,800	2,800	2,770	2,770	2.8	2.8	2.8	2.8	.5	.5	.4	0.4

[1] Civilian employment includes wage and salary employment, self employed and unpaid family workers.
[2] The 200,000 lower civilian employment in the high durables alternative, results from the Armed Forces' levels of 2.9 million being higher than the 2.7 million in the basic model.
[3] Compound interest rates between terminal years.

as well as for technical schools that train medical and dental technicians, in addition to technical aids in such areas as computer software technology or architectural engineering technology.

Large employment increases are also projected for personal services and wholesale and retail trade. These sectors employ hotel and motel workers and other service-oriented workers in addition to the workers needed to staff the expanding retail trade sector. Both of these areas have had difficulty in attracting personnel, because of the nature of the work and because of the pay scales. Both sectors will need to adjust wages or change the manner of doing business, or they will experience increasing difficulties in completing for talented and trained employees.

Construction, a sector currently experiencing shortages of skilled workers, will require, according to the 1980 projections, over 1.4 million additional employees. In order to meet this need, unquestionably more training will be needed, as well as increased apprenticeship opportunities and the elimination of unreasonable restrictions of entry in the skilled trades. Providing trained construction workers has been a question of increasing concern. It is one which must be answered if the Nation is to meet the critical needs in housing and public facilities.

Since the largest employment increases are projected for those areas in which serious shortages of highly trained and skilled personnel, already exist, the projections imply a need for a serious look at training and educational facilities to insure that they can meet the requirements of the 1970's.

14

Franklin James and James W. Hughes

MODELING REGIONAL GROWTH

INTRODUCTION

The phenomenon of inconsistency at the national level, as projections of regional models done for many states and metropolitan areas are aggregated, is just now being investigated. The sum total of the employment and population projections of individual regional plan studies is considerably higher than independent national forecasts. This type of pattern, at a lower scale of aggregation, has occurred within states as well. The costs of this lack of consistency are difficult to quantify because they are chiefly the opportunity costs of better information, but they certainly are not insignificant. The development of a state economic growth model should provide a framework of consistent and accurate building blocks of fact required by state and local policymakers to evaluate the immediacies of alternative approaches aimed at achieving certain objectives.

This section reviews alternative methodologies for forecasting statewide economic growth. The predictive approach recommended, shift and share analysis, overcomes the limitation highlighted above by assuming that statewide growth is a direct function of national growth. This type of methodology may then limit the bias of inconsistency of aggregative projections. The basic input into this submodel then, is the national employment projection for each particular industry. The output, correspondingly, is the state's share of the national growth forecast for each industrial category.

REGIONAL GROWTH MODELS

Models of regional growth are as much tools of understanding as they are predictive tools. This fact cannot be over-emphasized. As predictors, these models have not been subjected to thorough and competent testing.*

An extensive literature appraising these models is developing.** The principal accomplishment so far is the cataloguing and classification of techniques currently being used in regional growth models. Although they have been used most importantly in predictive applications, the test of appropriateness of techniques employed in this mode has been the "reasonableness"

---

*The design of the models projecting employment growth for a state will be one exception. These models will be designed on the basis of an appraisal of simple techniques coming into fairly wide usage. Unfortunately, all alternatives cannot be subjected to similar testing, because of the great expense this would entail. These tests will be of the absolute accuracy of the tool, other than its relative advantage over possible alternatives.

**See Models of Urban Land Use: A Survey and Critique (New York: National Bureau of Economic Research, forthcoming); and David Boyce, et al., Metropolitan Plan Making (Philadelphia: Regional Science Research Institute, 1970).

of the model. The question addressed in these critiques has been the extent
to which the model structure appears to represent the behavior of participants in the process of regional change. No attempt has been made to measure thoroughly the accuracy of these models as predictive devices.

In general, this emphasis on the descriptive power of the model appears to
be quite useful in itself.* These models are powerful analytical devices.
The design and use of models of regional growth educates participants by
exposing relationships in the process of growth which are not necessarily
obvious on the basis of casual or even thorough investigation. These models
represent a type of general analysis impossible without them. The interrelationships which form their basis are of sufficient importance that their
delineation in the model structure is a very valuable achievement in itself.
The incorporation of these relationships into a closed system also makes it
possible to simulate the impact of various phenomena, and to describe the
results of alternative events, and the phenomena operating jointly which
produced the results. A "descriptive" model of regional growth can thus
serve as an enormously powerful educational tool, as well as a predictive one.
As a matter of fact, for many purpsoses quantitative predictive accuracy is
less important than the descriptive content of the model. Thus, a state may
require a model of its growth both to obtain accurate and consistent projections of this process, and also to delineate the forces operating on and
within the state for change.

The classical structure of regional models of land use, which has remained
substantially unaltered over the last decade, is of the following form:

1. In general, projections of regional employment, population,
    and households are made;

2. sub-models allocate the "basic" or non-population serving
    employment projected level within the region;

3. population and households are then distributed within the
    region on the basis of the distribution of basic employment;**

4. on the basis of this geographic distribution of population
    and basic employment, population-serving employment is allo-
    cated geographically. There are, of course, several variants
    of this overall process, but this basic structure is almost
    universally employed.

---

*Of course, while it is impossible to test the accuracy of predictions
of future events, it is possible to test the basic structure of the models
by using back casting techniques, in which the model is employed to predict the recent past using data drawn from the past, and comparing the
"predictions" of these past events with the events which actually occurred.
This type of testing is necessary for progress in "scientific" predictive
tools, i.e., those tools using clearly defined and reproducible techniques.

**This first generation model consists only of these first three
steps.

Two major assumptions implicit in this structure raise some questions as it is adapted to corridor-type states, such as New Jersey. First, employment levels and employment distribution within the region are assumed to be independent.* This assumption is problematic for New Jersey, for example, because to a large extent a major determinant of the level of economic activity within the state is the locational decisions of economic activity within the New York and Philadelphia Metropolitan Areas. For New Jersey and other similar states there is no well defined or perhaps even defineable demarcation between inter- and intra-regional locational decisions. The traditional models of regional development focus on this dichotomy.

The second assumption involves the proposition that population levels and location are independent, and that both are to a major extent dependent on the level and location of employment. Again this is inapplicable to many states. In New Jersey in 1960, for instance, approximately 150,000 residents commuted to jobs in New York State.** At the same time, almost 60,000 persons residing in New York commuted to New Jersey jobs, and almost 31,000 Pennsylvania residents worked in New Jersey. In that year apparently five percent of New Jersey's jobs were held by out-of-state residents, while a considerably larger portion of the New Jersey labor force was employed out-of-state. A large portion, of course, was employed in Manhattan and Philadelphia.

This heavy interdependence of New Jersey's population and jobs in the activity in New York State and City, and Pennsylvania and Philadelphia, (and similar situations in many other states) makes the traditional modeling framework to some extent inadequate for the analysis of a single state alone. Obviously, this interdependence of economic activity must be an explicit portion of any analytical framework for any state.

REGIONAL EMPLOYMENT PROJECTION MODELS

Shift and Share Analysis

A class of techniques currently used to project employment can be subsumed under the rubric "extrapolations." Obviously these techniques are of limited but varying sophistication. It is this specific limitation which leads to their principal advantage: extreme simplicity and economy. Although the

---

*Employment levels are considered a function of macro-variables and employment distribution a function of micro-variables. That is, employment levels are a function of national trends while the distribution is considered a function of local characteristics.

**Commuting Patterns of Workers Employed in New Jersey, (Trenton: New Jersey Department of Labor and Industry Research, Series No. 3, February 1961), p. 38.

class of extrapolative methodologies lacks substantive theoretical underpinnings, a variant of the technique designated shift and share analysis has
become quite popular and has received some theoretical advocacy.*

The difference between basic extrapolation and the shift and share technique
is relatively straightforward. The extrapolation methodology assumes that
industrial employment growth rates in the future will be identical to those
of the past. The shift and share technique asserts that patterns of variation in industrial growth rates among regions will remain constant through
time, but that absolute growth rates must be normalized by the anticipated
growth of all regions combined. Thus, shift and share analysis maintains
patterns of differences among regional growth rates, but adjusts all regional growth rates by some constant factor to make them consistent with the
growth anticipated for all regions combined.

The shift and share technique decomposes economic growth in a region into
two principal components. The first is the growth anticipated in the market
for the output of the region. If the region maintains its share of the
markets in which its output is sold, the rate of growth of regional output
will be identical to that anticipated in the entire market. If this share
is not maintained (if there is a shift in the share of the market satisfied
by the region) then the region's growth is asserted to respond to a so-
called "competitive component," which can, of course, be positive or negative, depending on whether the region is growing more or less rapidly than
its markets. The shift and share model is best thought of as a variant of
extrapolation. If the expected market growth is anticipated to be constant
through time, the region's growth in the shift and share model is also projected as constant. The model rests on the stability of the competitive
component. The advantage of this model is chiefly its simplicity and its
relative inexpensiveness to estimate.

Thus the technique partitions economic growth into two components. The first
is the "expected" or average rate of growth for all regions. This is often
the rate of growth in the nation as a whole.** The second component is the
deviation of the actual growth of the region from this average. This difference is termed the "competitive component" of the region's growth. It is
asserted that these growth rate differences among regions result from
characteristics of the regions making them more or less attractive to the
growing activity.

------

*See Victor R. Fuchs, Changes in the Location of Manufacturing in the
United States since 1929. (New Haven, Conn.: Yale University Press, 1962),
and Harvey S. Perloff, et al. Regions, Resources, and Economic Growth,
(Baltimore: Johns Hopkins Press, [1961, c 1960]) In both works, shift
and share analysis is used quite extensively.

**
The National Planning Association has employed the growth of so-called
market areas" in its implementation of the shift-share techniques as estimates of the expected rate of growth. These market areas are defined as the
area in which the region's products are sold, and are estimated using Census
of Transportation data on the origin and destination of shipments of various
products. The validity of this approach is somewhat questionable, however.
For an excellent theoretical analysis of the problems facing such definitions
of market areas within housing markets, see William Grigsby, Housing Markets
and Public Policy (Philadelphia: University of Pennsylvania, 1963) pp. 33-36.
While Grigsby's arguments were made in a different context, they apply equally
to interregional market relations.

Algebraically, the shift-share model is:

$$E_{ijt} = E_{ijt-1} \quad (B_i + \alpha_j)$$

E is employment, value added sales, or some other variable.

  B_i is the expected rate variable.

  α is the "competitive component."

  i refers to industry.

  j refers to region.

  t refers to time period.

Theoretical criticism of this model has concentrated on two aspects of this formulation. First, questions have been raised about the choice of B_i. Because α_j and B_i are connected in an algebraic identity, questions about the proper choice of B_i inevitably have raised questions about the interpretation of α_j. A separately identifiable challenge has concerned the analytical propriety of the partition. It has been asserted that because presumably both components B and α_j are functions of the same variables--supply and demand changes, technological shifts, etc.--the partition is meaningless.* These theoretical arguments thus center around the necessity of developing some sort of analytical framework devised to estimate directly the expected rate of growth of some economic activity in a region, and question the ability of shift-share analysis to provide a useful framework for the accomplishment of this theoretical task.

These questions have not been adequately addressed, and will not be addressed here. Increasingly, shift-share is being used as a predictive tool of regional growth. This transition is methodologically quite simple. In general, these predictive models assert that the "competitive component" (α_j) is stable through time, and that variations in regional growth rates can be, in large part, attributed to variation in the expected growth rates (B_i). The model thus becomes:

$$E_{ijt+2} = E_{ijt+1} \quad (\alpha_{jt,t+1} + B_{i_{t+1}, t+2})$$

Because quite often the projections made for regional growth employing this model are used in the making of important public and private decisions, analysis of the adequacy of shift-share predictive models is of crucial importance. An empirical analysis in regard to the task at hand is presented in Appendix B.

Economic Base Analysis

In addition to these mechanistic projection models of regional growth, three general models of the regional growth process have been employed as projecting devices: these are economic base studies, input-output analysis, and mathematical programming models. The economic base argument is quite simple.

---

*See D. Houston, "The Shift and Share Analysis of Regional Growth: A Critique." Southern Economic Journal, 32 (1967) 577-581.

The basic concept was first employed by Homer Hoyt and has been developed along Keynesian lines since.*

In this growth model some group of industries is identified as primarily serving export markets. This identification is usually quite ad hoc. Identification procedures commonly employed are: (1) The portion of total regional economic activity in the industry relative to some expected portion (usually the portion of activity in the industry in the national economy). Their difference is usually called the export ratio; (2) information from secondary data sources on shipments from the region of an industry as a portion of total shipments is employed; and (3) actual interviews with a sample of establishments, to determine the location of their markets, and of their sources of supply. This information is not, unfortunately, conclusive in the demarcation of export oriented industries, because, in general, the degree of export activity varies continuously across industries--the dividing line between basic and non-basic industries is unclear. The general operation of these discriminating devices is to determine that most manufacturing activity is basic, and most non-manufacturing activity is non-basic.

The purpose of this partition is to develop a group of industries for which the demand for its output can be taken as substantially exogenous to the economic events in the region itself, while at the same time changes in the demand and output of these industries have important secondary impacts on the nonbasic sector. In general, simple Keynesian tools are used to estimate "multipliers" relating changes in activity of the basic industries to changes in total or nonbasic activity. The magnitude of these multipliers are a function of the propensity of the region to import goods and services from beyond the region (MPI). A typical multiplier computation would be the $1 added output in the basic industries would result in ($1-MPI) of additional income generated in the nonbasic sector. This first round effect would in turn produce ($1-MPI) additional income. Because the MPI is assumed to be between zero and one, each round's effect is less than that of its predecessor, and in equilibrium the total impact of the change in output of the basic industry is $\frac{1}{(MPI)}$.**

This type of multiplier is usually considered excessively crude because it is difficult to introduce inter-industry difference in interregional trade balances. This multiplier need not be estimated directly, of course. It can be approximated quite simply using time series information on activity levels in "basic " exporting industry and in regional population-serving industries. Change in the employment activity of export industries can be related to change in the employment of population-serving industry. These estimated relationships can then be applied to projected employment changes in basic industries to project employment in non-basic industries.***

_____
*See H. Hoyt, "Homer Hoyt on Development of Economic Base Concept," Land Economics 41 (1954), 182-191, for a description of his work in this area.

**This approach has been generalized into an interregional income model and employed for a number of analytical purposes. See H. Richardson, Elements of Regional Economics (Baltimore, Md.: Penguin Books, 1969), Chapter 1, for an excellent summary of these developments and applications.

***Edwin Terry, "Linear Estimators of the Export Employment Multiplier", Journal of Regional Science 6 (1965) pp. 17-34, for a description of these techniques.

Input-Output Analysis

An input-output formulation has been imposed upon the attractively simple notion of the economic base. The study by Walter Isard and Robert Kuene on the impact of the expansion of steel output in the New York-Philadelphia region is a classical example of this technique.* Isard employed expansion plans in progress by U.S. Steel and Bethlehem Steel in the New York-Philadelphia area as the "exogenous" change in a regional basic industry, and used input-output analysis and assumed importing behavior of industries in the region to predict the impact of the plans on economic activity in the entire region.

This classic approach to regional analysis is one simplification of a general inter-regional input-output design of which there exist a considerable number of variants. The basic model which includes this family of approaches is as follows. Instead of the simple structure of the above analysis, in the generalized inter-regional model an inter-regional matrix like that below is specified:

EXHIBIT II-1

GENERALIZED INTERREGIONAL INPUT-OUTPUT MATRIX

		Region 1 Industry A	Region 1 Industry B	Region 2 Industry A	Region 2 Industry B	Region 3 Industry A	Region 3 Industry B
Region 1 Industry	A	a_{11} 1	a_{21}	a_{31}	a_{41}	a_{51}	a_{61}
	B	a_{12}	"	"	"	"	"
Region 2 Industry	A	a_{13}	"	" 2	"	"	"
	B	a_{14}	"	"	"	"	"
Region 3 Industry	A	a_{15}	"	"	"	"	"
	B	a_{16}	"	"	"	" 3	"

*Walter Isard and Robert E. Kuene "The Impact of Steel Upon the Greater New York, Philadelphia and Industrial Regions," which first appeared in The Review of Economics and Statistics 35 (1953), 289-301 and republished in Location Analysis for Manufacturing, (eds. Karaska and Bramhall) The MIT Press, 1969.

The matrix specifies along the diagonal the simple input-output relationships employed in the earlier work by Isard. The other submatrices specify
the extra-regional import-export relations of the economy.

Column one, for example, shows the breakdown of the input required for the
expansion of a unit of output of industry A in region one. The sum of the
entries in column one is equal to one. Each of the entries in column one
can be interpreted as the percent of input into industry A coming from a
given industry and region. A one dollar increase in the output of industry
A in region one requires total input of $(a_{11} + a_{13} + a_{15})$ cents of additional
input of the product of industry A, and an increase of $(a_{12} + a_{14} + a_{16})$ in
the input of industry B. Of these increased inputs, $a_{11}/ (a_{11} + a_{13} + a_{15})$
percent of the additional input of industry A will be produced within the
region, and the residual will be imported from regions two and three.
$(a_{12}/ (a_{12} + a_{14} + a_{16}))$ percent of the increased demand for industry B's
production will be satisfied from "domestic" production.

This is not the final result of the response of the increased production in
region one. The increased demand for the products of industry for inputs
into the expanded production must be satisfied by increased output of the
regional economies. The matrix is employed with a projection of the final
economic demand of the region to determine the nature of the final adjustment. This interregional input-output model thus simulates the impact of
change in any single region on the economies and trade relations of all
regions. Interregional input-output analysis can be a powerful tool
of economic analysis. This general formulation has been approximated most
ingeniously by Leontief and Strout, and has been implemented by the National
Planning Association for New York State Office of Planning Coordination.*
This model employs gravity-model estimates of interregional trade, in which
trade between two regions is directly proportional to the product of the
input requirements of the first and the output of the second; and inversely
proportional to some measure of trade impedence separating the regions.

One of the chief difficulties of input-output analysis has been the definition of inter-sectoral relations active in a region. More often than not,
national tables are employed. This is a highly questionable assumption.
Due to relative price differentials, resource differences, and technological
variation, it can be expected that these I-O relations will vary significantly among regions. Aside from analytical complexity, the I-O techniques
applied conscientiously can be quite expensive because of its relatively
large requirements for primary data.**

---

*The model was developed by W. W. Leontief and A. Strout, "Multi-regional
Input-Output Analysis." Paper presented at the International Conference on
Input-Output Techniques, Geneva, 1961; its implementation in a somewhat simpli-
fied form by the N.P.A. (National Planning Association) is described by
Marshall K. Wood, "The Sequential Economic Modeling System." Paper presented
at the Symposium on Regional and Multi-Regional Input-Output Studies, New
York 1970.

**See W. Isard, T.W. Landford, E. Romanoff, Working Papers, Philadelphia
Region Input-Output Study, Volumes I, II, III, and IV (Philadelphia: Regional
Science Research Institute, 1967 and 1968), for a report on the process of
estimating an input-output model for the Philadelphia metropolitan area. The
data requirements for the estimation of an inter-regional input-output matrix
are enormous. If, for instance, the nine major Census regions were employed,
and a fifty industry breakdown were desired, the matrix would contain
9x9x50x50, or over 200,000 elements.

Despite its apparent complexity and cost, and its apparent popularity, input-output analysis is subject to a number of rather severe shortcomings. The most obvious shortcomings concern the stability and interpretation of the input coefficients. The first question concerns industry definitions. These definitions are crucial, of course, for the interpretation of coefficients. Within even four-digit industries, there exists considerable variation in input requirements of constituent industries. The acceptable degrees of industrial aggregation is essentially an empirical question, depending on region and industry, and is not a conceptual difficulty of the technique. The major conceptual difficulty of the analysis is the assumption of a constant and invariant mix of input requirements of an industry through time. The input requirements of an industry employed in the analysis are those observed at the point in time at which the input table was estimated. Obviously these input requirements change through time as technology and relative price variation among these inputs change. These changes cannot easily be introduced into the model. The extreme case of this shortcoming of the technique is when industries require input of some factor which is available to a region in only a fixed and finite amount. In this case, the I-0 technique could very well project industrial growth requiring impossible utilization of this resource. This problem is a special and extreme case of factor price changes, of course.

The input-output technique is both a crude and complex procedure. In addition, its use for a corridor state such as New Jersey for instance, seems highly questionable because the technique somewhat artificially includes locational factors into the model only through trade relations. It is undoubtedly true that a major source of this state's growth is directly attributable to explicitly locational decisions of establishements operating within the New York and Philadelphia metropolitan regions. To analyze them as "domestic" establishments "exporting" their product to meet the input requirements of New York and Pennsylvania establishments and households seems highly artificial.

Mathematical Programming Models

The basic tools of input-output analysis have been employed in two highly related techniques of regional planning: (1) comparative industry cost estimation, including industrial complex analysis; and (2) mathematical (linear) programming optimizing models of regional and interregional developments.

The first group of these is fairly obvious. Comparative cost analysis, whether of a single industry or an industrial complex, involves simply estimating the profitability or cost advantage of an industry or group of industries in a region, based on the assumption in general that input and output can be purchased or disposed of at known prices. It is a partial analysis and, like most partial analyses, can be extraordinarily misleading in the analysis of regional growth.*

---

*For a discussion of these techniques, see W. Isard, op. cit., chapter 9, pp. 375-413, and W. Isard, E. Schooler, and T. Vietorisz, Industrial Complex Analysis and Regional Development (Cambridge: The M.I.T. Press, 1959).

A more general analysis with an optimizing framework is interregional linear programming. This optimizing model follows the structure of the linear programming problem: The function to be optimized is a linear function of a number of variables, which are themselves linear combinations of "inputs" subject to upper limit constraints on their availability. Objective functions are typically designed to maximize the sum of regional incomes, minimize transportation costs required to supply a product, and many others. The technique is optimizing in only a partial sense, as is true of comparative cost analysis, because it does not, in fact, include such factors as household and labor adjustment to response to regional economic change. In addition its data requirements can be immense, just as interregional input-output analysis. Consequently, the technique has never been applied operationally in planning applications.*

METHODOLOGY SELECTION

These commonly employed procedures to project regional employment vary greatly in their complexity and costs and in their analytical elegance. It is not clear, however, that they vary greatly in accuracy or reliability as predictive models, or in their economic content. To a large extent these models remain untested, despite controversy about their relative accuracy. In this uncertain condition, it is difficult to select on rational grounds between alternative possibilities, because the trade-off between cost and accuracy, if any, is impossible to specify. Though a "highly tooled, multi-jeweled... creation"** has great appeal both because of the intellectual satisfaction available from its design, and because its very complexity offers some extra-rational credence to its value, simplicity and low cost are very real advantages of regional forecasting models.

The underlying philosophy is that a simple tool is preferable to one that is more complex unless it can be shown that either the simple tool is useless, or that the more complex model is sufficiently more accurate to justify its greater cost of implementations. For this reason, the conditional implementation of shift-share techniques for the projection of manufacturing employment in the Regional Plan is proposed. The implementation of this projection device will be conditional on a test of the accuracy of this model of regional growth as a predictive device for states in the post-war period.*** These tests indicate significant predictive ability of the model in "backcasting" experiments, and thus it satisfies the above criterion of simplicity. Thus shift and share analysis is the technique to be used in the first submodel, Primary Employment Projection.

---

*For an introduction to the linear programming technique, see R. Dorfman, P.A. Samuelson, and R. Solow, Linear Programming and Economic Analysis (New York: McGraw Hill, 1958); and for its application to regional problems, see Isard, op. cit., Chapter 10, pp. 413-492.

**B. Berman, "Analysis of Urban Problems-Discussion", American Economic Review 51 (1961) p. 300; as quoted in J.R. Meyer, "Regional Economics: A Survey," L. Needleman Regional Analysis (New York: Penquin Books, 1968) p. 43

***This test is fully described in Appendix B, where the model was tested for New Jersey. The context of the entire model testing procedure is described in Appendix A.

SECTION III

PRIMARY EMPLOYMENT ALLOCATION AND HOUSEHOLD GENERATION

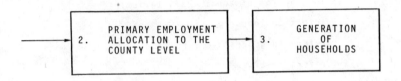

INTRODUCTION

The output of the models projecting regional employment is utilized as inputs into sub-models designed to allocate these activities geographically within the region. This demarcation is made on the assumption that the factors determining regional and intra-regional location decisions are quite different and can be adequately modeled as independent decisions.

EMPLOYMENT ALLOCATION

The principal determinants of intra-regional location of employment have as yet not been precisely isolated. As a result, empirical models of these determinants have been somewhat lacking in sophistication. The utilization of such limited models, at times, tended to compromise the value of enormously expensive quantitative regional models. Although there is some variation among regional models, the general structure of these intra-regional employment allocation models is generally either:

$$(1) \quad E_{ijt} = AX_{t-1}$$

or

$$(2) \quad E_{ijt} = bE_{ijt-1} + AX_{t-1}$$

where E is employment,

> X is a vector of zonal characteristics,
>
> i refers to industry,
>
> j refers to geographic zone, and
>
> t refers to time

The only difference of importance, but one of potentially great significance, is that the first model is estimated on cross-section data, and the second relies on time series or longitudinal data. The vector of zonal characteristics (X) includes such attributes as population density, land availability and land price; access to markets for output, and to inputs, including labor; zoning constraints; and public service and tax levels.*

---

*For examples of the first model type, see: (1) the models employed by the Delaware Valley Regional Planning Commission to allocate non-manufacturing employment presented in 1985 Regional Projections for the Delaware Valley (DVRPC Plan Report No. 1: 1967); (2) the models employed in the Bay Area Transportation Study, as reported in BATSC Locational Model System (August 1969); (3) the models employed in the Bay Area Simulation Study, as reported in Jobs, People and Land: Bay Area Simulation Study Special Report Number 6.

For two examples of the second type, see: (1) the models employed by the Delaware Valley Regional Planning Commission to allocate manufacturing employment, which are also presented in 1985 Regional Projections for the Delaware Valley; (2) the models employed in the Detroit Traffic and Land Use Study reported in An Urban-Regional Model of Small Area Change for Southeastern Michigan, Consad Research Corporation, July 1969.

The results of the first model are biased toward replicating the initial distribution of employment. This holds because the model is based on the assumption that concentration of economic activity in a zone implies attractiveness of the zone to such activity. Because the present distribution of activity is the result of decisions made over a substantial length of time, and under a wide range of conditions, this assumption need not be true.*

The second model is probably a more accurate predictive device.** For short time periods, it is evidently a variant of a "shift-share" predictive device. If only small changes occur in the characteristics of zones, then the relative rate of growth of activity of a zone is projected substantially unchanged through time. In essence models of the second type project into the future the trends in activity occurring during the study period. When study resources are limited, or for preliminary projections, this technique is most appropriate.

One principal difficulty with this second approach is that the intra-regional distribution of employment is possibly subject to random and cyclical variations which may be highly misleading for long-term projections and for understanding of the determinants of the locations of economic activity. For example, as a result of the secular trend toward suburbanization of manufacturing activity, there possibly exists considerable amounts of excess industrial capacity in core areas of cities. This capacity may be used on a short-term basis during business cycle booms, when prices and demand for manufactured products are high and be unused substantially in recessionary periods when demand is low. As a result the direction of this bias would depend on the cyclical nature of the periods during which the two observations of employment required by the model were made.***

Under these circumstances it is important to employ in the calibration of any model of employment location indicators of the current locational desires of industry which are based to as large an extent as possible on the long-term consideration of locational advantages. At least three such indicators are available and appropriate for the estimation of a model of intra-regional employment location. These are (1) the location choices of new establishments; (2) the origin and destination of moving establishments; (3) and the location of new industrial construction.

---

*This so-called "cross-section bias" is more fully discussed in John F. Kain, "The Distribution and movement of Jobs and Industry," in James Q. Wilson The Metropolitan Enigma (New York: Anchor Books, 1970) and H. James Brown, et al, Models of Urban Land Use: A Survey and Critique (New York: National Bureau of Economic Research, forthcoming).

**The Detroit Talus employment projection seems highly questionable. See F. James and R. Struyk, "Recent Trends in Industrial Composition and Location," the NBER Urban Simulation Model: Volume II (National Bureau of Economic Research, mimeo). Their problem was perhaps produced by exogenous constraints imposed on the operation of the model, expressly to increase the inertia of the distribution of employment.

***For a more complete discussion of these problems, see J.F. Kain, "The Distribution and Movement of Jobs and Industry," op. cit.

The location of new establishments offers an implicit ranking of all alternative locations. Presumably, each new establishment chooses, or tends to
choose, the location which is optimal. Moreover, because the decision is
substantially irrevocable, or it can only be changed at great cost, it is
made on the basis of long-term considerations. If new establishments have
locational desires similar to those of all establishments, then their locational decisions appear to meet the requirements set above for an indicator
of the locational desires of industry.*

Moving establishments offer an explicit ranking of their origin and destination zones, and implicit ranking of their destination zone and all other
zones. The direct expenses of moving can be large and the indirect expenses,
in terms of possible disruption of established relations with suppliers and
markets for output, can be substantial as well.** The locational decisions
of moving establishments should contain information similar in usefulness to
that obtainable from the location of new establishments.

A major determinant of the location of economic activity is the existing stock
of production facilities. Industrial and commercial buildings are physically
very long-lived and geographically immobile.

The income of these buildings, once constructed is in economic terms a
"quasi-rent;" i.e., the price of these buildings will tend to be their value
to the user who places on them the highest value. This rent need not bear
any relationship to the construction costs of the building. As a result,
changes in the locational desires of employers can to a large extent be reflected in rental changes of the stock of real capital, rather than changes
in the actual locational patterns of production. New construction can be
presumed to take place in those locations where the builder believes that
the value of the building will through time, justify the construction costs
of the facility. Because the life of a facility is long, new construction
can be assumed to be made on the basis of long-term expectations, and so
again appears to meet the criteria set above for a satisfactory indicator of
the long term.

-----

*Considerable discussion has, of course, been made of reasons why new
establishments might be expected to have different locational desires from
those of all manufacturing. This discussion has centered around the incubator hypothesis of E. Hoover, which suggests that new establishments tend
to be more dependent on the market provision of several sorts of services
which established firms can provide themselves internally. Examples of these
services are legal and financial services, rentable space, and knowledge of
markets for inputs and outputs. No substantial evidence has been presented
to support this hypothesis, and some has been presented which does not support it. See R. Struyk and F. James, The Process of Change in the Intrametropolitan Location of Industry (NBER manuscript) Hoover's incubator
hypothesis is presented in Anatomy of a Metropolis (See footnote below).

**Edgar Hoover described establishment movement as "traumatic" in
Anatomy of a Metropolis (New York: Anchor Books, 1962) p. 28.

The translation of new construction into new employment offers some difficulty, of course, but this problem can be handled adequately by estimating capital-labor or space-per-laborer relationships using available data. The analysis of new construction has a corresponding advantage. The explicit output of function relating new construction to zonal characteristics may be transformed into a function relating location-rents and zonal characteristics. This relation is of considerable analytical interest and can serve as the basis of a satisfactory model of the determinants of employment location desires, and thus as a tool for the projection of employment location.

Data are available in many states which make possible the analysis of all three indicators of the locational desires of employers, as well as the time series data on the intra-state distributions of employment necessary for the estimation of the traditional model of intra-regional employment location. Because so little satisfactory analysis has been completed on the determinants of the locational patterns of employment, in Appendix C the patterns and process of employment growth within New Jersey are examined.

The results indicate that the growth or decline of individual establishments dominates the process of employment location change. This basic process is thus of greater significance than the relocation, birth, and death of in-dustries in terms of the distribution of employment within the state. Re-location therefore is <u>not</u> the most powerful process altering employment dis-tribution in the case area, New Jersey.

<u>It would not be unreasonable, based on this analysis, to employ the allo-cation model which relies on longitudinal data</u>; this model is essentially a variant of a "shift-share" predictive device.

$$E_{ijt} = bE_{ijt} + AX_{t-1}$$

As described earlier in this chapter, models of this type project the trends of activity occurring during the study period into the future. This is a suitable technique for initial projections and when implementation resources are limited. <u>Thus a variation of the shift-share methodology developed in Appendix B should be employed as a first approximation Employment Allocation sub-model</u>.

GENERATION OF HOUSEHOLDS

The output of the above model allocating employment to the county level (Employment Allocation sub-model) is used as inputs into models (Household Generation sub-models) which will convert county employment into heads-of-households and consequently, households. A household is by definition the group of persons residing in a housing unit. Because a substantial portion of employees are not heads-of-households, but rather wives or young persons who are employed and live with their families, the growth of households should be less than the growth in employment, other factors held constant. Additionally, the number of employees who are heads-of-household varies by occupational type. Thus employment must be converted initially into occu-pations and consequently into household heads.

The first sub-model of the Household Generation sub-model involves the adjustment of present occupational distributions* by industry to reflect 1980 technological conditions. Each industry, it should be emphasized, requires a specific occupational mix. As an economy matures and evolves, changing technological factors result in adjustments to each industry's occupational structure. Recognizing this fact, the Bureau of Labor Statistics has developed a series of change coefficients to project the industry occupational matrix.** It is possible to employ these coefficients in a sub-model which is methodologically straightforward. Each cell in the industry occupational matrix is multiplied by the corresponding cell of the change factor matrix. This operation generates the 1980 industry occupational matrix.

$$\boxed{\begin{array}{c} 1970 \\ \text{Industry} \\ \text{Occupational} \\ \text{Matrix***} \end{array}} \quad X \quad \boxed{\begin{array}{c} \text{Change} \\ \text{Coefficient} \\ \text{Matrix} \end{array}} \quad = \quad \boxed{\begin{array}{c} 1980 \\ \text{Industry} \\ \text{Occupational} \\ \text{Matrix} \end{array}}$$

If each column of the 1980 industry occupational matrix is multiplied by the 1980 employment growth forecast for the industry corresponding to each column, then the growth in employment by occupation for each industry is obtained. If each of the rows is then aggregated, the total employment growth by occupation becomes available. This can be done for all county or sub-regional areas.

For each of these occupational groupings, a varying proportion tends to be heads-of-household. These proportions can be determined from the 1970 Census data or from investigations by such regional agencies as the Tri State Regional Planning Commission which encompasses broad portions of New York, New Jersey, and Connecticut. In the initial calibration of the larger model, the sub-model converting occupations to heads-of-household can be determined by applying constant proportions over time. While further refinements obviously are desired in more advanced models, certain important questions have to be answered. For example, if more women choose careers, as presently seems to be the case, and if marriage rates remain constant, then a decreasing proportion in each occupation will be heads-of-household. Unless the Bureau of Labor Statistics or other national agency undertakes rigorous investigations of such trends, little definitive work can be done within a study of limited financial means. Nevertheless, to assume a constant proportion of each occupational group who are heads-of-household should not introduce significant error in a first approximation of household heads. This latter category, obviously, is a surrogate for the total number of households.

By use of two sub-models, the total number of households and the number of households by occupation can be determined. These outputs are important inputs into the Household Characteristics and Housing Demand sub-model, the subject concern of the next section.

---

*Available from the 1970 United States Census.

**Source: U.S. Department of Labor, Bureau of Labor Statistics, Tomorrow's Manpower Needs, Vol. IV, The National Industry-Occupational Matrix and Other Manpower Data, Bulletin No. 1606, February 1969, pp. 221-247.

***Occupational distribution (percentages) in each column for each industry.

15

Management and Economics Research, Inc.

ECONOMIC AND FISCAL IMPACTS
OF A NEW AUTONOMOUS ENTERPRISE IN AN AREA

An autonomous enterprise is an "export" industry in that it serves customers outside the area in which it is located. Nevertheless, an autonomous enterprise has direct economic and fiscal impacts on the area in which it is located, and these impacts may be measured.

The Economic Impact

The economic impact of a new autonomous enterprise may be measured in total income generated in the area by such an enterprise. In doing so, three time periods must be distinguished:

1. The construction phase: Income is generated by the construction of facilities to house the new enterprise and by the other expansions that derive from this enterprise. Although the construction phase may generate income for local businesses, the income effects are essentially transitory, in that the income stops upon completion of the construction phase.

2. The short-run phase: An increase in total income and employment results rather quickly from new spending in the local economy, but there is no change in the basic structure of the local economy. Rather, income is generated by expansion of existing local industries in response to demands of the new autonomous enterprise.

3. The long-run dynamic phase: The basic structure of the local economy may change in response to the original stimulus. New industries may be established to provide goods and services previously imported. Others may be established to make use of new labor pools that arise because of the expanded activities of the autonomous enterprise and its suppliers. Such effects change the economic structure of the area and may even result in a long-run increase in the area's growth rate that becomes independent of the original stimulus.

the impact of income increases during the construction phase is transi-
y and will therefore be omitted from further discussion. Income impacts
in the short and long run need further explanation.

The Short-Run Impact

The short-run impact has three distinct components:[1]

1. The direct income impact: the wage, salary, and other income pay-
    ments (such as profits and interest) of the new autonomous enter-
    prise.

2. The indirect income impact: the wage, salary, and other income pay-
    ments of those local industries and suppliers who provide goods and
    services to the new enterprise.

3. The induced income impact: the increases in wage, salary, and other
    income payments of local consumer goods industries and their local
    suppliers brought about by consumption spending out of augmented
    incomes.

To follow the complex web of income payments, a hypothetical example is
offered of a new firm, manufacturing lead pencils for shipment to a nationwide
market. The firm is assumed to be moderately small, with a payroll of 230 persons, and sales of approximately 1.25 million gross of pencils per year at a
wholesale value of $3.5 million. Assumed operating expenses, profits, and
revenues for this firm are shown in Table 4.

Direct and Indirect Income Impacts. If we assume that local entrepreneurs
have established the plant, the direct income impact will include the profits
of the enterprise, as well as wage and salary payments, for a total direct impact of $1.4 million.

The indirect impact is that part of the $2.1 million spent by the pencil
manufacturer on goods and services that remain in the local economy as income
payments. In other words, it is that portion of the $2.1 million that does
not leak out of the local economy through purchases of goods and services from
firms outside the local area.

To determine the indirect impact, it is necessary to first determine the
portion of the $2.1 million that is spent by the pencil manufacturer in the
local economy. It is then necessary to estimate the leakages for the purchase

1/ Hansen et al., Markets for California Products (Ref. 49).

FIGURE 1

DIRECT AND INDIRECT INCOME IMPACT OF A HYPOTHETICAL
PLANT IN A "LARGE" AREA
Dollar Amounts in Millions

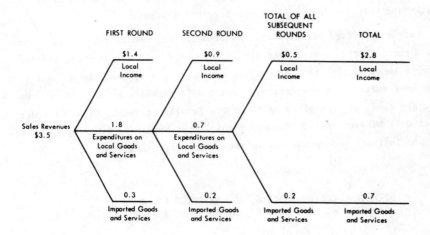

FIGURE 2

DIRECT AND INDIRECT INCOME IMPACT OF A HYPOTHETICAL
PLANT IN A "SMALL" AREA
Dollar Amounts in Millions

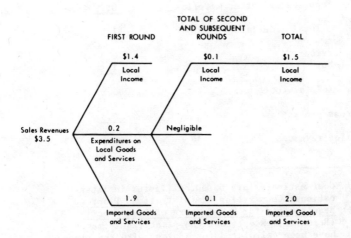

of imports that would occur at each subsequent round of purchases: for example, the pencil manufacturer may purchase pencil slats from a local lumber mill, which in turn buys rough lumber from a mill outside the area. To fully evaluate the leakages, data describing the complex of interindustry relations in the local area are required. As will be discussed later, input-output is a technique that provides a framework for this analysis.

Four specialized products are required for the manufacture of lead pencils: pencil slats, leads, ferrules, and erasers. If all of these are manufactured locally, then the import leakages will be very small in the first round of spending, and the indirect impact will probably be very large. On the other hand, if none of these items are locally produced, then the indirect impact will be very small. Figures 1 and 2 show hypothetical examples of direct and indirect income impacts in two alternative situations:

Table 4

OPERATING COSTS, PROFITS, AND REVENUES FOR A
HYPOTHETICAL LEAD PENCIL MANUFACTURING FIRM[1]/

	Millions of Dollars
Costs	
Materials	
Pencil slats	$0.7
Leads	0.5
Ferrules	0.25
Erasers	0.25
Supplies and other material	0.1
Total materials	$1.8
Services	0.3
Labor	1.1
Total costs	$3.2
Gross profits	0.3
Sales revenues	$3.5

1/ Cost estimates are based on figures in International Cooperation Administration, Plant Requirements for Manufacture of Lead Pencils (Ref. 61), except that the plant requirements have been calculated for a plant with ten times the volume of the one in Ref. 61. Annual price and wage inflation factors of 2 percent and 3 percent respectively have been added.

1. Location in a "large" metropolitan area, one that is capable of
    supplying three of the four specialized products needed by the
    pencil manufacturer; many of the more generalized needs, such as
    office supplies, maintenance materials, packing boxes, and busi-
    ness services; and a large part of the needs of the subsidiary
    industries.

2. Location in a "small" metropolitan area, one that is incapable of
    supplying any of the specialized products needed for pencil manu-
    facturing, and also providing fewer of the generalized needs.

As the figures show, the total direct and indirect income impacts are
much greater in the "large" area, with 80 percent of sales revenues providing
income to local persons and businesses. In contrast, almost no indirect
income is generated in the "small" area without industries to supply the needs
of the pencil manufacturer. Therefore, only 43 percent of the revenues of the
pencil manufacturer provide income to local inhabitants; the remainder provides income to residents of other areas.

Induced Income Impact. The direct and indirect increases in income are
augmented by the induced income that stems from the consumption expenditures
of the income recipients. It was estimated in the 1963 Economic Report of
the President that $0.50 of each dollar of national income is spent on con-
sumption, the other $0.50 going for taxes, savings, and imports from foreign
countries. The multiple effects on income of increases in autonomous spending (direct and indirect) are measured by a consumption or income multiplier,[1] which may be defined as:

$$\frac{1}{1 - \text{proportion of income spent on locally produced consumption goods and services}}$$

For the nation, the multiplier is 2.0; that is, $\frac{1}{1 - 0.50}$.

Other things being equal, the income multiplier for any local area will
be smaller than the national multiplier, since many of the goods and services
consumed in the local area are imported from other areas of the country.
Therefore, if an area provides only half of its own U.S. consumption goods,
only $0.25 will be spent on local consumption goods and services in each
spending round, and the multiplier is 1.33; that is, $\frac{1}{1 - 0.25}$.

---

[1] For further definition and description of the income multiplier, see
     International Cooperation Administration, Plant Requirements for Manu-
     facture of Lead Pencils (Ref. 61), and Tiebout, "A Method for Determining
     Incomes and Their Variations in Small Regions" (Ref. 96).

Thus, the more self-sufficient a local economy, the closer the local consumption multiplier will be to the national multiplier. The general thesis, as reported in the literature, is that the size of the consumption multiplier increases with the size of the area's population.[1] However, an accurate estimate of an area's multiplier requires statistical verification, since factors other than size enter into the determination of relative self-sufficiency, such as proximity to other producing centers, diversity of the industrial structure, and consumption patterns of the local inhabitants. Under no conditions can the simplistic view that each employee in an autonomous industry requires an additional employee in support industries be accepted as a meaningful approximation of the income multiplier for communities.[2]

On the basis of the studies available, it may be assumed that a large, diversified, metropolitan area will have an income multiplier of about 1.8. This means that in each round of consumption, $0.44 of each dollar of local income will be spent on locally produced consumption goods and services ($1.8 = \frac{1}{1 - 0.44}$). On the other hand, a small, modestly diversified metropolitan area would have a multiplier of about 1.3, equivalent to spending $0.23 out of each additional dollar of income on locally produced consumption goods and services.

Total Income Impact. The total income impact of the pencil plant is found by applying the appropriate income multiplier to the sum of direct and indirect income. There is no automatic correlation between the size of the indirect impact and the size of the consumption multiplier; a small area specializing in lumber products may provide many of the specialized needs of a pencil plant, and a large, diversified area may not. For purposes of this illustration, the 1.8 multiplier is assumed to apply in the case of the "large" area (Figure 1), and the 1.3 multiplier is assumed to apply in the case of the "small" area (Figure 2). The "large" area, then, would have total

---

[1] See Ullman, "The Basic-Service Ratio and the Area Support of Cities" (Ref. 99).

[2] Chamber of Commerce of the United States, What New Industrial Jobs Mean to a Community (Ref. 21).

income of about $5.0 million generated by the pencil plant ($2.8 million in direct and indirect income times 1.8), whereas the "small" area would have total income of only $1.95 million.

The Long-Run Impact

For many areas, the long-run impact may be of greater importance than the short-run impact, because the long-run impact may be a dynamic one resulting not only from economic growth but also from an increase in the rate of growth. This change in the rate of growth stems from a change in the economic structure and environment of an area, that is, a change in the mix of industries located in the area and a change in the attractiveness of the area to new people and new enterprises.

Whether or not a new plant will act as a catalyst in the growth process to bring about a change in the economy out of proportion to the short-run stimulus will depend on the way the new plant interacts with other activities in the area and on other circumstances. Thus, two areas experiencing similar short-run impacts could have very different long-run impacts. Only a detailed study of conditions in each area will yield reasonable hypotheses about the dynamic impact of plant location.[1]

Techniques for Analyzing Economic Impact

The principal tools currently in use for the study of economic impact are multiplier and interindustry (input-output) analyses. In their present forms, these tools use short-run static analyses, with change in the economic structure of areas introduced exogenously, i.e., as data given to the models.

As noted in the example, the multiplier is an expression of the multiple effects on income of increases in autonomous spending.[2] The form of multiplier analysis most commonly used for regional impact analysis is called

---

1/ Examples of such studies appear in Committee for Economic Development, Community Economic Development Efforts: Five Case Studies (Ref. 24).

2/ Tiebout, "Community Income Multipliers: A Population Growth Model" (Ref. 97).

"base theory"; it identifies "exports" to places outside the area as the only autonomous element to be considered.[1]

In the classification scheme posed earlier in this report, the autonomous elements include the direct and indirect impacts, and the non-autonomous (often termed non-basic or service) elements include the induced impacts. There are many studies of small areas in which efforts have been made to derive base-service multipliers, but most of these have relied on very crude techniques of analysis in which whole industries or whole industry sectors (i.e., manu-facturing, trade, service, government) are classified as either basic or service (non-basic). In general, there is great confusion in the literature as to how to identify and classify the indirect impacts.

Input-output is a form of interindustry analysis used to aid in deter-mining the indirect and induced economic impacts of an autonomous enterprise. The first function of an input-output analysis is to provide an accounting system to trace the short-run flow of goods and services from one productive sector to another.

Many regional studies employing input-output analysis rely for their interindustry coefficients on studies at the national level, specifically the U.S. Interindustry Study of 1947.[2] The difficulty with using national co-efficients for regional analysis is that there are no studies to show whether such use is justified for all regions of the country. More reliable regional

[1] The concept of base theory and its use for small area analysis has been set forth in Andrews, "Mechanics of the Urban Economic Base" (Ref. 2). Reasons for concentrating on exports as the crucial autonomous variable are discussed in North, "Locational Theory and Regional Economic Growth" (Ref. 80). Further discussion and critique of base theory appears in Spiegelman, "A Method for Determining the Location of Footloose Indus-tries" (Ref. 94).

[2] Examples are given in Cumberland, A Regional Interindustry Study of Maryland (Ref. 27), and in Moore and Peterson, "Regional Analysis: An Inter-Industry Study of Utah" (Ref. 75).

input-output studies are probably those primarily using locally collected data on production and trade to create a truly local accounts table.[1]

It is important to analyze industries and their markets separately in order to develop an accurate estimate of economic impact. For instance, in the case of the hypothetical example used here, the pencil plant must purchase rubber erasers, the manufacture of which is included in an industry whose standard industrial classification number is SIC 3069. In the 80 x 80 U.S. Interindustry Table for 1958, this industry is part of the two-digit classification SIC 30, which includes all industries manufacturing rubber and plastic products. Another plant in the same area manufacturing tires (SIC 3011) will also be in the same two-digit category. Thus, without more detailed information, the fact that rubber erasers would have to be imported is disguised.

Except for the forthcoming Philadelphia study, there are no regional input-output tables of sufficient detail to delineate local purchase of any particular new plant.[2] Existing tables could at best be used to determine the second and subsequent rounds of indirect impact. These subsequent rounds, however, are of only small importance in determining the income impact of a new plant on an area. As can be seen in Figures 1 and 2, the direct income impact and the first round of indirect impact account for more than 80 percent of the total direct and indirect impact in the case of the large area, and about 100 percent in the case of the small area. However, an input-output table can be useful in estimating the income multiplier as a basis for determining induced income impacts.

---

[1] Examples are given in Hansen et al., Markets for California Products (Ref. 49); Hirsch, "Interindustry Relations of a Metropolitan Area (Ref. 56); and Hochwald et al., Local Impact of Foreign Trade (Ref. 57).

[2] Currently a very large and detailed interindustry study is being conducted by Professor Walter Isard at the University of Pennsylvania, which will develop an accounts table for Philadelphia distinguishing about 500 industries. This will be the most detailed in the country.

The apparent economic impact on an area depends on where the boundary lines defining the area are drawn, and the boundaries relevant for a particular analysis will depend on the policy purposes for which the analysis is being made. Thus, a multistate region, a state, a metropolitan area, a county, or a city may be the area of analysis at different times. The impact of any single plant location will be less as one moves down the size scale of areas. However, the task of projecting the impact of a single location becomes increasingly difficult as one moves down the size scale of areas, because there will be more alternative sources of supply to meet new demands. Thus, a pencil plant located in a particular city may be supplied by one of several lumber mills located in the same state but in different cities and counties. Analysis of the state would consider the supplies as part of local production; analysis of the city would consider them as imports.

Another aspect of area delineation that relates to relative impact is commuting to work. We have assumed that the economic impact in an area is given by the wage, salary, and other income payments of the enterprise. But these payments may be considered as income generated in an area only if the workers who receive them live in that area. Thus, if a plant generates $1 million in wage payments to workers all of whom live in other communities, the impact on the community containing the plant will be zero. A possible rule for meaningful impact analysis, therefore, might be that no area being analyzed should be smaller than that necessary to encompass the homes of most of the workers in the establishments studied. Thus, it is unlikely that meaningful impact analyses could be conducted for areas smaller than counties or even groups of counties.

The Fiscal Impact

Fiscal impacts, like economic impacts, vary according to the characteristics of the area and those of the new enterprise; they also vary according to the nature of the economic impacts. It is frequently contended that any new autonomous investment will result in a net fiscal benefit to a community. This contention, if supported by numerical data at all, is based on a comparison of local government revenues accruing directly from the new establishment with costs directly chargeable to it. Empirical cost studies of this type have estimated that industry produces a ratio of revenues to costs of about three to one in Greenwich, Connecticut,[1] and Evanston, Illinois;[2] five to one in Arlington, Virginia;[3] and four to one in Yorktown, New York.[4]

However, the fiscal impact is a function not only of the costs and revenues attributable to the new establishment but also of the costs and revenues attributable to the households of employees establishing residence in the area. Furthermore, both the new establishment and its resident employees stimulate other activities and employment with which costs and revenues are associated. In other words, evaluation of the fiscal impact of a new autonomous investment should consider each level of economic impact identified in the preceding discussion--direct, indirect, and induced.

Because of the complex interrelationships involved, a definition of the area of interest is critical. For example, if a new plant locates in one area, its employees reside in another, and supporting commercial or industrial activities are established or expanded in a third, the fiscal impacts will differ sharply from the case where all these are in the same area. Some studies of fiscal impact have avoided the problem of area definition by the expedient of starting with a well-defined, relatively homogeneous area. Others have been concerned primarily with the fiscal impact in a specific political entity, and as a result do not provide an estimate of total impact.[5]

---

[1] Frederick P. Clark and Associates, Economic Study (Ref. 37).

[2] Homer Hoyt Associates, Economic Survey of the Land Uses for Evanston, Illinois (Ref. 58).

[3] Homer Hoyt Associates, Economic Survey of the Land Uses of Arlington County, Virginia (Ref. 59).

[4] Frederick P. Clark and Associates, Land Use and Community Taxes (Ref. 38).

[5] See Isard and Coughlin, Municipal Costs and Revenues Resulting from Community Growth (Ref. 65); Hirsch, "Fiscal Impact of Industrialization on Local Schools" (Ref. 55); and Sosnick, "The Local Tax Impact of a New Plant" (Ref. 93).

Some studies of fiscal impact dealing primarily with specific political entities suggest that major inequities can result within a metropolitan complex when men and the capital with which they work are separated.[1] One study found that certain types of economic activity were advantageous to an area only if a large proportion of the prospective employees lived in this area.[2]

Although no hard and fast rule can be suggested for delineating the appropriate area to use, in general the area should be large enough to include the major fiscal impacts--those associated with the industrial activity, with its employees, with the supporting activities generated, and with their employees. For practical purposes, it is probably sufficient to limit the study area to one that includes 80 to 90 percent of the commuting pattern.

Studies on fiscal impact indicate that the following factors, listed roughly in the order of their importance, should be considered:

1. Assessed value of the autonomous enterprise (land, plant, equipment, and inventory) per employee.

2. Proportion of employees who establish new households in the area.

3. Average earnings per employee.

4. Non-property tax revenues per employee, reflecting sales to residents or enterprises in other areas.

5. Requirements of the enterprise for special government services, particularly those involving large capital expenditures.

6. Impact on subventions and shared revenues from higher levels of government.

_____

[1] See Loewenstein, "The Impact of New Industry on the Fiscal Revenues and Expenditures of Suburban Communities" (Ref. 70); and Groves and Riew, "The Impact of Industry on Local Taxes--A Simple Model" (Ref. 47).

[2] Harvey, Types of Economic Activity Suitable for Marin County (Ref. 52).

Assessment of the revenue-cost balance attributable directly to a new establishment involves consideration of (1), (4), and (5) above. Assessment of the balance attributable directly to employees involves consideration of (3) and (4). In addition, as indicated earlier, further adjustment should be made to reflect economic activities and added employment stimulated by the new enterprise and its resident employment.

These factors are interrelated and none is controlling. However, they are discussed separately below to indicate their major elements.

Assessed Value per Employee

Assessed value per employee varies widely among industry groups and among firms within these groups. It is a function of land, improvements, equipment, and inventory values. Published data, such as those available in the Census of Manufactures, reflect this variation but are of limited usefulness in assessing potential fiscal contribution of specific new establishments. For example, data on net depreciable assets are underestimates of true value for industries where rental or leasing is widespread. Furthermore, average inventory values may substantially overestimate taxable inventories in industries that can adopt a flexible inventory policy.

A study of fiscal impact of assessed value per employee of autonomous enterprise in Marin County, California,[1]/ indicated that even if analysis is limited to a new firm, the result can be positive or negative. The breakeven point will vary according to applicable tax rates, level of government services in the area of concern, and other factors.

Proportion of Employees Establishing Residence in the Area

In allocating government costs and revenues to households in an area, the largest single cost item is education. This item typically varies widely within relatively small areas because of differences among school districts in average cost per pupil and in average daily attendance (ADA), and because of differences in ADA per household.

1/ Harvey, Types of Economic Activity Suitable for Marin County (Ref. 52).

In the Marin County study referred to above, government costs were allocated to households by function (education, general government, charities and corrections, protection, sanitation, roads, and "other"). Since Marin County is heavily residential, about 90 percent of total government expenditure was so allocated to households, with a resulting total per-household cost of $449.

An analysis of the results indicated that the net revenue generated by a new firm increases rapidly as investment per employee increases, but decreases rapidly as percent of employees establishing new residences in the county increases.

A small proportion of the employees of a new activity will consist of new residents if the labor requirements are substantially met either (1) by those living within the area of interest who are unemployed or underemployed, who have been hitherto commuting elsewhere to work, or who are in the pool of secondary wage earners[1] or (2) by new employees commuting to work from outside the area. The second condition is irrelevant if the area studied includes most of the commuting area.

Average Earnings per Employee

In general, as family income levels increase, investment for housing tends to increase.[2] Thus, property tax revenue accruing from a new residence should typically be higher for employees of high-wage industries than for those of low-wage industries. However, an upward shift in residential assessed value may also result from the establishment of a low-wage industry if a large proportion of the employment consists of secondary wage earners, thereby increasing disposable family income available for housing. The latter impact on assessed value can be expected to materialize less rapidly than the former.

1/ Defined as wage earners who are not heads of households and therefore not primarily responsible for establishing a residence in the area.

2/ See Groves and Riew, "The Impact of Industry on Local Taxes--A Simple Model" (Ref. 47), for statistical information on this relationship.

However, there is also an offsetting tendency for the level of government expenditures, particularly those for education, to increase as average assessed value increases. Methods have not been developed for predicting the net fiscal result of these offsetting tendencies.

Higher local incomes, whether generated by a high-wage industry (as opposed to a low-wage industry) or by increased secondary employment, result, typically, in higher consumer expenditures in the area than would otherwise be the case. As a result, sales tax revenues (if a sales tax is levied) are proportionately higher than otherwise. These revenues are unevenly distributed within the area according to the location of the commercial establishments. For those jurisdictions containing the establishments and for the area as a whole, there is a favorable fiscal impact.

Non-Property Tax Revenues per Employee

In areas in which a sales tax is levied, a new autonomous enterprise may provide a direct contribution to government revenue in addition to the property tax. The impact will vary according to the applicable law. In California, sales taxes are payable with respect to non-retail sales of some enterprises, but the location of the office of record determines the locality that receives credit for the tax. This is an important consideration where branch plants are involved, since the office of record typically is located elsewhere.

Many localities use business licenses or similar levies as a revenue device. In the aggregate, the amounts collected are relatively small, but for some political jurisdictions they constitute a sizable revenue item. Other jurisdictions levy a wage tax on employees of firms located in their area. These revenues, like sales tax revenues, are unevenly distributed within the area affected by the new industry.

Requirements for Special Government Services

The fiscal advantage of a specific industrial activity may be substantially reduced if its location will require special government services, particularly those involving large capital expenditures. In general, a new

activity requiring minimal capital expenditures by local government is preferable to one with equal assessed value requiring a large capital expenditure.

However, the policy adopted by local government regarding such expenditures is critical in the determination of fiscal impact. In some areas,
major capital expenditures, such as those for streets and sidewalks in housing tracts or industrial parks, must be met by the developer or industry involved. Since these expenditures become a part of the assessed value of the
developed properties, local government, in effect, benefits twice--capital
expenditures are avoided, and property tax revenues are increased (at the
same tax rate).

Local government policies vary widely regarding capital expenditures not
so directly identified with specific developments. In some areas, local
jurisdictions will attempt to recover expenditures for extension or improvement of roads, expansion of utility services, and so on. The proportion of
total cost attributable to a specific development is frequently difficult to
estimate and may be the subject of negotiation.

Population growth in general, whether initially generated by a new
autonomous investment or by the development of residential areas for persons
commuting elsewhere to work will cause continual expansion of government services and increasing capital expenditures. These capital expenditures, although typically made in large increments, can be converted into an expenditure stream. But estimation of the increment to this expenditure stream
attributable to a new autonomous investment presents difficult conceptual
problems and requires first the identification of economic impacts attributable to that investment.

Impact on Subventions and Shared Revenues

Development in an area resulting from a new autonomous investment may
affect subventions and shared revenues received by the local government from
higher levels of government. State formulas for distributing funds from the
various motor vehicle and gasoline taxes (usually earmarked for streets and
roads) are frequently based upon population and motor vehicle registrations.
Thus, growth rates and income levels influence such distributions; they are,
therefore, roughly responsive to need.

State subventions for education are also related to growth and frequently reflect both number of pupils and assessed value per pupil. The impact of growth in population and assessed value on these subventions will vary from state to state, depending on the state aid formula. In the case of California, increases in assessed value per pupil result in decreases in state equalization aid. The effect varies somewhat by formula and according to certain locational variables, but, in general, the aggregate property tax gain from increased assessed value far exceeds the reduction in revenues from the state under current financing procedures.[1]

The impact of a single autonomous investment on distributions and subventions from higher levels of government cannot be assessed precisely unless the full economic impact discussed in the first part of this chapter is traced.

The preceding discussion of fiscal impact has concerned primarily the effects of short-run income impacts--direct, indirect, and induced--referred to earlier. Even in this limited area of interest it is clear that fiscal impacts are highly variable and that analysis is both complex and difficult. In fact, little research has been undertaken in this field. However, most research efforts have identified as major determinants of short-run fiscal impact (1) the assessed value per employee of the autonomous establishment, and (2) the proportion of the new employment requirement that is met by area residents.

---

[1] However, Hirsch, in "Fiscal Impact of Industrialization on Local Schools" (Ref. 55), found that increased investment in 7 of the 16 industries he studied did not improve the fiscal health of the school district unless state aid was included as a revenue source.

V

Environmental Degradation
of Urban Regions

16

U. S. Council on Environmental Quality

AREAS OF
CRITICAL ENVIRONMENTAL CONCERN

There is growing consensus that control over land use is probably the most important single factor in improving the quality of the environment in the United States. Land use is a term which encompasses many dimensions; as we develop indicators for land use problems, it is essential to be clear about what these problems are.

Land use indicators, like land use regulation, usually focus on competing uses for the same land. Because each of the competing uses is likely to serve some socially beneficial purpose, it is often difficult to interpret indicators in any absolute way. For example, an increase in agricultural land may or may not be desirable, depending on the competing demands. There may be a few absolutes—for example, increases in the amount of unreclaimed surface-mined land are undesirable—but there are not many. The interpretation of data on land use changes usually requires a more complex framework.

One concept used in interpreting land use indicators is "carrying capacity," the intensity of use which, if exceeded, will cause adverse environmental consequences. When deciding among conflicting land uses, one must know an area's natural carrying capacity so that the adverse consequences of exceeding that capacity may be considered. In many cases, one cannot say that this natural carrying capacity should not be exceeded because the adverse consequences usually can be overcome by engineering or other adjustments. Then the relevant question becomes whether the costs of exceeding the natural carrying capacity are worthwhile. Or, put another way, is the "conversion cost" to increase the capacity of land, plus the other costs involved, less than the anticipated benefits?

A report to the Council by Development Sciences, Inc., illustrates this view of carrying capacity with the example of Washington, D.C.:

> The Potomac River and the land which it drains have a certain limited natural capacity to deal with human land use patterns. There are lands of certain soil types and there are water-bearing areas of specific limited quality and quantity. Before World War II and the accompanying population growth of the federal government, the natural cleansing capacity of the river was such that most human wastes were "treated" by natural forces, and low density land use patterns were sustained without excessive pollution or threats to the supply of water.
>
> If the land were zoned according to the carrying capacity of the soil and the river's capacity to handle wastes and supply water, the Potomac could not have sustained the growth in land use which the demands of the growth in government placed on the natural environment. Instead, the society paid the "cost of conversion" from using land in its natural state by applying technology such as sewage treatment systems and dams and reservoirs to ensure water quantity and quality for the new population.[17]

When the natural carrying capacity of an area is exceeded, the consequent costs can be paid in the form of remedial measures, such as constructing sewage treatment plants, or in the form of increased environmental damages, such as water pollution. In the Washington, D.C., area, some of the costs of conversion clearly have been paid in the form of reduced environmental quality—more water pollution, air pollution alerts, and threatened shortages of water, for example.

Given the small number of absolute prohibitions on land uses and the limitations of the concept of carrying capacity, most land use data must be put in some type of cost-benefit or supply-demand framework if they are to indicate environmental quality. But in most cases such a framework and the relevant costs and benefits are likely to be local or regional. Many land use indicators would have limited, if any, meaning on a national scale unless they were aggregates of rather complex local or regional indicators.

For example, there is no national policy against converting agricultural or forest land to residential use, and thus national figures on such conversions do not indicate whether land use is improving or deteriorating. To make such an evaluation, one would need to look at each area where conversion is taking place and evaluate the demand for housing in the area, the regional need for open space, the value of the crops or timber produced there, the effect of the conversion on transportation routes and commercial development, the methods for disposing of the wastes generated by the residences, and several other factors. The Federal Government cannot evaluate such changes on a national basis.

The large number of factors to be considered in making and evaluating land use decisions may mean that computer-based models, which can simulate the results of alternative decisions, will be a necessary adjunct to a system of indicators. Several projects to develop such models are underway or have been completed. For example, the National Science Foundation sponsored development of a national model linking agricultural policy, land use, and water quality by Dr. Earl Heady of Iowa State University. NSF is also supporting work at Oak Ridge National Laboratory to develop regional models that can be used to determine the environmental impact resulting from the location of industrial, commercial, residential, and recreational development. The OBERS model, developed by the Departments of Commerce and Agriculture for the Water Resources Council, projects estimated population, economic activity, and land use for regions of the United States. It may also be useful for considering alternative land use policies. The Strategic Environmental Assessment System being developed by EPA is using the OBERS projections, economic and environmental models, and forecasts of land use and other changes to estimate the condition of national and regional environments 10 to 15 years in the future.

Problems of land use in the United States may be arbitrarily classified into three categories. First, we are concerned about the availability of certain types of land, such as enough agricultural land to grow food, adequate open space for recreation in densely populated areas, and sufficient timberland to meet national pulp and lumber demands. Second, we need to control development in areas of critical environmental concern, including areas of particular environmental value such as wetlands, other rare or valuable ecosystems, and scenic or historic areas. Such areas also include land which, if developed, may pose a direct hazard to man: for example, flood plains, steep slopes, soils unsuitable for development, and earthquake fault zones. Third, there are types of land use development and practices that lead to other problems which, in turn, may have adverse environmental consequences. These include unreclaimed surface mining, practices that lead to soil erosion, urban development patterns which produce pollution, and the spread of areas impervious to water.

Each of the three categories will be discussed after they are put in the context of national trends in land use.

Areas of Critical Environmental Concern

Areas may be of critical environmental concern because they serve a vital ecological, cultural, biological, or aesthetic function. A good example of this type of area is the Nation's wetlands. Areas are also of concern if they pose dangers when developed. Development in flood plains and development on unsuitable soils are examples of this type of problem.

Wetlands—Wetlands are a vital natural resource, characterized by fragile biological and ecological regimes. Some serve as important recharge areas for replenishing ground water. Coastal wetlands may provide a natural barrier that prevents subsurface fresh drinking water supplies from mixing with undrinkable ocean waters. In many shore areas, the mud, sand, and vegetation of wetlands create natural buffer zones to dampen the force of storm-driven waves, thus providing a barrier for areas farther inland. Wetlands are also prime habitat and breeding grounds for both aquatic and airborne wildlife; an estimated 60 to 70 percent of fish caught in U.S. coastal waters, either commercially or for sport, would not be there if at one time they had been unable to find shelter, safe spawning, or nutrients in a wetland.[30] Further, coastal wetlands are unique in appearance, contrasting sharply with both developed and other natural areas; they offer a high degree of diversity in the natural landscape.

Because of their beauty and their accessibility to water transportation, wetlands have always been targets for development. In the past, their development has been abetted by government. The Federal Swamp Land Acts of 1849, 1850, and 1860 paved the way for the transfer of nearly 65 million acres of wetlands in 15 states from Federal to state administration in order to expedite their drainage.[31] In recent years, however, the Federal Government and several coastal states have proposed or enacted legislation to ensure that future wetlands development will be consistent with the ecology of the wetlands environment. (See the land use section of Chapter 5.)

Figure 25, which shows an area of New Jersey south of Raritan Bay, demonstrates dramatically five types of development that can impinge on wetlands: A) a saline wetland extends from the bottom left of the photograph to the upper right; it has been extensively ditched in an effort to control mosquitoes; B) the Garden State Parkway is seen cutting across the wetlands; C) in three areas, as noted, surface mining is evident; such activities have caused erosion problems and have affected the viability of the wetlands and local water quality; D) in the center left, a solid waste disposal site imperils both land and water quality; suspended sediment runoff from cleared areas is apparent on the original photograph; and E) high-density housing developments are encroaching onto the wetlands in the upper right of the photograph. New Jersey is one of the States that has enacted legislation to control wetlands development.

The study conducted by the Earth Satellite Corporation for the Council examined three areas to trace patterns of urban growth in coastal wetlands: Ocean County, N.J.; Orange County, Calif.; and Hillsborough County, Fla. In the Ocean County study area, several major high-density residential developments on which construction began in the 1960's consumed 14 percent of the wetlands area and

Figure 25

Development in New Jersey Wetlands

Source: Earth Satellite Corporation

affected a substantial additional area in the wetlands and shallow coastal waters before State legislation halted them in 1970. The rate and character of development in Florida were similar.[32]

In Southern California, the extent of coastal wetlands is more limited than in the East. The area studied contained three tidal lagoons. By 1947, they had been contained by dikes and one had been ditched and diked for intensive oil production. By 1972, another lagoon had disappeared, replaced by high-density residential development.

Development on Flood Plains—Urbanization of flood plains has been a continual process in the United States. In many large cities the locational advantages of easy transportation, power supply, and waste disposal have favored development on the flood plains. All too often, such development has taken place without adequate consideration of the associated hazards and problems.

Historically, the flood plains were intensively developed because of the need of industries to be near water. In more recent years, the pressure of increased population on land resources has been a major factor leading to encroachment on flood plains. Land availability figures prominently in the use or nonuse of flood plains, although even in some places with declining populations, new development takes place in the flood plain. When city populations grow to between 5,000 and 25,000, the pressure to use vacant land begins to encourage development in the flood plains.[33] Industrial and transportation uses have usually accounted for the most significant development. But with further growth of urban areas, residential development in flood plains also becomes significant.

Three areas were picked in the Earth Satellite study to illustrate the changes in flood plain land use characteristics between 1960 and 1970: Baltimore, Denver, and Kansas City. In each city, residential development in the flood plains increased substantially over the 10-year period, even encroaching on tributaries and upstream areas. Industrial and commercial uses increased only slightly, apparently because many new businesses preferred more accessible suburban locations.

Land uses appropriate for flood plains, especially public parks, increased in Kansas City and Denver. Both cities have encouraged open space conservation in flood plains and other environmentally hazardous areas. However, neither city has prevented residential development on the flood plain.

In the Denver urbanized area, the estimated portion of flood plain land in residential use increased from 9.2 percent in 1960 to 29.9 percent in 1970. This 225 percent increase in residential use compares to a 50 percent increase for the region as a whole. Part of this increase in flood plain development was due to the beginning of construction of the Chatfield Dam after major floods hit the area in 1965.

Despite the fact that the Federal Government has funded flood protection and prevention projects since 1936, national losses from floods have increased because flood plains have been put to residential and other intensive land uses. Such losses now amount to a national average of almost $2 billion annually.[34] Although Federal flood control funding was implemented to protect already existing properties, it has had the effect of encouraging new development projects which increased flood plain occupancy.

The Army Corps of Engineers—the primary agency responsible for building Federal flood control projects—has recognized the problem of flood plain development. It has established a Flood Plain Management Services Program, with units in each of the 47 Corps field offices, to encourage and assist communities that desire to control land use in flood plains. The Federal Government has taken a number of other steps to deal with flood plain development. For example, Executive Order 11296 calls on all agencies to recognize flood hazards in their construction and grant programs. (See the discussion of proposed new legislation in the land use section of Chapter 5.)

As we noted earlier, most land use questions must be considered in a supply-demand or cost-benefit context. In a few cases, the advantages of locating on a flood plain may outweigh the intermittent cost of damage. There can be little question, however, that there are many locations where millions of dollars could be saved by locating high-value industrial, commercial, and residential developments outside the flood plain and developing the land along the rivers for parks and other low-density uses.

Development on Unsuitable Soils—Some of the problems discussed above, such as erosion and flooding, are due in part to the type of soil on which development takes place. Development on unsuitable soils can also cause a variety of other problems—from water pollution by septic tanks to destruction of buildings by landslides.

The nature of the soil differs widely across the United States, and the types of problems that characterize development on unsuitable soils vary from area to area. Three areas with quite different soils were examined in the Earth Satellite study: Montgomery County, Md.; Hillsborough County (Tampa), Fla.; and Ventura County, Calif. Within each of these counties some soils are well suited for development and others are not.

In Montgomery County, the most common soil problems are shallow bedrock which results in water pollution by septic tanks, poor internal soil drainage which causes basement flooding, and "shrink-swell" properties in some of the clays which can cause postconstruction damage to building foundations, roads, and other installations. In Hillsborough County, the most common kinds of unsuitable soils are those with a high water table. In such soils the pollution of ground water by septic tanks and the likelihood of flooded basements are distinct hazards. In Ventura County, the main limitations on urban uses are steep slopes, susceptibility to erosion, internal drainage problems, and the hardpan or water table depth. Within the Southern California valley and mountain coastal region, where Ventura County is located, the serious land-related hazards to urban uses are damage from floods, erosion, and landslides. Construction on earthquake faults also poses obvious dangers.

In each of the three study areas, the Earth Satellite study divided the soil areas into four categories of suitability for development: good, fair, poor, and very poor. The amount of development taking place in each category was then determined.

In Montgomery County, as much development took place on unsuitable soils as on suitable soils (see Table 6). Recent urban expansion appears to have proceeded without much consideration of soil properties that relate to urban use. It also appears that development

Table 6

Development by Class of Soil, Montgomery County, Md.

[Mileage zone from city center [1]]

	8.5	11.0	13.5	16.0	18.5	21.0
Percent of soils in urban use—1957						
Good and fair soils	83	59	27	10	4	1
Poor and very poor soils	45	32	24	7	3	1
Percent of soils in urban use—1971						
Good and fair soils	86	67	47	20	18	3
Poor and very poor soils	45	40	48	13	17	1
Percent increase in urban use, 1957–71						
Good and fair soils	4	14	74	100	450	300
Poor and very poor soils	0	24	100	86	565	0

[1] City center defined as the zero mile marker just south of the White House, Washington, D.C.

Source: Earth Satellite Corporation, "Land Use Change and Environmental Quality in Urban Areas," prepared for the Council on Environmental Quality, April 30, 1973. p. 174.

on unsuitable soil did not occur because land with more suitable soil was lacking.

In Hillsborough County, better (good and fair categories) soils have been brought into urban use at about twice the rate of unsuitable (poor and very poor) soils. Developers and home purchasers in this area were more sensitive to the costs of building on unsuitable soils than those in Montgomery County, in part because the severity of the soil problems in Hillsborough was very obvious.

Many inhabitants of Ventura County have chosen the status of a hillside home over the greater safety of more suitable land. Substantial residential building has taken place on areas of steeply sloping soils subject to erosion, gullying, and landslides, while areas with soils more suitable for urban development have been left unused.

Development on unsuitable soils is the cause of many environmental problems of major concern to homeowners and local communities across the entire Nation. Many problems could be avoided if the unfavorable soil properties were identified before development through the use of soil surveys such as those prepared by the Soil Conservation Service of the U.S. Department of Agriculture. The potential benefits of such surveys can be illustrated by examples of what happens when they are not used. A school in Fairfax County, Va., suffered $250,000 in structural damage because the school site was selected without a soil survey. Soils only 500 feet away were favorable. Communities have lost hundreds of thousands of dollars because pipes were laid in unsuitable soils. In a 7-county area of southeastern Wisconsin, it was estimated that use of soil surveys would save $300 million over the next 25 years in the cost of residential land development by ensuring that new homes were not built on soils unsuitable for septic tanks.[35] The Soil Conservation Service estimates that soil surveys cost only 50 cents to $1 per acre, so the cost-benefit ratio of making and using such surveys to guide development is very high.

Land Use Effects

The broadest, and probably the most significant, land-related problems are secondary consequences of land use patterns and practices. These patterns and practices create problems such as pollution, which in turn endanger man and his environment.

Patterns of land use are a major determinant of pollution levels in any area. The greater the distances that must be traveled between home, workplace, and shops, the more air pollution will be generated by automobile travel. Significant water pollution problems can be generated by development on lakeshores or by placement of septic tanks in unsuitable soil. Many forms of industrial pollution may be reduced by siting a plant so that its wastes can be productively utilized by a neighboring plant. For all types of pollution the degree of concentration of principal pollution sources is a key factor in the level of pollution to which the population is exposed.

Land use patterns also play a significant role in the consumption and availability of natural resources. Pollution often represents misplaced resources. Thus, for example, the added air pollution generated because of longer travel distances also means wasted gasoline. Land development can lead to reduced water supply (by building over ground water recharge areas, for example), reduced soil capability for growing crops (by erosion and poor farming practices), and reduced ability to extract mineral resources (by building in areas where such resources are found).

The Council, in cooperation with EPA and HUD, is conducting several studies to determine more precisely the secondary impacts of development on the environment. These studies include the impacts of highway and sewer construction, second-home developments, and the costs of alternative residential development patterns.

Three problems are covered in this section—erosion, unreclaimed surface mining, and the increasing land area covered by impervious surfaces such as roads, buildings, and parking lots. Erosion is an environmental problem arising from a variety of land use practices; surface mining is a particular type of land use which gives rise to a number of environmental problems; impervious surfaces are a characteristic of all types of urban development. Thus each is a different type of land use issue, but each represents patterns of development which can create adverse environmental impacts.

Erosion—Each day huge amounts of soil in the United States are washed off the land into rivers and streams. The results are a reduction in quality of the remaining soil and water pollution in the form of sediment, nutrients, and other contaminants attached to the sediment.

The Soil Conservation Service (SCS) estimates that more than 3.5 billion tons of soil is lost each year through erosion from the approximately two-thirds of U.S. land that is privately owned. About 40 percent of this soil becomes waterborne sediment in streams.[36]

Although no fully accurate data are available, it appears that total soil erosion losses have been sharply reduced in recent years. SCS considers cropland adequately treated against erosion if soil loss from the land is less than 5 tons per acre per year. It estimates that soil loss from properly treated pastureland averages less than 2 tons per acre per year; from rangeland, about 1.5 tons per acre per year; and from forest land, about 0.5 tons per acre per year. The portion of privately controlled land which is adequately treated to minimize erosion has risen from 35 percent in fiscal year 1965 to over 50 percent in fiscal year 1972.[37] However, this measure of overall progress does not take into account such major problems as huge sediment losses at suburban construction sites which can cause severe local water quality problems.

The dimensions of the erosion problem may be seen from Geological Survey data on sediment discharged to the oceans.[38] Each year, on the average, more than 490 million tons of sediment, 185 tons for each square mile of the conterminous United States, washes into the oceans. Fourteen million tons is discharged to the Atlantic Ocean, 378 million tons to the Gulf of Mexico, and 99 million tons to the Pacific Ocean. If this sediment were transported by train, it would fill an average of 27,000 boxcars per day. These figures underestimate the amount of soil that is eroded, because in many areas reservoirs and diversions may trap up to 75 to 95 percent of the sediment. However, it should also be kept in mind that there is a significant amount of sediment that occurs naturally and that is probably uncontrollable.

Despite the staggering size of these figures, it appears that the amount of sediment discharged to the oceans has lessened over the past years. No overall figures are available, but it would appear, for example, that the average annual suspended sediment discharge carried by the Mississippi River to the Gulf of Mexico has been reduced by about 30 percent during the past 100 years. The annual sediment discharge of the Colorado River has fallen from 234 million tons during 1911–16 to 152,000 tons during 1966–67. This dramatic reduction in the Colorado is due largely to the construction of reservoirs which trap the sediment and to diversion of more water for irrigation. Improved land use practices have also helped, but much of the sediment has simply been retained upstream rather than carried to the oceans. The reservoirs and irrigation, of course, may create or aggravate other problems, such as salinity.

It is not known whether it is better to have the sediment trapped behind dams or to have it flow to the oceans. Both situations are undesirable, and the key goal is to reduce the amount of sediment which gets into rivers in the first place. It appears that progress has been made in reaching this goal.

Surface Mining—Surface mining unaccompanied by reclamation has many serious environmental consequences. It can cause severe erosion, pollute water with acid drainage, cause aesthetic blight, and destroy land for other productive uses unless adequate reclamation is undertaken. In last year's Annual Report, we indicated that the acreage being surface mined in the United States is increasing rapidly. Current energy supply shortages and the rising demand for low sulfur coal to meet the 1975 deadline for Federal air quality standards make it likely that surface mining will grow at an even faster rate. About 75 percent of the country's economically strippable coal reserves lies in 13 states west of the Mississippi, and it is likely that large new western areas will be opened to mining.[39] How much will be reclaimed depends heavily on the effectiveness of regulation at all levels of government.

New monitoring technology should be a major help in the enforcement of surface mining laws and in keeping track of the problem. Figure 26 shows the rapid increase in surface mined area which has occurred in a portion of southern Indiana. It also shows the potentially great value of earth-orbiting satellites to monitor environmental problems. The map is based on pictures taken from the ERTS–1 satellite, which photographs the entire United States once every 18 days. Such satellites can be used for this type of comparatively small-area analysis as well as for the type of macroscale picture reproduced in Figure 19.

Impervious Surfaces—As urban development spreads, buildings, streets, and pavement cover land where water once percolated into the soil, rendering the urban surface increasingly impervious to rainfall. This means much faster and greater water runoff, which increases the likelihood of erosion and flooding. Impervious surfaces can reduce urban water supply by decreasing the flow of water to natural aquifers. They can also impair water quality by increasing the amount of water discharged directly into a stream without treatment.

In many urban areas, small creeks or rivers have become major flood hazards. Because so much of the land around them is covered with concrete, very little of the rain from a storm is absorbed into the ground. Instead, it is channeled directly into the river. Rock Creek in Washington, D.C., is a good example of this phenomenon. A study by the U.S. Geological Survey estimated that if 80 percent of an area is sewered and 60 percent is covered by impervious surfaces, the water runoff occurring in the average once-a-year flood will be more than four times greater than if none of the area were sewered or impervious.[40]

Figure 26

Mined Land Inventory Map,
Pike, Warrick, and Gibson Counties, Ind.

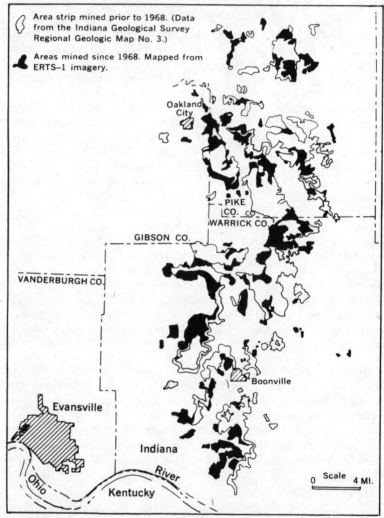

Source: Earth Satellite Corporation and the Indiana Geological Survey, *Application of ERTS–A Imagery to Fracture Related Mine Safety Hazards in the Coal Mining Industry,* prepared for the National Aeronautics and Space Administration under contract #NAS5–21795

A combination of impervious surfaces and inadequately designed storm sewers can also cause local, intra-urban flooding. Although a serious problem, it has received little attention. Especially in older cities, such as Baltimore, more flood damage incidents occur from inadequate drainage within the city than from rivers overflowing their banks. Forty percent of the 800 reports to the Office of Civil Defense and Emergency Preparedness of damage from Hurricane Agnes and another major Baltimore flood in 1971 involved flooded basements where drains backed up, raw sewage collected, and property damage and health hazards resulted. The vast majority of the other 60 percent was connected with wind and rain water damage. There were few reports of damage caused by running water from streams.

One might think that newer suburban developments, because they are of lower density, would contain less impervious surface. However, a study of Riverside, Calif., indicates that this may not be the case. Almost 60 percent of the built-up land area in Riverside is paved or covered by buildings, and almost one-third of the built-up area is more than 90 percent impervious. Wider streets, more parking area, and lower and broader buildings more than compensate for the lower density.

Clearly many of the problems that we have discussed are closely interrelated. More impervious surface, for example, may make flood plain development more hazardous and may increase erosion. The three categories of problems—land availability, areas of critical environmental concern, and land use effects—interact with each other in numerous and complex ways. Their interactions reflect the complexity of land use problems and the difficulty of developing satisfactory land use indicators.

Land Use Indicators

The discussion so far illustrates the importance of land use in determining environmental quality. But it also demonstrates the difficulty of establishing a set of national environmental land use indicators.

Land use policies, whether at the local, state, or Federal level, are designed to accommodate many conflicting and often poorly defined social goals. These include economic profit, suitable living conditions at reasonable prices, aesthetic and environmental improvement, and siting of necessary facilities such as roads, industry, and powerplants. Unlike air and water pollution programs, the goals of land use programs and policies do not lend themselves to simple description or to indicators for which the desired direction of change is obvious.

The context of land use conflicts and decisions is usually local or regional, not national. Construction of housing on agricultural land may be desirable in one city but not in another. Steep slopes or earthquake faults are problems for some regions of the country but not for others. Large parks may be a major factor in the environmental quality of Washington, D.C., but they are not what attracts people to midtown Manhattan. In addition, the basic regulatory authority over land use rests with state and local governments.

Yet it is possible to develop some indicators of land use and environmental quality. For uses such as unreclaimed surface-mined land and wetlands, simple acreage increases or decreases have meaning. Some land use problems will be reflected in other environmental indicators. For example, a significant increase in erosion may show up as increased water pollution from sediment. If automobile-related air pollutants increase despite emission controls, land use patterns must clearly be examined.

Some land use decisions, such as the siting of airports, powerplants, and deepwater ports, are becoming questions of national concern. The Federal Government owns about one-third of the land in the United States, and the use of this land will be determined by national policy. But the majority of land use decisions must be made in a local or regional context because both the costs and benefits of the decisions are primarily local or regional. Insofar as national indicators are developed, they will have to be aggregated from a series of local indicators.

Land use, for the most part, is simply the culmination of a large number of individual decisions about how to allocate space. But like the state of the economy, which is also a cumulation of many uncoordinated decisions, land use can be guided so that the outcome is more consistent with the public interest. If such guidance is to be effective, there must be agreement on what constitutes satisfactory land use before indicators can be developed to measure whether the use of land is being better regulated. While we have identified above certain areas for which national indicators would be appropriate, most measures or indicators will have to be developed and applied primarily by local, State, and regional authorities.

Population

Population size is clearly one of the major factors underlying many environmental problems. Rapid growth in population provides impetus for growth in GNP and for the development of new technologies as well as increasing the demand on natural resources.

In 1972, for the first time in the Nation's history (see Figure 27), the total fertility rate (the number of births that a woman would have in her lifetime based on the birth rate occurring in a specified year) dropped below the replacement level (the level of fertility required for the population to replace itself exactly under projected mortality rates and in the absence of immigration). The total fertility rate was estimated at 2.0 in 1972, compared to the replacement level of 2.1.

The birth rate began to decline in the late 1950's. After leveling off in the 1968 to 1970 period, it has continued its sharp decline. This trend is most encouraging, but it must be kept in mind that the national birth rate has fluctuated sharply in the past. Thus, it cannot

Figure 27

Total Fertility Rate, 5-Year Averages
1920–1959 and Single-Year Data 1960–1972

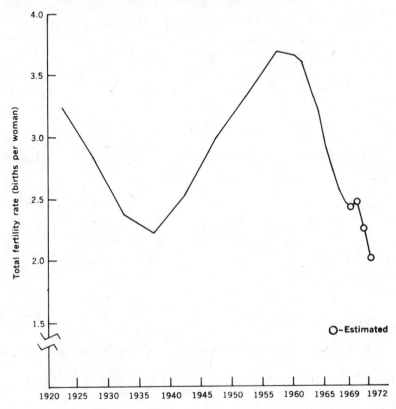

Source: Department of Commerce, Bureau of the Census, *Special Studies, Fertility Indicators: 1970,* Series P–23, No. 36, April 6, 1971, p. 9. Estimates for 1971 and 1972 from unpublished Bureau of the Census data

be predicted how long the current trend will continue.

Responding to the recent decline in fertility and to the sharp decline in the birth expectations of young wives, in December 1972 the Census Bureau issued revised projections of the U.S. population. The current U.S. population is estimated at 210 million. Previous projections had estimated the population level in 2020 at between 307 million and 447 million.[41] The new figures revise these estimates downward to a range of 264 million to 392 million by 2020 (see Figure 28).

Even with the current low birth rate, the U.S. population is increasing and is likely to continue to increase for several decades because of the proportionally large number of women of child-

Figure 28

Projection of Total Population, 1972–2020

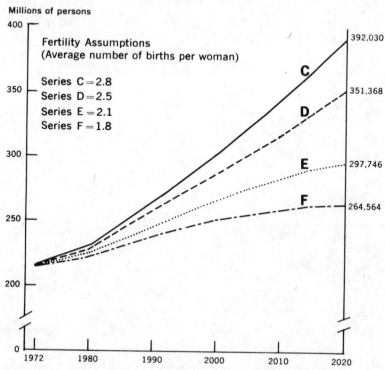

Millions of persons

Fertility Assumptions
(Average number of births per woman)

Series C = 2.8
Series D = 2.5
Series E = 2.1
Series F = 1.8

392,030

351,368

297,746

264,564

1972   1980   1990   2000   2010   2020

Source: Department of Commerce, Bureau of the Census, *Population Estimates and Projections*, Series P-25, No. 493, December 1972, p. 1

bearing age in the population. Assuming the lowest Census Bureau projection, there will be 40 million more people in the United States in 2000 than there are now.

Other industrialized nations are experiencing declines in the birth rate. But in many less-developed countries, which account for the bulk of the world's population, birth rates continue at high levels, often substantially negating hard-earned economic growth. At the current rate of growth, world population will double in less than 40 years. This will mean a staggering 4 billion additional people to feed, clothe, and shelter.

Summary

At some time in the distant future it may be possible to aggregate all aspects of environmental quality and issue a definitive pronouncement that, for example, the quality of the environment improved 3.68 percent during the past year. Such a statement is not possible now, and, even if it were, it would not be very informative. The environment encompasses too many diverse aspects to make any single overall expression of quality meaningful.

Even within the discrete areas discussed in this chapter, generalizations are not easy. There are wide variations in the type and severity of problems among different geographical locations. For any one aspect of the environment, some problems may be lessening and others worsening. For example, the problem of water pollution from nitrates may be getting worse while water pollution from sediment may be showing improvement. There is also the question of relating environmental trends to baselines. Although there may be steady improvement in a particular aspect of the environment, the magnitude of the problem may still remain substantial. Conversely, there may be deterioration in some problem area; yet the quality of the environment may still be good.

In both air and water pollution, major obstacles still stand in the way of obtaining adequate data on national status and trends. But perhaps for the first time, there is good reason to expect that a thorough description of where the Nation stands with respect to pollution will soon be available.

The data presented in this chapter continue to lend support to the conclusion of the Council's 1972 Annual Report that air quality is improving. There has been a continuing decline in the levels of sulfur oxides, due to the use of lower sulfur content fuels. The automobile-related pollutants are also declining as cars with emission controls replace the older models.

Neither the Geological Survey data nor the other information in the water pollution section yet provides a basis for generalizing about water quality. Chapter 2 shows that dramatic improvements in water quality can take place, and the Willamette River is not unique. But the extent to which the Nation's waters have improved or degraded remains largely a question for speculation.

We have discussed a number of aspects of land use in the United States. The dominant trend is the "spread city." The pervasive influence of the automobile has led to urban areas which occupy increasing amounts of land at lower densities than any previous type of development. This is not to say that we are becoming a nation paved over with concrete. There is no national shortage of land—only an increasing shortage of the right kind of land in the right places. There are so many interrelationships between land use and the environment that they are almost inseparable concepts. We are beginning to have a greater appreciation and understanding of these interrelationships.

While progress has been made in describing, understanding, and improving the environment, there remain obvious gaps. There is still a long way to go before we can be satisfied with our effort. But our improved ability to describe and understand trends in the quality of the environment lays the groundwork for even more progress in achieving better environmental quality.

Footnotes

1. A. B. Toan, Jr., "Social Measurement," *The New York Times,* Mar. 18, 1973, Sec. 8, p. 14, col. 3.
2. The Directory may be purchased at the Government Printing Office.
3. For a full description, see Lyndon R. Babcock, Jr., "A Combined Pollution Index for Measurement of Total Air Pollution," *Journal of the Air Pollution Control Association* 20:653–59, October 1970, and Lyndon R. Babcock, Jr., and Niren L. Nagda, "Cost-Effectiveness of Emission Control," *Journal of the Air Pollution Control Association* 23:173–79, March 1973.
4. These data will be published as part of the forthcoming EPA document, "The National Air Monitoring Program: A Status Report on Trends in Air Quality and Emissions." The document is being compiled by the EPA Office of Air Programs, Research Triangle Park, N.C.
5. See Thomas R. Hauser and Carl M. Shy, "Position Paper: NO_x Measurement," *Environmental Science and Technology* 6:890–94, Oct. 1972, and EPA press release of the statement of William D. Ruckelshaus (EPA Administrator), April 11, 1973.
6. Ralph M. Rotty (Old Dominion University, Norfolk, Va.), "Global Production of CO_2 from Fossil Fuels and Possible Changes in the World's Climate," paper to be presented at the American Society of Mechanical Engineers, New Orleans, La., September 1973 (unpublished).
7. T. D. Steele, E. J. Gilroy, and R. O. Hawkinson, "A Nationwide Assessment of Areal and Temporal Variations in Quality, Using Selected Data from the National Stream Quality Accounting Network," U.S. Geological Survey Open File Report, 1973.
8. See Council on Environmental Quality, *Third Annual Report* (Washington: Government Printing Office, 1972), pp. 44–46.
9. The same kind of analysis has been used successfully in many academic studies, such as M. G. Wolman, "The Nation's Rivers," *Science* 174:905–918, Nov. 26, 1971, and in the detailed technical studies of rivers often performed prior to establishing standards and abatement plans for dischargers.
10. Environmental Protection Agency, Division of Water Planning, Office of Air and Water Programs, "Priority Basin Accomplishment Report," Feb. 28, 1973.
11. Most of the data in this section come from Great Lakes Basin Commission, Great Lakes Basin Framework Study, "Limnology of Lakes and Embayments," Draft 2, Vol. I, Appendix 4, December 1972. We are also indebted to the Great Lakes Basin Commission and Professor Alfred M. Beeton for their help in preparing this section of the report.
12. U.S. Department of Commerce, National Oceanic and Atmospheric Administration, "Fish Larvae Found in Environment Contaminated with Oil and Plastic," MARMAP Red Flag Report No. 1, Jan. 18, 1973 (available from NOAA).
13. "NMFS Finds Tons of Plastic Debris on Alaskan Island," *NOAA Week* 4:1, Mar. 30, 1973.
14. P.L. 92–532, 86 Stat. 1052 (1972).
15. "Baseline Studies of Pollutants in the Marine Environment and Research Recommendations" (unpublished report available from the National

Science Foundation, International Decade of Ocean Exploration, May 1972).

16. Much of the material in this section is derived from two 1973 reports commissioned by the Council: Development Sciences, Inc., "Criteria for National Land Use Planning Indicators," and Earth Satellite Corporation, "Land Use Change and Environmental Quality in Urban Areas" (available from the National Technical Information Service, Springfield, Virginia 22151, PB–220 650 and PB–220 742).

17. Development Sciences, *supra* note 15.

18. See CEQ, *Third Annual Report, supra* note 8, at 24.

19. Robert C. Otte, "Competing Uses for Rural Land Near Cities" (unpublished paper from U.S. Department of Agriculture, Economic Research Service).

20. "Urban uses" are defined as all "urbanized areas" (as defined by the Census Bureau) plus "urban places" over 2,500 population not included in urbanized areas.

21. The Census Bureau's definition of an SMSA is "a county or group of contiguous counties (except in New England) which contains at least one central city of 50,000 inhabitants or more or 'twin cities' with a combined population of at least 50,000. Other contiguous counties are included in an SMSA if, according to certain criteria, they are essentially metropolitan in character and are socially and economically integrated with the central city. In New England, towns and cities are used in defining SMSA's." U.S. Department of Commerce, Bureau of the Census, *Statistical Abstract of the United States—1972* (Washington: Government Printing Office, 1972), p. 2.

22. Otte, *supra* note 18.

23. Density for all SMSA's in 1960 was 364 persons per square mile; in 1970, 360 persons per square mile. *1960 Census of Population,* Vol. 1, Part A, Table 34; *1970 Census of Population,* Vol. 1, Part A, Table 35.

24. U.S. Department of Commerce, Bureau of the Census, *Statistical Abstract of the United States—1972* (Washington: Government Printing Office, 1972), Table 15, p. 16.

25. *Id.*

26. U.S. Department of Agriculture, Economic Research Service, "1972 Changes in Farm Production and Efficiency," Statistical Bulletin No. 233 (Washington: Government Printing Office, 1972), Table 6, p. 10, and Table 7, p. 11.

27. *1972 OBERS Projections: Economic Activity in the United States,* Vol. I, *Concepts, Methodology, and Summary Data* (Washington: U.S. Water Resources Council, 1972). These figures exclude cropland not used for raising crops, such as cropland used for grazing.

28. U.S. Department of Agriculture, Economic Research Service, "1972 Changes in Farm Production and Efficiency," Statistical Bulletin No. 233 (Washington: Government Printing Office, 1972); 1972 figure, unpublished Economic Research Service information.

29. Earth Satellite, *supra* note 15.

30. Communication from U.S. Department of Commerce, National Oceanic and Atmospheric Administration, National Marine Fisheries Service, April 23, 1973.

31. S. P. Shaw and C. G. Fredline, "Wetlands of the United States, Their Extent and Their Value to Waterfowl and Other Wildlife," U.S. Fish and Wildlife Service Circular No. 39 (Washington: Government Printing Office, 1956).

32. For an account of some of the effects of wetlands development in Hillsborough County, see John L. Taylor and Carl H. Saloman, "Some Effects of Hydraulic Dredging and Coastal Development in Boca Ciega Bay, Florida," *Fishery Bulletin* 67: 213, Spring 1969.

33. Gilbert F. White, "Changes in Urban Occupancy of Flood Plains in the United States" (University of Chicago, Department of Geography, unpublished Research Paper 57, 1957).

34. U.S. Water Resources Council, "First National Assessment of the Nation's Water Resources" (Washington: Water Resources Council, 1968), p. 5-2-6.

35. The examples are from A. A. Klingebiel, "Costs and Returns of Soil Surveys," *Soil Conservation* 32:3-6, Aug. 1966.

36. U.S. Department of Agriculture, Soil Conservation Service, unpublished data based on "National Inventory of Soil and Water Conservation Needs," 1967.

37. U.S. Department of Agriculture, Soil Conservation Service, unpublished data, 1973.

38. W. F. Curtis et al., "Fluvial-Sediment Discharge to the Oceans from the Conterminous United States," Geological Survey Circular 670 (Washington: Government Printing Office, 1973).

39. U.S. Department of the Interior, U.S. Geological Survey, "Stripping Coal Resources of the United States—January 1, 1970," U.S. Geological Survey Bulletin No. 1322 (Washington: Government Printing Office, 1970).

40. L. B. Leopold, "Hydrology for Urban Planning—A Guidebook on the Hydrologic Effects of Urban Land Use," U.S. Geological Survey Circular 554 (Washington: Government Printing Office, 1968).

41. See U.S. Department of Commerce, Bureau of the Census, "Population Estimates and Projections," Series P-25, No. 470, November 1971, p. 1.

17

Richard Slavin

TOWARD A STATE LAND USE POLICY: HARMONIZING DEVELOPMENT AND CONSERVATION

The function of state land-use policy in making development compatible with preservation of the environment is discussed in this article by Dr. Richard H. Slavin, Director of the Planning and Community Affairs Agency of the State of Washington. Dr. Slavin is President of the Council of State Planning Agencies.

EVERY STATE IS CURRENTLY INVOLVED in an environmental crisis. This crisis indicates a need for state government to develop methods to resolve the constant conflicts that arise between development processes and the needs for environmental preservation and resource conservation.

Rapidly increasing populations are escalating demands on space for housing, industry, commerce, transportation, recreation, agriculture, forestry, mining, water, power and waste disposal. Continuation of present development processes will result in further deterioration of our land, air and water resources to such a point that we may be courting major natural disasters jeopardizing human life itself.

Presently, state land-use policy is an aggregate of thousands of unrelated decisions made by single-purpose agencies, local governments and private developers without regard for each other or regional, state and national concerns.

The goal, therefore, should be to evolve and promote development policies and programs taking into account both people's and nature's needs for the purpose of minimizing the areas of conflict and discovering and enhancing the areas of harmony.

and delta lands, the building of beaches and dunes and wearing away of lands along oceans, and the uplifting and gradual subsidence of lands. Rapid geological changes are volcanic eruptions, earthquakes, landslides, floods and tidal waves. Respect for earthquakes has brought improved structural standards into building codes. Respect for floods and tidal waves has brought special use zones into being. Respect for landslides and severe erosion has port the processes that support human life are the smaller animals, plants and organisms— the mosses, lichens, soil bacteria, insects and plankton. Management of the renewable species requires the knowledge of and care for the entire related world of resources.

Natural geological processes generally operate at such a glacial pace that man tends to ignore them—frequently to his consternation and disadvantage. These are the erosion of hills and mountains and the building of valley plains

ENVIRONMENTAL PRESERVATION AND RESOURCE CONSERVATION ISSUES

Some natural resources are limited, and once used are no longer available. It is, therefore, prudent that these be placed under a management system that seeks the most efficient use of the resource while protecting reserves for the future.

Some resources are renewable if properly managed and, therefore, are considered permanently available if not overused. We are most familiar with the plants and animals used for food, fibre, building, medicines and so forth. Of equal importance because they sup-

283

brought special hillside development requirements into being. Lack of sufficient respect for these natural processes, however, results in enormous losses, some of which are measured quickly when a landslide kills a family or blocks a highway or a flood wipes out a town. Some losses are more difficult to measure, such as the loss of beaches due to the damming of rivers or the damage to a city because of its gradual subsidence.

All of these problems are of a collective nature requiring collective action. However, government typically reacts to situations after the fact. It has not been able to anticipate and respond to potential problems and gives little consideration to gradual changes which man is effecting. The crux of the environmental crisis is that it may now be too late to continue a policy of reacting only. Government should escalate its position in relation to the environment and natural resources.

Some of the areas demanding continued or new attention are the State's water and air; its seacoast and tidelands; its rivers; its forests and agricultural lands; its wetlands, swamps and estuaries; its fisheries; and its mineral extraction areas.

Public concern has resulted in new legislation dealing with air and water pollution, but has yet to link up its concern on these subjects to land-use issues.

URBAN DEVELOPMENT ISSUES AND PROBLEMS

Characteristic of the last few decades has been the decline of rural areas, deterioration of central city cores and thriving growth of city suburbs in the Nation. It has been a period of gross social and economic inequity, degrading poverty, a crisis in race relations, alienation of youth, enormous environmental pollution, high taxes, high spending, and tremendous industrial and building activity.

An in-city migration of the rural poor with an out-city migration of high- and moderate-income people together with business and industry has resulted in social polarization; inequity in job, educational and recreational opportunities; and a phenomenon called the urban crisis. Lack of job and housing opportunities in the suburbs for the unskilled poor and minorities reinforce the polarization. Land-use controls, specifically exclusionary zoning, have helped to direct the division of society into ghettos and moderately well-off suburbs.

Old city residential, commercial and industrial centers deteriorate into slums and blighted areas far faster than they can be rehabilitated by public or private institutions. Reliance on the automobile and removal of transportation services have created hardening of traffic arteries. Population pressures on inadequately designed sewerage facilities and gaseous wastes pollute streams, lakes, oceans and the air. In the city fringe areas vegetation is stripped, topsoil is buried, streams are channeled into culverts, hills are leveled, valleys and marshes are filled and whole new communities occupy areas which were formerly forested or farmed. The adverse impact of these phenomena on human and natural life and resources is what we call the environmental crisis.

The urban and environmental crises are part of a general crisis involving the economic and social conditions and values of the entire society. Efforts to deal with either part of the crisis inevitably involves the other.

Problems of Urban Growth

The way in which cities have grown of late has been characterized in various ways, but "leap-frogging" is one of the most descriptive phrases for the sprawling pattern resulting from the private ownership of land and the "bundle of rights" which goes with that ownership. Many attribute urban sprawl to speculative activity, but the root cause of urban sprawl is the right to buy and sell land and develop it, for all intents and purposes at will, for lack of other public goals for development. Local governments, under their present planning and zoning regulations, have been unable to cope with sprawl. So, if more reasonable urban development patterns are to be encouraged, it is essential to control the timing and location of growth.

A brief summary of the problems of urban sprawl follows.

• Premature characterization of an area by the prior development of housing, factories or commercial development which subsequently make the area unfavorable for anything but compatible uses. Such characterization is done quite unintentionally by those trying to avoid high land prices or restrictive regulations in other areas.

• The high costs or poor quality of public services; costly and wasteful extensions of or lack of sewer, water, gas and electric services; similar wasteful costs of or inadequate transportation, educational, fire, police and other community services.

• Unregulated growth of poor quality rural subdivisions and trailer courts in areas where public agencies are not prepared or able to regulate decent subdivision, housing, building and health codes.

• Waste of land resources in bypassed areas suitable for no economically productive use, either for housing, industry or farming, nor for public recreation.

• Monotony, lack of community identity and inadequate social and cultural opportunities.

Problems of Established Communities

The following is a list of major problems facing many established communities. They appear to stem in large part from lack of sufficient municipal revenues, overcompetitiveness in the exercise of local powers, lack of mechanisms for dealing with problems that do not recognize jurisdictional boundaries (regional problems), and inability to forecast and act on emerging issues.

1. Deterioration of older residential neighborhoods with subsequent loss of tax base, loss of purchasing power, social and economic segregation and need for increased health, welfare and safety services.

2. Lack of community facilities such as park and recreation areas where they are needed and public transportation facilities to serve the needs of the young, aged and poor.

3. Deterioration of central industrial and commercial districts with resultant erosion of tax base because of competition from new outlying areas.

4. Exclusionary zoning practices on the part of some communities for the purpose of social control and protection of property values resulting in forcing the poor and minorities into older sections.

5. Proliferation of special improvement districts for a multitude of single purposes. These districts operate without coordination, each with their own taxing power and administrative mechanisms. They are not publicly "visible" or responsive and frequently outlive their original purpose because there is no public check on their usefulness.

LAND DEVELOPMENT PRACTICES

The development process has four general phases: programming (planning), design, construction, and maintenance. From a policy standpoint, the programming phase is the most important because that is where locational decisions are made. In general, economics takes precedence in this phase, but political-legal constraints such as deed restrictions, zoning, building, and subdivision codes, and varying taxes have been effective in directing and timing growth as well. If new objectives could be agreed upon, and if these could be translated into new policy levels, our old political-legal institutions could be improved upon and new ones developed to help both public and private sectors structure better communities.

Private Sector

The private development sector initiates and carries out the bulk of our urbanization in thousands of relatively independent actions. It has an enormous capacity for discovering opportunities for profitable effort. Its goal is legitimately and necessarily making profits, but while profits are essential, the profit motive has provided the basis for a simplistic measurement of values.

In this system, the cost-benefit analysis and the making of money have resulted in a distortion of values wherein we have allowed profit making to become equated with social benefit. As a result, there are great efforts being made to translate social costs and benefits into dollar terms to help measure the real impact of alternative developments.

The hue and cry for social considerations comes from one sector, while others call for increased concern for aesthetics, others call for increased concern for natural factors, and others point out the need to be concerned with economic, political and legal factors. Arising from the need for comprehensive understanding of all issues, it has become obvious to many development companies, industries, and government agencies that an "interdisciplinary approach" should be used in solving complex problems.

The "interdisciplinary approach" brings to bear on the planning and design of a project— whether it be an industry, freeway or community—the knowledge and skills necessary to assure that the planned results meet the cross section of needs of its time, place and purpose. Almost any project has both local and regional impact and should be inspected from these aspects. Once considered the exclusive bailiwick of the engineer, the urban freeway now also employs in its planning and design: planners, sociologists, economists, architects and landscape architects. A community development plan can employ planners, lawyers, sociologists, foresters, zoologists, geologists, hydrologists and economists in addition to experts in architectural and landscape design and a host of engineering specialists, to name but a few.

This approach to planning is becoming "standard" with state highway commissions, advanced land developers, large industries and federal agencies. It is the only way to insure that all important phases of a problem will receive the attention they deserve and that the final solution will be affected by consideration of them.

The general factors requiring attention in any project of major importance can be briefly listed.

1. Social-cultural
2. Political-legal
3. Economic—that is, the economic feasibility of the development itself as well as the public costs and benefits
4. Natural—air, water, land, fish and wildlife
5. Physical—man-made factors such as existing structures, systems and services
6. Aesthetic—mass, form, color and texture.

Each of these factors has within it sub-factors generally known only to experts in their fields. It is almost impossible for one administrator to know which considerations should be studied in depth because of their importance to the project and which can be set aside as relatively unrelated. This is why it is so important to get a broad perspective of all facets at the beginning of planning. A legislative mandate requiring an interdisciplinary approach to urban development and review processes would go far toward changing the face of urban environments.

Public Sector

Federal, state and local agencies, as well as the private sector, initiate and finance enormous amounts of construction. The public sector plays two roles, that of developer and that of controller of private development.

In the role of developer, all public agencies should be subject to the same disciplinary methods as the private sector. In fact, they should play leading roles that the private sector would emulate. The National Environmental Policy Act of 1969 requires that federal agencies "utilize a systematic, interdisciplinary approach."

State governments should do no less; but they, as well as the federal and local levels, also have other opportunities. One of these is to use investment programs to guide better development. The State, for instance, is involved in an investment program including state highways and transportation, urban arterials, public schools, colleges and universities, sewer lines and treatment plants, state parks and recreation lands, local facilities and open space, institutions, land reclamation, airport subsidy, trust lands, bridges and ferries, and nuclear siting.

Obviously all of these expenditures have land-use implications, but rarely, if ever, are these programs administered with concern for coordinated land use as such. The State should develop an urbanization policy as a good business practice so that state investments are used to assist in directing more orderly development, rather than following the uncoordinated development we now have.

By the Tenth Amendment to the Constitution, States have authority for management of state and private lands within their territory. However, they have distributed much of this responsibility to city and county governments in the form of powers for planning and zoning so that land-use decisions are made in the localities affected by them.

In the last few decades a very large gap has appeared in this land-use control mechanism with respect to multijurisdictional issues that do not coincide with city and county boundaries. Decisions of small communities adversely affect the environment, economies and social conditions of entire regions and no way has been found to deal with them effectively. The solution to this problem requires that the State realign its development planning and control mechanisms and those of city and county governments. This realignment appears to require the State to increase its policy-making role and provide higher standards for public agencies performance.

AREAS OF CRITICAL CONCERN

State government should take the responsibility for identifying areas of critical concern and monitoring land uses within them.

Specifically, the State should develop:

• An overall land-use policy and plan for environmental preservation and resource conservation including the living natural systems and state-owned lands, uplands, forests, watersheds, shorelands, arid lands, agricultural lands, geologically or otherwise unique areas, water-use and development, air quality and mineral development.

• An urbanization policy and plan covering areas of state investment and grants-in-aid.

• Performance standards and guidelines for local government of delegated responsibilities for land-use planning and control.

• A method for coordination and review of local plans and development legislation to insure that they relate to state and regional goals.

PLANNING, DESIGN AND REVIEW

In the land and water areas of critical concern, land-use guidelines covering development principles should be developed by the State. These should be administered by the local government having jurisdiction over the particular area of concern under methods to be designated by the State. In order to surmount the inflexibility of present zoning techniques, it is proposed that land developers, local regulatory agencies and state government be involved in a comprehensive planning, design and review system. The interdisciplinary approach previously discussed should be made a mandatory part of the system at both planning and review phases.

Once areas of critical concern are identified by the State, these concerns and land-use guidelines would be forwarded to local governments. Counties and cities of jurisdiction would prepare plans and regulations within a set time period. These would be reviewed, approved or rejected by the State as dictated by state objectives. Once plans and regulations are approved, local government would administer all land uses, except extraordinary ones. Extraordinary land-use proposals would have to receive both local government and state approval since they would not be covered by the original plan.

In the case of state projects it is recommended that local government act in areas of critical concern in an advisory capacity to the State.

Technical assistance and financial support to local governments should be a part of the new planning, design and review process in order to assist in the extra-administrative operations required as well as in various other ways that may be necessary to make the new control mechanisms more effective.

A STATE POLICY

State land-use policy might be defined in the following terms.

1. The social and economic well-being of the people of the State is closely related to the condition of the environment and to resource management. It is therefore urgent, in the face of rapidly increasing demands on the environment, that the State develop a land-use policy for protection of the environment and conservation of its resources, and develop an urbanization policy related to it.

2. The people of the State have a fundamental interest in the orderly development of the entire State consistent with the protection and enhancement of its natural, land, air and water resources. Therefore, there should be a legislative declaration of state environmental policy modeled after the National Environmental Policy Act of 1969. Such policy should require state and state-chartered agencies to conform to the standards established to effectively, with proper monitoring, head all agencies in the same direction and to unify federal and state policy.

3. Although state government has constitutional authority and responsibility to manage its land resources, it should be its policy to depend upon local government and private landowners to exercise state objectives toward preservation and conservation of land resources insofar as is possible, and the State should assist local government and private landowners in the pursuit of these objectives.

4. Each level of government should be responsible for those areas under its jurisdiction which are primarily the concern of its own citizens. In areas of concern to citizens of multi-city or multi-county jurisdictions, or the State at large, the State should take the primary responsibility unless the cities and counties do so under joint powers agreements. In order for there to be a consistent policy and direction, the State should provide guidance, authority where needed, and financial assistance to help overcome local deficiencies and disparities.

5. At the earliest possible moment, state, county and city governments should identify areas to be preserved and take positive actions toward preserving them in accordance with local objectives and state policy.

6. The actions of all agencies, in order to be consistent with these objectives, should be subject to statewide review and coordinating procedures.

7. It should be the policy of state government to take direct remedial action when local government and private landowners are powerless or reluctant to act in behalf of objectives.

8. State and local tax policies should be designed to support these environmental protection and resource conservation objectives.

LEGISLATIVE ALTERNATIVES

The following alternatives demonstrate directions that might be taken. The first alternative is little more than doing as we always have. The last three alternatives propose to insert state or regional policy-making into land-use decision processes more than in the past, but in varying degrees. All alternatives depend upon local government taking increased land-use planning and control responsibilities and all alternatives could be modified to contain certain elements of the others.

Alternate I: Information and Individual Issues

This alternate presents the possibility of continuing to act on one issue at a time in a relatively unrelated way.

There is no doubt but that there are many important issues competing for legislative action. All those listed will meet some requirement and, even if more comprehensive legislation is adopted, some would still be desirable for their stated purposes.

—An extensive inventory and research program into the actual extent and scope of environmental deterioration and future needs should be undertaken. This would draw attention on areas not now known and would lead to solutions based upon more knowledge than now exists. However, it would be prudent to combine this level of research with an action program so that it does not go to waste.

—There appears to be a need for better special district and local agency formation control and review of need for continued existence.

—A number of beneficial improvements should be made to assist local government in exercising its present zoning ordinances, such as (a) compensable regulations, (b) a provision that local governments could enter into development contracts with private owners in "planned development zones," and (c) a provision permitting local government to charge for up-zoning (English method).

—Mandatory dedication of park, open space and school sites or the payment of in-lieu fees to help resolve local agencies fiscal needs should be required.

—Provision should be made for use of the "official map" technique for open space and other public facilities space acquisitions.

—A requirement should stipulate that local governments include conservations and open space elements in their general plans.

—Provision should be made for a state or regional development agency to buy, plan and sell land to developers so as to control the location, timing and development of it.

—A significant emergency rotating fund should be established to buy already impacted areas and otherwise assist local government in exercising land-use controls through compensable regulations.

—Adjustment of tax programs should be undertaken to provide more equity among local agencies.

Alternate II: State or Regional Review

Place new responsibilities for land-use planning and control on local governments together with a new state [or regional] review [or approval] system.

As can be seen by the above use of brackets this proposal contains some interior alternatives of its own.

The State (or the State together with regional agencies that might be established in the same legislation) should establish state and regional objectives, policies, priorities and guidelines for local governments' use in preparing conservation and development plans which would be new mandatory elements of their general plans. They would be given a deadline for completing these plans. If they could not or chose not to prepare the plans for themselves, the state or regional agency could be authorized to prepare the plans for them.

The plans prepared by the local agencies would then be submitted to the state or regional planning agency for review and approval, request for modification, or rejection if unsuitable. Two alternative courses lie open at this point.

Alternate A. It would be possible to give the regional or the state agency only an advisory and persuasive role in which case the state or regional agency could only recommend to local governments. This power to recommend could have considerable influence, particularly if the regional or state agency is required to evaluate and make recommendations to federal and state agencies being petitioned for aid funds.

Alternate B. The state or regional agency could be given very strong powers for review and approval of plans and implementation programs. In this case, in the absence of an approved plan, the local agency would not be eligible for state or federal grant funds or loans related to the elements of the conservation and development plan.

Implementation of the plan in either of the above cases would be entirely in the hands of the local agency. However, deviations from its requirements would be by special permit only. Special permits would have to receive the approval of the local and review agencies where the state or regional agency had been given strong review powers.

Alternate III: State Guidelines

Require the State to establish areas of critical concern together with guidelines for land uses within them. Local government to plan and administer land uses in areas of critical concern but plans to be subject to a state review system before becoming effective.

In this case the State would prepare plans and policies showing areas of critical concern (dealt with in more detail elsewhere). The reasons for, and guidelines governing the kinds of land uses permitted in, the various areas of critical concern would be forwarded to the local government. Plans and development regulations would be prepared by the local government having jurisdiction. The plans and regulations would then be forwarded to the State for approval or modification. Once they were approved, local governments would administer land uses in the areas of critical concern in compliance with the regulations applying to them. Any unusual developments not covered by the plans would be treated as special permits and would require the State's approval. All applications including those of special districts for development within the areas of critical concern would be processed by the local government having territorial jurisdiction. No development permits would be issued until the state review body approval was received by the local government and no state agency could take any action within the area of critical concern unless the state review body approval was given.

It is recommended that the state review body consist of the Governor and principal agency administrators. The Governor with agency support would define the areas of critical concern and guidelines.

Alternate IV: State Land-Use Commission

A proposal to establish a State Land-Use Commission which would designate settlement, conservation and agricultural districts.

This alternative is to establish a Land-Use Commission much along the lines of that established by Hawaii about ten years ago. Because the Hawaii system would have certain shortcomings in some States with a much more complicated system of government, certain differences can be recommended. Basically these would be (1) to establish a state land development and settlement policy as a basis for planning and districting, (2) to provide for a different number of districts than the four in the State of Hawaii, (3) to simplify the administrative procedures, and (4) to provide for yearly review.

This is a statewide zoning system based upon a state "plan" which would be updated yearly in accordance with a review and with policy changes that may be enunciated by the Governor. The State Land-Use Commission would develop regulations governing land uses within the conservation and agriculture dis-

tricts. Local government would retain its land-use regulatory powers within the settlement districts and would administer land uses within the conservation and agriculture districts on a special permit basis subject to State Land-Use Commission approval. (This is different from Hawaii where the State Department of Land and Natural Resources regulates land uses within the Conservation District.)

The Hawaii system has acted as a restraint on leapfrogging and scatteration and thus has provided protection to its important agricultural districts and natural and scenic resources.

This is an excellent state land-use control mechanism. It has an advantage in having been successfully tested. Although in Hawaii it has certain built-in problems that are difficult to change, it can be observed in operation and improved upon for other States' applications. The review processes, regional planning and other concepts herein discussed under separate sections could all be included in a comprehensive Land-Use Law along these lines.

There is also the possibility of avoiding the lay commission aspect by having the Governor and principal department heads act instead.

SUMMARY

Almost constant conflict exists between urban development and conservation principles. The profit goals of private enterprise and the requirements for economy placed on public agencies have caused developments of all kinds to take an unnecessarily contradictory position toward environmental preservation and enhancement.

Municipal and county governments make land-use decisions adversely affecting areas far beyond their borders because no other mechanisms exist for making these decisions. They also find themselves unable to be fully objective because under the present tax laws revenues from property taxes accruing from development are essential to their fiscal well-being.

The use of land as a relatively unregulated commodity, the desires of owners to realize maximum economic benefit from its sale, use or development, and the economic penalties if they do not, generate intense demands on land resources. The dilemmas caused by these problems and the lack of mechanisms for adequately dealing with them have resulted in serious environmental deterioration with prospects for continuation if remedies are not forthcoming.

Because cities and counties receive their authority from state government, studies conducted throughout the Nation are calling for States to develop urbanization policies giving priority to conservation, social and aesthetic requirements. Public reaction to air and water pollution has resulted in legislative action to correct those problems. The next targets are the problems connected with environmental deterioration related to uncoordinated, ill-conceived, poorly planned and wasteful land-use practices.

While more equitable public financing methods will go far toward mollifying the problems of established communities, and while a change in public attitudes toward land ownership may make land-use controls easier to accommodate, most urban developments fail because they are shortsightedly measured only in economic terms. They are, therefore, incapable of fulfilling social, aesthetic and natural needs no matter what reforms might be made in the tax and landownership patterns.

For these reasons, a comprehensive, interdisciplinary approach to planning, design and review of developments should be required of all public and private builders. This approach is already gaining favor among the private sector, has been used successfully many times by public agencies, and is required of all federal agencies under the Environmental Policy Act of 1969. Such an approach by the State Legislature would make it mandatory to consider social, legal, economic, natural and aesthetic factors in the planning and review of public works and private developments.

State government's goal, therefore, should be to develop urbanization policies and programs that take into account both people's and nature's needs for the purpose of minimizing the areas of conflict and discovering and enhancing the areas of harmony.

REFERENCES

The following books, laws, pamphlets, study documents, etc. are related to state, regional and local land-use management, planning and control issues.

Alternatives to Urban Sprawl, Fred P. Bosselman. Prepared for the National Commission on Urban Problems. Washington, D.C.: U.S. Government Printing Office.
A careful look at the constitutional validity of three promising new methods of controlling urban development: Planned Development Zones; Compensative Regulations; Public Land Assembly.

Building the American City. Report of the National Commission on Urban Problems to the Congress and to the President of the United States. Washington, D.C.: U.S. Government Printing Office.
Summary of two years of study of building and housing codes, zoning, local and federal tax policies and development standards. Contains many recommendations for new policies at local and state levels.

Design with Nature, Ian L. McHarg. Garden City, N.Y.: Natural History Press, 1969.
A brilliant exposition of the reasons for and methods of relating urban development to natural factors.

Final Report. California Legislative Joint Committee on Open Space Land. Sacramento: California Office of State Printing, February 1970.
While dealing specifically with open space, it is of such a comprehensive nature that many of its findings and concepts related to local, regional and state government are pertinent to this subject.

Land, People and Policy, Gordon Edwards. Trenton, N.J.: Chandler-Davis, 1969.
Analyzes the current problems and recommends a unique public-private partnership for land development. Reviews European experiences in land-use management.

A Model Land Development Code. Tentative draft # 1. Philadelphia: American Law Institute, April 24, 1968.
Still incomplete, but eight years of work have gone into this draft which is the result of critical examination and reworking of law relating to public control of land use and development.

The National Environmental Policy Act of 1969, Public Law 91-190, 91st Congress, S. 1075, January 1, 1970.
The national policy act establishing the Council on Environmental Quality together with policies and goals, administration, review and reporting to Congress.

National Land-Use Policy Act of 1970, S.3354.

Now in hearings. Requires that States develop land-use policies and plans and implement them in order to receive federal aid. Hearings are published in: *National Land-Use Policy*, part I, printed for use of the Committee on Interior and Insular Affairs. Washington, D.C.: U.S. Government Printing Office, 1970.

State Planning in the 60's. Report of the Committee on State Planning in the 60's. A.I.P. Newsletter, vol. 4, no. 10, October 1969.

A summary report by the committee covering historical viewpoint, objectives, place of planning in the state and matters of professional concern.

State of Hawaii Land-Use Law, Act 187, Session Laws of Hawaii 1961 amended by Act 32 and Act 205.

This law, as amended, establishes the State Land-Use Commission with zoning powers to district the State into Urban, Rural, Conservation and Agricultural Districts, together with regulations. It also establishes a complementary assessment practice to apply to "dedicated" lands. The first and most comprehensive such law in the Nation.

State of Maine Land Use Regulation Commission, Chapter 494, Public Law, July 1969.

Establishes a Land-Use Regulation Commission with zoning powers in unorganized and deorganized areas of the State to prevent detrimental land uses in those areas.

State of Rhode Island "Compensatory Regulation" Law, P.L. 1965, Ch. 140; Rhode Island Gen. L. Sec. 2-1-13-17.

Establishes a program for protection of coastal wetlands and for payment of damages to any owner suffering same and who recovers in an action in the superior court.

Study Document No. 4, Summary and Legislative Proposals, New York State Planning Law Revision Study. Albany, New York: New York State Office of Planning Coordination, February 1970.

This is the summary document of a concentrated four-year study by the office and an eminent panel of consultants. It is distributed for study and criticism. It states the problems and need for reform, the recommended land-use legislation, and contains many interesting new concepts.

1970 Suggested State Legislation, Lexington, Kentucky: The Council of State Governments.

Drafts of timely state legislation including: State Highway Interchange Planning Districts, Planned Unit Development, Mandatory Dedication of Park and School Sites, Joint Legislative Committee on State Planning, State and Regional Planning, Official Map, Urban Development Corporation.

The Zoning Game, Richard F. Babcock. Madision, Wisconsin: University of Wisconsin Press.

The most stimulating work on the problems and paradoxes of land-use decision-making at the local level by a famous lawyer in the field. Exposes the capriciousness entirely too common among those involved in zoning issues.

Toward a More Effective Land-Use Guidance System, 1969, David Heeter. Chicago, Illinois: American State Planning Office. A summary and analysis of five major studies.

18

George Carey, Leonard Zobler,
Michael Greenberg and Robert Hordon

TOWARD AN ENVIRONMENTAL
MONITORING SYSTEM

The previous sections of this chapter have detailed the actual operations
of a water quality surveillance network in the NYMR. The network's
structure and behavior, as an information-gathering system for urban water
management decisions, reflect the interplay of numerous forces and
interests -- political and jurisdictional fragmentation, official over-
optimism based on an assumed abundance of the water resource, state of
hydrologic knowledge, a pattern of crisis-inspired responses, bureaucratic
competition, and the inertia of habit. The present arrangements cannot be
regarded as a network if by that word we mean coordinated entities responsible for gathering information on events or conditions and for relating
all the bits of raw and spent water data to one another so that they bear
on local and regional water management and policy decisions.

The following recommendations, based on our field experiences, describe the
elements of a metropolitan area water surveillance network and their integration into a goal-oriented information system.* Among the advantages
of reducing the current disorder are: transferability of data from one
agency to another, feasibility of simulating the responses of water
bodies to natural and man-induced hydrologic events, evaluation of
alternative abatement methods, reduction of the time period between the
recognition of a pollution problem and its solution, prediction of undesirable quality levels, identification of appropriate preventive measures,
environmental impact review of short term and long-term regional land and
water policy decisions.

The organization of a hydrologic data base would provide essential inputs
into a managerial structure in charge of long-term water policy formulation
and short-term regulatory and allocational decisions. The ten elements of
such a data base purposely bypass the difficulties associated with actual
sample collection and laboratory analysis, not because we wish to minimize
these problems, but because we wish to stress the broader design components
of a monitoring network.

   (1) Parameter identification
   (2) Selection of water bodies and effluent dischargers
   (3) Location of sample points
   (4) Observation frequencies
   (5) Selection of sample sites
   (6) Choice of sampler and sensing instruments
   (7) Analyzing samples and scaling results
   (8) Bookkeeping practices
   (9) Data storage and retrieval
  (10) Systemic properties of data

---

*The importance of the subject is indicated by a recent symposium
(Kerrigan, 1970).

1. Parameter Identification

A first crucial element is the selection of the parameter set appropriate
to the existing or anticipated uses of the water body. The total set of
possible parameters probably amounts to at least 93 variables
(Porterfield, 1970). They are divisible into several categories:
hydrological and meteorological -11; physical -14, inorganic chemical -33;
organic chemical -9; nutrient -9; microbiological -10; biological -7.
The list could undoubtedly be expanded, as knowledge of toxic, trace, and
radioactive materials and the use of synthetic compounds grow. It seems
neither necessary nor feasible to monitor all the parameters. Some adjustment of parameters to land use, industry and the hydrology of the water
body can be made. For example, trace metals could be monitored in the
spent water prior to discharge; meteorological variables would be more
significant in estuaries and impoundments than in free-flowing streams.

Our screening of large masses of data revealed that substantial economies
are possible of the monitoring effort because of high intercorrelations
among some variables. The number of variables to be monitored in the water
body is also closely tied to the operational efficiency of the regulatory
agencies responsible for inspecting industrial and municipal discharges.
If potential sources are kept under reliable surveillance, the number of
episodic events may be reduced to a level which would obviate constant
monitoring of the water body for a large number of parameters.

There is also evidence that some widely sampled variables yield information
that is superfluous, misleading or unreliable. Among the suspect variables,
institutionalized by virtue of their long histories as water quality indicators, are: color, odor, carbon dioxide, air temperature, and coliform
counts -- the latter as a criterion of contact recreational uses.

2. Selection of Water Bodies and Effluent Discharges

As an interconnected water network characterized by hydrologic subunits,
the urban water regime should be monitored in a way that reflects its
diversity. It is composed of free-flowing streams; impounded streams;
impoundments (lakes and reservoirs); tidal fresh water; estuaries;
aquifers; and nodes or confluences at which flows mix, water is withdrawn
and spent water is discharged. Water bodies that are unique aquatic
environments should be monitored separately. In addition, each use zone --
existing or planned -- should be included in the sample. In establishing
such use zones, outfall locations of municipal treatment plants and large
industries, discharge of bypass wet weather-flows and surface runoff all
merit consideration as man-designed junctions.

The urban water regime is a complex aquatic system both in its natural
hydrologic behavior and in its response to effluent receipts. The surveillance network should take cognizance of these variations.

3. Location of Sample Points

The places at which samples are withdrawn should reflect the hydrologic
diversity so that the contribution of one sector to its adjacent sector
can be evaluated. In a stream, these flows are unidirectional, though
residual time or unit-travel time within a sector may vary. In the lower
tidal reaches of the streams and in the estuary, flows are multidirectional
In other words, the sample locations should be arranged to form a pattern
that resembles the hydrologic structure, including engineering works.
Figure 8 is a schematic diagram of one possible sampling pattern. Within
a hydrologic unit, additional subdivisions that merit sampling may be
identified to trace flows and observe offshore and near-shore gradients.

4. Observation Frequencies

The interval of time between successive samples should be regular and un-

interrupted, except for good cause. Repeatedly, we have observed that
time periods between samples have been uneven because of weekends and/or
holidays. Such irregularities reduce the utility of the data set.
Several types of time series analysis -- e.g., harmonic analysis -- require
constant observation intervals. In addition, breaks in the record
increase the probability of unrecorded events.

The two ends of the observation frequency continuum are "grab" samples
and continuous monitoring. Grab sampling -- widely used for spot
inspections by regulatory agencies or as a politically-inspired cosmetic
response to crises -- yields instantaneous information about specific
parameters. It is extremely hazardous to attempt to relate grab findings
to the same or different parameters for the same water body and for other
water bodies.

At the other end of the spectrum, continuous monitoring at short time
intervals -- usually 15 minutes -- is possible with robot instrumentation.
It is doubtful if so frequent a sampling is worth the effort, even if it
can be carried out for extended periods. The resulting avalanche of
information would be a deterrent to meaningful analysis. Our limited
examination of such continuous records indicates that many breaks occur
in the record despite impressive statements about the capabilities of
robots.

Between the two end points lies a vast range of possible sampling time
intervals. The question of deciding on the best frequency is not resolved
easily. It depends on the behavior of the parameter, the response time of
the water body and the object of surveillance activities. (In one study
of a data set on the Raritan River, New Jersey, composed of daily, weekly
and monthly observations, we found parameter correlations and trends similar
for daily and weekly frequencies.) Hydraulic behavior of water bodies
influences response time to given waste loadings and this will affect both
sampling frequency and evaluation of findings. Streams, lakes and estuaries
differ in their magnitudes of quality responses. Similarly, the variability
of load fluctuations in waste effluents is important in determining sample
size (Thomann, 1970).

If the purpose of monitoring is to record long-term trends and changes in
the state of the water body, the sampling texture can be coarser than if
the object is regulatory or the recording of episodic events. Detection of
episodic occurrences is more effectively achieved by direct, frequent
monitoring of the effluent rather than the receiving water. This method
has the added advantage of identifying the source.

Our experience indicates that daily or weekly observations are adequate
for most purposes. The actual time of sampling should also be recorded
and every effort made to keep the interval of time constant to reduce
sampling bias.

Observation frequency, geographical location and site selection jointly
determine the field sample design, which must be sensitive to the
spatial and temporal variabilities of water quality and waste loadings.
In organizing sampling strategies, some prior knowledge is assumed. If
this is not available, preliminary investigations will be needed.

5.   Selection of Sample Sites

Once the water body and the sample location have been selected, the precise
point at which the sample is withdrawn must be determined. There are at
least two alternatives that reflect lateral and vertical stratification in
water quality: (a) horizontal distance from shore banks, or obstacles,
and (b) depth. Both are important. Additional study is needed to
evaluate midstream and bank sampling. It is possible for slugs of pol-
luted water to be missed entirely if they pass downstream beyond the reach
of the sample site. Depth variations also return contrasting results,
particularly in estuaries and deep-standing bodies of water. The tendency

SAMPLING PATTERN AND HYDROLOGIC STRUCTURE

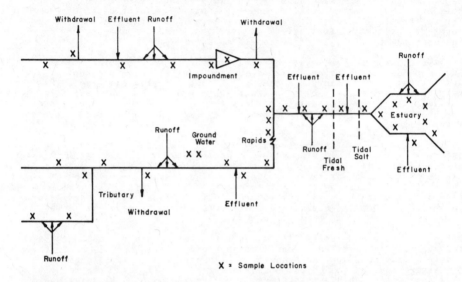

X = Sample Locations

to employ convenient sample sites at accessible locations -- particularly
from bridges where abutments may cause turbulence -- is to be avoided.

6. Choice of the Sampler and Sensing Instrument

The two sampling methods available involve either people or machines. Each
is subject to failure due to the instrument's reliability. Caprice,
perversity and illness are some of the shortcomings of people as sampling
instruments. Their behavior patterns may become institutionalized into
systematic omissions, as when, for instance, samples are not taken on
weekends and holidays, even though waste discharge and water flows are
continuous.

How reliable is the alternative of automatic sampling? Robots are subject
to equally serious failures caused by the mechanical analogues of caprice,
fatigue and breakdown. In addition, robots are subject to vandalism.
However attractive automatic sampling may appear -- especially when touted
by equipment manufacturers -- recent experience, in our study area and
elsewhere, indicates that the state of the art is still too primitive for
robots to be entrusted with the responsibility of guarding our waterways
(Kerrigan, 1970, panel no. 3). Moreover, robots require backup human
support and cannot themselves respond to changing conditions. Though
automatic electrochemical monitoring is more reliable than wet chemical
methods, the number of parameters that can be analyzed is still limited.
We have observed that this rigidity may include the establishment of information bounds, as when the uses of automated instrumentation often confine
the parameter set to the variables that can be sensed. Our understanding
of water pollution is not sufficiently developed at this time to permit the
installation of a rigid instrument package that is also delicate,
unreliable and dependent upon human maintenance.

7. Analyzing Samples and Scale Results

Even if all the foregoing requirements are met, the absence of common
analytical methods and variable scaling will cause confusion. Intra- and
interbasin comparisons are not possible without the use of transformation
coefficients. In a metropolitan area where many different agencies are

sampling water, disparate analytical methods may introduce errors in the comparison of two data sets.

Sometimes, it may be necessary to change laboratory procedures. To avoid a break in the continuity of the record, the replacement of one method by another should be preceded by a period of time during which the two methods are used simultaneously, in order that transformation coefficients can be derived. We have observed several instances in which coliform methods changed abruptly, causing a break in the data stream.

8. Bookkeeping Practices

Our field experiences revealed that data recording on field sheets and in files differed widely throughout the region in ways that reflected the special interests of the collecting agency, historical events, random choices and indifference on the part of the collection agency. The variation added greatly to the burden of reducing the information to a common format. We recommend strongly that field and office file storage forms be arranged in a uniform format. The raw record should also indicate where breaks occur in the whole file or for particular parameters.

In a metropolitan area water-monitoring scheme, several categories can be established depending on whether the data pertains to sample location and site, agency responsible for collection, political and geographical unit, land use information, ambient parameters, and variables describing inherent water properties. Among the latter variables are those pertaining to hydrology (discharge, stage or surface elevation, velocity), physical properties (color, turbidity, odor), chemical properties (dissolved gases and solids, metals), as well as conductivity, temperature, radioactivity, biochemical attributes, and macro- and microbiological populations, etc. Although no one observation will contain complete information, it is recommended that uniform data sheets be used to record the raw information in format field clusters.

9. Data Storage and Retrieval

Our experience has shown that handling raw data is a three-step process -- the recording of data on field sheets, their manual transfer to files for office storage, and the subsequent assemblage of the accumulated information into a data bank. The first two steps involve intermediate, and, often, temporary data in states of limited accessibility and use. With the accumulation of data sheets, the passage of time enhances the utility of the information. We have observed that lost records and the destruction of files -- by design or through indifference -- are serious obstacles to the compilation of a reliable historic record. It is important, therefore, to aggregate the data into a bank as soon as they have been collected.

The term data bank implies a highly-structured arrangement of information and the ability to identify data receipts and storage. The data bank should have the capability of responding on demand to queries for information on specified accounts and on the state of the whole account for selected time periods -- from the first to the last input. Its organization requires back-sighting to field observations and record keeping, and fore-sighting to information needs. Hence, it is imperative that the detailed arrangement of each record be linked closely to the sensing instrument and the original field data. Where automatic sensing instruments transmit information by telemetry to a storage bank, the units are, of course, functionally coupled. When field sheets are used, information transfer is facilitated by format compatability between the field sheet and the storage file.

Rapid retrieval of the masses of stored data generated by a metropolitan area water-monitoring system requires the use of punch cards, tapes or disks for machine processing. Data storage should be arranged in simple formats to service the needs of a variety of users and should also be able to satisfy the input needs of software package programs without requiring

intermediate output or reformatting. Retrieval difficulties with the
EPA's STORET format have already been noted.

In an urban area as hydrologically and managerially diverse as the NYMR, it
is useful to think of a data bank composed of two linked modules. The
first would contain information about the bank's status, including location
by geographical coordinates, political unit, water body address, collecting
agency, water intake, treatment, effluent, tax monies, sample frequency,
land use and parameters sampled. This would provide a potential user with
information about the character of the sample available at a given point
and the status of the information system.

The second module, whose files would be linked to the first by a sample
identification number, would contain the actual data. This record could
be maintained by the collecting agency, while the status record could be
housed in a central service organization. Both modules would be open-
ended so that new information could be inserted into the record.

10.   Systemic Properties of Data

All of the previous elements should be related systemically to form a network of sampling installations that expose water spatial and temporal
quality states and patterns for the metropolitan area. To erect the framework, the objectives of the surveillance program must be stated clearly.
Raw data generated by the sampling program should be analyzed, scaled and
processed in ways that satisfy the objectives. The output should be
reviewed against the demands of old and new goals. A feedback loop to the
field sampling net should update raw information and prevent the accumulation and collection of useless data.

For system viability, each sample location, site and variable should be
related to:

        a) all other sample locations and sites
        b) all other like variables and selected other variables
        c) waste loadings and land uses
        d) water uses and water goals

The waterway is a sink for receiving and responding to waste loadings from
given land uses and a vector for transmitting the impact of these waste
discharges to other water bodies and land uses. The surveillance system
must not violate the systemic character of the metropolitan area water
environment. In collecting the data for the NYMR taken by a pre-existing
monitoring net -- a situation that undoubtedly is found elsewhere -- we
have followed a dual framework of hydrologic and geographic hierarchies
with a common data base. The former is composed of natural hydrologic
elements whose states (historic, contemporary and simulated), are to be
defined for selected parameters. The latter hierarchy is imposed on the
natural hydrography; it consists of major and minor political divisions
whose decisions and policies affect water use and quality goals, land uses
and waste loadings (through population, employment, water supply, industry
and sewage treatment) and the operations of water agencies. By interfacing
the two hierarchies -- the hydrologic and functional -- unity of the metropolitan area water system is preserved.*

_____
      *A similar but more formal approach to the same question has been
developed for Kentucky by WAMIS, the Water Management Information System
(Sena, 1970).

19

Michael Greenberg and Robert Hordon

ENVIRONMENTAL IMPACT
STATEMENTS: SOME ANNOYING QUESTIONS

ABSTRACT

The National Environmental Policy Act of 1969 (NEPA) may prove to be a
double-edged sword. On the one hand, it may be of great importance in
managing the environment by providing a stimulus to organized, multi-
disciplinary research. On the other hand, NEPA opens the door to
decisions made with misplaced concreteness and, more importantly, to
the false justification of decisions motivated by political concerns
and bureaucratic vested interests. The adequacy of the theoretical,
data bank, and mathematical underpinnings of the impact studies, and
the institutional responses to using and to evaluating the projected
environmental impacts are analyzed in the context of the Suburban
Action Institute proposal to construct moderate and low income housing
in Mahwah, New Jersey.

ENVIRONMENTAL IMPACT STATEMENTS: SOME ANNOYING QUESTIONS

The National Environmental Policy Act (NEPA) outlines the necessity
of preserving the natural environment and important cultural artifacts
for succeeding generations.[1] The law requires with every proposal for
federal funds a report which identifies unavoidable, adverse environmental impacts, alternatives to the proposed plan, and an accounting
of long-term damages versus short-term gains.[2] Although the courts
conducted proceedings which included environmental evidence prior
to NEPA, the Act is especially significant because the burden of
proof is shifted from the plaintiff to both parties and the government. Any potential violation of environmental standards is potential
grounds for halting development.

The purpose of this article is to suggest serious misgivings about the
process by identifying six points at which a lack of information,
misplaced faith in the ability of science to understand the environment, and agency reluctance to identify points of discrepancy may lead
to faulty decisions by even the most open-minded judges and funding
agencies. The six points are each associated with a question. The
questions are in the order in which they should be faced in the process.
If any question cannot be answered with assurance, the difficulty of
answering the subsequent questions is likely to increase.

1. What environmental impacts are likely to result from alternative development patterns?

2. Do we have indicators of environmental damage and standards
   for these indicators which reflect the threshold beyond
   which serious and possibly irreversible environmental damage
   may result?

3. Have enough data been collected to determine the present and probable future environmental status given alternative development plans?

4. Will mathematical simulation models adequately specify environmental impacts?

5. Will agencies responsible for preparing and evaluating impact statements attempt to avoid any manifestations of internal disagreements or disagreements with other agencies regarding impacts?

6. Will the court system be able to adequately weigh information of varying quality and quantity from a widely divergent set of disciplines and from persons with different value systems?

We shall illustrate the difficulty of answering these six questions by reference to a specific case and to a specific set of impacts: the potential water resources impacts of the Suburban Action Institute's attempt to build 6,000 housing units on Ramapo Mountain in Mahwah, New Jersey.[3] In contrast to a piecemeal overview of a set of prototype of actual cases, the use of a single case has the advantage of providing an in-depth view of the process through specific sets of impacts, data, models, agencies, and decision-making bodies. The advantage of this particular case is its potential implications for the case of a suburban, high-economic-status community versus a developer seeking to build moderate-income housing at densities above the present zoning regulations.

There are two general disadvantages. First, the construction of housing may be the most typical issue, but it may be less revealing from the environmental perspective than the case of an oil refinery, chemical plant, or other land uses which introduce a complex variety of pollutants. Second, any site will have some unique physical, social, political, and economic characteristics. Ramapo Mountain is an unusually large project on a difficult site and carries with it extremely strong emotional ties and legal implications. We have attempted to treat the case objectively and have used Ramapo Mountain as an illustrative point of reference rather than as a single focus.[4]

1. <u>What environmental impacts are likely to result from alternative development patterns?</u>

Until very recently, the search for water resources environmental impacts was tied to a legacy of diseases which had decimated urban nodes during the industrial revolution. Human wastes associated with pathogens, oxygen depletion, and sedimentation were considered critical and were monitored almost to the exclusion of other indicators of environmental damage. In the late 1960s, the potentially serious implications of pollutants such as phosphates, mercury, and lead were publicized and began to receive some, if only minimal and discontinuous, attention.

The promulgation of NEPA has forced researchers to add to the list of impacts. In 1971, the United States Geological Survey published a document offered as a "sincere but still preliminary effort to fill an interim need" (Leopold, <u>et al.</u>, 1971). The need was, and is, to know

what the important environmental impacts are and how they are to be
weighted. The thirteen page document provides a format of presentation, a scale for a numerical weighting system, and an 88 x 100 matrix
of existing conditions and of actions which could cause impacts. The
information matrix is like a gourmet chef's list of recipes and the
costs of the ingredients are not supplied.

The potential impacts of a proposed housing development may be vaguely
gleaned from the one to six word categories along the rows and columns
of the matrix. The matrix may serve as a checklist, but in this role
the user must be prepared to search for indirect effects among the
categories. For example, a single row and column intersection is
present for urbanization and water quality. However, about thirty
other causative actions listed in the matrix may be associated with
urbanization, and these proposed actions may, in turn, affect about
sixty of the eighty-eight existing characteristics of the present environment. In addition, the categories are too general (for example,
one water quality category). Thus, this publication and other publications dealing with general categories of impacts are useful, but
they can provide only some of the larger bones in a complex body of
literature that spans the physical and social sciences.

Research focusing on the specific impacts of alternative developments
is badly needed. For example, the indirect effects of a large, residential development would include increased traffic generation and
commercial development. These land uses, in turn, are likely to lead
to identifiable environmental impacts: in the first case to an increase, from gasoline stations and vehicles, of hydrocarbon discharge,
which would flow either directly or through storm sewers into streams,
and to chloride runoff from snowmelt traced to road salting; in the
second case to increased flooding and the deterioration of the quality
of the runoff linked to the increase in paved parking lots. While we
are able to pinpoint indirect effects such as these, we are unable to
estimate the impacts with adequate precision.

An input-output model theoretically should be capable of providing a
measure of direct and indirect effects. Isard and his associates (1972)
and three articles in an input-output symposium (Bergman, 1972; Hirsch,
Sonenblum, and St. Dennis, 1972; and Leontief and Ford, 1972) illustrate that input-output methods can be used to simulate an array of
impacts ranging from air pollution to workers' accidents to women's
employment goals.

Although these studies are beacons of light, the estimates that they
yield must be used with great caution because of the questionable
nature of the coefficients that fill the technological coefficient
matrix. Each of the column and row intersections between a node of
development and a pollutant implies a constant relationship. In interindustry analysis this problem has been treated by developing
dynamic matrices based on updated information and "best practice
plants" (Miernyk, et al., 1970). As will be detailed below, the
information needed to prepare accurate and alternative economic-
ecologic matrices is not available. We do not know, for example, to
what extent substitutions between forms of disposal are likely to
take place.[5] Similarly, in an input-output model the pollutants will
be accumulated in a constant ratio. In the real world, the pollutants
and the impacts of the discharges may be concentrated or dispersed
at non-linear rates.

Finally, although the study of presently known pollutants is being expanded, additional environmental impacts are likely to be revealed in the near future through the isolation of new pollutants. The recent publicity given to toxic metallic compounds like mercury and lead, and the reincarnation of asbestos as a pollutant with grievous effects may be only the precursors to the identification of other impacts traced to the effluents from the petroleum refining and chemical industry complex, the metal fabricating industry, and others.

The implications of synergistic effects will also have to be studied with greater intensity because the greater variety of discharges from industries makes possible the potentially unfortunate joining of two or more relatively harmless effluents to form one dangerous pollutant. For example, the discharge of water vapor from a cooling tower, when combined under specific weather conditions with a discharge of nitric oxide from a metal fabricating plant may lead to a rainfall of dilute nitric acid.

Summarizing, our knowledge of the full extent of environmental impacts resulting from alternative developments has expanded rapidly in recent years but remains cursory in too many cases.

2. Do we have indicators of environmental damage and standards for these indicators which reflect the threshold beyond which serious and possibly irreversible environmental damage will result?

Beyond the identification of potentially important impacts, the state of the art presents an unclear sketch of definitions, indicators, standards, data, and models from which to isolate the critical impacts Reference to the four impacts of the proposed Ramapo Mountain development should illustrate this conclusion.

In a typical geology or physical geography text, a floodplain is characterized as a strip of flat land alongside a river channel which has been constructed by a river during floods. This simple definition is a misleading introduction to a complex issue involving changing definitions and jurisdictions and, overall, a trend to limit building in the floodplain.

Jurisdictional Questions

A developer may design a subdivision with a municipality floodplain ordinance in mind, only to discover that another level of government has assumed control of the floodplain and indeed does not even recognize the word floodplain. In New Jersey, future building in the "floodway" is likely to be severely limited because this portion of the floodplain constitutes an area in which flood waters must be allowed to pass. The floodway is to be distinguished from the "flood fringe," an area whose outer boundaries may or may not coincide with the boundaries of the floodplain and in which building may be permitted a specified distance above the likely reach of the expected flood waters and with restricted land fill.[6]

Beyond the initial problem of defining the floodplain, the question arises as to its delineation: should one use the river stage associated with the maximum probable flood, the flood of record, an empirically-derived multiple of the mean annual flood, or the probable 25-, 50- or 100-year flood?

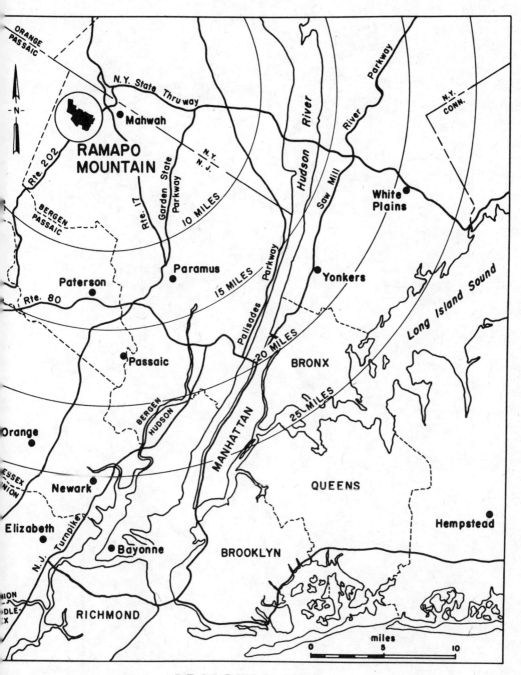

REGIONAL MAP

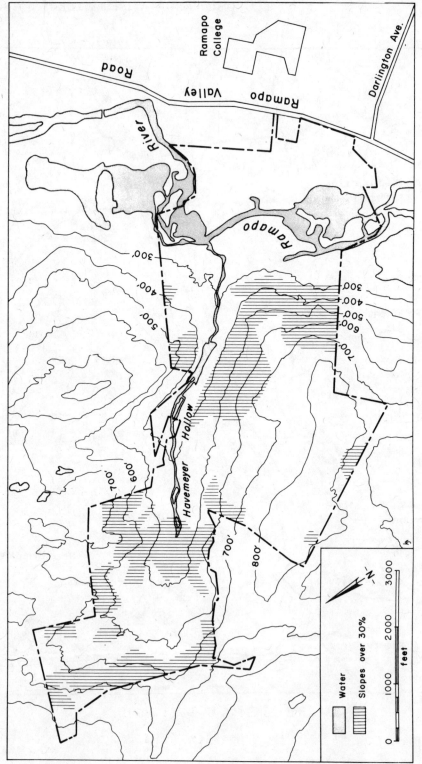

SITE MAP

Ramapo College

Ramapo Valley Road

Darlington Ave.

River

Ramapo

Havemeyer Hollow

300'
400'
500'
600'
700'

300'
400'
500'
600'
700'

700'
600'

700'
800'

N

Water

Slopes over 30%

0   1000   2000   3000

feet

At present, the Soil Conservation Service, the United States Geological Survey, and the State of New Jersey use different methods to estimate flood frequency and magnitude. This, in turn, leads to alternative floodplain areas, and, in turn, to varying developability potentials for the same land.

Hopefully, the confusion may end if and when the respective agencies agree on a uniform method for estimating flood frequency and magnitude, in accord with the Pearson Type 3 distribution recommended by the United States Water Resources Council (1967). However, in the interim, the State Department of Transportation designs bridge culverts with a 25-year flood in mind, the consulting engineer for Suburban Action uses a recurrence interval of 50 years in his designed use of the floodplain (Stubee, 1972), and the National Flood Insurance Act of 1968, and amendments thereto, refers to the 100-year flood as the design flood (U.S. Federal Register, 36, Sept. 10, 1971, 18175). Suffice it to say that the landowners and the environmentalists will argue for opposite poles of the definition, and either side may argue with perhaps some degree of legitimacy that the definition adopted by the responsible agency or agencies is inadequate for its particular case. Some of the legal aspects of using flood prone land in New Jersey are discussed by Rose (1973b).

Suburban Action Institute has submitted an introductory plan for a site which has steep slopes. The regional setting of the Ramapo Mountain plan and the detailed topography of the site are shown in Figures 1 and 2. About half of the 720-acre site has slopes greater than 15 percent, a figure considered to denote a "critical environmental impact area" by the state of New Jersey (New Jersey, Department of Environmental Protection, Guidelines for Interceptor Sewers, 1972). In addition, the site has sizable areas in which rock outcrops appear and soil cover is thin. Although the developer may be prepared to avoid these areas of obvious difficulty, the increase in sediment during construction and the increase in runoff following construction should rise considerably.

Although sediment and runoff are likely to increase substantially, one is once again faced with the choice of methods of estimating the increased yield. Even if a single figure or meaningful range could be agreed upon, the translation of sediment into an increase in stream turbidity and into effects on stream flora and fauna, and into a potential for increased downstream flooding is a highly debatable issue. We discuss it below in response to the question on the effectiveness of water quality models.

Water supply and water quality considerations associated with human effluents combine to form an intricate problem which overrides any single development of the size under consideration. The amount of water to be used and the effluent loading from the proposed site may be estimated with a reasonable degree of accuracy. However, regional water demands and effluent generation are not as easily estimated and are of great importance because the water supply for the proposed community would be drawn from the Ramapo River, one of the major tributaries to the Passaic which crosses a state boundary. At present, the two states, New York and New Jersey, do not have an agreement on the use of the water. If local agencies in New York State were to remove water from the basin by piping the effluent to treatment plants on the Hudson or, alternatively, were to use and degrade the quality of the stream by inadequate treatment as population grows, the water supply for not only the proposed development, but also for a major portion of northeastern New Jersey would be threatened. The above possibilities are real and are likely to result in court proceedings if they materialize.

An equally complex problem of the use of the water exists downstream from the site. The water is used by two major water supply agencies who want to keep the water in the basin. At the same time, the initial franchise for sewerage was granted to a sewerage system which would pump the effluent out of the Ramapo basin to a recently constructed but underutilized treatment plant in the Saddle River basin. Finally, the State of New Jersey is attempting to increase its own control over development and water quality in the region. This case will be discussed in greater detail in the context of interagency evaluation.

Overall, at the heart of the use of this site of slightly more than one square mile is a set of initial jurisdictional questions over which the weighting of environmental, economic, and political factors may not be in the order indicated in this sentence.

Water Quality Standards

Beyond questions regarding jurisdiction, one looks to water quality goals. Water quality is a subjective concept which implies a host of physical, biological, and chemical properties affecting the utility of water at a given time and location. To the manager of an iron and steel plant who is interested in cooling water, domestic effluent may be desirable to dilute water with a high salt content; to the brewer of malt liquor only water from the distant pristine reservoir may be suitable. To the jogger and stroller, water quality in the nearby river may be irrelevant; but the presence of bacteria and oxygen-demanding wastes may be acutely perceived by the fisherman and wader (Coughlin, et al., 1972.)

A definitive set of pollutants and their impacts on water uses have not been determined. Instead, several hundred parameters have been categorized of which the following types are commonly observed in the literature: heat, oxygen consumers, minerals, organic and inorganic chemicals, oils, infectious agents, sediments, and salts.

Increases in temperature and oxygen-demanding wastes reduce the capability of the water to support plant and fish life. Metallic compounds, chemicals, and oils are usually associated with the presence of industries. Oils can coat the gills of fish, cover birds, interfere with the processing of drinking water, deplete oxygen, and create serious fire hazards. Detergents and other commonly used chemicals containing nitrogen and phosphorous cause algae growth which in turn leads through eutrophication to oxygen depletion and channel blockage. Wastes with high or low pH values (a measure of acidity and alkalinity) can corrode structures, kill aquatic life, and create unfavorable tastes and odors. The long term impacts of small doses of heavy metals, phenols, and radioactive releases are not known. However, large discharges have been toxic to aquatic life. Infectious agents carried in wastewater were once responsible for major epidemics and must be kept under control by chlorination, a process which hopefully will continue to be effective.[7] Sediments and salts released from treatment facilities and washed into water bodies from roads reduce the penetration of light, cover fish nets, produce sludge banks, and retard the decomposition of organic wastes by smothering anaerobic organisms and by creating benthic deposits on the channel bottoms.

In 1965, the Federal government ordered the states to promulgate surface water quality standards and a means of enforcement. As of 1970, all state standards had been approved.

Present standards generally contain average or threshold instream values for oxygen-demanding, thermal, sediment, pH, and infectious agent parameters. Qualitative standards may exist for floating solids, toxic substance, odor and taste-producing substances. Conspicuously absent from many standards are chemicals and heavy metals because of a paucity of data, the high cost of sampling, and the fact that present treatment plants cannot deal with these pollutants. Fortunately, this problem is likely to be substantially reduced in the near future because the Environmental Protection Agency has been sponsoring research into the environmental implications of pollutants and has recently published proposed water quality criteria based on the latest scientific research (1973).

A satisfactory method of weighting the pollutants has not yet been developed. The United States Environmental Protection Agency prepared the "PDI indexes" (prevalence-duration-intensity) which, in essence, estimate the severity of water quality problems by determining the extent to which a water body falls short of its water quality goals (Council of Environmental Quality, 1972, pp. 11-16). The index has, however, a number of important weaknesses including an inability to weight the relative importance of each pollutant and a reliance on questionable sample survey data. Most recently, Batelle Memorial Institute (1973) has developed an interesting weighting scheme which shows some promise as a general guide. Overall, however, a systematic means of distinguishing the importance of specific pollutants for particular bodies of water at specific times is not available. Accordingly, the researcher must fall back on individual standards.

The portions of the Ramapo River in the vicinity of the site are classified by the State of New Jersey as suitable for public potable water supply, for the maintenance, migration, and propagation of the natural and established vegetation, for primary contact recreation, for industrial and agricultural water supplies, and for any other reasonable uses (New Jersey, Department of Environmental Protection, Classification-Surface Waters, 1966; Rules and Regulations Establishing Surface Water Quality Criteria, 1971).

Dissolved oxygen is the most common indicator of water quality and the most specified standard in New Jersey. The imperfect state of water quality standards at the present time may be illustrated with reference to this standard. Average and minimum standards based on the breeding and maintenance of trout have been issued. The minimum threshold of 4.0 ppm may be a reasonable average minimum goal; however, evidence suggests that readings below 4.0 ppm are not necessarily fatal to fish. However, oxygen depletion may reduce their

size and cause them to swim closer to the surface where they are
subject to injury from the weather and from birds. Thus, the amount
of oxygen must be considered in the context of temperature fluctuations and the degree of fish acclimation to their environment
(Dorfman and Westman, 1970). Such evidence is an added complication
for the decision-maker. A reduction of life in a stream may warrant
a different legal response from a reduction in the size of selected
flora and fauna. The other water quality standards are far less
precise and appear to be more easily subject to challenge on scientific grounds.

In our view, present standards are not scientific absolutes; rather,
they are educated guesses about the environmental implications of
alternative land uses and the financial and administrative practical-
ities of enforcing the standards.[8] In addition to a potential legal
challenge, we pose the moral question of how equitable are a set
of environmental standards which may have the effect of drastically
hindering the mobility choices of lower and lower middle income
populations. One might assume that the mobility of people is more
significant than that of fish, especially when the standards seem to
rest so completely on only a few species.

3. Have enough data been collected to determine the present and
    probable future environmental status given alternative develop-
    ment plans?

The extent to which water bodies in northwest Bergen County meet the
New Jersey State standards is not easily determined because of a
paucity of data and the vagueness of some of the standards. In a
previous study, the authors concluded that the New York Metropolitan
Region's water quality data bank is characterized by a lack of homo-
geneity (Carey, Zobler, Greenberg, and Hordon, 1972). A variety of
public and private agencies sample raw water at different frequencies
with different laboratory techniques, collecting different variables at different locations. The collected information is recorded on a host of non-standardized formats. Some of the data is
lost, and other information is available only in extremely confusing
forms. No single centralized agency is responsible for organizing,
storing, and retrieving data. Most of the best data is collected by
large water supply agencies.

Water quality data for northwest Bergen County closely fit these generalizations. Relatively good data are available for the Ramapo
River because two large public water supply agencies have major downstream diversion rights.[9] Their vested interest in the costs of
treating raw water results in frequent sampling along the Ramapo.

With this data we were able to conclude that water quality along the
Ramapo presently ranks among the best in New Jersey. However, this
conclusion must be tempered because the data are far from complete.
For example, the presence of fecal coliforms is regarded as an indicator of recent and dangerous pollution. Yet an insufficient amount
of data has been collected to determine whether the standard for this
variable is being met on the Ramapo.

Total coliform data were available. Total coliform is a much less
desired indicator because high readings may be associated with non-
human wastes and long-term decay of other organic sources. In lieu of

a New Jersey standard for total coliform, a federal guide was used
(National Technical Advisory Committee, 1968). The means of the lower
90 percent of all the sampling stations fall well within the federal
permissible limit, but above the desirable. Episodes of high coliform
pollution do occur. Overall, the river may meet the federal guidelines. However, our own research suggests that, in contrast to the
general belief, total coliform counts may not be consistently correlated with counts of fecal coliform, streptococcus, and other infectious agents. In short, validating the fact that low total coliform
pollution is present in the river may not be a sufficient demonstra-
tion that potentially harmful organisms are not present.

Information about the release of effluents varies from insufficient
to almost nothing. Data on non-point sources of pollution are neglig-
ible. As development has spread, pollutants from malfunctioning septic
tanks, runoff from storm sewers, unauthorized bypasses, dumping and
discharges, and leaching from solid waste disposal sites have become
major effluent sources. For example, in the study region, Whipple
(1969) found that a majority of the organic pollutants in the upland
Passaic basin were from non-point sources.

Other than the almost total absence of information about non-point
sources of pollution, sewage treatment plant effluent data sets are
easily the worst water quality information series in the region.
Monthly operators' reports are often missing, either because they
were not submitted or they were lost or discarded. The record sheets
on the reports contain space for more than a dozen indicators of effluent. Generally, only one, flow, has been recorded and on occasion
the same flow has been reported in every month. In some counties,
the design capacities, type of equipment, and even the watercourse
into which the effluent is discharged are known to only a few persons
and contradictory information is obtained from several sources.

Sewage treatment plant data in northwest Bergen County closely fit
the above generalizations. Most of the useful data were abstracted
from quarterly samples made by the New Jersey Bureau of Water Pollution Control. These data suggest that the vast majority of the population in the area is not served by sewer systems and most of the
small package plants seem to operate efficiently. However, because
of the infrequent sampling, we are unable to estimate the periodicity
of plant malfunctions which create the most serious impacts on the
stream.

In general, the reporting, recording, and storage of water quality
and effluent data is spotty and in most areas in the New York Metropolitan Region is an inadequate data base upon which to rest solutions
for maintaining or improving water quality.

4. Will mathematical simulation models adequately specify environ-
    mental impacts?

The environmental impact of a particular effluent is dependent upon
the uses of the water body and is a complex combination of the flow,
the dispersion, and the assimilative properties of the water body.
These characteristics are, in turn, related to such factors as the
underlying geologic and soil properties, the presence of diversions
and of man-made structures, the presence and location of other point
and non-point effluent discharges, and naturally occurring rates of

oxygenation and deoxygenation. Our knowledge of water quality at specific locations and times has increased due to the development of mathematical simulation models. However, such models frequently prove to be unsatisfactory or must be recalibrated to address specific time-place-pollutant relationships. In addition, the development of the mathematical model is dependent upon the availability of detailed and costly data inventories. The application of mathematical modeling techniques to water quality is a recent endeavor. Most of the studies have focused on dissolved oxygen and biochemical oxygen demand. The studies may, for purposes of convenience, be divided into two groups: causal and statistical. The causal mass balance approach is the standard one. Models are developed from causal biological, chemical, and physical relationships (Pence, 1968; Whipple, 1970). The mass balance approach requires precise information about the location of domestic and industrial outfalls and runoff channels, and utilizes parameters that describe oxygenation and deoxygenation rates. The causal approach also can be adapted to other measures of pollution, such as coliform bacteria, nutrients, and suspended solids (Hydroscience, 1971), and can be modified to include stochastic elements (Thayer and Krutchkoff, 1967).

A second approach is empirical. Relationships among parameters are examined through stepwise regression analysis (Lesser, Spinner, and Tirabassi, 1970). Thus, the complexities of the mass balance model are not faced and any statistical dependence does not necessarily imply causality. Clearly, however, causality must be traced and modeled. Therefore, the statistical model should incorporate expected relationships between water quality and land use.

In a previous study the authors were able to develop a model of the second type for two basins in New Jersey, including the Passaic, which includes the Ramapo River (Carey, Zobler, Greenberg and Hordon, 1972). However, the data base was judged to be inadequate, especially with respect to non-point effluent sources, for more than the simplest test of attentive policies.

While the data were not firm enough for policy analysis on the Passaic, we tested three hypotheses for thirty-eight stations in the Raritan River Basin in New Jersey. The hypotheses and conclusions are briefly stated in order to demonstrate that water quality models do have the potential to severely test environmental policies.

    1.   Hypothesis: Secondary treatment is sufficient to meet required water quality goals.

       Conclusion: Secondary and in some cases even tertiary treatment of point pollution sources is not always sufficient to bring all stations up to the desired water quality standard.

    2.   Hypothesis: Large regional sewage treatment plants are salutary with respect to water quality goals.

       Conclusion: Regional plants may improve the already clean upstream waters at the cost of further deteriorating the already polluted downstream waters.

3. Hypothesis: Present zoning ordinances are not at variance
    with water resources planning goals.

    Conclusion: Zoning and water quality regulations fre-
    quently conflict.

Our model results clearly question some working government hypotheses.
We are not, however, confident enough about the model structure and
the data base upon which it rests to unabashedly advocate that our
findings be adopted as new policies.

The State of New Jersey is presently applying mathematical mass
balance models and is committed to developing a model for each basin
(N. J. Department of Environmental Protection, Interim Millstone Plan,
1972). Whether the statistical or mass balance model approach is
used, the utility of the models will ultimately depend upon the accuracy
of the input data, a fact which seems not to have deterred many
advocates of the mass balance approach from developing models of
ever-increasing complexity.

We believe that land use and environmental planners are better off
with models than without. However, we suggest that before the mathematical model becomes the new rule of thumb, efforts should be made
to validate model conclusions either through another mathematical
model which should be based on a different approach or through
iconic physical models of the basin, or through both.

Next, the authors wonder to what purpose the models will be put. Will
they be utilized to test important policy alternatives such as centralization or dispersion of plants? Or alternatively, will agencies
responsible for critically reviewing each others' policies reach
accommodations that will actually obscure underlying policy alternatives? Can we expect that the mathematical models will be used to
establish the practicality of already developed standards, or will
they be used to develop solutions for unreasonable standards which
should be discarded? In short, one wonders to what extent inflexible
policy stances by agencies will blunt the possible uses of mathematical models.

5. Will agencies responsible for preparing and evaluating impact
    statements attempt to avoid any manifestation of internal dis-
    agreements with other agencies regarding impacts?

After the initial impact statement is prepared, an authorized official
is obligated to seek comments from federal, state, and local agencies
involved in developing and enforcing environmental codes. Such
comments become part of the statement. The final version is submitted
to the President, the Council on Environmental Quality, and the general public. A draft and final statement (other than actual legislation) must be made available to the general public thirty and ninety
days, respectively, before action is to be initiated.

The presentation of the report, however, need not draw any comments
and the sponsoring agency may legally ignore any comments that it
does draw. At this time, it is unfair to suggest that agencies will
behave so as to minimize review. However, based on thirty-five years
of observing the review of water resources projects, White suggests

that agencies do develop accommodations and often make decisions with
rule-of-thumb coefficients which are treated as gospel (White, 1972).
If rule-of-thumb coefficients are used in lieu of too costly or difficult to calibrate mathematical models, or if the models are restricted
in the policy questions that they might explore, and if intra- and
interagency differences are minimized, the authors would argue that
final decisions will probably not be the most desirable from the environmental perspective.

The decision about where to send the effluents from the town of Mahwah,
including the proposed Ramapo Mountain development, may be used to
illustrate the forces which are conducive to environmental factors
taking a back seat in the decision. We are not, however, suggesting
that non-environmental factors will in fact dominate the decision in
this particular case.

Four plans have been considered for treating the effluents from
Mahwah. The decision will have to consider the disparate views of
at least four major parties. The State of New Jersey has been committed
to regionalization of sewage treatment plants and has given recent
notice that it is moving from a reactive and passive role to a position of leadership.[10] Two water supply agencies with diversion
rights dating back several decades can be expected to oppose any
regionalization plan which would result in the piping of effluent out
of the basin. They would prefer to see the effluent highly treated
and then released back into the river upstream of their intakes. In
contrast, the Northwest Bergen County Sewerage Authority, which is
presently operating at 35 percent capacity, would prefer to see the
effluent piped out of the Ramapo basin to its plant on Hohokus Brook
in the Saddle River basin. Finally, the citizens of the township of
Mahwah probably prefer the least costly solution, which may or may
not correspond with any of the above.

The key to the ultimate decision may be the extent to which the state
will adhere to regionalization. The regional approach to water resources planning would ideally deal with multiple and often disparate
water uses. Federal funding programs directly encourage regional concepts by awarding an additional monetary inducement to projects cer-
tified as regional, and discourage unilateral planning by towns by
specifying that construction grants will be given only for facilities
which conform with the basin-wide plans developed by the states
(U. S. Federal Register, 35, July 2, 1970, p. 10756).

In practice, regionalization has meant centralization: reducing the
number of plants and locating the plants as closely as possible to
the downstream or lowest point in the basin. The advantages of this
policy that are especially relevant to northwest Bergen County include
economies of scale in treatment plant construction, the preservation
of upstream water quality, the maintenance of better work standards,
and greater ease of administration and enforcement. Some of the
less frequently publicized disadvantages include the removal of water
for water supply, the high cost of interceptors, and the potential
of greater environmental damage from a plant malfunction.[11]

In 1968, about 750 treatment plants in New Jersey discharged more
than one billion gallons of effluent per day. To secure Federal
funds the State has adopted the regionalization policy. The implications of this policy are graphically exhibited in a 1969 capital needs

report which has two maps, one with about 750 dots representing the present treatment facilities, the second with about 170 dots representing the proposed system of plants (N. J. Department of Health, 1969).

At the county scale, engineering firms were retained to develop regional plans which would receive both Federal and State funding and therefore be less of a burden to local taxpayers. Having read more than two dozen master plans, the authors would characterize many of them as intrinsically not regional because county and basin boundaries frequently do not coincide and because the consultants are placing undue emphasis on engineering and short-term economic considerations.

The drawbacks of applying regionalization as implied in some of the county master plans are, we believe, causing a reconsideration of the policy at the state scale. Mahwah and the proposed Ramapo Mountain development have definitely been affected by this reconsideration.

On July 24, 1972, the State published a memo entitled "Discussion of Regional Concepts for Wanaque, Ramapo and Pequannock Basins." The report concludes that Oakland and Mahwah should join the downstream Pompton Lakes MUA treatment plant (N. J. Department of Environmental Protection, Regional Concepts, 1972). This statement reversed an earlier policy which had the influents from Mahwah and Oakland coming into the underutilized Northwest Bergen County Sewer Authority plant. The reasons given for the reversal of the earlier policy are capital cost savings and the requirement for reuse of the water by the Passaic Valley Water Commission.

On December 1, 1972, the State backed further away from the large treatment plant concept on the Ramapo. Following personal interviews with pertinent officials of the Division of Water Resources in Trenton, it was determined that the destination of Mahwah's wastewater had not been decided.[12] Four possibilities are being considered. Whatever plan is chosen will have to receive careful scrutiny with respect to environmental quality because of the water supply function of the river. At this time, however, we cannot say to what extent environmental, economic, jurisdictional, and political factors will be weighed in the decision.

Summarizing, agencies responsible for preparing impact statements and developing policies may have an overriding concern for the environment. However, jurisdictional, budgetary, and political pressures can force them into inflexible policy positions which may undermine their original goals.

6.   Will the court system be able to adequately weigh information of
     varying quality and quantity from a widely divergent set of dis-
     ciplines and from persons with different value systems?

From the perspective of the social scientist trying to understand legal decisions, an examination of selected cases dealing with potential environmental impacts leads us to conclude that the courts have been influenced both by the amount and quality of evidence and by the same personal value judgments as those that affect the concerned citizen.[13]

In New Jersey, environmental justifications for large lot zoning have been recognized in a number of cases dating back to 1949: for example, Duffcon Concrete Products v. Borough of Cresskill, 1 N. J. 509, 1949; Vickers v. Twp. Comm. of Gloucester Twp., 37 N. J. 232, 1962; and Oakwood at Madison, Inc. v. Madison Twp., 117 N. J. Super. 11, 1971. In the last case, the ordinance was voided as exclusionary. Justice Furman recognized the environmental argument; however, he dismissed it because insufficient data were brought to bear upon the claim that low population density would be an important environmental aid.

More recently, in cases dealing specifically with water resources questions, courts have upheld increasing lot sizes and zoning against multi-unit dwellings on the basis of potential drainage and water quality impacts: see Nattin Realty, Inv. v. Ludewig, 2d, 828 ERC 1121, N.Y.S. Sup. Ct., 1971; and Salamar Builders Corp. v. Tuttle, 275 N.E. 2d 585, N.Y.S. Ct. App., 1971.

Conversely, other environmentally based cases have been rejected. In Pennsylvania, for example, arguments for the protection of water supplies and water quality along with the preservation of natural and cultural sites were rejected: see National Land and Investment Co. v. Kohn, 215 A. 2d 597, Pa. Sup. Ct., 1966; and Eaton Quarries, Inc. v. Zoning Bd. of Adjustment, 228 A. 2d 169, Pa. Sup. Ct., 1967.

Overall, the courts seem to reflect the uncertainty and concerns that frustrate the authors and many social and physical scientists. The authors do not feel adequately enough informed about the cases to evaluate these decisions, other than to point out that the judgments have not been consistent and minority opinions have prevailed in a number of the cases.

Conclusion

The drafting of six questions regarding the preparation and use of environmental impact statements reveals our belief that the law is not going to be a savior to those advocating the environmental position. At this point, it might be typical to conclude with a pithy statement condemning all parties for hypocritically trying to use the concept of environmental impact to serve their own vested interests. Although such a cynicism might be partially or totally warranted, we believe that the concept of weighting environmental factors along with economic and political considerations will force otherwise negligent developers, industrial powers, and government agencies to reluctantly consider environmental degradation prior to making land use commitments. If NEPA indeed accomplishes this task, it will go down in history as landmark legislation.

FOOTNOTES

[1]Signed into law on January 1, 1970 (P.L. 91-190, 42 U.S.C. 4321-4347).

[2]There has been a "multiplier" effect from the NEPA legislation. For example, local municipalities, such as Franklin Township in New Jersey, now require that an environmental impact statement be prepared by a developer prior to approval and construction of a subdivision, even though federal funds are not involved.

[3]See Davidoff, Davidoff, and Gold (1971) for a presentation of Suburban Actions' arguments. A specific plan by the Garden Cities Development Corporation (1972) has been prepared for the Ramapo Mountain site.

[4]One final preliminary note that the reader should be alerted to is the fact that the authors are not lawyers and have not worked directly for a government agency. Therefore, the comments relative to questions 5 and 6 reflect discussions, reading, and educated guesses rather than actual working experience.

[5]Ethan T. Smith of the Environmental Protection Agency (Region II) is working on such a model.

[6]See New Jersey Flood Hazard Report (1972) for a discussion of the New Jersey approach. Briefly, the state defines a flood hazard area as a zone on either side of a stream channel that may be flooded during a storm. The flood hazard area consists of a floodway which carries the major portion of the flood flow and a flood fringe area further away from the stream which is inundated to a lesser degree. Both the flood hazard area and the flood fringe area are elements of the floodplain.

[7]Note that there is increasing evidence that chlorination does not kill all water-borne viruses. For a further discussion of the role of chlorination in metropolitan water management systems, see Carey, Zobler, Greenberg, and Hordon (1972).

[8]A similar view is taken in the classic article by Harold Thomas (1963).

[9]The two agencies are the North Jersey District Water Supply Commission, which supplements its supply from the Wanaque Reservoir with Ramapo water, and the Passaic Valley Water Commission, which depends upon the better quality Ramapo water to mix with and dilute the lower quality Passaic water.

[10]All applications for federal construction grants must now be accompanied by an interim basin plan which considers economic, demographic, institutional and environmental factors and presents technically feasible alternatives. The interim plan is to be followed by a comprehensive basin plan which among other improvements must contain a mathematical water quality model. See Interim Basin Plan for the Millstone River Basin (1972) for a presentation of the state's new role.

[11]See Michael Greenberg (1972) for a brief review of these issues.

[12]Conversations with John Gaston, Principal Environmental Planning Engineer, Division of Water Resources, Department of Environmental Protection (DEP), Trenton, N.J., letter to the files, December 1, 1972 and interview, December 22, 1972. Other corroborating and helpful interviews were held with Neil Goldfine, Rocco Guerrieri, and Steve Nieswand, Senior Environmental Engineers, Bureau of Water Pollution Control, DEP, Trenton, N.J., December 20, 1972.

[13]Two extremely helpful discussions have been prepared by Richard Sullivan (1972) and Jerome Rose (1973a).

REFERENCES

Batelle Memorial Institute (1973) Environmental Evaluation System for Water Quality Management Planning, Columbus, Ohio.

Bergman, B. R. (1972) "Assessing the Impact of Alternative Economic Outcomes on Social Objectives," in A. Brody and A. Carter, eds., Input-Output Techniques. New York: North Holland, pp. 31-43.

Carey, G. W. et al. (1972) Urbanization, Water Pollution, and Public Policy. New Brunswick, N.J.: Center for Urban Policy Research.

Coughlin, R. et al. (1972) Perception and Use of Streams in Suburban Areas: Effects of Water Quality and of Distance from Residence to Stream. Philadelphia: RSRI Discussion Paper Series No. 53.

Council of Environmental Quality. (1972) Environmental Quality - Third Annual Report of the CEQ Washington, D.C.: Government Printing Office.

Davidoff, L., P. Davidoff, and N. Gold (1971) "The Suburbs Have to Open Their Gates," New York Times Magazine, November 7, p. 40.

Dorfman, D. and J. Westman (1970) Responses of Some Anadromous Fishes to Varied Oxygen Concentrations and Increased Temperatures. New Brunswick, N.J.: New Jersey Water Resources Research Institute.

Garden Cities Development Corporation (1972) Ramapo Mountain. White Plains, N.Y.: Garden Cities Development Corporation.

Greenberg, M. (1972) "Regional vs. Local: Issues in Waste Water Treatment Facility Location," Growth and Change 3 (January): 38-43.

Hirsch, W., S. Sonenblum, and J. St. Dennis (1972) "Estimating the Quality of Urban Life with Input-Output," in A. Brody and A. Carter, eds., Input-Output Techniques. New York: North Holland, pp. 44-60.

Hydroscience (1971) Simplified Mathematical Modeling of Water Quality. Washington, D. C.: EPA Water Quality Office.

Isard, W. (1972) Ecologic-Economic Analysis for Regional Development. New York: Free Press.

Leontief, W. and D. Ford (1972) "Air Pollution and the Economic Structure: Empirical Results of Input-Output Computations," in A. Brody and A. Carter, eds., Input-Output Techniques. New York: North Holland, pp. 9-30.

Leopold, L. et al. (1971) A Procedure for Evaluating Environmental Impact. Washington, D.C.: U. S. Geological Survey Circular 645.

Lesser, A., A. Spinner, and M. Tirabassi (1970) An Engineering Economic Study of the Industrial Growth Potential of the Upper Passaic River Basin. Hoboken, N.J.: Stevens Institute of Technology.

Miernyk, W. et al. (1970) Simulating Regional Economic Development. Lexington, Mass.: D. C. Heath.

National Technical Advisory Committee (1968) Report of the Committee on Water Quality Standards. Washington, D. C.: FWPCA.

New Jersey, Department of Environmental Protection (1966) Classifications - Surface Waters. Trenton, N.J.: Department of Environmental Protection.

_____ (1971) Rules and Regulations Establishing Surface Water Quality Criteria. Trenton, N.J.: Department of Environmental Protection.

_____ (1972) "Discussion of Regional Concepts for Wanaque, Ramapo, and Pequannock Basins," mimeographed, Trenton, N.J.: Department of Environmental Protection.

_____ (1972) Interim Plan for the Millstone River Basin. Trenton, N.J.: Department of Environmental Protection.

_____ (1972) New Jersey Environmental Guideline for Planning, Designing, and Constructing Interceptor Sewers. Trenton, N.J.: Department of Environmental Protection.

_____ (1972) New Jersey Flood Hazard Report No. 2 - Raritan River. Trenton, N.J.: Department of Environmental Protection.

New Jersey, Department of Health, Division of Clean Air and Water (1969) Anticipated Capital Needs for Sewerage Facilities in New Jersey. Trenton, N.J.: Department of Health.

Pence, G., Jr., J. Jeglic, and R. Thomann (1968) "Time-Varying Dissolved Oxygen Model," Journal of the Sanitary Engineering Division, Proceedings of the American Society of Civil Engineers 94 (April): 381-402.

Rose, J. (1973a) "Judicial Trends in New Jersey Zoning Laws: The Balanced Community," Paper presented at a Conference on Land Use Problems in New Jersey at Ramapo College, March 27.

Rose, J. (1973b) "From the Legislatures: Use of Flood Prone Land,"
    Real Estate Law Journal 1, 4 (Spring): 382-384.

Stubee, A. H. (1972) "Preliminary Hydrologic Study of the Ramapo
    River from Mile 10.8 to Mile 12.1 in Mahwah, New Jersey," mime-
    ographed, Willingboro, N.J., March 30.

Sullivan, R., Commissioner, Department of Environmental Protection,
    State of New Jersey (1972) brief amicus curiae in case of Allan-
    Dean Corporation vs. Bedminster Township.

Thayer, R. P. and R. C. Krutchkoff (1967) "Stochastic Model for BOD
    and DO in Streams," Journal of the Sanitary Engineering Division,
    Proceedings of the American Society of Civil Engineers, (June):
    59-72.

Thomas, H. A., Jr. (1963) "The Animal Farm: A Mathematical Model for
    the Discussion of Social Standards for Control of the Environ-
    ment," Quarterly Journal of Economics, reprinted in R. Dorfman
    and N. Dorfman, eds., (1972), Economics of the Environment.
    New York: W. W. Norton, pp. 250-256.

U. S. Environmental Protection Agency (1973) Proposed Criteria for
    Water Quality, Volumes 1 and 2, Washington, D.C.: U.S.E.P.A.

U. S. Federal Register (1970) 35 F.R., p. 10756, July 2.

U. S. Federal Register (1971) 36 F.R., pp. 18175-18186, September 10.

U. S. Water Resources Council (1967) A Uniform Technique for Deter-
    mining Flood Flow Frequencies. Washington, D.C.: Water Re-
    sources Council Bulletin 15.

Whipple, W., Jr. (1969) Preliminary Mass Balance of BOD on Three
    Major New Jersey Rivers. New Brunswick, N.J.: New Jersey Water
    Resources Research Institute.

Whipple, W., Jr. (1970) "BOD Mass Balance and Water Quality Standards,"
    Water Resources Research 6, 3 (June): 827-837.

White, G. (1972) "Environmental Impact Statements," Professional
    Geographer 24, 4 (November): 302-309.

VI

Supplementary Bibliography

INTRA-URBAN LAND USE

Introductory

Burgess, "The Growth of the City: An Introduction to a Research Project,"
Ch. 2 of R. Park, et al., The City, Chicago, 1925/1967, pp. 47-62.

Carey, G. W., "Density, Crowding, Stress and the Ghetto," American Behavioral
Scientist, March/April 1972, pp. 495-509.

Glazer, N. and D. P. Moynihan, Beyond the Melting Pot, M.I.T., 1963.

Harris, C. and E. Ullman, The Nature of Cities," AAAPSS, 1945, pp. 7-17,
also reprinted in H. Mayer and C. Kohn, Readings in Urban Geography,
Univ. Chicago, 1959.

Hoover, E. M., and R. Vernon, Anatomy of a Metropolis, Anchor, 1959/1962,
ch. 8.

Jacobs, J., The Death and Life of Great American Cities, Vintage, 1961.

Nourse, H., Regional Economics, McGraw-Hill, 1968, ch. 5.

Rose, H., The Black Ghetto, McGraw-Hill, 1971.

Sjoberg, G., The Preindustrial City, Free Press, 1965.

Wirth, L., "Urbanism as a Way of Life," AJS, 44,1938, pp. 8-20, also
reprinted in Louis Wirth, On Cities and Social Life, Phoenix Books, 1964.

Intermediate

Bourne, L. S., Internal Structure of the City, Oxford, 1971, articles
in Sections 2, 3, and 5.

Boventer, E.v, "Land Values and Spatial Structure: A Comparative Presentation of Agricultural, Urban, and Tourist Location Theories,"
PPRSA, 18, 1967, pp. 231-42.

Downs, A., Urban Problems and Prospects, Markham, 1970.

Sinclair, R., "Von Thünen and Urban Sprawl," AAAG, 57, 1, 1967, pp. 72-87.

STK: articles by Chisholm, Haig, and Hoover.

Sternlieb, G., The Tenement Landlord, Rutgers Univ. Press, 1966.

Taeuber, K. E., and A. F. Taeuber, Negroes in Cities, Aldine, 1965.

Ward, D., Cities and Immigrants, Oxford, 1971.

Warner, S., Streetcar Suburbs, Atheneum, 1970.

Wingo, L., Cities and Space: The Future Use of Urban Land, Johns Hopkins, 1963.

Advanced

Alonso, W., Location and Land Use, Harvard, 1964.

Andrews, R. B. (ed), Urban Land Use Policy, Free Press, 1972.

Brown, H. J., J. R. Ginn, F. J. James, J. F. Kain, and M. R. Straszheim, Empirical Models of Urban Land Use: Suggestions on Research Objectives and Organization, National Bureau of Economic Research, 1972.

Carey, G. W., L. Macomber, and M. Greenberg, "Educational and Demographic Factors in the Urban Geography of Washington, D. C.," GR, 58, 4, 1968, pp. 515-37.

Deskins, D., Residential Mobility of Negroes in Detroit: 1837-1965, Univ. of Michigan, Dept. of Geography, 1972.

Earickson, R., The Spatial Behavior of Hospital Patients, Dept. of Geography Research Paper No. 124, Univ. of Chicago, 1970.

Hughes, J., Urban Indicators, Metropolitan Evolution and Public Policy, Center for Urban Policy Research, Rutgers Univ., 1972.

Murdie, R. A., Factorial Ecology of Metropolitan Toronto, Dept. of Geography Research paper No. 116, Univ. of Chicago, 1969.

Muth, R. F., "Urban Residential Land and Housing Markets," in PW.

STK: articles by Alonso, Dunn, Stevens, and Yeates.

Sudman, S., N. Bradburn, G. Gockel, "The Extent and Characteristics of Racially Integrated Housing in the U.S.," Journal of Business, January, 1969, pp. 50-92.

SITING OF INDUSTRY AND COMMERICAL ACTIVITY IN URBAN CENTERS

Introductory

Berry, B., Geography of Market Centers and Retail Distribution, Prentice-Hall, 1967.

Colby, C. C., "Centrifugal and Centripetal Forces in Urban Geography," AAAG, 23, March, 1933, pp. 1-20, also reprinted in H. Mayer and C. Kohn, Readings in Urban Geography, Univ. of Chicago, 1959.

Estall, R. C., and R. Buchanan, Industrial Activity and Economic Activity, Wiley, 1961.

Miller, E. W., A Geography of Industrial Location, W. C. Brown, 1970.

Nourse, H., op. cit., chs. 3, 4, and 9.

Smith, D. M., Industrial Location, Wiley, 1971.

Intermediate

Berry, B., "Cities as Systems Within Systems of Cities," PPRSA, 13, 1964, pp. 147-63.

Bourne, L. S., op.cit., articles in section 6 - Berry, Boal and Johnson, Morrill and Earickson.

Christaller, W., Central Places in Southern Germany, trans. Carlisle W. Baskin, Prentice-Hall, 1967.

Cyert, R. M., and J. G. March, A Behavioral Theory of the Firm, Prentice-Hall, 1963.

Greenhut, M. L., Plant Location in Theory and Practice: The Economics of Space, North Carolina Press, 1956.

Karaska, G. J., and D. F. Bramhall, Locational Analysis for Manufacturing, M.I.T., 1969.

Kinnard, W. N., Jr., and S. D. Messner, Effective Business Relocation, Heath, 1970.

Losch, A., The Economics of Location, trans, Wolfgang Stolper, Wiley, 1967.

Pred, A. R., The Spatial Dynamics of U. S. Urban-Industrial Growth, 1800-1914, M.I.T., 1966.

STK: Daggett; Kennelly; Pred; Isard and Cumberland; Berry and Pred; Valavanis; Brush; Berry, Barnum and Tennant; and Morrill.

Weber, A., Theory of the Location of Industries, trans. Carl J. Friedrich, Chicago, 1929/1969.

Weber, A. F., The Growth of Cities in the Nineteenth Century, Cornell Univ. Press, 1965.

Advanced

Applebaum, W., Shopping Center Strategy, International Council of Shopping Centers, 1970.

Berry, B., Commercial Structure and Commercial Blight, Univ. of Chicago, Dept. of Geography Research Paper No. 85, 1963.

Berry, B., S. Parsons, and R. Platt, The Impact of Urban Renewal on Small Business, Center for Urban Studies, Univ. of Chicago, 1968.

Burrows, J. C., C. E. Metcalf, and J. B. Kaler, Industrial Location in the United States, Heath, 1971.

Garner, B., The Internal Structure of Retail Nucleations, Northwestern Univ. Studies in Geography, No. 12, 1966.

Guigou, J.-L.,"On French Location Models for Production Units," RUE, 1, 1970, pp. 107-38.

Hamer, A. M., Industrial Exodus from Central City, Heath, 1973.

Harris, C., and F. Hopkins, Locational Analysis, Heath, 1972.

Olsson, G., "Central Place Systems, Spatial Interaction, and Stochastic Processes," PPRSA, 18, 1966, pp. 13-45.

Pred, A., Behavior and Location: Foundations for a Geographic and Dynamic Location Theory, Lund studies in Geography, series B: Human Geography, No. 27, 1967.

Simmons, J., The Changing Pattern of Retail Location, Univ. of Chicago Dept. of Geography Research Paper, No. 92, 1964.

Rose, H. M., "The Structure of Retail Trade in a Racially Changing Neighborhood," GA, 2, 2, April 1970, pp. 135-48.

Webber, M. J., Impact of Uncertainty on Location, M.I.T., 1972.

REGIONAL ECONOMIC DEVELOPMENT

Introductory

Ashby, L., "The Geographical Redistribution of Employment: An Examination of the Elements of Change," Survey of Current Business, 44, 1964, pp. 13-20.

Chinitz, B., "Contrasts in Agglomeration: New York and Pittsburgh," AER, May 1961, pp. 279-89.

Morrissett, I., "The Economic Structure of American Cities," PPRSA, 4, 1958, pp. 239-56.

Myrdal, G., Rich Lands and Poor, Harper, 1957.

Perloff, H. S., and V. W. Dodds, How a Region Grows, Supplementary Paper No. 17, Committee for Economic Development, March 1963.

Pfouts, R., (ed.), The Techniques of Urban Economic Analysis, Chandler-Davis, 1960.

Pittsburgh Regional Planning Association, Region With a Future, Vol.3 of the Economic Study of the Pittsburgh Region, Univ. of Pittsburgh Press, 1963.

Sonenblum, S., "The Uses and Development of Regional Projections," in Perloff, H., and L. Wingo, Jr., Issues in Urban Economics, Johns Hopkins, 1968, pp. 141-86.

Thompson, W., A Preface to Urban Economics, Johns Hopkins, 1965.

Ullman, E., M. Dacey, and H. Brodsky, The Economic Base of American Cities, Univ. of Washington (Seattle) Press, 1969.

Intermediate

Berry, B., Growth Centers in the American Urban System, Ballinger, 1973.

Greenberg, M., "A Test of Alternative Models for Projecting County Industrial Production at the 2, 3, and 4 - Digit Standard Industrial Code Levels," RUE, February 1972, pp. 397-417.

Hansen, N. M., Intermediate Size Cities as Growth Centers, Praeger, 1971

Hansen, N. M., Location Preferences, Migration, and Regional Growth, Praeger, 1973.

Harmstron, F., and R. Lund, Application of an Input-Output Framework to a Community Economic System, Univ. of Missouri, 1967.

Hirschman, A. O., The Strategy of Economic Development, Yale, 1958.

Isard, W., Methods of Regional Analysis: An Introduction to Regional Science, M.I.T., 1960.

Little, A. D., Inc., Fostering Industrial Growth in Massachusetts: Strategies for Development of Selected Industries in the 1970's, NTIS October, 1970.

Miernyk, W., The Elements of Input-Output Analysis, Random House, 1965.

Tiebout, C., The Community Economic Base Study, Supplementary Paper No. 16, Committee for Economic Development, 1962.

Advanced

Brody, A., and A. P. Carter, (eds.), Input-Output Techniques, American Elsevier, 1972.

Chenery, H., and P. Clark, Interindustry Economics, Wiley, 1959.

Czamanski, S., Regional Science Techniques in Practice: The Case of Nova Scotia, Heath, 1972.

Garnick, D. H., "Disaggregated Basic-Service Models and Regional Input-Output Models in Multiregional Projections," JRS, Vol. 9, No. 1, April 1969, pp. 87-100.

Glickman, N., "An Econometric Forecasting Model for the Philadelphia Region," JRS, Vol. 11, No. 1, April 1971, pp. 15-32.

Haber, W., W. A. Spivey, and M. R. Warshaw (eds.), Michigan in the 1970's: An Economic Forecast, Univ. of Michigan, 1965.

Harris, C. C., Jr., The Urban Economies, 1985, Heath, 1973.

Hewings, G., "Input-Output Models: Aggregation for Regional Impact Analysis," GC, 3, 1, January 1972, pp. 15-19.

James, F. J., and J. W. Hughes, Modeling State Growth: New Jersey 1980, Center for Urban Policy Research, Rutgers Univ., 1973.

Lee, T., J. Moore, and D. Lewis, Regional and Interregional Intersectoral Flow Analysis: The Method and an Application to the Tennessee Economy, Univ. of Tennessee Press, 1973.

Miernyk, W. H., K. L. Shellhammer, D. M. Brown, R. L. Coccari, L. Gallagher, and W. H. Wineman, Simulating Regional Economic Development, Heath, 1970.

Udis, B. (ed.), The Economic Consequences of Reduced Military Spending, Heath, 1973.

ENVIRONMENTAL CONSEQUENCES OF URBAN-INDUSTRIAL DEVELOPMENT

Introductory

Curtis, V., (ed.), Land Use and the Environment, American Society of Planning Officials, 1973.

Darling, J. F., and J. Milton, Future Environments of North America, Natural History Press, 1966.

Fallows, J. M., The Water Lords, Bantam, 1971.

Firey, W., Man, Mind and Land, Free Press, 1960.

Kapp, K. W., The Social Costs of Private Enterprise, Schocken, 1960/1971.

National Academy of Sciences, Waste Management & Control, 1966.

Olson, M., The Logic of Collective Action, Schocken, 1968.

Purdom, P. W., (ed.), Environmental Health, Academic Press, 1971.

Sax, J., Defending the Environment, Knopf, 1971.

Intermediate

Baldwin, M., and J. Page, Law and the Environment, Walker, 1970.

Bosselman, F., and D. Callies, The Quiet Revolution in Land Use Control,
U.S. Government Printing Office, 1971.

Burton, I. and R. Kates, Readings in Resource Management and Conservation,
Univ. of Chicago Press, 1965.

Brown, W. H., How to Stop Corporate Pollution and Make Money Doing It,
Bellerophon, 1972.

Caldwell, L., Environment-Challange to Modern Society, Anchor, 1971.

Hagevik, G., Decision-Making in Air Pollution Control, Praeger, 1970.

Kneese, A., and B. Bower (eds.), Environmental Quality Analysis, Johns Hopkins
Press, 1972.

Margolis, J., (ed.), The Public Economy of Urban Communities, Johns Hopkins
Press. 1965.

Moore, G., (ed.), Emerging Methods in Environmental Design & Planning,
M.I.T. Press, 1971.

Advanced

Carey, G. W., L. Zobler, M. Greenberg and R. Hordon, Urbanization, Public
Policy, and Water Pollution, Center for Urban Policy Research, Rutgers Univ.,
1972.

Chase Econometric Associates, The Economic Impact of Pollution Control:
A Summary of Recent Studies, prepared for the Council on Environmental
Quality, NTIS, 1972.

Dee, N., N. L. Drobny, J. K. Baker, K. M. Duke, and D. C. Fahringer,
Planning Methodology for Water Quality Management, Battelle for EPA, July 1973.

Department of the Army, North Atlantic Division, Corps of Engineers,
Northeastern United States Water Supply Study, Vols. 1-3, July 1972.

Dorfman, R., H. D. Jacoby, and H. A. Thomas, Jr., (eds.) Models for
Managing Regional Water Quality, Harvard, 1972.

Downing, P., The Economics of Urban Sewage Disposal, Praeger, 1969.

Greenberg, M., and R. Zimmerman, "Estimating Industrial Water Pollution in∙Small Regions," Journal Water Pollution Control Federation, 45, 3, March 1973, 462-69.

Isard, W., Economic-Ecologic Analysis for Regional Development, Free Press, 1972.

James, L. D., and R. R. Lee, Economics of Water Resource Planning, McGraw-Hill, 1971.

Krutilla, J. V., (ed.), Natural Environments: Studies in Theoretical and Applied Analysis, Johns Hopkins, 1973.

Little, A. D., Inc., Potential On-Shore Effects of Deepwater Oil Terminal - Related Industrial Development, 4 Vols., NTIS, 1973.

Prest, A. R., and R. Turvey, "Cost-Benefit Analysis: A Survey," Economic Journal, December 1965, pp. 683-736.

Thomann, R. V., Systems Analysis and Water Quality Management, Environmental Research and Applications, Inc., 1972.

Van Tassel, A. F. (ed.), Environmental Side Effects of Rising Industrial Output, Heath, 1970.

SUPPLEMENTARY BIBLIOGRAPHIC MATERIAL

ABBREVIATIONS

AAAG	Annals of the Association of American Geographers
AAAPSS	Annals of the American Academy of Political and Social Science
AER	American Economic Review
AJS	American Journal of Sociology
EG	Economic Geography
GA	Geographical Analysis
GC	Growth & Change
GR	Geographical Review
IESS	International Encyclopedia of the Social Sciences
JAIP	Journal of the American Insitute of Planners
JASS	Journal of the American Statistical Association
JRS	Journal of Regional Science
NTIS	National Technical Information Service
PPRSA	Papers and Proceedings of the Regional Science Association
PW ∙	Perloff, H., and L. Wingo (ed.), Issues in Urban Economics, Johns Hopkins Univ. Press, 1968.
RES	Review of Economics and Statistics
RUE	Regional and Urban Economics
RSRI	Regional Science Research Institute
STK	Smith, R., E. Taaffe, and L. King, (eds.), Readings in Economic Geography, Rand McNally, 1968.